MODERNISM IN EUROPEAN DRAMA: IBSEN, STRINDBERG, PIRANDELLO, BECKETT
ESSAYS FROM MODERN DRAMA

EDITED BY
FREDERICK J. MARKER   CHRISTOPHER INNES

This collection of essays, drawn from scholarship over the last forty years, explores the drama of four of the most influential proponents of modernism in European drama: Ibsen, Strindberg, Pirandello, and Beckett. Although there are other dramatists who also contributed to Modernism, these four illustrate widely different and contrasting aspects of the movement. Since discussions of Modernism are generally restricted to poetry, novels, or the fine arts (painting, sculpture), examining theatre from this perspective covers new ground.

The choice of these four dramatists as the subjects of the volume reflects the large percentage of essays dealing with their work published by *Modern Drama*, the leading scholarly journal in the field, which in turn is a measure of the centrality of these particular playwrights in critical discourse. The essays here have been selected to cover the main elements of the work of each of the four dramatists, with the aim of creating a useful teaching tool for university courses. Since some of the essays selected go back to the 1960s, while others are very contemporary, this volume also offers a perspective on the historical development of critical theory.

FREDERICK J. MARKER is Professor of English and Drama, University of Toronto.

CHRISTOPHER INNES is Distinguished Research Professor, York University.

Modernism in European Drama: Ibsen, Strindberg, Pirandello, Beckett

Essays from *Modern Drama*

Edited by
Frederick J. Marker   Christopher Innes

UNIVERSITY OF TORONTO PRESS
Toronto Buffalo London

© University of Toronto Press Incorporated 1998
Toronto Buffalo London
Printed in Canada

ISBN 0-8020-4399-2 (cloth)
ISBN 0-8020-8206-8 (paper)

Printed on acid-free paper

Canadian Cataloguing in Publication Data

Main entry under title:

Modernism in European drama : Ibsen, Strindberg, Pirandello, Beckett :
essays from Modern drama

Includes index.
ISBN 0-8020-4399-2 (bound)   ISBN 0-8020-8206-8 (pbk.)

1. European drama – 19th century – History and criticism.   2. European
drama – 20th century – History and criticism.   3. Modernism (Literature) – Europe.   4. Ibsen, Henrik, 1828–1906 – Criticism and interpretation.   5. Strindberg, August, 1849–1912 – Criticism and interpretation.
6. Pirandello, Luigi, 1867–1936 – Criticism and interpretation.   7. Beckett,
Samuel, 1906–1989 – Criticism and interpretation.   I. Marker, Frederick J.,
1936–   .   II. Innes, Christopher.   III. Title: Modern drama.

PN1851/M64 1998   809.2   c98-932218-1

University of Toronto Press acknowledges the financial assistance to its publishing program of the Canada Council for the Arts and the Ontario Arts Council.

Contents

Dates of Original Publication

The Dangerous Seductions of the Past: Ibsen's Counter-Discourse
to Modernity
BRIAN JOHNSTON
  First published in *Modern Drama*, 37 (1994), 651–64
Patterns of Structure and Character in Ibsen's *Rosmersholm*
MARVIN CARLSON
  First published in *Modern Drama*, 17 (1974), 267–76
Marriage, Metaphysics and *The Lady from the Sea* Problem
ELINOR FUCHS
  First published in *Modern Drama*, 33 (1990), 434–44
The Unspoken Text in *Hedda Gabler*
EVERT SPRINCHORN
  First published in *Modern Drama*, 36 (1993), 353–67
Ibsen's Endgame: A Reconsideration of *When We Dead Awaken*
M.S. BARRANGER
  First published in *Modern Drama*, 17 (1974), 289–300
Strindberg and Ibsen: Toward a Cubism of Time in Drama
BENJAMIN K. BENNETT
  First published in *Modern Drama*, 26 (1983), 262–81
Strindberg's *Miss Julie* and the Legend of Salomé
BRIAN PARKER
  First published in *Modern Drama*, 32(1989), 469–84
Strindberg's *To Damascus*: Archetypal Autobiography
DIANE FILBY GILLESPIE
  First published in *Modern Drama*, 26 (1983), 290–304
Pirandello's Mirror
MARVIN ROSENBERG
  First published in *Modern Drama*, 6 (1963–4), 346–67

Introduction

Volumes have been written on the subject of modernism, but our intention here is to provide a brief introductory comment which will prepare the way for the essays that follow. This collection of articles explores, from widely differing points of view, the contributions of Henrik Ibsen, August Strindberg, Luigi Pirandello, and Samuel Beckett to the complex and eclectic cultural phenomenon we have come to call the modernist movement. As a movement in art it has been identified with the sculptures of Gaudier-Brzeska and the paintings of Kandinsky, while in literature it has been defined through the work of poets and novelists such as Ezra Pound, T.S. Eliot, James Joyce, and Virginia Woolf. The start of the movement is usually associated with the symbolists of the last decade of the nineteenth century. But, although there were a number of French symbolist plays and some of the modernist painters and poets also wrote for the theatre, such as Wyndham Lewis or T.S. Eliot, few of the general studies of modernism published over the last half-century even mention drama.

This is partly because the theatre's intrinsic connection to physical reality, literally incorporated in the bodies of the actors, contradicts some of the key modernist principles. Simply presenting a sequence of actions in a temporal and spatial frame evokes the "narrative method" that both Eliot and Kandinsky rejected. On the stage, art could not be autonomous, abstract, or aspire to pure form. The combination of all these qualities has been seen as the stylistic mark of modernism in poetry and the novel. Yet, taking account of the different medium, the same underlying perception of existence that inspired the art of modernist poets and painters was expressed by dramatists.

In addition, the almost exclusively English and American purview that has characterized literary studies of modernism has helped to exclude the theatre from discussion, since in drama the main impetus for the movement has come from Europe. Bernard Shaw was influenced by Ibsen, O'Neill by Strindberg, Pinter by Beckett, and so on. Thus this collection of essays focuses specifically on four of the major European dramatists, each of whom responded to the sense of cultural crisis that propelled the modernist vision.

Ibsen, Strindberg, Pirandello, and Beckett are by no means the only European exponents of modernism. In addition to including the symbolists and futurists, a comprehensive history would also deal with Dada and the surrealists, as well as Chekhov, Hauptmann, Brecht, Ionesco, and others, crossing over into the contributions of directors and non-text-based performances. However, in place of the overview represented by such an approach, a more concentrated analysis of key figures gives a fuller sense of their work and place within the movement. These four have been selected not only because they remain among the most widely studied of modern European dramatists, but also because in meeting the challenge of modernism each initiated a clearly identifiable style of theatre that has been highly influential. In addition, while all four created radically different styles of theatrical expression, which serve to outline the parameters of modernism in drama, there are identifiable links between their work that help to show the evolution of this movement in our genre.

The idea of modernism in drama and theatre involves a range of different but related issues. On a very basic level, as expounded with great vigour by Emile Zola in the 1880s, it was at the outset a matter of eliminating constraints, dismantling what Zola calls "the decayed scaffoldings of the drama of yesterday," and making way for an extension of both theme and subject matter into new and previously "forbidden" areas. In a profounder sense, however, the real well-spring of modernism is a radically altered *Weltanschauung* born of a perceived loss of such values and beliefs as the rationality, purposefulness, and dignity of the human condition. In Ibsen's plays, Kierkegaard's existential vision of the isolation, self-scrutiny, and despair of the modern tragic protagonist finds its first and fullest expression. But, as in music and painting, perhaps the most striking manifestation of the modernist spirit in drama has been as a technical revolution – an ongoing search for new forms and techniques capable of exteriorizing the inner sense of dissonance and dislocation inherent in this new world-view. The spirit of experimentation engendered by this search embraces the whole history of the modern period. Thus the truly "absurd" qualities of disjuncture, apparent randomness, and unresolved (and unresolvable) dissonance that we take for granted in Beckett's dramaturgy are directly foreshadowed in Strindberg's dream plays and even in the late plays of Ibsen.

The four writers represented in this anthology have each, in their distinct ways, defined and given direction to the development of modernism in European drama. They expose the critical crisis that characterizes the modernist experience. But beyond documenting the increasing breakdown of faith in human reason and belief in the dignity of the human condition, through their work they offer modes of vision to supersede the old outdated certainties. The progressively bleaker view of existence, which finds its most extreme expression in Beckett, is given purpose by what Andrew Kennedy, writing in an essay on Pirandello, refers to as "creative nihilism." Hardly surprisingly, both Pirandello and Beckett were given the Nobel Prize for literature, while Strindberg holds the singular distinction of having been awarded an Anti-Nobel Prize, conferred by popular acclaim and national subscription, when he (like Ibsen) was unjustly passed over in the early years of the Nobel Prize's history. The ongoing artistic revolution represented by the work of these playwrights has won wide acceptance, to the point where all four are recognized as contemporary classics. However strange their plays initially appeared, they are now part of the standard repertoire and have become reference points for twentieth-century drama criticism. It would seem that each succeeding generation of critics, readers, and playgoers rediscovers elements in their work that revive the dialogue in which the past and the present continue to meet.

As the most recent (1997) International Ibsen Conference again demonstrated, it has been the symbolic and mythopoetic universe within Ibsen's late plays that has often tended to provoke the strongest critical and intellectual (as distinct, perhaps, from theatrical) interest. In her feminist reading of *The Lady from the Sea*, which seeks in fact to set aside these philosophical and symbolic interpretations of the play in order to restore its "gendered specificity," Elinor Fuchs draws an interesting general distinction between two broad stages of Ibsen criticism: "Realist critics wrote character studies. Modern critics have focussed on the symbolic elements submerged in realistic structures." Most of the Ibsen commentators represented in the present collection would seem to belong in the latter category. Marvin Carlson's essay on *Rosmersholm* identifies the hidden patterning at work "even in the plays of the middle period, where a basically realistic approach tends to mask its importance." In his article on *Hedda Gabler*, Evert Sprinchorn performs a rather similar service in his explication of the "unspoken text" developed by the visual elements and effects in the play. In her discussion of *When We Dead Awaken*, M.S. Barranger explores an underlying pattern of games and game-playing which, in turn, brings to mind Beckett's later use of similar strategies for an essentially different purpose. In quite another vein, Brian Johnston's broad overview of Ibsen's drama as a whole explores its opposition to modernism's rejection of a past and its consequent determination to confront this limited "modernity" with "those archetypal forces and possibilities whose rights it would prefer to deny."

Strindberg's approach to modern theatre was essentially protean and pragmatic, shaped by his restless search for new forms of drama capable of articulating the changing spirit of the times. In a widely ranging comparison between Ibsen and Strindberg, Benjamin K. Bennett focuses on the concept of time and the use of "temporal perspective" by these two playwrights as indicative of "a deeper level of dramatic form on which Strindberg follows Ibsen and measurably surpasses him." Subsequent essays by Brian Parker and Diane Filby Gillespie concentrate on two of Strindberg's best-known works. *Miss Julie* – otherwise almost invariably discussed as a naturalistic tragedy that is "explicated" by Strindberg himself in his famous Preface – is explored by Parker from an entirely different perspective, as a symbolist-inspired "exploitation and repudiation" of the legend of Salomé and John the Baptist, one of the central myths of the *fin de siècle* period. In her discussion of *To Damascus*, Gillespie likewise tries to push beyond conventional readings of Strindberg's first dream play as "a kind of case study or personal confession," in order to look instead at the more universalized effect of the trilogy as archetypal autobiography, "a work in which Strindberg draws attention to the elements in his personal life which are the fundamental patterns of human experience as a whole."

Broadly speaking, although Ibsen's influence on twentieth-century drama has been decisive and indisputable, it could be argued that both Pirandello and Beckett seem more obviously and closely related to Strindberg, both in spirit and in technique. While Ibsen appeared content, even in his last plays, to operate within a traditional framework of verisimilitude, his great Swedish contemporary wrestled continually both with shifting conceptions of theatrical representation and with the paradoxical tension he perceived between the reality of drama and dream and the illusory nature of external reality – the very problems, in fact, that are the essence of Pirandello's theatre. From *The Wild Duck* onward, Ibsen's drama became increasingly preoccupied with human isolation, the relativity of memory, and the ultimate unknowability of the past. In Ibsen, however, these concerns constitute a persistent thematic pattern submerged beneath the realistic surface of his action. In Strindberg's dream plays and chamber plays – as in all of Beckett's work – these same concerns *are* the action, acquiring direct structural expression in the dramatic form itself.

It is worth noting, on the other hand, that the four playwrights explored in this volume represent successive generations in the development of modernism. Born in 1867, just three years before Strindberg's first plays appeared, Pirandello only began writing for the theatre shortly after Strindberg's last play was performed, while Beckett drafted his earliest dramatic script barely a decade after Pirandello's final play, which was produced posthumously in 1937. Despite thematic continuities however, there is a significant shift in the modernist experience between the earlier pair of playwrights and the later two. Ibsen and Strindberg were writing against the apparently monolithic and all-dominating bourgeois society of the late nineteenth century; and as an alternative to its materialism, in their later plays both turned to spiritual realities. By contrast Pirandello's first full-length dramas were written in the middle of one world war, Beckett's in the immediate aftermath of a second; and in such a context of global destruction their questioning of reality is more radical, challenging spiritual as well as external existence. Even the concept of individuality, on which the subjective and increasingly autobiographical works of Ibsen and Strindberg are based, is put into question.

Marvin Rosenberg's overview of Pirandello's plays focuses on just this questioning of personality, associating Pirandello's own psychological state with the illusory constructs of the self dramatized in his protagonists. Picking up on the same theme, Anne Paolucci argues the liberating potential in these transformations of identity, and in drawing out the connections between Pirandello's plays and his novels she reminds us that – like Beckett – Pirandello had already established a reputation as a novelist before he turned to drama. Pirandello's deconstruction of character undermined one of the fundamental conventions of Western drama; and in conjunction with his emphasis on illusion, which destabilized the nature of theatrical representation, this liberated the stage from naturalism. Each of the other essays deals with central aspects of the open theatricality that Pirandello introduced as the direct embodiment of his themes. J.L. Styan analyses the way Pirandello breaks out of the dramatic frame through the impact of the 1924 Pitöeff performance of *Six Characters in Search of an Author*, while James Fisher illustrates the extent to which the nonliterary structure of the *commedia dell'arte* underlies his philosophical comedy. Both also set Pirandello in context, comparing his shock effects with those of the surrealists and Artaud, and relating his reworking of a traditional theatricalized form to similar experiments by Meyerhold or Copeau. Paralleling Fisher's point, Andrew Kennedy uses the same play as Styan to examine the crisis in dramatic language that was highlighted by Pirandello's work. As Kennedy indicates, the way Pirandello resolves this crisis points forward to Beckett; and each of the other essays also draws connections with Beckett's anti-illusionistic metatheatre, and his existential clown figures.

In many ways the modernist movement in theatre culminates with Beckett. When *Waiting for Godot* was first performed (in Paris in 1953, and two years later in London) it was met with critical incomprehension, largely because it established a completely new stage language. But, like Pirandello's *Six Characters in Search of an Author*, its theatrical influence was immediate and explosive; and by now the weight of critical analysis devoted to Beckett's work is overwhelming. The essays selected here represent the development of Beckett criticism, ranging from the 1960s to the 1990s, in addition to covering the main aspects of his work. The early essays established the unity of form and subject, theatrical presentation and philosophical statement in Beckett's plays, highlighting the fundamental quality of his drama. Richard Schechner, himself an avant-garde theatre practitioner, points out the way one of the dominant themes in *Waiting for Godot*, Time, is embodied in both action and structure. Schechner also relates this to the game-playing element that John Fletcher explores in his overview of the popular presentational forms – clownery, music hall, mime – on which Beckett, paralleling Pirandello's use of *commedia* traditions, bases his plays from *Waiting for Godot* to *Play*. In a brief note from the journal's earliest period, Ruby Cohn calls attention to the importance of considering the theatrical dimension in Beckett's work. As Strindberg aspired to do, Beckett directed definitive productions of his own plays. Cohn's comments on the style of acting required by Beckett's texts leads into James Knowlson's discussion of the insights into the plays provided by Beckett's directing notebooks, which show the playwright's evolving view of his own earlier plays. In analysing *Not I* Hersh Zeifman draws on the whole range of Beckett's previous writings to reveal both the thematic and theatrical complexities of his minimalist pieces, while H. Porter Abbott uses *Ohio Impromptu* to demonstrate the fusion of performance and text in Beckett's late plays. Another aspect of Beckett's drama – his work for radio, film, and television – is covered by Linda Ben-Zvi, who underlines this writer's sensitivity to the formal requirements of different media and his conscious reflection of that form within a work.

As these essays demonstrate, then, all four of the dramatists showcased here have been truly seminal figures, revolutionizing the stage in their search for new theatrical forms to express a new consciousness. Their centrality is indicated by the fact that Ibsen, Strindberg, Pirandello, and Beckett have each been the subject of a special issue of *Modern Drama*. It is largely for this reason, although it generally remains an unstated subtext, that their plays have continued to be among the most frequently discussed in the pages of the journal throughout the past four decades since its first issue. The necessarily modest handful of these studies selected for republication here represent developing trends in the critical treatment of these dramatists, on one level offering a history of criticism dating, with the earliest of the essays, from the beginning of the sixties. While all still retain their relevance, the fact that several were the first statements of a particular theme, or the first application of a theoretical approach, adds an extra dimension. However, in the process of selection, the primary objective of the editors has been to create a thought-provoking interface of different critical methods and ideas. The essays have thus been chosen on the basis of both excellence and diversity of views. It should also be noted that a conscious effort has been made to preserve the integrity of each contribution as a historical document; no attempt has been made, in other words, to "update" the papers or to impose a homogeneous style of writing or expression upon them.

More essays have been published in *Modern Drama* on Beckett's work than on that of any other dramatist; and in recognition of the close relationship with him fostered by one of its early associate editors, the late Laure Rièse, Beckett gave the journal a new piece of his for publication. This is "Roundelay," with which we have chosen to close this critical selection marking the fortieth anniversary of *Modern Drama*.

CHRISTOPHER INNES   FREDERICK J. MARKER
Toronto, 1998

MODERNISM IN EUROPEAN DRAMA

The Dangerous Seductions of the Past: Ibsen's Counter-Discourse to Modernity

BRIAN JOHNSTON

Culture is to set man free and help him be equal to his concept.

(Friedrich Schiller)

Ibsen adopted the theater decisively as his medium under the aegis of Ole Bull's Norwegian (Norske) Theatre in Bergen. A fundraiser for this theater was held in 1851 in Christiania, and Ibsen wrote an enthusiastic verse Prologue for the occasion in which he proclaimed dramatic art would awaken the Norwegian people from the long winter's sleep in which it had forgotten its glorious Viking heritage. Viking life had itself been a poem "of sword and shield," which then was sublimated into the art of the skald and minstrel. But then an "awesome winter fell over the north," the noble skald fell silent, "dedicated to death like one bewitched who has forgotten the word with which he can find release from his enchantment." There remained a "harp of longing" within the people who could never be satisfied by alien customs and arts. A native art alone could interpret the longing of the people and its forgotten music, and this art would sing both about the past and the re-awakened life of the present.[1]

In the same year, somewhat more soberly, in defense of Paludan-Müller's poems against the criticism of Johan Welhaven, Ibsen strongly defends the use of ancient myths in modern literature, insisting that their life continues into the present – especially as material for poets. These are, I think, the first expressions by Ibsen of the theme of the power of the past to awaken the life of the present. The cause of the new theater and of an awakened Norwegian cultural consciousness stretching back into the distant past were, therefore, intimately linked from the beginning.

One impetus behind this venture was the Norwegian people's desire to be free from cultural dependence on Denmark, whose theater in Copenhagen was one of the most accomplished in Europe. To quote Bjørnstjerne Bjørnson, also writing in 1851, a Norwegian theater would permit Norway "to enjoy its own language and its own poetry on its own stage": conditions which are essential if Norway is "to join the ranks of the other nations."[2] Or, in the words of M.J. Monrad in 1854, it originated in a conviction of "the deep national significance of theaters, the necessity of a truly national theater as a part of the self-revelation and development of nationality."[3] Here, the "self" to be revealed and developed is an objective, collective one, and a national poet's self-determination would require an analysis of this shared collective identity.

We know from his own critical writings that the youthful Ibsen endorsed these nationalist aspirations, though he later was to look on them less ardently. The domain of national identity would be something Ibsen's art could share with his public in a form of mutual self-discovery. And it would better justify the founding of a national or Norwegian theater in which to perform the poet's work.

For all its limitations as an orientation to the world, nationalism had one great advantage for the dramatic poet – it extended the audience's imagination beyond the immediate, contemporary world, the world busily revealed everyday in, say, *Morgenbladet* or *Aftenbladet*, and into a wider and imaginatively more resonant world of history, folklore and myth.

Above all, it adds an alternative dimension – of time – to the experience of our identities. The presence of this living but exiled spiritual past, seeking to regain the stage of his theater and thus to regain its place in modern consciousness, is a feature of Ibsen's drama from the earliest plays to *When We Dead Awaken*. And this preoccupation of Ibsen with the recovery of the past is shared, for example, with the theaters of Richard Wagner and W.B. Yeats.

It would be simplistic to attribute Ibsen's nationalism – apparent in the revised 1854 version of *The Burial Mound* as well as in the argument and imagery of *Lady Inger of Østråt* – to an attempt by the poet to ingratiate himself with the Norwegian public. For one thing, the Norwegian theater public much preferred the confections of Scribe and Co.

Because it encourages an imaginative extension into cultural history, myth and legend, nationalism permits the dramatic poet an enrichment of the terms of his art beyond the everyday here and now. In other words, it permits the poet to be a better and bigger poet, to enlarge the scope of his subject matter and thus create a more liberating "space" for his imagination to operate within. Once that metaphoric territory has been mapped out, it gradually can be extended and enriched. And it was a territory Ibsen never relinquished.

In 1857, in an essay on the heroic ballad, Ibsen contrasted the condition of mind of fashionable theatergoers with the actual spirit of the Norwegian people. The former, he writes: "visit the theater only when offered the opportunity of being titillated by some novel situation or excited by some novel intrigue."[4] The people, on the other hand, are less interested in fashionable modernity than in recognizing aspects of their identity stretching far back into the past:

If the new is to appeal to the people, it must also in a certain sense be old; it must not be invented, but rediscovered; ... it must not appear as something strange and incongruous in the conceptual range inherited by the people from their ancestors, and in which our national strength mainly resides.[5]

The conceptual range inherited by the people is richer and deeper than the modernity of the fashionable theatergoers. Within the popular imagination, Ibsen adds to the passage quoted above, the old, pre-Christian religion and its figures "continue to live until our own day." The young Ibsen, I suggest, like many early nationalist poets and dramatists, hoped to transform his theater into one that could sustain a major dramatic art by addressing a people whose consciousness was attuned to the rich spiritual past, that is, to a bigger subject matter for dramatic art.

This belief that the people were a rich repository of buried spiritual ore for the poet as miner to unearth by digging beneath the superficial consciousness of modernity was a necessary stage on the road of Ibsen's later disillusionment. He was to discover, with many other believers in the rich buried treasures of folk-consciousness, that the living dead – one's contemporaries – were most unwilling to be awakened to their full cultural heritage. The everyday business of modernity, then as now, always was more alluring.

There is a similarity here with the situation of W.B. Yeats, as described by Edward Said, citing Seamus Deane, in *Culture and Imperialism*.[6] In order to escape the degraded modernity of colonized Ireland, Yeats invented a mythopoeic Ireland "amenable to his imagination" and in alliance with an imagined "people," only to find the Irish in actuality recalcitrant to his mythic reconstruction. Unable to ignore modern history, Edward Said notes, Yeats tended to render actual historical events into occult events: and, I shall claim, this is the course Ibsen pursued, recreating modern Norway as an occult or archetype-filled space in his twelve-play realist cycle.

At first, the people in alliance with the poet were seen as the possessors of a consciousness rich with a past that would redeem dramatic art from the degradation of modernity. Richard Wagner, similarly, attempted to bypass alienated modernity in his music dramas and to return to myth, "that native, nameless poem of the folk."[7] His then disciple (later scourge) Friedrich Nietzsche, in *The Birth of Tragedy*, turned in revulsion from a modernity that comprised

abstract man stripped of myth, abstract education, abstract mores, abstract law, abstract government; the random vagaries of the artistic imagination unchannelled by any native myth. ... Man today, stripped of myth, stands famished among all his pasts and must dig frantically for roots, be it among the most remote antiquities.[8]

These strictures, long earlier uttered by Ibsen in his account of the frivolity of modernity and the need to return to myth, taken together, might supply some idea of *one* tradition of hostility to "modernity." They are repeated by many artists seeking to "awaken from" what Stephen Daedelus in *Ulysses* calls "the nightmare of history" – of merely abstract and arbitrary time. T.S. Eliot hailed Joyce's use in *Ulysses* of "the mythical method" as making possible for art "the immense panorama of futility and anarchy which is contemporary history."[9]

In *Cosmos and History*, Mircea Eliade notes how modernists like Joyce and Eliot sought to return to archaic thinking, to the concept, for example, of the myth of the eternal return.[10] This led many artists at first to believe that a lifeline to this significant and abiding spiritual past lay in the conceptual range of the people uncorrupted and undistracted by modernity, allowing the creation of that alliance of poet and peasant that Ibsen forges in his essay on the heroic ballad. Such an idea is present, for example, in T.S. Eliot's *Murder in the Cathedral*, in the spiritual and mythopoeic bond between Thomas and the Women of Canterbury against the Knights, who justify their crime with the political and psychological clichés of modernity. This hopeful union of poet and people was bound to be dissolved as the work of the poets and scholars recreating the past became more and more esoteric and removed from the conceptual range of the people.

There are two conflicting programs involved in this remembrance of things past. The first is a form of Platonic or Hegelian *anamnesis* or "unforgetting," a recollection of living spiritual truths which the soul, in its modern and fallen state, has lost sight of. Here, artists such as Wagner and Ibsen and philosophers such as Hegel and Nietzsche try to bring the past compellingly into the life of the present. The second program is the methodical reproduction of the past in sober and meticulous detail. The first mode is mythopoeic and rejects modernity's claim to represent reality; the second is historical and scholarly and forces the past to conform to modern reality's requirements of sober diligence. The mythopoeic and the scholarly recreations of the past interacted. And, as with the famous quarrel between Nietzsche and Wilamowitz-Moellendorf over *The Birth of Tragedy*, over the spirit and the letter of Greek culture, they could momentously collide.

The investigation and recreation of the Past by artists and scholars (and by archaeologists) was as important a factor in nineteenth century culture as the extraordinary scientific-industrial and social transformation of the Present. And Ibsen's career from *Catilina* to *Emperor and Galilean* reflects this; almost twice as many plays are set in the distant past as are set in the present. And these are not escapist costume dramas in the manner of Victor Hugo's *Hernani*. Whatever their success, they are serious attempts by the poet to recover for the modern theater the past forms of cultural life in terms of aesthetic consciousness. In the essay "On the Heroic Ballad," Ibsen insists on an unbroken chain of consciousness in the people, from earliest times to the present, in which the old mythic presences continue to live.[11] This should be the modern poet's subject matter. The essay itself is an example of the poetic imagination working upon the material of scholarship to bring it to life, like a sculptor working on clay.

This union of the mythopoeic and the scholarly visions makes for an uneasy alliance, for their agendas are bound continually to clash. These two agendas (and, I have claimed, much of the argument and imagery of *The Birth of Tragedy*) seem yoked together with beautiful incongruity in the marriage of Hedda and Tesman: of a Hedda who, as Errol Durbach observes, wants to escape the "world of generation, time and death"[12] (history, that is) and to live mythically; and of a Tesman who wishes to bury himself utterly among the archives of insignificant history. And *Hedda Gabler* is followed by a play in which the two lovers, Hilde and Solness, attempt to defy the constricting facts of their histories and to live mythically, validating visionary memory and visionary possibility.[13]

Emperor and Galilean, which explores far beyond the conceptual range of most Norwegian – or European – imaginations, combines, like Flaubert's *Salammbô*, the imaginative and the scholarly enterprises (Hedda and Tesman). It is a compelling account of Julian's futile attempt to recover the life of the spiritual past against the inertia, absurdity, mendacity and pedantry of intractable history. And the play, for all its great qualities, seems, like Julian's quest itself, to sink under the weight of its burden of historical detail (which many also think true of *Salammbô*). The mythopoeic impulse of the play, especially in Part Two, is smothered by its scholarly conscientiousness. It is not surprising that actions, character-types and themes of *Emperor and Galilean* re-emerge in *Hedda Gabler*.

There seems to be a clear continuity between Ibsen's early and later work, though it is a continuity of evolution, development, in which the relations between past and present in his art become absolutely inverted. In the early work up to *Emperor and Galilean*, Ibsen is looking at the past from the standpoint of his contemporary world and its needs; in the later work he is looking at the contemporary world from the standpoint of the past and its requirements. The later Ibsen has gone over to the ranks of the occult, of the reproachful ghosts.

The series of dramas from *Lady Inger of Østråt* (1855) to *The Vikings at Helgeland* (1858) performs a dual purpose. First, it represents an aesthetic recovery of the Norwegian past in reverse sequence, from Renaissance, through medieval to Viking times; second, this series of four plays also is an exercise in the literary styles or phases of aesthetic consciousness appropriate to each period: dramatic for *Lady Inger*, lyric for *The Feast at Solhoug*, lyric-balladic for *Olaf Liliekrans*, and epic for *The Vikings at Helgeland*.[14]

These plays are the young poet's attempted mastery simultaneously of his art form and of his subject – Norwegian consciousness as it has evolved through the phases of its cultural history. Knowing the stages of this evolution is essential to an adequate understanding of modern conscious- ness itself.

This reversed historical sequence of the plays is not altered if we add *St. John's Night*, or subtract *Olaf Liliekrans*, neither of which Ibsen wanted to be included among his published works. For *St. John's Night*, set in Ibsen's own day (and remarkably prefiguring scenes, characters, actions, images in *The Wild Duck*), has as its subject the problematic presence of that very past – as disputed inheritance – which the following plays will explore. And *Olaf Liliekrans* (oddly prefiguring details in *The Master Builder*) merely extends the medieval consciousness of *The Feast of Solhoug* into a more remote and fantastic medievalism. Ibsen's first plays for the Norwegian theater,[15] therefore, appropriately represented a layer-by-layer excavation of the national consciousness. As Ibsen explained his procedure, regarding *Lady Inger*, in a preface to *The Feast of Solhoug*, "I tried as far as possible to live myself into the ways and customs of that period, into the emotional life of the people, into their patterns of thought and modes of expression."[16]

For Hegel, it was in its arts and philosophy, its cultural artefacts (forms of consciousness) rather than in its historical actions, that a people grasped its essential reality and so made it available for later generations to possess. This, in fact, is the cornerstone of Hegel's whole Philosophy of History: the discourse of past cultures can and indeed must be recovered and relived by the present. Whatever the soundness of the idea (it has been put into question by Jacques Derrida), Ibsen plausibly could claim that by recovering past modes of aesthetic expression – quintessential consciousness – he was incorporating these past spiritual phases of the people into the modern consciousness of his own art and that of his public. This might sound too abstract an intention for a dramatist, who must create living characters for the stage, but how else *would* he be able to make the past live unless he believed it could be recollected imaginatively as consciousness?

From this standpoint, the conceptual range of his art ideally would mirror and even awaken, at the deepest levels, the conceptual range of the people. These layers of the cultural and national past would make up a conflict-filled continuum within the modern individual and communal psyches which could be realized as dramatic art. In this imaginative-cultural space the poet could find metaphors more adequate for his own psychic life and for the conflicts within his society. And, by maintaining historical perspectives, shared by us all, behind modern psychological and social phenomena, Ibsen was able to offer a saner and more comprehensive image of human life than one that fastened exclusively on the problems of the present.

But what then follows, I want to suggest, is a phenomenon that could be described even as somewhat sinister: as the dramatist more deeply and widely explores the cultural past, a past now extending beyond Scandinavia, this starts taking on the nature of an alternative *world*, a world of presences and forces with at least as much attractive power as that which the everyday world can offer. This world develops a symbolic vocabulary independent of and even hostile to that employed by the modern world.

Roland Barthes observed of Greek drama that the total corpus of myths upon which it drew made up "a second-order semiotic system," which, Charles Segal in *Interpreting Greek Tragedy* glosses, "creates its own language, its own system of relations between signifier and signified."[17] Ibsen would be repeating, in his own program of imaginative emancipation, what Barthes observes occurred with the very origins of drama in Greece:

Associated with the "loosening" of work time, the theater installed another time, a time of myth and of consciousness, which could be experienced not as leisure but as another life. For this suspended time, by its very duration, became a saturated time.[18]

In classical Athens, this addition to everyday reality of myth-saturated consciousness, whereby the theater of Dionysos became filled with the ghosts of the cultural past and of previous performances within that theater space, was one the whole community could share. In the modern world, however, beginning with Romanticism, no such cultural consensus exists. Theater shares the modern world's division between conventional and unconventional cultures – often facing each other in mutual hostility or bafflement.

Once Ibsen embarked upon the intellectual journey that extended his imagination into the rich supertext of post-Revolutionary European culture, he would be brought into greater alienation from modernity. He would fashion out of the Past, which was to include the huge subversive terrain of *Emperor and Galilean*, not only an occult *alternative* to modernity but, more startling, a dramatic method of transforming the people, events and things of the modern world back into mythic people, events and things, returning lost modernity to its more adequate archetypal origins. James Joyce, in *Ulysses*, infiltrated the archetypes of Western culture into the seemingly densely intractable quotidian banalities of Dublin life: Ibsen already had performed a similar service for modern Norway. In each of the plays in the twelve-play cycle the quotidian world of contemporary bourgeois life is reconstructed to express the numinous life of the archetypal realm.

The Romantic and post-Romantic supertext has built within it an allegiance to an idea of Nature and to an idea of the Past, both betrayed by modernity; it therefore also has built within it a profound quarrel with the modern world. W.B. Yeats' comment – that he and Ibsen did not have the same friends but they had the same enemies – reveals how even opponents within the modernist tradition shared an antipathy towards the mainstream culture – an antipathy often vehemently reciprocated.

Drawn first to the nationalist agenda, that is, to the deepest accord *with* his culture, Ibsen embarked upon an exploration of the spiritual past that would lead him into the deepest alienation *from* his culture, one consequence of which, surely, was twenty-seven years of exile in which his most significant work was achieved. This exile was to the antiquities of Italy and to the new world order of evolving Germany. The exile itself, therefore, supplied Ibsen with the widest and most potent arena Europe could offer for the abiding subject of his art: the clash of Past and Present, between human possibilities revealed by the Past and the likely degradation or distortion of that identity by the ideologies, blindnesses and demands of modernity.

I suggest that when Ibsen took up the realist method, it was less to imitate or record the tremors within a modernity for which he then expressed little regard than to *transform* this modernity so that it would take on the identity of the mythopoeic, myth-saturated world of his imagination, to render reality occult, in fact. A world in which, to take the last four plays alone, a Valkyrie-like Hilde Wangel descends from the mountains in response to Solness's fearful summons, in which a Rat Wife and her black dog emerge from the sea to lure to his death an unwanted child, in which Borkman can address the spirits of his mountain kingdom, and in which the white-clad Irene can emerge from her tomb to confront her artist-betrayer, is a world responsive to occult dimensions of reality that everyday modern life is not attuned to. And this is true of all the plays in the Realist Cycle, beginning with *Pillars of Society*. Reality is reshaped by Ibsen's art better to conform to dimensions of human identity derived from the Past. It means the contemporary world that lay to Ibsen's hand is refashioned by him into a more adequate one. This is the Ibsen, after all, who in 1871 advised his friend Georg Brandes:

What I recommend for you is a thoroughgoing, full-blooded egoism, which will force you for a time to regard yourself and your work as the only things of consequence in this world, and everything else as simply non-existent. ... There are actually moments when the whole history of the world reminds one of a sinking ship; the only thing to do is to save oneself.[19]

I have borrowed the term "counter-discourse" from Michel Foucault, who sees this Schillerian stance as the essential mode of modern literature:

throughout the nineteenth century, and right up to our own day – from Hölderlin to Mallarmé and on to Antonin Artaud – literature achieved autonomous existence, and separated itself from all other language with a deep scission, only by forming a sort of "counter-discourse". ... In the modern age, literature is that which compensates for (and not that which confirms) the signifying function of language.[20]

Romantic and post-Romantic thought, in other words, is a deliberately *subversive*, second-order semiotic system, aware of how much is left out by the discourse of modernity; how much the vocabulary employed by a materialist culture is repressively limited; how much of what is invaluable to our human identity has been sacrificed in order to further modernity's projects – political, social, financial, academic, domestic and so on. This is the nightmare Herbert Marcuse designated "one-dimensional man" which is, among other things, humanity without living cultural memory.

The alienated artist will see the everyday world *only* in terms of its capacity to take on the forms of the alternative imaginative world he or she more intensely inhabits. This, I believe, is what happens by the time Ibsen embarks upon his cycle of twelve realist plays: that their realist details of action, character, dialogue, scene, are metaphors selected *only* insofar as they can take on archetypal identity, and can enact the archetypal action the play sets out. In Ibsen's realist method there is a continuous interplay between the mythopoeic story and the modern reality that frustrates its manifestation; but, ultimately, the archetypal dimension is able to assert itself and to give reality a shape and significance which the dispiritualized consciousness of the modern world seeks to evade. As Ibsen's son Sigurd writes in *Human Quintessence*:

[Art] gives liberty of action to forces and possibilities to which life does not grant the chance of coming into their rights.[21]

The past will come to seem dual: on the one hand, it is seen as the historical process by which "all mankind is on the wrong track," as Ibsen writes in a note to *Ghosts*; on the other, it is seen as the neglected repository of forces and possibilities whose restoration to their rights might contribute towards a new humanity created out of what Brand calls the "torsoes of amputated mind." At its extreme this vision will see modern humanity as a walking dead that needs to be awakened, as in Edvard Munch's painting *Evening on Karl Johan Street.*

Against the random anarchy and futility of inchoate history, art sets up the coherency and significance of mythic and archetypal identity. This, for the orthodox after all, already is a major function of religion. The Christian's or Muslim's experience of individual identity and destiny in the world is rescued from the anarchy and futility of modern history by an abiding and transcendent interpretation of the world whose perspectives transform his or her experience of modernity. Artists like Ibsen and Joyce, or philosophers like Hegel and Nietzsche, who have cut loose from the certitude of orthodoxy, will seek its equivalent. But not by means of new dogmas. Writers such as Ibsen and Joyce assign to themselves the validation of the worlds they create, and so their work will claim much once considered the province of religion. After all, it was Ibsen's far more cautious contemporary, Matthew Arnold, who nevertheless wrote, in *The*

Study of Poetry (1880), "Most of what now passes with us for religion and philosophy will be replaced by poetry."

What gives such great value to the work of Ibsen, Yeats, Joyce, Pound or Beckett is that, whatever sources or disciplines they draw into their work, they never fall back on sustaining systems or dogmas; they share no "solidarity" (as Ibsen declared) with given modes of thought or value. They may employ, as I claim Ibsen employs Hegel, structures that can serve as the scaffolding of their projects; but the structure of Hegel's *Phenomenology* or of Homer's *The Odyssey* are springboards, only, for the author's most audacious artistic explorations.

The everyday modern world that confronts such an artist (which naïve realists believe is the proper object of the artist's *mimesis*) is neither natural nor true but is itself an ill-constructed artefact, made by the blundering human consciousness, a bad artist, through a long, conflict-filled history of repression, evasion, deception and distortion. Modernity, then, is itself at work on the human spirit spoiling and falsifying the material bequeathed by the Past. The alienated artist will try to restore this material to a more adequate shape or identity. At the end of his long life's work, Ibsen has the artist Rubek comment on his portraits that really were of "alle de kaere husdyr" – all the dear domestic animals – and continues: "all the animals that humanity [menneskene] has warped [forkvaklet] in its own image. And have warped humanity in return."[22]

These images of a distorted animalic humanity stand in stark contrast to Rubek's masterpiece, "Resurrection Day," the naked young Irene, uncorrupted by the world and its unhappy history, "awakening to light and glory with nothing ugly or unclean to cast from her."[23] This also reminds us of Brand's vision of a regenerate humanity arising from our disastrously fragmented human identity:

> Forth from all these stumps of Soul,
> Torsoes of amputated Mind,
> These separated heads and hands,
> A hero strong and whole shall rise
> In whom God finds his greatest work
> His heir, his Adam, young and free.[24]

Both the naked Irene and this Michangelesque Adam are, I think, metaphors for the humanity which is our birthright, but which we can only glimpse behind the unhappy portraiture of our distorted (forkvaklet) humanity that has experienced the Fall into Time. Ibsen's realism had to depict these distortions as well as indicate more adequate, if less comfortable, dimensions of our identity, just as Rubek could not be content with the figure of Irene but had to surround it with images of animal-faced humans swarming up from the earth crust.

We glimpse the image of our lost and our potential humanity by means of the archetypal presences that take over Ibsen's realistic stage and, assembled like the broken torsoes and limbs of Brand's vision, hint at the scale and power of our potential identity as well as at the extent of our loss. Truly to appreciate Ibsen's art, especially the art of the great twelve-play Cycle, we need to keep in sight both perspectives: our fallen reality, and the past and potential reality from which we have fallen. Schiller wrote, and I think Ibsen agreed, "Culture is to set man free and to help him be equal to his concept."[25] This concept lies behind modernity as an unfulfilled project.

The everyday world is an inferior or bungled work of art because it does not know itself, does not know what of itself it has sacrificed and maimed: because it does not give "liberty of action to forces and possibilities" that the artist might consider indispensable to human truth and freedom. Hegel remarked that the known, just because it is known, is the unknown. That is, familiarity has hidden from us the monstrous strangeness of what we have made of life, and Ibsen wishes to *estrange* us from this familiar unreality, to make us see it as riddled with contradiction and as filled with neglected spiritual presence. This, we might say, is his version of the Brechtian *Verfremdungseffekt*.

In conventional melodrama the spirit world is the fearful realm. Peter Brooks, in *The Melodramatic Imagination,* describes how the early melodrama of France created the terms of a new "moral-occult" universe to replace the metaphysically sanctioned world of pre-revolutionary culture. This melodrama was "a drama of emblems,"[26] of violently opposed typological characters and actions, of astonishing manifestations from a natural world engaged in the human conflict of Good and Evil. Storms, earthquakes, fires, floods were all elements of an extravagant and thrilling theatrical code, "an architecture of pure signifiers" within which the morally stereotypical characters menaced or were menaced. Miraculous "signs" could reveal the presence of good or evil and of providential intervention. Brooks notes how "in a novel by Dickens or a play by Ibsen" there is a "movement of the plot toward discovery of identity, and the moral anagnorisis that accompanies it"[27] which is wholly inappropriate to the melodrama's dynamic interplay of bipolar, competitive signs. In the more Gothic versions of this melodrama, the spirit world mostly was demonic. Menacing the moral-human world (also bipolar in terms of good and evil), it had to be defeated by heroes and heroines of a reassuring conventionality. Every encounter with the demonic was an ultimately triumphant reinforcement of conventionality.

In a Copernican reversal, Ibsen takes the side of the reproachful and importunate ghosts, the archetypes that wish to possess and awakens us, and it is the normal and conventional world that is perhaps looked upon with horror. Ibsen also wishes to create a drama of occult presences and of the interplay of human and natural forces and one might say that he recovers for "high culture" much of the power of the older popular melodrama. His "metaphysical landscape" is invested with a personally authenticated symbology, a drama of signs in which the "archetypal text" engages with the "realistic text" for possession of the play's dominant language.[28] And the combat is a mortal one. For the world of modernity seems to menace that potential identity that justifies human existence. It is the occult world that possesses the "forces and possibilities" that should come into their rights and redeem us through a struggle more gigantic than the hopeful project of a Norwegian theater, back in 1851, ever could have forseen. It is Ibsen's major triumph as a dramatist, I think, that he was able to make available for modern drama a new occult space, a metaphysical landscape as ambitious as, and far more credible than, that of the older melodrama described by Brooks. It is a landscape of the existential drama of the modern spirit first mapped out in the non-theatrical dramas *Brand* and *Peer Gynt* and extended in history in *Emperor and Galilean*. In the last four plays and in *The Lady from the Sea* Ibsen recovered this metaphysical landscape and historical perspective for the modern theater, making it a space where the modern spirit – modernity – is lured into a confrontation with those archetypal forces and possibilities whose rights it would prefer to deny.

Modernity dearly would like to be rid of the challenge of the past, to erase it in a form of cultural lobotomy and so get on with the frightfully maimed (forkvaklet) and limited agendas of our contemporary world. The media of modernity seek to persuade us of the adequacy of culturally lobotomized human identity. Recidivisms such as nationalism seek to resurrect only a lethal fragment of our identity, truncating it from our wider humanity. Ibsen's lifelong struggle against what he termed "the trolls that infest the mind and heart" required his modern theater to be a spiritual battlefield whose ghostly combats beneath the realistic surface are fought to prevent the triumph of one-dimensional humanity. John Gabriel Borkman's lament that the treasure-filled kingdom he sought to bring into being now lies leaderless, given over to the pillage of mediocre and visionless plunderers, might well be the lament of the poet himself at seeing the spiritual heritage of the past as recklessly and as fatally devastated as the natural world we have inherited. A note to a draft of *When We Dead Awaken* reads: "In this country, it is only the mountains that give an echo, not the people."[29]

NOTES

1 *The Oxford Ibsen*, ed. James Walter McFarlane (London, 1960), 1:608–9.
2 Cited in *National Theaters in Northern and Eastern Europe, 1746–1900*, ed. Laurence Senelick (Cambridge, 1991), 151.
3 Cited ibid., 165.
4 "On the Heroic Ballad and its Significance for Serious Poetry," *The Oxford Ibsen*, 1:672.
5 Ibid.
6 Edward W. Said, *Culture and Imperialism* (New York, 1993), 227.
7 *Wagner on Music and Drama: A Compendium of Richard Wagner's Prose Works*, ed. Albert Goldman and Evert Sprinchorn (New York, 1964), 91.
8 Friedrich Nietzsche, *The Birth of Tragedy* and *The Geneaology of Morals*, trans. Francis Golffing (New York, 1956), 137.
9 *Selected Prose of T.S. Eliot*, ed. Frank Kermode (London, 1975), 178, 177.
10 Mircea Eliade, *Cosmos and History: The Myth of the Eternal Return* (New York, 1959, 153.
11 *The Oxford Ibsen*, 1:672–84 *passim*.
12 Errol Durbach, *Ibsen the Romantic* (London, 1982), 35 and 34–52 *passim*.
13 Cf. James L. Calderwood, "*The Master Builder* and the Failure of Symbolic Success," *Modern Drama*, 27 (1984), 616–36.
14 Cf. Brian Johnson, *To the Third Empire: Ibsen's Early Drama* (Minneapolis, 1980), 58–101 *passim*.
15 Though *The Vikings at Helgeland* was first performed in Christiania, the play was conceived in Bergen.
16 *The Oxford Ibsen*, 1:372.
17 Charles Segal, *Interpreting Greek Tragedy: Myth, Poetry, Text* (New York, 1986), 49.
18 Roland Barthes, *The Responsibility of Forms* trans. Richard Howard (New York, 1985), 77.
19 Henrik Ibsen, *Letters and Speeches*, ed. Evert Sprinchorn (London, 1965), 114.
20 Michel Foucault, *The Order of Things: An Archaeology of the Human Sciences* (New York, 1973), 43–44.

21 Sigurd Ibsen, *Human Quintessence*, trans. Marcia Hargis Janson (New York, 1912), 92.

22 Henrik Ibsen, *Samlede Værker*, Mindeudgave (Kristiania, 1908). V: 367.

23 *When We Dead Awaken*, Act 2, my translation. This whole immense metaphoric art, especially that of the twelve-play cycle, is fundamentally misread if seen in terms of modern realism. If one took one figure alone, for example, the "devil" identity as it profoundly but playfully travels through the Cycle (after a debut in *Peer Gynt*), in the varying figures of Nils Krogstad, Jakob Engstrand, Morten Kiil, Dr. Relling (living below with his "demonisk" companion Molvik), Ulrik Brendel, Judge Brack, Hinkel and Ulfheim, we will glimpse an idea of both Ibsen's use of a major metaphoric presence in European art and the wonderful audacity of his variations on this satanic theme within the mythopoeic polyphony of the Realist Cycle.

24 *Samlede Væker* 11:22. My translation.

25 "On the Sublime," in *Two Essays by Friedrich von Schiller: Naïve and Sentimental Poetry: On the Sublime* (New York, 1966), 194.

26 Peter Brooks, *The Melodramatic Imagination* (New Haven and London, 1976), 53.

27 Ibid.

28 *The Wild Duck* presents the richest polyphony – or cacophony – of competing vocabularies, each speaker offering a single perspective upon a drastically fragmented reality. Hedvig Ekdal alone can respond to all of them, as Hedda alone engages with all the speakers in *Hedda Gabler*, and neither play allows any one mode, or perspective, ultimately to predominate.

29 *The Oxford Ibsen*, 8:355.

Patterns of Structure and Character in Ibsen's *Rosmersholm*

MARVIN CARLSON

In Henrik Ibsen's final play, *When We Dead Awaken,* the reader can scarcely escape an impression of careful and conscious arrangement of elements. The progression of the settings from a veranda near the fjords to the high fells, then to the mountain site of the final apotheosis, has the clear symbolic shape of a Strindberg pilgrimage drama. The main characters form complementary and contrasting patterns so consciously balanced that some critics have likened the working out of the play to the construction of a string quartet.[1]

Ibsen's last drama, however, merely brings to the surface a concern with the careful patterning of character and situation which can be found throughout the dramatist's work, even in the plays of his middle period, where a basically realistic approach tends to mask its importance. Taking *Rosmersholm* as an example, I propose to demonstrate how an awareness of the patterns beneath the surface of this play, perhaps the most complex Ibsen every created, can guide us through much of its dynamic.

From a technical point of view, the first thing that strikes one about *Rosmersholm* is its remarkable concentration. The action covers approximately forty-eight hours; the sole setting is Rosmersholm itself, three acts in the living room and one in Rosmer's study; and there are only six characters to develop the extremely complicated action. There is more than a hint here of the practice of classic tragedy, an impression strongly reinforced by Ibsen's use of Madame Helseth. Were we concerned only with the play's plot she would be clearly the least important of the characters, except of course, for her closing speech, but it is obvious that she contributes significantly to deepening the drama. Little wonder, for Ibsen has entrusted her with the duties assigned in classic tragedy to a whole group of characters. Most obviously, she serves as confidante to

Rebekka, but she doubles as oracle (so that she more than anyone else explains to us the nature and the effects of the "curse" on the house of Rosmer), as chorus, and, in describing the catastrophe, as the traditional messenger.

Madame Helseth's scenes, moreover, give us a first suggestion of the sort of patterning we can observe throughout the play. She opens and closes the play, of course (describing to us the view of the millrace from the window in both cases), but she opens and closes three of the four acts as well. Every act but the second begins with a dialogue between Madame Helseth and Rebekka and every act but the second closes in the same way until Madame Helseth, left alone at last, reports Rebekka's death. This pattern of repetition becomes more striking as we realize that these are essentially Madame Helseth's only scenes in the play. Except for these six times, she makes only three brief appearances, all strictly utilitarian – to announce Brendel in Act One, to look for Rebekka and to announce Mortensgaard in Act Two.

The three acts "framed" by the Rebekka–Madame Helseth scenes have not only this structural feature in common. They are also the three which take place in the Rosmersholm living room, and Rebekka is the character who holds them together. Act Two, set in Rosmer's study, is also the only act in which Rosmer, not Rebekka, is continuously on stage. Rosmer, a victim of his tradition, needs no Madame Helseth to remind him of his white horses. His act, however, is arranged in harmony with a more complicated structural dynamic, which we may best approach by considering the relations between several of the central characters.

Kroll's statement in the first act, "You are so terribly susceptible to outside influence," provides the key to Rosmer's character, and indirectly to much of the action of *Rosmersholm,* where influence often takes the form of unconscious repetition or echo. When the play begins, Rosmer is intellectually under the influence of Rebekka, though his inability to cross the bridge reminds her that she has still not entirely freed him from his past. Further and stronger confirmation comes when Kroll appears and Rosmer is unable to confess to him his new liberal beliefs. It is as if the psychic forces working on Rosmer from opposite directions, represented at this point by Kroll and Rebekka, cancel each other out and produce in Rosmer a kind of intellectual paralysis. To move past this position of stasis, Ibsen introduces the strange, exaggerated, but engaging figure of Ulrik Brendel. He arrives fired with new enthusiasms, a liberal *deus ex machina,* and when he leaves the scene we find that his arrival somehow provided Rosmer with the impetus previously lacking. He now confesses to Kroll, and though Rosmer is saddened by his old friend's bitter rejection, he confesses to Rebekka after Kroll leaves that he feels now purged and calm. The Brendel scene thus serves as the emotional center of the act, and it is the structural center as well, the capstone of a symmetrically balanced arrangement of character confrontations as we may see by laying out the scenes in order:

Rebekka – Madame Helseth
    Rebekka – Kroll
        Rebekka – Kroll – Rosmer
            Rebekka – Kroll – Rosmer – Brendel
        Rebekka – Kroll – Rosmer
    Rebekka – Kroll
Rebekka – Madame Helseth

The structure of the fourth act is a distinct echo of the first, but with emotional forces reversed, like a negative of Act One's positive. Now Rosmer begins the act under the intellectual influence of Kroll, but prevented from complete commitment by his remaining feelings for Rebekka. His confrontation with her reduces him once more to psychic paralysis, since she can cancel Kroll's force but not overcome it. Once again Brendel arrives to break the deadlock, but this time he appears shattered and defeated, opting for death instead of life, and it is that impetus he delivers to Rosmer. When the strange figure departs, Rosmer demands the sacrifice of Rebekka and then joins in her immolation. The arrangement of scenes is simpler than in the first act, but balanced in the same manner:

Rebekka – Madame Helseth
    Rebekka – Rosmer
        Rebekka – Rosmer – Brendel
    Rebekka – Rosmer
Madame Helseth

The middle two acts, in which Brendel does not appear, have another system of organization, but it is similarly consistent, so that Act Three is a structural echo of Two just as Four was of One. To trace its development, we need to consider briefly the conflict of forces within the two central characters. In a key speech in the third act Rebekka seeks to explain the dynamic of her destruction of Beata. "I believe that there are two sorts of will in each of us," she suggests. "I wanted to be rid of Beata, one way or another. But even so, I never believed it would happen. Each time I was tempted to risk going another step I seemed to hear something cry out within me: 'No further! Not a step further!' And yet I couldn't stop."[2]

Ibsen's critical pronouncements on his plays are rare, but he did elaborate on this conflict of wills in a letter to Bjørn Kristensen of February 13, 1887:

The play deals with the internal struggle of any serious-minded man who wishes to reconcile his way of life with his beliefs. The different functions of the spirit do not develop uniformly or comparably in any one individual. The acquisitive instinct rushes forward from gain to gain, but moral consciousness, "the conscience," is, on the other hand, very conservative. It has roots deep in tradition and in past events. From this arises the conflict within an individual.[3]

These contradictory "functions of the spirit" are old friends to students of Ibsen. The acquisitive instinct (*tilegnelsesdriften*) is the instinct of the reformer, the idealist, the bringer of light and truth. Moral consciousness (*moralbevidstheden*) is the driving force of the conservative elements, the powers of tradition. In the early social dramas, Ibsen encourages us to sympathize with the first and condemn the second, but *An Enemy of the People* and even more clearly *The Wild Duck* take a more balanced view. In *Rosmersholm* we find a still more complex development. Mortensgaard and Kroll seem at first glance to suggest these opposing positions, but the play reveals them as morally indistinguishable. The real conflict between the functions of the spirit has become internal, as Rebekka suggests, and is played out within her and within Rosmer. Contrasts and balances are correspondingly more complex, but in the overall action of the play we may describe Rosmer as fundamentally a conservative spirit in the process of being, as he calls it, "purified" by the acquisitive instinct, while Rebekka is fundamentally an acquisitive spirit in the process of being, in her expression, "infected" with moral consciousness.

One act is devoted to exploring the effects of this dilemma on each of these leading characters. Act Two, as we have already noted, focuses on Rosmer. After a scene with Rebekka which serves as a sort of overture to the act, the parallel scenes with Kroll and Mortensgaard reveal to Rosmer that the weight of the past prevents both him and others from ever acting as free agents, and that the idealism of which he dreamed has no place in the practical world. In desperation he turns to Rebekka with an offer of marriage, but at this point, a victim of the conflict of wills, she is unable to help either Rosmer or herself. She at first reacts with a cry of joy, her "old driving spirit fighting to free itself" as she explains in the final act, but this urge is immediately checked by the power of the "Rosmer philosophy of life."

Neither Rosmer nor the audience yet has this explanation at hand as the second act closes, however, and Rebekka's reaction seems unmotivated and puzzling. The tension thus created carries on into the third act where the conflicting forces working on Rebekka defeat and isolate her as Rosmer was defeated and isolated in Act Two. After the opening scene with Madame Helseth, Rebekka confronts Rosmer in a scene paralleling the Rosmer-Kroll scene of Act Two. Her resolution is undermined by Rosmer's obsession with guilt and shattered completely in the following Kroll scene where Rebekka finds that she also is a moral prisoner of the past. Now it is her turn for a desperate action, and she turns to Rosmer as he turned to her at the same point in the previous act. Her confession of guilt for Beata's death is a terrible gamble, since it frees Rosmer only at the risk of his turning from her in revulsion. The gambler loses: Rosmer is still not capable of standing alone, and he falls back immediately under the influence of the now more dominant Kroll. Rebekka is left alone, to confess her defeat to Madame Helseth. In summary, the parallel development of these middle acts runs as follows:

ACT TWO		ACT THREE
Rosmer – Rebekka	preparatory scene	Rebekka – Madame Helseth
Rosmer – Kroll	the hero's resolution undermined	Rebekka – Rosmer
Rosmer – Mortensgaard	the resolution collapses, leading to a desperate bid to the other hero for affirmation and stability	Rebekka – Rosmer – Kroll
Rosmer – Rebekka	rejection and isolation	Rebekka – Madame Helseth

Symmetrical arrangements of action and character development can be found wherever we look in the play. Probably the most obvious balanced elements are the two politicians, the liberal Mortensgaard and the conservative Kroll, with the ironic twist already noted that these two enemies are far more like each other than either is like Rosmer, whom both attempt to use. Their twin scenes with Rosmer in the second act are so similar in development as to border on the comic, precisely the sort of borderline comedy Ibsen loved to use. Both are quick to think the worst of Rosmer, but more disconcerting to him, both are quite willing to accept this so long as he remains quiet and lends them his name.

There are clear parallels also between Brendel and Rosmer. Brendel's use as a psychic catalyst seems explicable largely because his emotional situation echoes Rosmer's almost to the point of caricature. In Act One he, like Rosmer, stands on the brink of carrying out a great dream. In Act Four he, like Rosmer, retreats shattered and disillusioned from the world of men. What Brendel says of Mortensgaard applies in significant measure to Kroll as well, and not in the slightest to Rosmer and Brendel: "Peder Mortensgaard is quite capable of living his life without ideals. And, don't you see, *that* is the great secret of action and success." Both action and success are denied to the dreamers Rosmer and Brendel, who share a repulsion for the physical, the real world. The very idea of actually setting pen to paper "arouses a nauseating disgust" in Brendel, while Beata's manifestation of passion "to which she expected me to respond" inspired "horror" in Rosmer. Thus we find that as early as the second act of the play a set of balanced positions has been defined which we might represent in this way:

conservative	*liberal*	
Kroll	Mortensgaard	*realist*
Rosmer	Brendel	*idealist*

Various parallel actions within this framework reinforce its symmetry. Both conservatives, for example, have publicly disgraced their liberal "opposites" in action antecedent to the play. So Brendel's expulsion from the debating society at the instigation of Kroll is an echo of Rosmer's more serious exposure of Mortensgaard. Within the play, both idealists are disillusioned by their realist counterparts at the same point in the action, the end of Act Three. Here Kroll seizes the opportunity offered to him by Rebekka's confession to take Rosmer off alone and convince him that he is incapable of "enobling the minds of men." At the same time, Montensgaard is similarly convincing Brendel of the futility of *his* mission, as we learn when Brendel reappears in the fourth act.

The Rebekka–Beata relationship provides an even more complicated illustration of balance and echo. The dead wife is of course a continuing presence in *Rosmersholm*, even more so than Captain Alving in *Ghosts*, and any reader of Ibsen will quickly recognize that we have here another variation of the arrangement of a man (usually somewhat neurotic) caught by the conflicting claims of two women of contrasting temperaments, an arrangement found as early as Ibsen's first play. Thus it is tempting, and in part justified, to align Rebekka West, who comes from pagan Finmark, with such Valkyrie figures as Hiördis of *The Vikings at Helgeland*, Gerd in *Brand* and Hedda Gabler, and to relate the self-sacrificing Beata to the angelic counterparts of these figures – Dagny, Agnes, and Thea. As we have already noted, however, Rebekka, like Rosmer, contains within herself two competing spirits. As the "Rosmer view of life" gains ascendency, she becomes, at least in her own eyes, more and more like Beata, a metamorphosis she views with mixed desperation and horror.

This dynamic is first clearly seen at work in the climax of Act Two, when Rosmer asks Rebekka to marry him. Clearly Rebekka undergoes a change between the moment when she "cries out in joy" and that when she tells Rosmer definitively "I will never be your wife." Here is the critical intervening interchange:

> *Rosmer.* Good. Let us try. We two shall be one. The place left by the dead must remain empty no longer.
> *Rebekka.* Me – in Beata's place – –!
> *Rosmer.* That will put her out of our lives. Completely out. Forever and always.
> *Rebekka.* [*softly and tremulously*] Do you believe that, Rosmer?
> *Rosmer.* It must be so! It must! I can not – I will not go through life with a corpse on my back. Help me to throw it off, Rebekka. And let us thus stifle all memories in freedom, in joy, in passion. You shall be for me the only wife I ever had.

It is clear that a major motive for Rebekka's refusal is her fear that despite Rosmer's disclaimer, he is attempting to recast her as a substitute Beata. Indeed the final impetus for her reaction may well be Rosmer's use of the word "passion," a word which he has already used unfavorably to describe Beata's feelings toward him. In the fourth act Rebekka confesses to this same feeling, and condemns it in herself as Rosmer condemned it in Beata. In any case, Rebekka realizes a danger and shuns it, for to be consistent with her own ideals, she could not accept this new role *without* condemning herself as she condemned the old Beata, as a barrier to Rosmer's freedom. Hence her final, and to Rosmer incomprehensible threat: "But if you ask me again, that's the end all the same. ... For then I go the way Beata went."

Recognition of this threat to Rebekka's personality, indeed to her very existence, should force us to look more closely at Beata and her precise role in the action of the play. Rebekka's description in Act Three of the process by which she led Beata to her death suggests a relationship of an active and a passive agent, but the situation is more complex than that. To begin with, Beata did not simply and passively go to her death, but made several unsuccessful attempts to promote a crisis and interrupt the flow of events. We know of four specific actions she performed, and although the reports of them are somewhat vague, it is possible to arrange them in a reasonably reliable chronological order. Mortensgaard gives an approximation of the time of her death and reports on one of her actions – sending him a letter. "It was toward the end of your late wife's life," he notes. "That must be about eighteen months ago now." Kroll provides information about two other actions, both visits to him: "Twice in the last year of her life she came to me to disclose her fear and bewilderment." On the first visit "she came to report that you had entered the road to apostasy. That you were about to abandon the faith of your fathers." The second visit was "about a month after." Then she mentioned the white horses and hinted at an illicit relationship between Rosmer and Rebekka, saying "now Johannes must marry Rebekka immediately." "That was a Thursday afternoon," Kroll concludes. "On Saturday evening she threw herself into the millstream." Beata's four reported actions may thus be arranged:

1. about 19 months ago – conversation with Kroll, in which she indicates that Rosmer is falling into apostasy.
2. a week or more later (assuming that by "toward the end" Mortensgaard means within the final weeks. Otherwise the action would antedate the Kroll visit, which seems unlikely) – letter to Mortensgaard.
3. about 18 months ago – second conversation with Kroll, in which she hints at a relationship between Rosmer and Rebekka.
4. two days later – Beata throws herself into the millstream.

When we turn to Rebekka, and to the present actions of the play, we find that whatever her dynamic may have been before, she is now no more capable than Beata of controlling external events. She begins the play, like Racine's Phèdre, with the infection of guilt already eroding her will, though she is not yet fully conscious of this. Like Beata she struggles, unsuccessfully, against the fate which is overtaking her, but the most striking thing about her struggle is that it precisely echoes Beata's. The four specific actions taken by the dead wife are precisely repeated, and in order, by Rebekka – indeed, they serve as one basis for the four-act arrangement of the play:

Act One – conversation with Kroll and Rosmer. Rebekka's aim, like Beata's,

is to expose Rosmer's apostasy to Kroll, though she forces Rosmer himself to do this.

Act Two – Rebekka's letter to Mortensgaard. Her letter, like Beata's, solicits Mortensgaard's aid against supposed enemies of Rosmer. Rebekka is thinking of Kroll; Beata, Madame Helseth reveals later, was thinking of Mrs. Kroll.

Act Three – conversation with Rosmer and Kroll. Rebekka reveals the relationship between herself and Rosmer.

Act Four – Rebekka follows Beata to the millstream.

So Rebekka comes, step by step, to precisely the situation she anticipated in the second act and has tried ever since that moment to escape. She has become another Beata, and hence another encumbrance to Rosmer, and she accepts death, as Beata did, to free him. Now it is Rosmer who plays Rebekka's former role as the tempter leading her to destruction. Rebekka's description of that former role accords perfectly with Rosmer's action upon her just before the catastrophe: "Each time I was tempted to risk going another step I seemed to hear something cry out within me: 'No further! Not a step further!' And yet I couldn't stop. I *had* to go just a little bit further. Only the smallest bit. And then a little further – and always a little further. And so it happened. That's how something like that does happen."

Nevertheless Rebekka attempts to shield Rosmer from the guilt of being responsible for this sacrifice by calling it an expiation demanded not by him but by the "Rosmersholm view of life" which she now embraces. Her explanation seems to achieve the enlightenment in Rosmer which she desires, but ironically, this too leads to death: "Very well," he responds. "Then I assume our emancipated view of life, Rebekka. There is no judge over us. Therefore we must see to it that we judge ourselves." If the play ended shortly after this affirmation, we should have little doubt as to Rebekka's success in ennobling Rosmer, for here he seems to recognize and accept a position close to the basic paradox of tragedy – that man's search for identity is fulfilled only through a form of self-destruction. But now, before the step is taken, doubts and qualifications are introduced. "Are you really certain?" asks Rebekka. "What if you are only deceiving yourself? What if it were only a delusion – one of those white horses of Rosmersholm?" "That could well be," Rosmer admits. "We never escape them, we of this house." Whether Rosmer has truly gained an enlightenment thus cannot be determined, as Ibsen is careful to point out in Rosmer's admitted indecision: "This is something we shall never discover." All that exists is the action, the death itself. Still, recognition of the play's patterns leaves one with the strong impression that Rosmer was, after all, never a free agent. Beata, says Rosmer, was swept into the millstream by Rebekka's desire, and Rebekka in her turn is driven to atonement in a parallel action. The cycle now established, how can the so-impressionable Rosmer escape the repeating pattern? His last role of the judge over himself represents thus no progress, but only the grim working out of the double heritage of guilt and fatalism which darken Rosmersholm. Even the sacrificial act becomes one more neurotic imitation, chillingly put in its place by Madame Helseth's dark benediction: "The dead mistress has taken them."

NOTES

1 Most recently and most engagingly James Hurt in *Catiline's Dream* (University of Illinois, 1972), pp. 194–95.
2 Translations from the play are by the author of this article, using volume X of the *Hundreårsutgave* of Henrik Ibsen's *Samlede Verker*, Oslo, 1938–1957.
3 *Samlede Verker*, 18:128.

Marriage, Metaphysics and
The Lady from the Sea Problem

ELINOR FUCHS

In other words, only by denying sexual difference (and gender) as components of subjectivity in real women ... can the philosophers see in "women" the privileged repository of "the future of mankind."[1]

Teresa de Lauretis, *Technologies of Gender*

There has always been a *Lady from the Sea* problem: for a drama of the immaterial, it is too material. Allegorical/realistic, philosophical/psychological: to critics, it has always been too much of the one to be enough of the other. The task of the more recent Ibsen scholars has been to redeem the play by finding a reading that accounts for the two tones of the play, the two water levels (open sea and carp pond) of Ibsen's dramaturgical landscape. But that continues to be difficult, for no matter what reading over the past one hundred years, one thing has always bothered critics. As Henry James grumbled, and Francis Fergusson agreed nearly seventy-five years later, "one winces considerably" when faced with those dratted "pert daughters." (Fergusson staged it, and had first-hand experience that the daughters don't play.)[2]

The most recent effort to rationalize the play's structure comes in a brilliant and deeply argued analysis by the Hegelian Brian Johnston. As he sees it, all strands of the play serve to explicate a central philosophical dilemma, which may be stated: the highest yearning of the human spirit for freedom are in tragic conflict with the demands of organized society.[3] The ballet among the three central characters – Ellida, Wangel and the Stranger – becomes an allegory dialectically working out this problematic. But what, oh what, to do with the "pert daughters"? In Johnston, they are also allegorized. Thus:

The community depicted in the play is one animated by yearning, by longing for release from confinement and finitude. It is restless, discontented (Boletta), unhappily malicious (Hilde), or, like Ellida, subject to extreme disorder.[4]

In the end, the "community" cannot stand too much freedom. Thus, "Humanity chooses to remain earthbound, to reject the lure of absolute freedom, and to remain *this* side of the third empire of spirit."[5]

In this resolution, as readers may notice, something gets lost on the way to the universal signifier. The gender of the female characters of the play – degendered here as "community," "it," "humanity" – has become invisible. Johnston is not alone. Perhaps falling into a pathetic fallacy, critics doing "supertextual" readings of the play treat Ibsen's dramaturgy here in much the same way the men in the play treat the women.[6] That is, the women are invisible as autonomous individuals, but flourish as idea, force, symbol, embodiment of desire.

In these allegorical readings, Ellida Wangel is caught in a philosophical contest between two opposing forces. These are sometimes figured absolute freedom v. contingency, the Erotic v. Love, the Infinite v. the Bounded: all imaged as an opposition of Sea and Land. However it is figured, this central conflict is seen as being embodied in the two men contending for Ellida's allegiance. The central interpretative quarrels about the play concern the opposed values we attach to these men, and the valuation of those values. In such readings, critics discuss the play as if it concerned "The Being from the Sea," the "Species from the Sea," "Modern Western Man from the Sea," and so forth. Ellida Wangel becomes interesting primarily as the instrument through which certain values triumph and others are crushed.

But there is another, devastating, battle of opposing forces below the surface of the action. In this battle the men assert authority and the women struggle for autonomy. *The Lady from the Sea* may be Ibsen's most painful play about the fate of women in male society. It is not only a play about freedom in the metaphysical sense, but about freedom within marriage, and about the way our philosophical ideals must be shaken when confronted with the bondage of half the race.

Without negating the philosophical debate at the loftier reaches of the play, I would like to restore its concrete social dimension, its gendered specificity. A gendered reading of *The Lady from the Sea* brings many surprises. In it, the transcendent turns ironic; male opponents suddenly appear as allies; and Bolette, the pertest daughter, becomes a figure of near-tragedy. Such a reading starts by acknowledging that the "fruen" of the *Fruen fra havet*, Ibsen's Norwegian title, means not just the implied madonna or mermaid (*havfrue*) of the English translation, but also at the more concrete end of the spectrum of possible meanings, the woman or wife, the just plain Frau from the sea.

Reading for gender, we can see an absence not otherwise visible. Ibsen literalizes (though of course *avant la lettre*) the discovery of feminist semioticians that in narrative structure the subject position of women is vacant, and "spoken" by men.[7] In the world of Ibsen's play, there is an eerie vacuum in woman's place, even her place as object or other. Wangel lost one wife and can't quite materialize the second. The Stranger lost a fiancée and never recovered. Lyngstrand lost his mother and for consolation lives with the local midwife. Desperate to marry, Arnholm will cheat to get a woman. The Wangel girls need a mother. Ellida's own mother died long ago. The women who do inhabit the starved, male air are almost fleeing their own bodies: Hilda would rather be a boy, Bolette is miserable as a girl. Ellida wants to be a mermaid. Her self-vacancy encourages men to want to own her, sculpt her, possess her will and her speech.

In Ibsen's story, Ellida Wangel's troubles began years ago with the appearance of so-called "Freeman." Most critics uncritically associate Freeman with freedom. Read for metaphysics, Freeman's "freedom" may be a spiritual challenge for the human race, as embodied in Ellida. But read for gender, this freedom is nothing but compulsion. Ellida had "no will of [her] own" when she was near him, but became engaged because "He said I must."[8] In a trance she permits herself to think that two rings thrown to sea – his idea, not her agreement – constitute an actual engagement. Why? It was "fated to be" (p. 261).

Years later, she flops out of this commitment and falls into another, apparently just the opposite, but from a gendered perspective, very much the same. With Wangel, it is more "he said I must" and "no will of my own." In Act One Wangel enlists Arnholm, behind Ellida's back, to help the "poor sick child" (p. 257). This is the right approach: "I'm sure of it" (p. 237). Like the Stranger, he ventriloquizes Ellida and induces Arholm to do the same. In the next scene, Arnholm "helps" Ellida by demanding a kind of speech control. "[Y]ou must tell me more about this!" he exclaims, and a moment later, "there's no other way: you've got to tell me everything," and still later, "you *must* tell me your troubles, freely and openly ..." (pp. 241, 242, 248).

The act culminates in Lyngstrand's account of the "betrayal" of the American sailor Johnson (alias "Freeman") by his fiancée. "[S]he's mine, and mine she'll always be," Lyngstrand recalls his outburst on the merchant steamer. "And if I go home and fetch her, she'll have to go off with me ..." (pp. 246–247). Lyngstrand may be weak and young, but never too young and weak to enjoy the dominant discourse. Thus Lyngstrand is aroused by fantasies of an archetypal scene of erotic domination, which he intends to sculpt, on the sailor's return: he "stands there over her bed, looking down at her ... dripping wet ..." (p. 245). Masterfully, Lyngstrand attributes his own sexual fantasy to the sleeping woman. It is *her* dream; *she* has summoned this menace from the vasty deep, an emblem of her miserable guilt.

In Act Two, Ellida attempts to explain Freeman to Wangel. Every word her kindly husband utters is an act of unconscious condescension or compulsion. Full of mistaken certainty, he says, "I think I understand."

"But you don't!" she exclaims.

"And yet, I do," he perseveres. He has "seen the whole thing, down to the bottom."

"[D]on't be too sure," she protests.

"[Y]ou can't bear these surroundings," he insists, "We're moving away."

She objects, but Wangel has decided. "It's all settled now ..." (pp. 256–257).

Ellida forces him to listen to her story. After a moment he jumps in again. "I begin to understand."

"No, dear, you're wrong!" she corrects him. She tells more. Finally he is sure again – this time that she's crazy, "much more than I thought," and heavily adds, more "than you can possibly know" (pp. 263–265).

In Act Three the scene changes from a vista of the distant sea to a close-up of a stagnant carp pond. Critics have liked to look for contrast between the land-locked Bolette and her sea-free stepmother and again for a sharp contrast between the two Wangel sisters. The women of the play may be at sea or on a pond, but as the old joke has it, they are in the same boat when it comes to the struggle for female autonomy.

Poor, maligned Bolette, whom Fergusson calls "green" because she doesn't want instantly to marry the manipulative Arnholm. Bolette wants more than anything in life to learn, to attend the university as Father once promised. Bolette carries all the duties of the Wangel household patiently, but at last she permits herself to flare, "I have obligations to myself ..." (p. 271), for which Prof. Fergusson attacks her as "self-absorbed."[9] In a classic "blame the victim" move, Arnholm assures Bolette she can have anything she wants if only she wants it enough. "It depends completely on you," he tells her. "The whole thing is there, right in your own hands." But

Bolette sees where the power lies. "[P]ut in a good word for me with Father" she implores Arnholm (p. 271). Bolette's freedom must be arranged, like – and probably through – a marriage. There is no such thing as an unmediated freedom, a freedom by birthright, for a woman. All the women share this knowledge. Even Hilda, young as she is, knows the facts of women's lives. The road to freedom is paved with husbands, preferably a dead one. In fact (Hilda's famous bridal fantasy) why not attend your own wedding in widow's weeds?

Arnholm has two excellent chances to speak to Wangel about Bolette, but knowing that any guarantee of independence will scotch his marriage plans, he does just the opposite when the opportunity presents itself. "You hardly need to worry about Bolette," he assures Wangel, who declares himself willing to make any sacrifice for his daughters, "if I only knew what" (p. 293). When Bolette asks whether he has talked over her needs with her father, Arnholm flatly lies, "Yes, I've done that ... you musn't be counting on any help from him" (p. 308). So powerful is the momentum of the supertextual for Johnston, however, that he must disregard this evidence and beatify Arnholm as a practitioner of "self-sacrificing" Christian love.[10]

For Arnholm, and all the other men, autonomy for women is literally unthinkable, at least until Act Five. Ibsen makes it painfully clear that in this world woman cannot be figured as other than some spirito-erotic furnishing of the male mind. Thus even when Bolette explains that Arnholm was mistaken about her supposed passion for him, he says, "It's no help, Bolette. Your image – as I carry it within me – will always be colored now by those mistaken emotions" (p. 311). And so Bolette is maneuvered into marriage. She tries to negotiate a narrow zone of self-determination. Remember, "I can study anything I want," she reminds him, after dubiously rising to the bait at the edge of the carp pond. He answers ever so smoothly, "I'll teach you, just as I used to" (p. 313).

No sooner has a stutter of agreement to marry this unsavory person, at least sixteen years her senior, crossed Bolette's lips, than he slides into an obtuse intimacy, "Ah, wait till you see how easy and comfortable we'll be with each other," he murmurs, his arms coiling around her waist (p. 313). "The progress of their affair," writes Fergusson of this gynicide, "is hardly worth the clear, sober light, and the long stage-time, that Ibsen devotes to it." Chekhov, he says, knew how to handle commonplace love affairs "by presenting them very briefly, and without asking the audience to take their outcomes too seriously."[11]

Orley Holtan thinks "five alternative ways of life" are offered in the play, each represented by a male figure.[12] Laying aside Holtan's uncritical assertion of male signifying power, one must at least conclude that he misses Ibsen's savage irony. Thus Holtan believes Arnholm's adaptive "realism," rather than Bolette's crushed life, is Ibsen's interest. Holtan also thinks Ibsen ridicules Lyngstrand as a "helpless dreamer," as if his "dreams" were not supported, however parodically, by a solid foundation of far from helpless male privilege.[13] The Stranger, Wangel and Arnholm all hold inflated, narcissistic views of male power in marriage; Lyngstrand differs only in his inability to act them out. "[M]arriage," he confides to Bolette,

has to be accounted almost a kind of miracle. The way a woman little by little makes herself over until she becomes like her husband. ... [A] woman must feel a profound happiness in that. ... [T]hat she can help [her husband] to create – that she can ease his work for him by being there and making him comfortable and taking care of him and seeing that his life is really enjoyable. I think that must be thoroughly satisfying for a woman. (pp. 284–285)

The only hope for women in this play, apart from their own slowly waking powers, is Dr. Wangel. Ibsen shows how hard it is for Wangel to learn, how excruciating the pressure must be for him to learn even a little, and what a victory it must be accounted when he does begin to learn. We left Wangel in Act Two convincing Ellida that she was mad. In Act Three the two contenders for her allegiance meet face to face and debate to whom she "belongs." The Stranger is as peremptory as ever: "be ready to travel tomorrow night" (p. 279), but he throws Ellida a life line in the form of a new idea: "Imagine –," she marvels, "he said I should go with him of my own free will" (p. 280). It has never occurred to her that she had such a thing to exercise. Overnight the idea grows. She didn't enter marriage of her own free will, she sees. "Everything came together in those words – like a beam of light – and I can see things now, as they are" (p. 297). Wangel is melancholy. "You've never belonged to me – never" (p. 298). The standard of possession is the opposite of the standard of concrete freedom that Ellida is proposing. She wants an unequivocal return of her freedom of choice. Wangel cannot do it. Or, he'll do it tomorrow, after the danger has passed. But by then, Ellida cries, "the future I was meant for may have been ruined! ... A whole, full life of freedom ruined, wasted ... " (p. 301).

We must understand what these words mean coming from a woman. Holtan recounts the story told by Ibsen's biographer Halvdan Koht, that shortly before writing *The Lady from the Sea*, Ibsen "heard of a local girl who, apparently out of frustration and unfulfilled longing to get out into the world and be a poet, had shot herself. This incident so fascinated Ibsen," he goes on, "that he called at her home, obtained pictures of her, read the books she left behind, and even visited her grave."[14] If we persist in reading Ellida as a universal being (that is, as a man) we cannot understand her sense of terrible injustice, what it would mean to suffer "a whole, full life of freedom ruined, wasted." Hers will be an abstract plaint, philosophically interesting perhaps, but which of us achieves absolute freedom in a human life? But read for gender this cry states the anguished preoccupation of Ellida, Bolette, and all woman who reflect on their condition: they want *their* possibility of freedom, not only humanity's in some abstract sense.

One of Ibsen's great spiritual traits is that he never gives up on human growth. Wangel undergoes a phenomenal growth for a limited and decidedly unheroic man. In a remarkable breakthrough at the last instant, he dissolves the contract. "Now you can choose your own path – in full freedom. ... I mean it – with all my miserable heart." Ellida is amazed, "You can let this *be*?" "Yes, I can. Because I love you so much." That does begin to sound like love, that is, reverence for another consciousness. It is, in its homely way, an expression of a man's love for a woman unparalleled in dramatic literature. And then the words with which Ellida grows past her inchoate drive for freedom. Wangel: "now you can choose in freedom – on your own responsibility" (p. 319).

We recall Ellida's new knowledge of Act Three: that she might exercise her own free will. Again, Ellida is incredulous: "responsible to myself! Responsible? How this – transforms everything!" (p. 319). Throughout the agonized attraction to the Stranger, Ellida didn't have a self to be responsible to. No wonder she was terrified. Romantic transcendence may be fine for an Egmont, stuffed and wearied with self, but Ellida Wangel, gendered as a woman, can't be nobody without becoming somebody. For the woman, if not the symbol, choosing land represents growth.

Now comes a telling detail. It is only after his great renunciation and Ellida's assumption of self-responsibility that Wangel for the first time in five acts actually asks Ellida what she wants instead of announcing what she needs. "[W]ill you be coming back to me, Ellida?" (p. 321).

The decision Ellida has made is as much about the girls as about her husband. The relationship with Wangel will be far from perfect. (Notice his regression when after all he's learned he tells Arnholm that Ellida is not leaving for Skjoldvik because "We changed our minds this evening" [p. 322]). But the relationship with the girls has the promise of creativity, especially with Hilda, for whom Ellida finally reaches out.

There was an earlier scene of female alliance, the only other one in the play. At the beginning of Act One, Bolette and Hilda joined briefly in a secret birthday celebration for their dead mother. But this alliance also demonstrated a rift between women; keeping faith with the girls' first mother meant deceiving their second. Women do not again join forces in this woman-depleted environment until the final moments of the play, when Ellida is able to offer Hilda the "[o]ne small expression of love" (p. 302) Bolette says she has been longing for. (How different from the behavior of Wangel and Arnholm, who easily support and consult each other at every turn.) Almost all contemporary critics regard the ending of *The Lady from the Sea* as a choice between philosophical positions embodied by male figures; many note as well the comic device of the coupled ending. The same-gender reconciliation at the end of the play has escaped critical notice, however, despite the fact that the connection between Ellida and Hilda represents a significant realignment of affections in the world of the play, a "something new" that Ibsen so often brings to his endings.

In the opening scene of Act One, when Wangel discovers his daughters' secret observance of their mother's birthday, Bolette explains with a wink and a nod, "Can't you imagine how we went and did all this for Mr. Arnholm's sake. When such a good old friend comes back to visit ... " (p. 234). Apparently, there are alternate possible readings of the festive signs of flag and flowers that decorate the stage. These readings correspond to narrative types that have their immemorial gendered associations. One is a variant of the hero's return (even if the "hero" is only Arnholm, and his hero's journey is only a modest progress from southern town to northern sea resort). The other concerns a domestic ritual commemorating the dead and celebrating family lineage through the maternal line. Perhaps these readings can be taken as trail markers, set out by Ibsen to point a somewhat more complex route through the play than either its admirers or its detractors usually take.

Like the Act One celebration, the play too has its heroic and its domestic signs, its universalizing "cover story," and its concrete, gendered reality. In a gendered reading of *The Lady from the Sea*, a subtext boiling with woman's struggle for autonomy itself struggles to be recognized against the claims of Ibsen's "supertext," which enacts the clash of freedom and contingency worked through scenographic opposites and male antagonists. In the supertextual reading of *The Lady from the Sea*, the debate between Sea and Land, with their manifold associations, becomes a romantic search for a transcendent principle to govern human existence. In this reading, both the question the play puts and the dialectic through which an answer emerges fall into the binary logic of the metaphysical inquiry.

Feminist critiques of such "logocentric" argumentation have been levelled in many fields. One of the first was published by Hélène Cixous in 1975:

Everywhere (where) ordering intervenes, where a law organizes what is thinkable by oppositions (dual, irreconcilable; or sublatable, dialectical). And all these pairs of oppositions are *couples*. Does that mean something? Is the fact that Logocentrism subjects thought – all concepts, codes and values – to a binary system, related to "the" couple, man/woman? ... We see that "victory" always comes down to the same thing: things get hierarchical. Organization by hierarchy makes all conceptual organization subject to man ... And if we consult literary history, it is the same story. It all comes back to man ... Back to the father ... Subordination of the feminine to the masculine order ... Now it has become rather urgent to question this solidarity between logocentrism and phallocentrism ... What would happen to logocentrism, to the great philosophical systems ... [i]f some fine day it suddenly came out that the logocentric plan had always ... been to create a foundation for ... phallocentrism, to guarantee the masculine order a rationale equal to history itself. *So all the history, all the stories would be there to retell differently.* (Emphasis mine.)[15]

Cixous reads logocentrism for gender, as I, in an exercise made possible by such radical re-reading, read *The Lady in the Sea*. Ibsen's play is among the myriad stories "there to retell differently." The play's gender conflict makes no ontological claims and asserts no inalienable first principles. The questions it poses are who has power, over whom is it exercised, and what can be done to begin to right the balance. Does the gendered reading supplant the metaphysical, or can the two readings coexist? I think Ibsen, the withering ironist, in a deflationary move, deliberately set ontological freedom and women's freedom in conflict. He pits the abstract "truth" of "man's" longing for freedom against the social fact of female subjection, the uncomfortable detail that puts the idealist vocabulary into question.[16]

There have been two stages of Ibsen criticism, realist and modern. Realist critics wrote character studies. Modern critics have focused on the symbolic elements often submerged in realist structures. Such critics rely on transcendental symbolic systems: Orley Holtan reads Ibsen against myth; Brian Johnston reads Ibsen against Hegel. I don't want to supplant such supertextual readings by Ibsen's modern champions who have been determined not to let their man sink into realism's banalities. However, I do want to put them into the context of a fresh dialectic. I want to undermine their "truth force," meanwhile allowing them to stand as a stage in the archeology of culture that is never far from Ibsen's dramatic concerns. My own reading could be seen as an effort at a postmodern Ibsen criticism, one that permits conflicting elements of Ibsen's dramaturgy to emerge, and even regards such conflicts as deliberate rather than the playwright's "failure" to totalize his dramatic scheme by reconciling its contradictions.

Critics marvel at the reversibility of *The Lady from the Sea*: we can read it as an argument for the sea values or for the land values, and it works either way! Of course it does, operating within the overdetermined dualities of the systematic reading. But the play does not merely embody "signs against signs," as Arnholm says of Wangel's predicament in Act Four; it embodies sign *systems* against sign systems, advancing an ironic, mutually relativizing, bi-focal vision of human culture (a way of seeing already fully developed in Ibsen as early as *Emperor and Galilean*).

In a paper given at the Ibsen Sesquicentennial celebration at Pratt Institute in 1978, Sandra Saari argues that the ending of *The Lady from the Sea* is a "human tragedy." Ellida has chosen the "bourgeois view of life as opposed to the artistic view of life."[17] She chooses to obliterate her own vestigial memory of a time when human potentialities were unbounded, when we might have developed, actually or metaphorically, as sea or amphibious creatures. To Johnston too, Ibsen marks in this play a human defeat, a moment when mankind shrinks back to the land, with all its associations of boundedness. Much evidence in the play supports such a conclusion. Yet suppose we set against that ending another ending and a different moment in human history, when woman finally emerges from the waters (from the amniotic fluid, the Imaginary, the consignment to the Pre-Oedipal), and begins the fraught process of discovering her own subjecthood. Different evidence in the play supports this conclusion. Indeed, relying on this evidence, realist critics (affirming marriage and responsibility) typically regarded Ellida's final decision as a positive act.[18] Such evidence doesn't destroy a supertextual reading such as Johnston's; but it revitalizes it, revealing it as a carrier of the very values it discovers in the text.

If both readings can be sustained, the metaphysical and the gendered, the play would extraordinarily prefigure the paradigm collision of our own cultural moment today. Coincidentally, *The Lady from the Sea* "problem," with which this discussion began, would perhaps dissolve into a new historical perspective. M.C. Bradbrook's mid-century complaint that Ibsen had set his own poetic vision in opposition to itself, her criticism that "there is a contradiction at the basis of the play," becomes an unwitting insight into Ibsen's dramatic method.[19]

NOTES

1 Teresa de Lauretis, "The Technology of Gender," in *Technologies of Gender* (Bloomington, 1987), p. 24.

2 Francis Fergusson, "The Lady from the Sea," *Contemporary Approaches to Ibsen, Ibsen Yearbook*, 8, 1965–66 (Oslo, 1966), p. 54. The James citation is in Henry James, "Henrik Ibsen," *Essays in London* (London, 1893), p. 249.

3 Brian Johnston, "The Turning Point in *The Lady from the Sea,"* Text and *Supertext in Ibsen's Drama* (University Park and London,1989).

4 Ibid., p. 205. Johnston's spelling of proper names differs from that used below, which follows the Fjelde translation (see Note 8).

5 Ibid., p. 223.

6 Johnston defines a dramatic "supertext" as "the store of cultural reference a poet or thinker can draw upon and from which is derived his or her own identity." Ibid., p. 77.

7 See Teresa De Lauretis, op. cit, p. 32.

8 Ibsen, *The Lady from the Sea*, in *Ibsen: Four Major Plays*, Vol. 2, trans. Rolf Fjelde (New York, 1970), p. 260. Subsequent references are to this edition and appear in the text.

9 Fergusson, op. cit., p. 54.

10 Johnston, op. cit., p. 225.

11 Fergusson, op. cit., pp. 54–5.

12 Orley I. Holtan, *Mythic Patterns in Ibsen's Last Plays* (Minneapolis 1970), p. 77.

13 See Sandra E. Saari, "'Hun, som ikke selv har noe riktig livskall. ... ': Women and the Role of the 'Ideal Woman' in Ibsen's Munich Trilogy," *Contemporary Approaches to Ibsen*, Vol. 5 (Oslo, 1985).

14 Holtan, op. cit., p. 66.

15 Hélène Cixous, "Sorties," in Hélène Cixous and Catherine Clement, *The Newly Born Woman*, trans. Betsy Wing (Minneapolis, 1986), pp. 64–5.

16 We read in Naomi Schor's *Reading in Detail: Aesthetics and the Feminine* (New York, 1987), p. 26, that to valourize the detail is to "aid in the dismantling of Idealist metaphysics."

17 Sandra Saari, "'The Mermaid's End' or the Domestication of the Species," unpubl., p. 13.

18 In 1892 Lou-Andreas Salome published an essay on Ellida Wangel, affirming
    Ellida's development away from the Stranger and characterizing as "vague
    and substanceless" Ellida's fantasies of boundless freedom, that remarkably
    lacks the nostalgia for the freedom of the sea that tugs at modern critics. See
    Lou-Andreas Salome, *Ibsen's Heroines*, trans. and ed. Siegfried Mandel (Lon-
    don, 1985), p. 121. See also Yvonne Shafer, "The Liberated Woman in Ibsen's
    The Lady from the Sea, " *Theatre Annual*, 40, 1985. Schafer sees the play as a
    positive version of *A Doll's House*, one in which "Ibsen presents a view of
    women and of marriage far in advance of his time."
19 M.C. Bradbrook, *Ibsen the Norwegian: A Revaluation* (London, 1966), pp. 108–9.
    The book was first published in 1946.

The Unspoken Text in *Hedda Gabler*

EVERT SPRINCHORN

Before the advent of realistic drama, a playwright found no difficulty in having his characters express their inmost thoughts. Shakespeare could write soliloquies for the introspective Hamlet, and Racine could let the spectators in on Phèdre's smouldering jealousy by letting her speak directly to them. But the nineteenth-century dramatist who wanted to present a photographic semblance of life on stage had to avoid the soliloquy and the aside. If the rules of the fully developed realistic drama were faithfully adhered to, the spectators had to be thought of as unseen guests, observing what happens on stage but ignored by the people up there. Since the characters onstage could not break through the fourth wall of the set, the viewer had to figure out what was going on in their minds by watching them as they engaged in the ordinary business of daily life, chatted with friends, poured tea, arranged flowers, and passed the time of day.

One of Ibsen's more remarkable achievements was to find ways of revealing the unspoken thoughts of his characters without violating the conventions of realistic theatre. Often there are overtones in his dialogue that hint at things not actually said. Just as often the stage properties and the costumes silently but eloquently comment on the spoken words and on the physical action. John Northam and Else Høst pioneered in the study of these visual elements in Ibsen's realistic plays, especially in *Hedda Gabler*, and others have followed in their footsteps.[1]

But there is yet another method that Ibsen used to express what his characters cannot say directly if they are to behave like real people and what he as author could not verbalize for the audience without breaking through the fourth wall of the set and turning himself into a novelist. In *Hedda Gabler*, and perhaps in other plays, Ibsen made the stage itself speak. He divided the stage into distinct areas that have special significance, especially when they are considered in relation to one another. A crude form of this technique was employed in the medieval drama, in which heaven and hell were sometimes set up at opposite ends of the playing area, and in the Elizabethan theatre, where in *Antony and Cleopatra*, for example, profligate Egypt was opposed to stolid and proper Rome by means of signs over the stage doors. This method is almost uniquely theatrical. It does not work for novelists and lyric poets and non-operatic composers, though painters have certainly made use of it. Ibsen, who had once set his heart on being a painter, may have been the first realistic dramatist to employ it rigorously throughout a whole play.

Although it could be used effectively in earlier times, a great drawback to its use in the realistic theatre of the nineteenth century was that explanatory signs could not be hung about the stage. Given the conventions of the peephole stage, what could not be blatantly labelled had to accrue meaning gradually through associations as the play progressed. The hidden drama had to come to light slowly, as in real life.

Ibsen helps the spectator as much as he legitimately can by calling attention in the first moments of the play to the significance of certain visual elements on the stage. When Hedda first appears, she objects to the sunlight flooding the room and asks that the curtain be drawn over the glass doors opening on the verandah. Her husband's aunt had opened the doors wide to let in the air and the sun. Hedda does not want nature to intrude that much into her life. On the other hand, she does not want the doors closed. She only wants the curtains drawn over the opening. Her husband, George Tesman, does her bidding, saying, "There you are, Hedda. Now you've got both shade and fresh air."[2]

A minute later she crosses the room to the side opposite to the glass doors and stands at the tile stove. She makes this cross when Tesman asks her to look at the old slippers that Aunt Juliane has brought him. Hedda is irritated. "I'm really not interested," she says, coldly (XI:306).

Her husband follows her across the stage, insisting that she show some interest for his sake; after all, the slippers call up so many pleasant memories for him. Hedda turns from him, moves to the table that occupies the centre of the room, and from that point makes her devastating remark about Aunt Juliane's new hat, spitefully and deliberately mistaking it for the maid's. "We shall never manage with that new maid. ... Look, she's left her old hat lying on that chair" (XI:306). This is her spontaneous retort to Tesman: the hat against the slippers: tit for tat.

Observing this little scene, the audience can see battle lines being drawn up in this quiet domestic setting: Hedda against the Tesman clan, those boring, well-intentioned, ever-so-good denizens of the middle class, who, in Ibsen's words, "stand as a hostile and alien power opposed to [Hedda's] fundamental nature" (xviii:280). Moreover, the stage has become a divided room. At the left (from the audience's point of view, as are all the stage directions in the play) the sun enters the room, while towards the right the room is comparatively dark. Dominating that side of the room is a large stove, faced with dark tiles. Hedda launches her sally on the Tesmans from that stove, moving from there to the table in the centre to point at the hat.

Each movement by itself seems insignificant, but, lingering in our minds, these movements acquire meaning and become signs in a theatrical language that is not difficult to read. Thea Elvsted is seated in the easy chair next to the porcelain stove as she tells Hedda of her unhappy marriage and of her leaving her husband. When Hedda expresses her surprise at this defiance of social morality – "I don't see how you dared!" – Thea rises from the chair, crosses the room, and sits in the sofa near the glass door. "I simply had to do what I did," she says (xi:318).

These little episodes point to the tensions and conflicts that will dominate the drama: the aristocratic Hedda against the middle-class Tesmans, and social propriety against natural instincts. When Judge Brack and Hedda have their tête-à-tête hinting at a *ménage à trois*, notoriously Norwegianized by Ibsen as *trekant* (triangle), they are seated on the sofa at the right, near the stove. But in act 2 when Hedda reminisces with Løvborg, recalling their titillating conversations in which the Bohemian, uninhibited Løvborg recounted his sexual escapades, they are seated on the sofa at the left, near the garden. Judge Brack, the embodiment of sexual and social hypocrisy, never sits on the sofa at the left. Similarly, when Thea, that seemingly proper woman who has flouted social convention by walking out on her husband, says, "People can say what they want" (xi:319), she sits down on the sofa at the left. In contrast, when Judge Brack utters his famous last line, "Such things just aren't done!" (xi:393), he is ensconced in the armchair near the stove on the side of the stage that connotes propriety and the repression of the instinctual life.

Going through the play scene by scene, one can find example after example supporting this interpretation of the division of the stage left and right. However, Ibsen's characters do not confine themselves to horizontal movements across the stage. They also move up and down it. In fact, the most obvious aspect of the set is the division of the playing space into a downstage area, a drawing room and an upstage area, the inner room where Hedda will shoot herself. This room is definitely Hedda's domain. She claims it by hanging the portrait of her father there and by having her piano moved into it. This room is her refuge. When Tesman wants her to show her friendliness by addressing his aunt with the familiar *du*, Hedda declines and goes towards the inner room as if to escape from the insufferably sweet Tesmans.

Yet it is obvious that the playgoer cannot identify the inner room exclusively with Hedda. Other people use it. In one of the central scenes in the play Tesman and Brack sit there while Hedda and Løvborg are seated downstage, pretending to be looking at pictures in a photograph album while actually reviving their old relationship as trusting comrades. In those days when they were seeing a lot of each other, Løvborg whispered his secrets to Hedda while General Gabler sat nearby, reading a newspaper. The tolerant father sat near the window in the light, while the two young people sat on the darker side of the room. Now, in the play as we see it, we are in another house and the past is imposed on the present. General Gabler's portrait in the inner room looks down on Hedda and Løvborg, while Judge Brack sits under the portrait, keeping a jealous eye on them. The inference to be drawn from this is that the inner room is not so much Hedda's refuge as it is a link to the past.[3] Ibsen has divided upstage from downstage, inner room from living room, to suggest that the past is ever present in the lives of these people. This is a variation on a technique he had employed in earlier realistic plays. In *Ghosts* he had brought the past to bear on the present by having Oswald make love to Regina, just as years before Oswald's father had made love to Regina's mother. And in *The Wild Duck* he had made the loft at the rear of the stage a repository of things from the past, imbuing it with an atmosphere that affects the living characters.

Behind the inner room are more rooms, yet even back there, where the bedrooms are located, a symbolic division exists between right and left. Tesman enters from the right when he first appears on stage, and Hedda from the left. Hedda's ancestors were Viking barbarians; George Tesman's were tillers of the soil (their first names, Hedda, a form of Hedvig, meaning battle, and George, meaning husbandman, point to this difference in their lineages). Even in representing the past, Ibsen remains consistent in having the left side stand for the free and untamed human being, and the right stand for the domesticated home dweller. Hedda wants to act like her barbarian ancestors by exerting her power over others, while Tesman, living up to his name ("Thesis-man"), is writing his doctoral dissertation on the domestic industries of Brabant.

If the rear area of the stage opens up a vista on the past, and if the main part of the stage where most of the action takes place represents the present, then the extension of the time line implies that the area farthest downstage might contain glimmerings of the future. It is hardly a matter of chance that in act 1 Judge Brack and Tesman discuss the latter's hopes for the future while they are seated at the oval table that is closest to the apron of the stage. Again, in act 3, when Brack, with barely concealed relish, informs Hedda that Løvborg is a ruined man who will be shunned by every decent person after the brawl in a madam's house, and insinuates that from now on he will take Løvborg's place in Hedda's life, he is seated at this same table at the longer and dominant upstage side, while Hedda is at the *left* side of it.

The end of act 2 also connects the downstage table with future events. As Løvborg leaves for Brack's bachelor party, the maid enters with a lighted lamp that she places on this table. Thea says uneasily, "Hedda, Hedda, how is this all going to end?" (II:355). There is really no need to bring on the lamp shortly before the curtain is to come down on the act except to emphasize Thea's words – and to call our attention to the table.

The table is not empty. The flowers that Thea brought to the Tesman house in the first act were moved from the piano (at the left, on the side of nature) and placed on that table. More to the point, the manuscript of Løvborg's revolutionary work, the book about the future course of civilization, lies on the table as Brack, Tesman, and its author discuss it (while the appurtenances of Tesman and Brack – books, hat, and coat – are grouped together upstage right). During a large part of the act, the manuscript and the flowers are displayed together on the table, a weighty image, considering that it was only through Thea's loving care that Løvborg was able to write the book.

At the end of the act the stage grows dark as the sun sets. Løvborg puts the manuscript in his pocket as the maid brings in the lamp that casts its light on the flowers. The connection between the flowers and the manuscript is now severed, and the viewer is left to wonder what indeed will happen to Løvborg's vision of the future.

Hedda herself is thinking about the immediate future. "At ten o'clock, Løvborg will be back," she says, "with vine leaves in his hair" (XI:355). The phrase is disconcerting, and was greeted with derisive laughter when the play was first produced in Munich and Copenhagen.[4] It comes without any preparation; up to this point no one has mentioned vine leaves. Now we both hear about Hedda's vine leaves and see Thea's flowers. Then, at the very end of the act, while Hedda repeats the phrase about vine leaves, she threatens to burn Thea's hair. She virtually drags Thea into the inner room, behaving like a ravaging Viking, while downstage the light falls on Thea's flowers. There is flow and counterflow to the action. The lamp, brought in from the rear room, comes in from out of the past, as it were, while Hedda hauls Thea back into the past, treating her as she did when they were schoolgirls and Hedda used to bully and torment her by pulling her hair.

Naturally, most of what we see and hear concerns the present – that is, the 1890s – and takes place on the main part of the stage. Behind the middle-class world of the late nineteenth century, spatially and chronologically, lies the world of the barbarians, the Vikings, the precursors of the aristocratic class that has been pretty much replaced by the bourgeoisie, leaving behind only a few relics like Hedda. But this middle class, although it has superseded the aristocracy, is divided against itself. Within it, there has sprung up a group, the Bohemians, that spurns the values of the tradesmen and has formulated its own code of ethics. These Bohemians see the upholders of middle-class values as hypocrites. In Hedda's drawing room the Philistines and the Bohemians collide. "I only wanted to show," said Ibsen, "what results from the contact between two social classes that do not understand each other."5

The Tesman family exemplifies the middle class at its best – gentle, considerate of one another, and self-sacrificing – whereas Judge Brack is the exemplary Philistine, the bourgeoisie at its worst, pharisaical, self-serving, and pretentious. His very name was the slangy Swedish contemptuous term for a Philistine (*brackan*). What made the Philistine so unpleasant was that he harbored *petit bourgeois* values while entertaining aristocratic pretensions. Georg Brandes in his lectures on Nietzsche in 1888 declared that the assault on the culture-Philistine mentality was a phenomenon of the nineteenth century. The culture-Philistines were, he said, responsible for the absence of true culture and the simultaneous belief that they actually possess it.

The repartee between Judge Brack and Hedda Gabler is a fencing match between one who is truly cultured and one who is not. Brack wants to acquire status by possessing Hedda, while she can have a better time duelling with Brack, with whom she has much in common, than prating with her husband. What she has, Brack wants.

What Hedda wants is quite another matter. Like Brack, she would like to be a free spirit, rising above the conventions and prejudices of a society that bores and frustrates her; but, also like Brack, she wants a secure position in that society. The result is hypocrisy in Brack and fretfulness, restiveness, malice, and resentment in Hedda. The child in her womb, now six months after conception beginnning to stir noticeably, only exacerbates her nervousness. It will commit her to all that she despises, while Løvborg offers the possibility of at least a momentary escape. She is a woman not only in conflict with the society in which she lives but also in conflict with herself. In one of his working notes for the play, Ibsen wrote, "The play is about 'the insuperable,' the aspiring to and striving for something that goes against convention, against what is allowed into the conscious mind – Hedda's mind included" (XI:500).

There are demons within Hedda that she cannot control, imps engendered by the intermingling of the Viking spirit with middle-class propriety and restraint. The aggressive barbarian will has been stifled and, finding no outlet in a social environment that confines women to the home, has turned against Hedda herself. Nietzsche in one of his proleptically Freudian remarks said that "All instincts that do not discharge themselves outwardly *turn inward*,"[6] and Ibsen's drama affords a vivid demonstration of those words.

Why did Hedda, an intelligent, sophisticated, stylishly handsome woman from a good family, one of the most admired women in town, accept in marriage the hand of George Tesman, a man whom she cannot help but ridicule in her chat with Judge Brack? She says it all happened because of an impulse of the moment. Walking home from a party one evening, Hedda, who was only trying to make conversation with Tesman, tongue-tied in the presence of this awesome woman, happened to remark as they passed a handsome town house that she would like to live there. That "brought on the engagement, and the marriage, and the honeymoon, and the whole lot" (II:336). The cruel irony is that she did not even like the house.

We can guess why she yielded to the impulse, and the stage arrangement provides a visual confirmation of our thoughts. The picture provides the subtext for the scene. During their conversation, Hedda sits in the armchair next to the tile stove, and Judge Brack stands behind the chair. The chair stands for middle-class conventionality and comfort, and the stove is the home of the imps and demons bred by thwarted instincts and desires. When Hedda says that "these impulses come over me all of a sudden, and I just can't resist them," she "*throws herself down in the easy chair by the stove*" (II:335). Though the stove suggests domesticity and protection against the elements, the man-made fire in it can be as destructive as any natural force, and more pernicious. Hedda's desire to be assured of the comforts of life and a good place in society led her to marry Tesman. Now she is bored and looking for some kind of excitement that will relieve the tensions within her. In the next act the demons will break loose, and the fire will blaze in the stove.

Hedda grows increasingly destructive as the drama unfolds. In fact the plot forms a crescendo of malignity, and each one of her wicked acts makes use of a different part of the stage. In act 1 she makes fun of Aunt Juliane's bonnet, moving from the stove to the table at stage centre to do so. In act 2 she induces Løvborg, the reformed alcoholic, to drink. This happens at the sofa on the left, the garden side, which suggests that Hedda regards it as a creative act: she hopes to transform Løvborg into Bacchus. In the third act she burns his manuscript in the stove, killing the "child" of Thea and Løvborg. In the final act she kills herself – and the child within her – in the room at the back of the stage.

The burning of the manuscript constitutes the climax of the drama, and in order to leave no doubts in the viewer's mind about Hedda's reasons, Ibsen for once resorts to the soliloquy, realistically motivated by the circumstances. Since Hedda's mind is exposed here, the scene provides the perfect occasion for a confirmation of the symbolic significance of the division of the stage space. The fire in the stove dominates the scene visually, emphasizing the right-hand side of the stage. The left side of the stage, however, is not dark. Earlier, Hedda had gone to the glass door and opened the drapes, letting the bright morning sun pour into the room. Her behaviour here contrasts with her dislike of the sun in act 1. Furthermore, the stove was not lit in the two previous acts. Although it would seem more true to life to have a fire in the afternoon of act 2 when guests were entertained, Ibsen has artfully saved the lighting of the fire for the third act in order to call attention to it. He also arranged for the curtain covering the opening to the inner room to be drawn shut. The viewer's eye, then, is caught by the shafts of sunlight to the left and the reddish light from the stove on the right. Pictorially, the stage presents a conflict between the sunlight and the firelight, between nature's light and artificial light, between nature and civilization or, more specifically, bearing in mind the time axis of the stage, society at the end of the nineteenth century.

At the beginning of the act, there are only a few embers glowing in the stove, and, in keeping with this, Hedda is asleep on the sofa at the left, the side of the natural instincts. The fire will grow brighter throughout the act, and Hedda will be feeding it with the manuscript at the end, burning the "child" of curly-haired Thea. Taking the scene in through our eyes, reading the ideograms of the stage, we see the natural emotions being repressed and perverted, becoming destructive rather than creative. Hedda burns the manuscript out of spite and jealousy. Resentful of Thea (Thea = Dorothea, "the gift of the god"), and envying her abundant hair, her life-giving spirit, and her caring nature, Hedda would rather kill new life and close off the future than see her rival accomplish what she herself could not. The image is that of a pregnant mother throwing the new-born babe of another mother into the fire. And in his inimitable fashion Ibsen combines the intellectual motive with the emotional. Unlike Thea, Hedda understands the significance of the manuscript; hence the destructive act is raised in our minds above the merely psychological. "Her act," as a perceptive French critic wrote, "is not one of simple female vengeance; it is an act of vandalism, a crime against humanity. In committing it, Hedda becomes something other than a mentally disturbed person [*une simple détraquée*]. She assumes in our eyes a superhuman stature; her role takes on a metaphysical aspect. Hedda is the genius of evil fighting against progress."[7]

Seen in the perspective of history, the Viking despoiler has degenerated into the Victorian spoiler. Just how true this is may be seen by comparing the early Ibsen play *The Vikings at Helgeland* (*Hærmændene på Helgeland*, 1858) with *Hedda Gabler* (1890).[8] In the former, the heroine Hjørdis (who is equivalent to Brünnhilde in Wagner's *Ring of the Nibelung*) prefers to slay herself and her lover rather than live on in a Christian world in which the Viking qualities of pride and self-assertion would be regarded as moral defects.

"The white god heads north," she laments. "I do not wish to meet him. The old gods are no longer strong. They sleep. They are but shadows, half-alive. With them shall we fight! Out of this life, Sigurd! I will set you on the throne of heaven, and I shall sit at your side" (4:94).

She kills Sigurd with an arrow from her bow, only to learn that Sigurd had become a convert to Christianity and that consequently they will not meet in the afterlife. Hedda's destruction of Løvborg contains a much greater irony, for Hedda at that moment is no Hjørdis. She burns the manuscript in resentment against the good Christian Thea, whereas Hjørdis acts out of regret, maintaining her nobility of character. But, like her Viking forbear, Hedda must face death alone, knowing that Thea and Løvborg will exist together in the future through the salvaging and recon-struction of the manuscript.

When Hedda burns the manuscript, exulting in this surrogate infanti-cide, she is at her worst. The admirable Viking attributes, the willingness to face a challenge unflinchingly and the ability to bear defeat without rancour, have deserted her. The stage picture tells as much. The rear room, the area representing her ancestral past, is closed off throughout the whole act so that we may see her as trapped in a middle-class Victorian parlour and motivated largely by middle-class standards of respectability, seeking an outlet for her energies not through brave deeds but through a cowardly, selfish, dog-in-the-manger act.

In the last part of the play, Ibsen attempts to redeem his heroine. Visually, the opening of the fourth act serves as a sharp contrast to the ending of the third. There the inner room was concealed; the sunlight entered from the left; the fire burned in the stove at the right. As the curtain rises on the fourth act, the drawing room is in darkness, and the inner room is lit by a lamp hanging over the table. The arrangement of light and dark is the reverse of what it was. The implication is that Hedda's Viking spirit is asserting itself. Having carried on like a hysterical, neurotic woman in the previous act, she will now perform with the pride and self-esteem of the barbarian and the hauteur of the aristocrat. Matthew Arnold's designation of the aristocratic class as barbarians applies here: "The Barbarians, to whom we all owe so much, and who reinvigorated and renewed our worn-out Europe. ... The Barbarians brought with them that staunch individualism ... and that passion for doing as one likes, for the assertion of personal liberty."9

In the last act, Hedda the barbarian asserts her personal freedom in the most extreme manner. When Judge Brack, the consummate Philistine, insinuates that he, knowing who owns the pistol that killed Løvborg, will blackmail Hedda, she realizes that she must either be forever sullied by public scandal or embraced by the unctuous Brack as his mistress. Either way, she loses her independence and purity. She takes the only way out – for a barbarian. She retreats into the inner room, goes back to her ancestral origins, sits at the piano, the family heirloom, and under the eyes of her father, whose portrait hangs in that room, blows her brains out with her father's pistol. Like Hjørdis, she vehemently rejects a world that does not measure up to her standards, preferring to join the shades of her ancestors.

The painter's eye and the psychologist's insight are at work in the scene in which Brack exerts his power over Hedda. Talking of Hedda's fear of scandal, Brack leans on the back of the armchair at the right, while Hedda, sitting on the ottoman belonging to the chair, is conspicuously at his feet. But she is near the stove in which the demons dwell. When Brack bends over her and whispers his threats, she says, "I'd rather die" (xi:390). The fact that the fire is out implies that she is no longer in the grip of her emotions, no longer *détraquée*. She is thinking clearly. Here the stage picture speaks more eloquently than the words because the properties –

the chair, the stool, and the stove – have gradually been accumulating symbolic weight during the first three acts.

There are, however, other symbols in the play that weave through the dialogue to create patterns of meaning. The most obvious of these, the one that stridently calls attention to itself, is the image of Løvborg as a Bacchic or Dionysian figure. Hedda visualizes him returning from Brack's bachelor party with vine leaves in his hair.[10] When that vision is shattered, she imagines him dying "in beauty," that is, by shooting himself in the temple.

Although men in those days did sometimes go to parties at which they wore wreaths of vine leaves on their heads, Hedda certainly does not have in mind one of those staid affairs, such as the Christmas banquet of the Scandinavian Society in Rome, with women wearing wreaths of roses accompanying the men.[11] She is conjuring up an image of Dionysus as Nietzsche pictured him. In *The Twilight of the Gods (Götzen-Dämmerungz)*, which appeared in print only a year before *Hedda Gabler*, the German philosopher described his Goethean superman as a "highly cultured human being who keeping himself in check and having reverence for himself, dares to allow himself the whole compass and wealth of natural being – a man to whom nothing is forbidden, except *weakness. ... He no longer denies. ...* Such faith is the highest of all possible faiths; I have baptized it with the name *Dionysus*" (chapter 9, section 49).[12]

Nietzsche had emerged as the most talked-about thinker in Scandinavia after Georg Brandes gave a series of public lectures on him in 1888, thus introducing the philosopher to an international audience. The lectures sparked a controversy between Brandes and the Danish philosopher Harald Høffding, who assailed "aristocratic radicalism," Brandes's term for Nietzsche's elitism, as immoral. Høffding was the comfortably placed academic, a professor of philosophy at the University of Copenhagen; Brandes the unregenerate defier of social convention and notorious defender of sexual licence, who some years before had been denied a professorship at the same university. The quarrel between these two is reflected in the competition between Tesman and Løvborg.[13] The latter's work on the history of social and cultural forces and what they portend sounds very much like Nietzsche's *Beyond Good and Evil*, which has the subtitle "Prelude to a Philosophy of the Future." Løvborg's manuscript is in two parts, the first on cultural forces in the past, the second on the future course of civilization.[14]

With Nietzsche's name on the lips of every literate person, contemporary critics immediately saw Hedda as a kind of superwoman, a higher being who places herself above society's moral standards, a woman liberated from conventional attitudes towards motherhood and family life. Not long after Ibsen's play was published, E.F. Lochman wrote:

Hedda Gabler corresponds to Nietzsche's man of the future. She belongs to the supermen, a coming higher stage in evolution. She has emerged a little too early, however, and goes down to defeat in that petty and confining modern society that has no place for these higher existences. ... Her death is, take note, a "death in beauty;" in actuality, a death without solace and without hope, a complete annihilation.[15]

For Lochman, Hedda is a destructive and cruel human being and her creator the incarnation of a maleficent force.

Nietzsche himself understood the double nature of his higher form of humanity. In a passage that reads like a commentary on *Hedda Gabler*, he said:

Superior spirits run no small danger of learning, one day or another, to look out for the terrible joy which is to be found in destruction ... in the event of creative activity being absolutely denied them. ... For such spirits, there then remains no other alternative; they may feel themselves constrained to destroy, gradually, insidiously, and with diabolical delight, just what they have loved most.[16]

Like one of these superior spirits, Hedda brings to ruin the one person she admires when he fails to live up to her ideal. When she challenges Løvborg to drink in act 2, she wants him to conform to her image of the strong man to whom nothing is forbidden, the superman who is able to retain control of himself while experiencing all that nature offers. She sends him off to Judge Brack's bacchanal for the same reason, convinced that he will return as master of himself, in her words, "a free man for the rest of his life." Seeing herself as a kind of goddess, above and apart from other morals, she is the uncompromising aesthete, and when her lost comrade falls short of her image of him as Nietzsche's Dionysus, she asks him to regain some of his lost glory by making his suicide a beautiful gesture, an aesthetic feat beyond the comprehension of shallow souls – "Une balle dans la tempe, voilà ce qu'il y a de mieux, le vrai chic!" as a French critic put it.[17] Like Nietzsche, she believes that only as a work of art and not as a moral product can the world be justified, and only as transmuted into music and not as reduced to reality can the world be redeemed.

At the beginning of the last act, she is waiting for the news that Løvborg has died "in beauty."[18] Understandably tense, Hedda paces the darkened room; then moves up into the inner room, which is lit; strikes a few chords on her piano; and comes back into the living room. She crosses to the glass door and looks out into the garden, which lies in darkness. Although she has received word that Tesman's Aunt Rina has died, her mind is occupied by other matters: Løvborg's suicide and her pregnancy. She must reconcile herself to a life with the most un-Dionysian of men. Yet her mood is not one of complete frustration. True, she will give birth to a child she does not want, but she is also about to enjoy the thrill of exerting her power over someone else's destiny. The child should have been Løvborg's. Now she must be content with Løvborg's poetic death – an aesthetic and sublime deed that she can savour again and again in the tiresome days and years that lie ahead.

To Judge Brack she expresses the sense of release and freedom she feels, believing that Løvborg died following her wishes. "I feel liberated, set free, knowing that a bold, gratuitous act is still possible in this world. An instinctive act, shimmering with pure beauty" (xi:387). She utters these Dionysian thoughts while seated in the easy chair near the stove.

Now it would seem that the more appropriate place for these thoughts would be on the garden side of the stage. Why does Ibsen have Hedda cross the stage and sit down at the stove when her mind is preoccupied by a bold, defiant, unconventional deed, completely in contrast to what the right-hand side has come to represent? If she is imagining her Dionysian Løvborg dying in beauty, why does she take her place with the Pharisees who do not appreciate true beauty and have no conception of the higher man?

Here the stage picture speaks more profoundly than the words. Hedda's physical movement exposes the substratum of her emotional life and betrays what has stirred her more deeply than Dionysian beauty. She returns to the place where she burned Løvborg's manuscript, and she burned the manuscript out of jealousy of Thea. Although she speaks to her confidant of a beautiful, audacious, convention-defying death, her inner being wants Løvborg dead because she cannot have him, because he belongs to someone else. She acts out of resentment, the most un-Nietzschean and un-Dionysian of sentiments. It was the one response to an unpleasant and demeaning world absolutely denied the superman. Carelessly destructive he might be, but never resentful. By putting Hedda in the armchair, Ibsen is pronouncing a Nietzschean judgment on her.

At that moment she is as mean in spirit as she was at the end of act 3 when she bade goodbye to Løvborg. "I want you to take something to remember me by," she had said, moving upstage (XI:387). It is a wonderfully revealing moment, its impact often lost in performance because it happens so quickly. Both the manuscript and the pistols are in the desk upstage, and when Hedda takes the one and not the other, the attentive viewer will understand exactly what it is that motivates Hedda and what underlies the talk about dying beautifully.

Equally revealing is her stage cross in the last act when she realizes she is in Brack's power. She rises from the easy chair and crosses to the writing desk, moving into the light, towards the garden of nature, and preparing through her suicide to rejoin the nobler races, who, as Nietzsche described them,

savor a freedom from all social constraints, they compensate themselves in the wilderness for the tension engendered by protracted confinement and enclosure within the peace of society, they go *back* to the innocent conscience of the beast of prey, as triumphant monsters who perhaps emerge from a disgusting procession of murder, arson, rape, and torture, exhilarated and undisturbed of soul, ... convinced they have provided the poets with a lot more material for song and praise. One cannot fail to see at the bottom of all these noble races the beast of prey, the splendid *blond beast* prowling about avidly in search of spoil and victory; this hidden core needs to erupt from time to time, the animal has to get out again and go back to the wilderness.[19]

Hedda takes the other of the two duelling pistols that belonged to her father and retreats into the inner room (off left) where she shoots herself after playing on the piano.

The final stage picture sums up the play. The characters onstage are clad in black in mourning for Tesman's aunt. The downstage table, pointing to the future, stands empty. The advance of culture envisioned by Løvborg and understood intuitively by Hedda seems doomed. The manuscript that would have adumbrated the future course of civilization has been destroyed by an undisciplined Løvborg and a spiteful Hedda. Judge Brack is in the armchair at the right, exclaiming, "Such things just aren't done!" (XI:393). That side of the stage was made relatively dark when Tesman moved the lamp from the table above the easy chair to Hedda's desk on the other side of the room. The light is on the left where Thea and Tesman sit, piecing together Løvborg's manuscript, which is entirely beyond their comprehension. Yet they are on the side of life. They belong among those who affirm human existence, regardless of its quality, often by sacrificing themselves for the sake of others. And ultimately, even for Ibsen, life itself is more decisive for the progress of humanity than are ideas about life.

For Ibsen, but not for Hedda. When she takes her own life, she escapes from the slave morality of those who surround her and becomes the magnificent barbarian. She takes time to play the Dionysian music for her own death, and she dies beneath her father's portrait. She asserts her Viking heritage while at the same time fulfilling her dream of an exalted life. When she shoots herself, she acts destructively and wantonly but without meanness or rancour. By her own standards and Nietzsche's, she dies in beauty.

NOTES

1 John Northam, *Ibsen's Dramatic Method* (London, 1953); Else Høst, *Hedda Gabler: En monografi* (Oslo, 1958). Among further contributions to the subject are Sigmund Skard, "Else Høsts doktordisputas om Hedda Gabler," *Edda* (1960), 24; Erik Østerud, "Lenestolysymbolet i 'Hedda Gabler,'" *Ibsenårbok* (1960–62), 82–92; Northam, "Hedda Gabler," *Ibsenårbok* (1968–69), 60–81; and James H. Clancy, "*Hedda Gabler*: Poetry in Action and in Object," in *Studies in Theatre and Drama: Essays in Honor of Hubert C. Heffner*, ed. Oscar G. Brockett (The Hague, 1972), 64–72.

2 Ibsen, *Samlede Verker*, ed. Francis Bull, Halvdan Koht, and Didrik Arup Seip, 22 vols. (Oslo, 1928–57), II:305. All translations from this edition are my own; volume and page numbers will be cited in the text.

3 In a stimulating discussion of Ibsen's use of the scenic space, Freddie Rokem (*Theatrical Space in Ibsen, Chekhov and Strindberg: Public forms of Privacy* [Ann Arbor, 1986]) sees the inner room as Hedda's own place and as the focal point of the play, a "metaphor for an inner self she is unwilling to share with anyone" (23). The application of this metaphor leads one to expect that the intimate dialogue between Hedda and Løvborg would take place in the inner room and not downstage. Rokem argues that Ibsen could not place them where logic requires them to be because they would be overheard by Tesman and Thea, and so Ibsen had to give them some privacy by hiding them behind a photograph album. But surely Ibsen could have found a way around this technical difficulty if he had wanted to put Hedda and Løvborg in the inner room. It is more likely that Ibsen desired to make use of the time axis of the stage as he imagined it. When Hedda and Løvborg talk about their comradeship, they belong in spirit to the present and the future and are trying to break with the past.

4 Wolfgang Brachvogel, "'Hedda Gabler' in München," *Freie Bühne für modernes*

Leben, 2 (1891), 117–18; Elisabeth Davidsen, *Henrik Ibsen og Det kongelige Teater* (Copenhagen, 1980), 177.

5 Ibsen, *Hedda Gabler*, French trans. M. Prozor (Paris, 1892), 5.

6 *On the Genealogy of Morals*, trans. Walter Kaufman and R.J. Hollingdale (New York, 1969), 84 (essay 2, section 16).

7 Auguste Ehrhard, *Henrik Ibsen et le théâtre contemporain* (Paris, 1892), 458. Ibsen praised this study of his works: "M. Ehrhard a fait tout un livre, qui ne sera pas, certes, de sitôt dépassé" (Maurice Bigeon, "Profils scandinaves: Henrik Ibsen," *Le Figaro*, 4 January 1893, 3).

8 The similarities between the two plays were immediately apparent to knowledgeable critics; for example, Henrick Jæger, "Hedda Gablers forhold til tidligere skuespil af Henrik Ibsen," *Folkebladet* (Christiana, 1891), #2; Jæger, *Henrik Ibsen og hans værker* (Christiania and Copenhagen, 1892), 190; and Emil Reich, "Ibsen und das Recht der Frau," *Jahresbericht des Vereins für erweitert Frauenbildung* (Vienna, 1891).

9 Arnold, *Culture and Anarchy*, ed. J. Dover Wilson (Cambridge, 1960), 102.

10 On the significance of the vine leaves, see Josef Faalund, *Henrik Ibsen og antikken* (Oslo, 1943), 74; Sigmund Skard and Paulus Svendsen, "Else Høsts doktordisputas om Hedda Gabler," *Edda*, 1960, pp. 25–28, 49–50; Lis Jacobsen, "En trilogi: Studie over tre Ibsen'ske trylleord," *Edda* (1960), 53–70; John Northam, "Hedda Gabler"; Eugene Webb, "The Radical Irony of *Hedda Gabler*," *Modern Language Quarterly*, 31 (1970), 53–63.

11 Ibsen's friend Ludvig Dietrichsen describes the Christmas banquet in Rome and attributes the source of the phrase "vine leaves in his hair" to Ibsen's recollection of the occasion (Dietrichsen, *Svundne Tider*, vol. I: *Bergen og Christiania i 40-og 50-Aarene*, 2nd ed. [Christiania, 1913], 366).

12 Friedrich Nietzsche, *Werke in drei Bänden*, ed. Karl Schlechta, 2nd ed. (Munich, 1960), 2:1025.

13 For a discussion of the Høffding-Brandes controversy and its impact on Ibsen, see Evert Sprinchorn, "Ibsen and the Immoralists," *Comparative Literature Studies*, 9 (1972), 58–79.

14 See Harald Beyer, *Nietzsche og Norden*, 2 vols. (Bergen, 1957–59), 2:36.

15 E.F. Lochman, *Populære opsatser* (Christiania, 1891), 214. Among others who remarked on the Nietzschean aspects of *Hedda Gabler* were Jules Lemaître, *Impressions de théâtre*, 6th series (Paris, 1898), 49–62 (a review that appeared originally in December 1891); J.A. Eklund, "Om 'Hedda Gabler' och 'esteticism,'" *Svensk Tidskrift*, 2 (1892), 606–16; and James Huneker, *Iconoclasts: A Book of Dramatists* (New York, 1905), 101. Else Høst in her monograph on the play viewed Hedda as the representative of a higher type of humanity; S. Skard rebutted her argument ("Høsts doktordisputas," 30–33).

16 Quoted in F.A. Lea, *The Tragic Philosopher: A Study of Friedrich Nietzsche* (London, 1957), 319.

17 Ehrhard, *Henrik Ibsen*, 456.

18 "Die in beauty," unlike "vine leaves in his hair," would probably not have caused any laughter or snickering in the theatre. The phrase would have been familiar, resounding with echoes of recent sensational events. Only the year before, in 1889, the circus performer Elvira Madigan and her married lover, Count Sixten Sparre of Sweden, had killed themselves in an idyllic setting in Denmark, preferring to die in beauty rather than to live a life that could never be free of scandal. Their tragic fate was the subject of newspaper stories and a popular ballad. Their decision to put their love above and beyond the reach of social convention was inspired by the Mayerling tragedy. Only six months earlier, Archduke Rupert, the crown prince of Austria, had killed the woman he loved, Marie Vetsera, and then shot himself, when the emperor had ordered him to end his liaison with her. An early commentator remarked that the audience upon hearing "die in beauty" would recall all the "theatrical death arrangements" of recent years (Eklund, 613). On the other hand, Max Harden, who read the play as undiluted satire, said that laughter was the only proper response to Hedda's asking Løvborg to die "in beauty." Harden also found humour in Løvborg's accidental death in *"ein lustiges Haus"* (M[ax] H[arden], "Hedda Gabler und ihre Kritiker," *Die Gegenwart*, 39:8 (21 Feb. 1891), 125–26.)

19 *On the Genealogy of Morals*, 40–41 (essay I, section II).

Ibsen's Endgame: A Reconsideration of *When We Dead Awaken*

M.S. BARRANGER

When We Dead Awaken, Ibsen's final play written seven years before his death, has been treated by critics as an epilogue to his previous work, as a personal confession, and as a forerunner of the symbolist movement in European drama. In two respects this last play, subtitled "A Dramatic Epilogue," is the conclusion to a series of four plays: *The Master Builder* (1892), *Little Eyolf* (1894), *John Gabriel Borkman* (1896), *When We Dead Awaken* (1899). In *When We Dead Awaken* are to be found such characteristic themes of the latterday Ibsen as the conflicting claims of artistic vocation and personal life as well as the incompatibility of the desire for success and the need for happiness. In addition, the opening out of the physical environment of the play sets the geography of *When We Dead Awaken* apart from the works of Ibsen's middle period. The open terraces and mountainous heights, which comprise the varied settings of his last plays, are suggestive of the retooling of the lives of his artist-heroes: Halvard Solness, Alfred Allmers, John Gabriel Borkman, Arnold Rubek. Ibsen's geography in these late plays suggests symbolically that in order to redress the spiritual imbalance of his past years, the Ibsen hero must allow the natural to take precedence over the artificial, life over art, the ethical over the aesthetic. Foreshadowed in *Rosmersholm* (1886) and *The Lady from the Sea* (1888), this pattern of development is accompanied by an expansion of the dramatic setting which, in turn, complements the hero's effort to come to terms with the stifling and injurious pattern of his existence. For instance, *When We Dead Awaken* opens outside a watering place on the Norwegian coast and moves into the mountains where Rubek and Irene, awakened to the wrongful pattern of their lives, die in a purifying avalanche. They are the resurrected of the play's title along with Maja, Rubek's young wife, and Ulfhejm, a country squire, who likewise are reawakened to the potential of their lives.

Despite new spatial patterns in these last plays, modern critics continue to make Ibsen's last works the subject of extensive thematic-biographical criticism. His four consecutive studies between 1892 and 1899 of the creative personality in conflict with the demands of his art upon his personal life lend themselves to this critical approach. In effect, these final plays are continually reviewed as rooted in the "facts of Ibsen's last years"[1] and treated as "mystical, symbolic, and autobiographical."[2]

Ibsen's final play, *When We Dead Awaken*, suggests a new dimension in the dramatist's work other than concern for biography and symbol; for Ibsen introduces in his last play the device of the sequential pastime and game in order to structure and give definition to the lives of his characters whose histories and motives are, at best, vague and contradictory.[3] He, therefore, achieves in 1899 a remarkable modernism. This unique thematic dimension which emerges in *When We Dead Awaken* has been peripherally explored under traditional approaches to motives of reality and illusion. Whereas these themes are without question at work in such plays as *Ghosts* and *The Wild Duck*, Ibsen devises the game in *When We Dead Awaken* not so much to comment on the role of illusion in the lives of his characters as to project the past in the present dramatic time in order to illustrate, in retrospect, the manner in which Irene and Rubek have sought to structure time, ward off guilt and despair, and, in Rubek's case, exploit the two women in his life for ulterior gains, i.e., artistic success and existential well-being.[4] The introduction of the game device in his final play suggests not so much a variation on the reality-illusion motive as a significant new approach to the problem of overcoming the limitations of the representational theatre. Ronald Gaskell suggests that as early as *Rosmersholm* the "subtlety of Ibsen's material has rebelled against the limits of the representational theatre."[5] *When We Dead Awaken*, moreover, suggests that Ibsen turned to what was, for him, a hitherto untried facet of theatrical experience – game devices – whereby to represent the complexities of existence. I have chosen to call this thematic and experiential motive in Ibsen's last play the endgame in the lives of Rubek and Irene.[6] Their terminal game, which ends in death, frames the play and contains the secondary games that externalize the responses of Rubek and Irene to the desiccated pattern of their lives.

Ibsen's pattern of development in Act I of *When We Dead Awaken* is a linear progression to Rubek's initial interview with Irene, the former model for his celebrated sculpture "The Day of Resurrection." Like many characters in modern drama, Arnold Rubek has reached a still point in his life. For some four to five years he has been married to Maja, a woman much younger than himself. Some two to three years before the present time, he has completed a sculpture which made him a wealthy and famous artist. He now occupies his professional life with accepting commissions for "portrait busts," an endeavor which he scorns but which is likewise an amusing game since he suggests bestial meanings beneath the features of the statuary. As the play opens, Maja catalogues the unsatisfactory quality of their lives together: her husband is restless and has lost interest in their marriage and his work as well. She reminds him of an earlier promise: "You said you would take me with you to the top of a high mountain, and show me all the glory of the world" (p. 322).[7]

Maja's echo here of Satan's words to Christ (Luke 4:5–7) and Rubek's startled response introduce the first references to the device of games in the play. Maja projects through the faintly suggestive allusion the grandiose selfishness of Rubek's schoolboy games in which he enticed and controlled others for his own self-gratification by vague promises of visionary delights. Ibsen's allusion here to Christ's temptation is not intended to equate literally the artist with Satan (although the suggestion is undeniably made), but rather to give dimension to the repetition of the errors of the past in the present and focus upon the serious ramifications of Rubek's sinister manipulations in the lives of others. In Act II this image is repeated in conjunction with the game of swans and lilies and the Satanic quality of the role in which Rubek is metaphorically cast becomes increasingly ominous.

In the present scene with Maja, Rubek recalls that he also made similar promises to someone else long ago: "It was a phrase I used to be fond of" (p. 323). During his schooldays Rubek used to make this promise in order to get other children to play with him in the mountains.

> *Maja.* Perhaps that was all you wanted me for? To play games with?
> *Rubek.* [*passing it off as a joke.*] Well, it's been quite an enjoyable game, hasn't it, Maja?
> *Maja.* [*coldly.*] I didn't go away with you just to play games. (p. 323)

This colloquy betrays Rubek's insensitive treatment of people and is to be echoed in Irene's ultimate condemnation of him; that is, he dismissed her love and commitment to him – symbolized by her nakedness before him as a model – as merely an "inspiring episode" in his life. Also his early discussion with his wife reveals that Rubek, despite his creative vocation, is insensitive to the needs of others. He has treated his wife like a child and his marriage as a diverting pastime. Although Solness, Allmers, and

Borkman have had children, Rubek and Maja are childless, a fact that
reinforces the suggestion that the marriage is without a mature commitment in love. Like his childhood games, this marriage for Rubek has been
little more than a selfish diversion to fill the vacuum of his declining years
which have been significantly without artistic satisfaction.

Rubek's lack of potential for love and children is brought to mind by the
unexpected entrance of Irene and by her association in the second act
with the village children. Rubek's initial interview with Irene establishes
her as a victim of unrequited love whose "child," the Resurrection Day
sculpture, has survived the mother's spiritual demise and made the father
famous: "I passed into the darkness. While our child stood transfigured in
the light" (p. 332). She asserts that Rubek's rejection of her love molded
her, like a clay form, into what she is: a desiccated, mentally ill woman
whose life has long been over and who travels from country to country
accompanied by her attendant nurse, a nun dressed in black. She holds
Rubek accountable for "leaving me no future but death."

> *Irene.* I was dead for many years. They came and tied me up, tied my arms
> together behind my back. Then they lowered me into a tomb, with iron bars
> across the door, and padded walls so that no one up above could hear the
> shrieks of the dead. But now, slowly, I am beginning to rise from the dead.
>
> (p. 334)

Like Ella Rentheim of *John Gabriel Borkman*, Irene has been sacrificed to
the ambition of the man she loves and holds him accountable for wrong-
ing her "inmost being." Just as Borkman defends his private vision, Rubek
reminds Irene that he was foremost an artist.

> *Rubek.* Before all else, I was an artist. And I was sick – sick with a longing to create
> the one great work of my life.
>
> ...
>
> And I was convinced that if I touched you, if I desired you sensually, my vision
> would be profaned so that I would never be able to achieve what I was striving
> after. ...   (pp. 335–36)

At this juncture, Rubek's comprehension of his destructive role in Irene's
life is only partial. Continuing to function as the artist – a divided self in
Ibsen's most condemning context – he rationalizes that she was not only
prodigal in giving him four years of her youth but also in displaying her
nakedness as his model. At the close of the scene Irene instructs Rubek in
his personal culpability:

Irene. I gave you my soul – young and alive. And left myself empty; soulless. Don't you see? That's why I died, Arnold. (p. 339)

Unlike Samuel Beckett's contemporary use of play in *Endgame* (1957) in which the diversions are external inventions enacted to fill the flow of time between sleeping and sleeping, the games in *When We Dead Awaken* grow linearly out of the interviews and define the goals of the characters as well as the spiritual vacuum that exists between them. Both ironic and sentimental, the game devices are, first, objective, theatrical means of revealing the subjective nature of the relationship past and present between Irene and Rubek. In one respect the games represent a variation on Ibsen's famous retrospective or analytic technique wherein the playwright reveals past events at the moment when their relation to the present is most significant and revelatory. In *When We Dead Awaken* play is a complex visual and thematic device in which Rubek's past actions may be illustratively repeated in the present in order to document his culpability and lack of any demonstrable spiritual change over the years. Play is also a technique whereby time can be realistically re-structured to mirror former interpersonal relationships while, in the same instance, the dramatic action continues to flow in the present toward the termination of the principals' lives.

Through such games as "swans and lilies," played out in the second act, Ibsen is able to suggest visually the interpersonal relationships of the characters and to reinforce theatrically the destructive role of neurotic pastimes and exploitive goals in the lives of his characters. These devices have served as inventions to mask the lack of communion and the denial of natural feelings on the part of Arnold Rubek in the pursuit of inspiration and artistry. The game devices in the play delineate the vacuity of his existence and, indirectly, suggest Rubek's progress toward the resurrection of his life. He must be a full participant in life; that is, prepared to set aside his self-centered and ulterior concerns and look to the needs of those around him. Ibsen develops this progression from self to other in three parts which correspond to the play's three acts. At the close of part one (I), Irene, in the spirit of initiating a game, challenges Rubek to meet her in the mountains. Her motive is the death of her exploiter, but the terms of this latter-day venture are clarified only in their second interview which takes place at the mountain health resort in the second act where Rubek and Irene are discovered sitting beside a mountain stream reflecting upon the past, the changes Rubek made in the sculpture after Irene left him, and their mutually forfeited lives. From time to time Irene punctuates her desire for vengeance on the man who destroyed her soul and hence her life by wielding a sharp stiletto behind his back. She produces the knife when she first realizes that Rubek changed his conception of the sculpture, their "child," after she left his studio. As he describes the completed group in which the dominant figure of Irene has been removed from the foreground and replaced by the figure of himself weighed down by guilt, she foregoes her revenge for the time. She realizes that he has already suffered beyond anything she can inflict upon him with the weapon.

In a calmer moment, Irene takes the petals of a mountain rose and scatters them in the stream beside them. This engages their mutual interest and initiates an elaborate game device. They pretend the petals are gulls and Rubek throws ships of green leaves after the birds. The action evokes thoughts of their former life together on Taunitzer See where Irene made swan-like water lilies swim in the stream and Rubek devised Lohengrin's boat out of a leaf and fastened it to the swan.

> *Rubek.* How you loved that game, Irene.
> *Irene.* We played it so many times.   (p. 358)

Irene reminds him that he thought of her as "the swan who was drawing your boat" (p. 358). Absorbed in the Lohengrin fantasy they continue to play for a time. This allusion makes vague use of the Parzival legend in which a Swan brings the mysterious knight, Lohengrin, to his lady and returns for him after his identity is unhappily made known to the princess. In one version, which Ibsen perhaps had in mind, the knight retransforms the Swan into the princess's brother who had earlier come under the spell of a sorceress. In Act III, Rubek will transform Irene, who as his model drew him toward his artistic goal (i.e., success), into his bride of light, but only after he has come to terms with his wasted humanity and his accountability for the destruction of Irene.

Although Ibsen does not invoke an exact analogue here, he does present us with another immurement-resurrection myth. The child, such as the youthful Irene, has been immured by enchantment in the artist's statue and experiences a resurrection in the play's action. If the situations of the legend are further analogized, then Rubek is cast as the enchanter of Irene (i.e., the analogue to the swan child's sorceress) and is not in the position of Lohengrin as Irene's fantasy would suggest. Thus we have a further iteration of the sinister quality of the Satan role which has appeared in the high mountain temptation fantasy of Act I, for Irene further tells Rubek:

Irene. High, high up on a dizzy mountain top. You enticed me up there and
promised you would show me all the glory of the world, if –
Rubek. If – ? Well?
Irene. I did as you told me. Followed you to the mountain top. And there I fell on
my knees and worshipped you. And served you. Then I saw the sunrise.

(pp. 359–60)

Despite these sublevels of meaning, the *primary* action taking place in
the swans and lilies pastime is a demonstration of the fantasy-level of their
lives together. Their role-playing in the past as model and artist and the
acceptance of the statue as their "child" was their substitute for life and for
their primary roles as male and female. In their first interview Irene told
Rubek that he placed "the child of the mind first; the child of the body
second" (p. 336). This denial of their sexual roles – which Maja and her
hunter in the secondary plot in no way sublimate – has resulted in the
death-in-life existences of both Rubek and Irene. Her subsequent degradation as a music-hall dancer, or worse, and Rubek's failed creativity and
self-isolation from those around him are partially the results of this denial.
Irene functions to bring Rubek to an awareness of his negative role in her
life and concomitantly to a perception of the quality of his own existence.

Rubek. ... it suddenly occurred to me that all this talk about the task of the artist
and the vocation of the artist was empty, hollow, and meaningless.
Maja. Well, what do you want instead?
Rubek. Life, Maja.
Maja. Life?
Rubek. Yes. Isn't life in sunshine and beauty far more worth-while than wasting
one's years in a raw, damp cellar, wearing oneself to death wrestling with
lumps of clay and blocks of stone?   (p. 347)

Although Rubek invites Irene to live with him and Maja on Taunitzer
See and pass the time as they are doing now, Irene perceives the truth:

Irene. Empty dreams. Idle, dead dreams. Our life together cannot be resurrected.
Rubek. [*curtly.*] Then let us go on with our game.
Irene. Our game, yes. Let us go on with our game. [*They sit throwing leaves and
petals into the stream, and watching them float and sail. ...*]   (p. 360)

As they mechanically throw leaves into the stream the action is transformed from a familiar pastime with romantic fantasies of mysterious knights, beautiful princesses, and magic charms into a self-conscious device for filling the void that exists between them. Moreover, the pastime now becomes a sinister game, for Rubek-the-artist wants to resurrect their former relationship so that Irene may again provide the inspiration for his work. He continues to view his existence through the priorities of artistic inspiration and success devoid of commitments other than to the piece of lifeless clay or marble with which he works. For a second time, Irene rejects Rubek-the-artist, and, as in the past, the game dissolves, but the effect for the characters as well as the audience has been that of *déja vu* – the mirroring of past actions in time present.

The scene is interrupted by Maja's announcement that she is going on an adventure with Ulfhejm whose name connotes a predatory beast. Her straightforward assertion underscores Rubek's inadequacies as a husband and their vacuous relationship together. At this point Irene issues her second invitation to Rubek: "Would you like to spend a summer night on the mountain? With me?" (p. 361). Rubek reiterates his sorrow for what their life together might have been, but she instructs him in his own wasted humanity in those famous lines:

Irene. We only find what we have lost when – [*Stops abruptly.*]
Rubek. When – ?
Irene. When we dead awaken.
Rubek. [*shakes his head sadly.*] What do we find then?
Irene. We find that we have never lived.   (p. 362)

In Ibsen's working drafts, the play was originally called *The Day of Resurrection*, which became *When The Dead Awaken*, and finally in the fair copy *When We Dead Awaken*. Michael Meyer suggests that Ibsen's self-identification with Arnold Rubek was made manifest in this final change from the article to the pronoun.[8] However, since the title comes directly from the line in Act II, it strengthens the fact that the play is not so much about Ibsen's personal evaluation of his own life as about the mutual destinies of Rubek and Irene, artist/man and model/woman. Indirectly, the play also speaks to the audience at large. Irene in her shroud-like white shawl and Rubek dressed in black suggest the several motifs of the play: ulterior motives, wasted lives, personal accountability together with the possibility for atonement. The game devices – artificial and external – momentarily re-create the errors of the past in the present and highlight those repeated errors of Rubek's existence; that is, the subordinating of his nature to his art, his personal life (and the lives of others) to his vocation.

In the second act we are introduced almost at once to another quality of *play*. Designed as studies in contrast to the aging Rubek and Irene, the hunter and Maja are life's creatures (variously described as vixen, faun, and bear) who, in their hedonistic pursuit of their quarry, their personal freedom, and sensual gratification, symbolize those forces in life rejected by Arnold Rubek. Their straightforward play evolves out of their natural drives and appetites. In contrast to the etiolated hue of Irene, her diet of milk and bread, and Rubek's funereal malaise, the ambience of Maja and Ulfhejm is that of blood, bone, and marrow. The quality of the games in this relationship is informed by the absence of fictive allusion. Ulfhejm woos Maja as a sportsman pursues his quarry. The interdependence of the players is delineated here as Maja flees her pursuer only to retrieve him as a mate. Thinly disguised as a childish retreat into athleticism, their sex-game leads to the archetypal mating of the pair. That they will return to the valley and its creatures to live sensually and procreate without the artifice of convention or even good manners is indicative that they represent one extreme of the complicated world view built into the play. Maja's description of her life with Rubek delineates the other extreme: "... he led her into a cold, damp cage, which the sun and fresh air never reached ... though the walls were gilded, and lined with great stone ghosts" (p. 367).

In the third act Rubek and Irene arrive on the mountain top and are warned by Ulfhejm to take shelter from the approaching storm whose winds sound to Rubek "like the Prelude to the Day of Resurrection" (p. 369). Irene's fragile mind is overwhelmed as she confuses their earlier playing by the mountain stream (II) with their past years on Taunitzer See, but the artifice of the childish pastime has, paradoxically, clarified in her mind the equation between Rubek and herself:

> *Irene.* I suddenly realised you were already dead. You've been dead for years.
> ...
> Dead, like me. We sat there by the Taunitzer See, two clammy corpses, playing our little game together. (p. 370)

This is the moment of Rubek's unavoidable realization of his responsibility for the ruin of Irene's life. This spiritual movement is missing in the person of John Gabriel Borkman who dreams on the mountain with his former love the old dreams of fortune and dies as "a hand of iron gripped his heart" (p. 301).[9] At the moment of death, Borkman is una-

ware and unredeemed. The heart of the matter in *When We Dead Awaken*
is Rubek's resurrection from his former self as well as Irene's transformation into a bride of light. Rubek confesses that he set "that dead figure of
clay above life, and happiness, and love" (p. 371), but perceives that there
is still time to live. Irene knows this to be impossible.

> *Irene.* [*looks at him sadly.*] The desire to live died in me, Arnold. Now I am risen
> from the dead, and look for you, and find you. And I find that you are dead,
> and life is dead – as I have been.   (p. 371)

Rubek insists that they flee the shroud-like mountain mists and go up into
the "light" to celebrate their wedding feast. Unlike his former promises to
show "the glory of the world" to those whom he wished to coerce, Rubek
has transcended in his awareness the need for the artifice. The sculptor
has become subordinate to the man. Whereas years earlier Rubek had
rejected Irene, he now leads her "up to the top of our tower, where it
shines in the sunrise" (p. 372). That tower, like Brand's Ice Church, is the
natural configuration of the mountain peak. Rubek has transcended his
desire to use Irene. Unlike the earlier games, the primary quality of the
marriage fantasy is personal and selfless and briefly reminiscent of Johannes
Rosmer and Rebecca West's marriage prior to their deaths in *Rosmersholm.*
Whereas Pastor Rosmer performs a brief ceremony over himself and
Rebecca, there is no such quality of realism at work here. Rubek and
Irene's roles as bride and bridegroom assume a mythic quality. The color
of Irene's shroud-like garments shifts momentarily from the hues of death
to those of life. Like Maja, who sings of freedom from the stifling cage of
her existence, Rubek and Irene have found release from their guilt and
despair. At this moment the avalanche descends. The Nun, Irene's constant shadow, blesses the dead and Maja's songs of freedom echoes in the
air as the play ends.

Although she sings of freedom, Maja, whom George Bernard Shaw
called a Stone Age woman,[10] is bound in sensual pleasure to her bear-
hunter and to that world of ordinary men that Rubek has secretly depicted
in his portrait busts as animalistic. Although he recognizes its satisfactions,
Ibsen does not appear to be greatly interested in this antithetical existence. His concern is with the aging artist who must reconcile, albeit
tragically, what *is* with what might have been. Rubek is able to depart this
life in visionary peace along with the woman he has loved and neglected by
holding himself accountable for the destruction of his life and art. As he
approaches the endgame of his existence, Rubek demonstrates the pat-

terned responses of his self-contained life which have brought him and Irene to this final crossroad.

When We Dead Awaken, unlike Beckett's *Endgame*, is not a single situation acting as a parable of universal human fate. Although the story of Rubek and Irene is, for the most part, a personal one, they likewise demonstrate the mutual interrelatedness of our lives while their childish-*cum*-adult games represent the most contemporary aspect of Ibsen's last play. Ibsen uses game devices (both by children and adults) as clues to the sequential progress of Rubek and Irene toward the momentary resurrection of their lives based on self-recognition, mutual trust, and shared understanding.

Throughout a lifetime, Rubek's games with the lives of others have been directed by ulterior motives and are catalogued here through reference to his schoolboy diversions, his use of Irene as a model and his subsequent rejection of her, his marriage to Maja, and, finally, his desire to use Irene again to open the "casket" of his creative inspiration. Irene, in turn, devises their sojourn on the mountain so that she can kill Rubek and be revenged for her own spiritual mutilation.

> *Irene.* Would you like to spend a summer night on the mountain? With me?
> *Rubek.* [*spreads his arms wide.*] Yes! Yes! Come!
> *Irene.* My love, my lord and master!
> *Rubek.* Oh, Irene!
> *Irene.* [*smiling, as she gropes for the knife.*] It will only be an episode. (p. 361)

At the moment that they renounce their ulterior motives – objectified by the conclusion of "swans and lilies" in the second act – their reformation is initiated. This spiritual progress may be traced from their sympathy with the children at play, through the sentimental game beside the brook, to the mystical wedding feast. In addition, Rubek and Irene's games are, like those of the children they encounter, a reflection of their non-sexual relationship. Their fantasy "child" has been that lifeless statue for which Irene modeled and which was the creation of Rubek's hands and vision. Paradoxically, as Rubek gave life to the statue, he deprived Irene of hers and left her to degradation and madness.

Whereas such secondary games as "Show me," "Casket," "Swans and lilies" delineate the errors of the past as they are repeated in the present because of the unchanged ulterior quality in the substructure of Rubek's life, the total concept of the endgame directs the linear progression of the play to the dramatic crisis – the awakening of the dead – and the multiple deaths on the mountain. Ibsen enriched this linear progression in *When*

We Dead Awaken and expanded the limits of the representational theatre at the close of the nineteenth century by utilizing games to structure the motives, histories, and problematic lives of his wasted principals.

NOTES

1 David Grene, *Reality and The Heroic Pattern: Last Plays of Ibsen, Shakespeare, and Sophocles*, Chicago, 1967, p. 9.
2 Orley I. Holtan, *Mythic Patterns in Ibsen's Last Plays*, Minneapolis, 1970, p. 16.
3 Ibsen's unusual approach to characterization in *When We Dead Awaken* prompted Hermann J. Weigand to argue that "Ibsen's organic unity of character is absent from this play." See *The Modern Ibsen: A Reconsideration*, New York, 1960, p. 391.
4 Eric Berne, *Transactional Analysis in Psychotherapy*, New York, 1961, p. 98.
5 Ronald Gaskell, *Drama and Reality: The European Theatre Since Ibsen*, London, 1972, p. 92.
6 Maurice Valency has argued that the game of Rubek and Irene is clearly to end in death. See *The Flower and the Castle: An Introduction to Modern Drama*, New York, 1963, p. 230.
7 All quotations are taken from *When We Dead Awaken and Three Other Plays*, trans. Michael Meyer, Garden City, New York, 1960, pp. 315–73.
8 *When We Dead Awaken*, p. 312.
9 *John Gabriel Borkman* from *When We Dead Awaken and Three Other Plays*.
10 George Bernard Shaw, *The Quintessence of Ibsenism*, New York, 1957, p. 144.

Strindberg and Ibsen:
Toward a Cubism of Time in Drama

BENJAMIN K. BENNETT

I

In some ways the relation between Strindberg and Ibsen is entirely obvious. The echoes of *Peer Gynt* in *Lucky Pehr's Journey* and the attack on *A Doll's House* in *Sir Bengt's Wife* require no comment: nor does it seem to me at all unlikely – even though the original titles are not as similar as their English translations – that *The Ghost Sonata* has to do with *Ghosts* in an oblique manner. In both the visionary and the realistic modes, the attempt to surpass Ibsen is a constant factor in Strindberg's intention; Strindberg is always more extreme, but the distance separating him from Ibsen is still finite, Ibsen's presence in his background still discernible.

My aim, however, is to show that the question of *time* suggests a deeper level of dramatic form on which Strindberg follows Ibsen and measurably surpasses him. It must be emphasized that the extent to which Strindberg was conscious of this particular relation to Ibsen has little bearing on the argument. The question of time belongs to the very essence of the dramatist's task and cannot be understood in terms of technical or thematic devices that might be regarded as the stock in trade of a particular poet or school. That Ibsen and Strindberg approach the question in basically the same way is certainly no accident. But it is not something Strindberg needs to have concentrated on in his relation to Ibsen; it is simply part of his striving to be a better dramatist.

Throughout the following I shall draw an analogy between time in drama and space in painting. It must be recognized, first, that a dramatic scene does not actually contain time in any more than the limited sense in which a painting contains space. A certain amount of time is required for performance, but the sharp formal boundedness of the scene, its containment between a beginning and an end beyond which it simply does not exist, fails to satisfy our notion of time as an unceasing and uninterruptible flow. The scene, or the play as a whole, has the character of an interlude, a segment of our existence that is separated artificially and devoted to a ritual, or an evoked reality, entirely distinct from the world in which we live the rest of our lives.

But reality includes time, and it follows that drama, if it seeks to imitate reality, must create an illusion of unrestricted time comparable to the illusion of unrestricted space created by the painter on his two-dimensional surface. This necessity produces what I shall call temporal perspectivism in Western drama. Just as the painter gives the impression of planes situated *behind* the plane of his canvas – by using lines that are assumed to be parallel in reality but converge in his drawing – so the dramatist, by making his plot depend on events in the relatively distant past, gives the impression of a temporal continuum extending beyond the limits of what is performed. This is not to say that all Western drama employs temporal perspective to the same degree. There are dramatic conventions in which the illusion of temporal depth is of no particular importance; in French classical drama and in German Classicism, the past is as a rule clearly subordinate to a present action on which our attention is focused. And even in those conventions where temporal depth is important, there are widely different ways of achieving it. In ancient and Renaissance drama, for example, the procedure tends to be highly formal, as it were geometrical, corresponding to the use of architectural outlines to define space in Renaissance painting. The past is narrated by a chorus or prologue, or else it is revealed in stylized dialogue, like Oedipus's questioning of witnesses in the *Tyrannos*. But with the growth of literary realism in the nineteenth century, the technique of temporal perspective, as a means of increasing the illusive power of staged fictions, was developed differently, since realist conventions exclude anything like the style of ancient tragedy. Hence the importance of what is usually called indirect exposition. The present is dominated by an oppressive, looming past, which is revealed only gradually, in fully motivated conversation and action. And the skillful application of this technique, the creation of temporal depth with an entirely seamless transition between depth and foreground, is an important part of what made Ibsen's reputation.

In Ibsen's career, however, the perspectivist phase is transitory. The preoccupation with he past not merely as an objective determinant of our destiny, but as an immediate presence in our mental and social life, leads of necessity to the question of how we see the past, and this question in turn leads to the dramatic equivalent of impressionism. The impressionist painters do not reject perspective; they do not neglect to show distant objects on a smaller scale than nearby objects. But they do question whether our perception of space is as objective and geometrical as perspective painting suggests: do we really see lines and contours, or do we not, rather, simply see light (or Cézanne's "volume and color") from which we then infer lines and contours? Ibsen, like the impressionists, without neglecting to indicate a past history for his plots, begins in his last plays to question whether there is such a thing as *the* past in our lives; is it not rather a pattern of private mental and emotional stirrings for which we merely infer an objective cause? This sense of time emerges clearly in the theme of Hjalmar Ekdal's ineradicable illusions, and also in the relation between Rosmer and Rebecca, which takes the form of a counterpoint built on differing and developing *ideas* of the past. Then, in *Lady from the Sea*, an ominous past is suddenly rendered innocuous, suddenly ceases to be an ominous past, by a simple mental development in those who perceive it; then Hedda Gabler attempts, as it were, actually to repair her past, to force Lövborg back into what she considers his proper place in it; and in *The Master Builder* it is not possible to establish beyond doubt even the bare facts of the past relation between Solness and Hilde. Just as the impressionists turn away from the direct conventional representation of space and seek, rather, to represent the raw sensory data from which we infer our idea of space in reality, so Ibsen turns from the representation of time to the adumbration of the mental processes by which an idea of time arises in us.

And it is in this mode of temporal impressionism that we find Strindberg's first major achievements, his main difference from Ibsen being that he prefers to show the relativity of the idea of time by a clash between the temporal or historical universes of different characters. This technique is applied consistently in *The Father*, even down to the level of the minor characters, and in *Miss Julie* it is developed in that we are shown not a clash between differing ideas of the past, but a collision between fundamentally different *types* of temporal experience: Julie has a past but no future, Jean a future but no past. Then, in *Creditors*, precisely the similarity between two characters' views of the past, not the difference, is employed in order to create doubt about the existence of *the* past. It is obvious that Adolf's idea of his own past is deeply influenced by Gustav, and that Gustav's past relation with Tekla, as we hear of it, is primarily an idea that he reinforces in himself by compelling Adolf to confirm it. Therefore precisely the area of agreement between Adolf's memory and Gustav's is suspect, and I think it is clear that we are meant to generalize from this. Even where the agreement between individuals, between witnesses, gives the past a kind of legal objectivity, still the pliability of human opinion is such that this evidence itself must cause us to doubt; the past as an objective entity remains as unattainable, in effect as nonexistent, as ever. Impressionism is Strindberg's natural approach to the theater, and it is a mode he never leaves entirely behind, even after he abandons mimetic realism in representation. Even after the first two parts of *To Damascus*, for example, we find a play like *The Dance of Death*, in which impressionistic technique is developed with unprecedented intensity, in which the past is not merely called into question but whipped about violently like a tattered pennant in a storm, utterly at the mercy of the particular human situations in which it is made to function.

Neither Strindberg nor Ibsen, however, remains entirely satisfied with impressionism as an artistic approach, and in Strindberg's case the reasons for his dissatisfaction, and its results, are quite clear. If our idea of time, hence a crucial component of our idea of ourselves and the world, is conditioned by our particular individuality and lacks all claim to being objectively valid, then mimetic realism becomes difficult to justify as a theatrical convention. If a drama even seems to present itself as imitating reality, while in the very process it demonstrates the relativity of its characters' idea of time, then the author is suggesting in effect that he and his audience are exempt from the human condition as he himself has portrayed it – since mimesis presupposes that we do see things as they are. It is this danger of logical conflict between style and meaning that moves Strindberg toward expressionism.

Whereas the impressionist, in drawing our attention to the questionability of our idea of space, still allows his composition as a whole to be guided by the mimetic conventions he is criticizing, the expressionist allows the mental or emotional content of his picture to distort the composition and so abandons all semblance of imitation. This distortion is what happens in Strindberg's quest and dream plays. Stage settings no longer represent believable locations but are stripped to their bare essentials as symbols emanating from the consciousness of a character; certain figures, like the Beggar in *To Damascus*, know more about the central character than they have any right to and so reveal the extent to which the whole fiction is a reflection of that character's inner life; the world is narrowed, by such devices as the past relationship between the Stranger and the Physician, to the point of an anguished constriction which in *To Damascus* we associate with the tight inner anguish of the Stranger himself. But above all, time is distorted. In *To Damascus I* the temporal succession of events is more or less plausible, but the direction of time's movement is very much in doubt: is it linear (progressive, cumulative, nonrepeating), or oscillating back and forth along the same path (seaside, hotel, Physician's house, street corner), or a circle of endless repetition – perhaps a Hegelian helix? Then, in *To Damascus II*, temporal continuity is simply exploded, especially by the banquet and prison scenes. And in *A Dream Play* time is made to move at bewilderingly different velocities, even with respect to itself, like the eddies, pools and currents in a swift, shallow stream.

Expressionism is one possible term for describing the way Strindberg goes beyond Ibsen. But once we understand that the term "naturalism," which is usually taken as the oppositive of expressionism, is not applicable at any depth to either Ibsen or Strindberg, once we understand that the essential historical phenomenon is a development toward expressionism by way of the temporal equivalents of perspective and impressionism, several interesting questions arise. Why does Ibsen not follow the same artistic path taken later by Strindberg? The impressionism of his later plays contains a definite force tending along that path. In *The Master Builder* there are several possible ways of accounting for the conversations Hilde "remembers" with Solness, but in her immediate effect Hilde is close to being one of those typical expressionist figures with mysterious inner knowledge of the hero; she is a projection of Solness, as the Rat Wife is a projection of the creeping things that inhabit the Allmers' psychological household. In *John Gabriel Borkman*, by contrast with the obtrusively strict temporal continuity, space (which is ordinarily less flexible than time in drama) suddenly becomes fluid in the last scene, when Borkman takes his walk; this relaxation of theatrical conventions is evidently a projection of the change taking place in Borkman himself. And in *When We Dead Awaken*, the quadrangular pattern of characters is a kind of moral coordinate system by which Rubek attempts to chart the position and contours of his true self.

For Ibsen, as for Strindberg, dramatic impressionism thus produces a tendency in the direction of expressionism, but Ibsen, to the end of his career, remains much closer to the cohesively mimetic. The question is: why? Surely the author of *Peer Gynt* was not incapable of expressionist style. The absence of a fully developed expressionism in late Ibsen must result from the playwright's *deliberate resistance* to a force he felt operating in his own work; and if we look at the thematic content of the late plays, this resistance is not difficult to understand.

Ellida Wangel, for example, when required to make an entirely free choice, chooses a quite thoroughly prosaic reality over the "terrible and alluring life" of poetic possibility offered by the Stranger. And a similar choice is made by Alfred and Rita Allmers at the end of *Little Eyolf*: after discussing various possible ways of poeticizing or tragedizing their existence – death, separation, infidelity, revenge on the poor who live below – they finally arrive at what seems to them a momentous decision: simply to go on living, and to try being decent with the people around them. In both cases, though with a certain irony in each, the ordinary, orderly operation of domestic or social reality is presented as the result of a serious ethical choice, not merely as unthinking routine. And *Hedda Gabler* stresses the negative aspect of the same idea by showing that normal human existence, if we consider it disinterestedly (that is, aesthetically, in terms of what Hedda calls "beauty"), is at its best intolerable. I do not mean that Hedda's attitudes are intended to be shared completely by the audience; but a quite improbable degree of bourgeois complacency would be required in order to assert that there is no truth whatever in her perception of things. Normal, everyday human life is inescapably a tedious affair, at least from the point of view of a disinterested observer, which means that the disinterested observer will not by nature be inclined to lead such a life; for the individual who has achieved any degree of detached perspective on his existence, as for Ellida or Allmers, normal human life cannot happen except as the result of a *free decision*, a deliberate abandonment of aesthetic disinterest in favor of ethical commitment.

This point, I think, explains Ibsen's resistance to the expressionistic tendency in his own development. We are meant to sense the latent expressionism in the last plays, and we are meant to understand that by remaining nonetheless within the conventional limits of the mimetic, we and the author are participating in an ethical decision similar to the decision suggested by the work's theme. The reason for this decision on our part, moreover, is indicated with perfect clarity in at least the final four plays. Solness, Allmers and Borkman all make a conscious effort to believe that they are devoting their lives to other people – Solness to the happy families he imagines living in his houses, Allmers to his son, Borkman to those whose prosperity he had dreamed of creating – and all three projects possess a certain basic logic. But each of the three men, as Solness puts it, must pay a price for his supposed altruism, and it becomes clear in each play that the reason this price is exacted is that the project is in truth self-directed, does not constitute a genuine approach to other people. This moral lesson concerning the ideas of self and other, however, is also an allegory of the artistic situation at which the author has arrived. Expressionism, or the elaboration of the symbolic at the expense of the mimetic, is a logical development of drama's attempt to achieve profound contact with its audience, the attempt to provide the audience not merely with a conventional picture of the world but with an understanding of the process by which our idea of world and time are generated. As in painting, the recognition that perspective is a mere convention gives rise to dramatic impressionism; and the recognition that impressionism is not strictly consistent, since its own nearness to the mimetic conflicts with its lesson about the nature of perception, leads onward to expressionism. Thus the expressionist, with some justification, can say that by distorting his images into symbols of the individual's inner life, he alone is showing things as they truly are, as mental or emotional projections, and he alone, therefore, is performing a true service for his audience.

But there is a difficulty here. In attempting to make contact with us, and in a sense to benefit us, the expressionist, like Solness, Allmers and Borkman, overshoots the mark. He aims for communication on the basis of the idea that no true communication is possible, that each individual lives in a world created by and for himself; we follow the expressionist, therefore, and learn from him, only by submitting to him, by surrendering to his vision, as those myriads whom Solness or Borkman dream of making happy would in essence only be contributing to their benefactor's self-magnification. The expressionist can teach me how *he* sees things, and perhaps even in a sense how *I* see things, but he has not grasped the secret of how *we* see things, the common ground where people meet and deal genuinely with one another. In the realm of artistic form, however, this common ground is represented for Ibsen by the conventions of the mimetic, to which he steadfastly adheres despite the pull of his stylistic development toward expressionism. That the mimetic is *only* a convention, without objective validity, is made clear to us by the strong expressionistic undertow in the late plays; but precisely the conventionality of the mimetic implies its nature as a *communal* phenomenon, a way of seeing which we more or less arbitrarily agree to keep in common with other people; and this is the source of its ethical value. It is our duty to understand reality in such a way that real contact with others becomes and remains possible. The conventionally mimetic does not reveal truth or even demonstrate facts; but it is a medium of communication, and functions the more perfectly as such when its lack of objectivity is generally recognized. If we imagine that "realistic" drama shows us reality, then our philosophical doubts about reality necessarily imply doubts about the actual communicativeness of such drama; but if the realistic is recognized from the outset as mere convention, then the conscious decision to accept that convention *is* undoubtedly communicative, shared with others, a communal process.

This argument, though perhaps abstract, is not at all speculative, for Ibsen himself incorporates it into his last play, *When We Dead Awaken.* The relation between Rubek's finished statue, with its supposedly hardheaded acceptance of the truth, and his original ideal conception, is the same as the relation between the expressionistic and the mimetic. From the expressionist's point of view, mimetic representation is an illogical idealism, comparable to Rubek's original style, for it assumes the existence of universally comprehensible entities or objects that can be imitated; the expressionist, with what he thinks of (in Rubek's words) as his greater "experience of life," has discarded the illusions on which the mimetic is based. But as in the case of the expressionist, Rubek's striving for truth is ultimately only a form of narcissism; the focus of his work is now a self-pitying vision of himself, surrounded by those human animals whom he despises and subjugates in his art. We must not be misled by an apparent connection between Rubek's late pretensions to "realism" and what we are accustomed to think of as Ibsen's own "realistic" style; the latter, as we have seen, is in truth not realistic so much as impressionistic, with a tendency toward expressionism, embodying the recognition that mimetic theatrical conventions do *not* communicate a true "experience of life." The mimetic, or the avoidance of the expressionistic, in late Ibsen – like Rubek's *original* statue, which he must now learn to reaffirm – is an ideal, a proposed rallying point for human communication in a genuine and joyful form (whether or not it agrees with "experience"), thus the hope for an awakening from our "death" as the encapsulated envisioners of narrow private worlds.

II

Ibsen the socially oriented artist, intent on understanding and communication; Strindberg the self-preoccupied expressionist, rescuing himself from insanity only by the repeated effort of re-creating his tortured inner life in the cool material of art. The argument so far thus appears to flatter some long established opinions on the two men. My main point, however, is that the ethical resistance to expressionism is found in Strindberg as well as in Ibsen, indeed in an even stronger form, which leads to artistic discoveries that are entirely beyond Ibsen's range, though still consistent with his principles.

Strindberg himself suggests something of this in his preface to *A Dream Play*, when he speaks of the dreamer's need to awaken, to rejoin and be reconciled with reality. The description of the dream play as a type, in that preface, reads like an expressionist manifesto: space and time are discarded or overcome in the theater; mental or inner realities assume physical shapes; the stage becomes the projection of a single governing consciousness. But still, we are told, even from the point of view of the governing consciousness, ordinary daylight reality is preferable to the dream or expressionist vision; and accordingly, in the very fabric of Strindberg's expressionist style, we can discern a tendency in the other direction, toward what appears in Ibsen as the ethical avoidance of expressionism.

The style of *To Damascus III*, for example, is still basically expressionistic. The scene visions are obviously symbolic; shapes and spaces, especially in Act III, Scene i, are permitted to change fantastically in accordance with the Stranger's inner needs; entrances and exits of characters are determined not by external causes but by the development of moods and thoughts in the central figure. And yet there are a number of touches that seem stylistically incongruous. The Tempter, for instance, who of all the characters is most exclusively a projection of the Stranger's inward state, is suddenly endowed, in Act III, Scenes i and iv, with a detailed past history, as if he were a human being in his own right. It is as if the dream were struggling back toward reality, as if the mental figments were striving to reveal themselves as real objects after all, as if the expressionistic were turning away from itself, toward the mimetic. Or we think of Caesar, who is introduced in *To Damascus I* as a projection of the Stranger's monomaniacal tendency, but now, as the Pilgrim, also receives his own three-dimensional being. Indeed, the whole use of plot complications in *To Damascus* bears thinking about. That there had once been a relationship between the Confessor and the Lady, or that the Stranger and the Physician had known each other as boys, tends to make the work's apparent expressionistic structure not more cohesive but less so. The symbolic or philosophical connections among these characters are quite sufficient to bear the weight of the work's development; therefore the connections via past history give the impression of being superfluous. But they are not superfluous; their function is to remind us of the possibility that the dream is merely a dream, the possibility that *all* those inner connections which make up the play's desperately pessimistic philosophical structure are merely the morbid mental distortions of simple facts in a solid real world to which we might conceivably awaken. That is, plot complication represents a counterforce to the expressionist notion that our world is never anything but our own mental construction.

Still more significant, however, is the nature of time in *To Damascus III*. In Parts I and II time is treated expressionistically. There is a sense of reversibility or circularity in Part I which confuses our sense of chronological direction; and in Part II inconsistent action sequences are made to collide, thus disrupting our sense even of chronological succession. But in Part III, despite the generally expressionistic style, time becomes strictly linear and cumulative. The action begins at the foot of a mountain and ends at the top, if with some delay. Earlier scenes, to the extent necessary, are recollected in scenes that follow, and later scenes are prepared for in what precedes. There is no chronological conflict; things happen one after the other and build toward the conclusion. It is clear, moreover, that this relatively rational ordering of time is related to the development of the Stranger's character; as the Stranger grows toward self-conquest, the time in which he lives straightens itself out into something approaching our conventional idea of time as progression. And this relation between character and style makes it clear that the counterforce operating against expressionism, in Strindberg as in Ibsen, is basically ethical in nature. The existence of a reality that is more than just the anguished projection of ourselves, reality as a medium of communication and understanding, may not be taken for granted; such a reality arises only as the result of an ethical growth or resolve on our part.

This sense of struggle between expressionist style and ethical or communicative resolve is central in Strindberg's later development. In some plays it is perfectly obvious, as in *Easter*, where Lindkvist's sensible directness and generosity dissipate the atmosphere created by our sense of his shadow as a relentless avenging force in Elis's inner life. In some plays, like *To Damascus*, it is woven subtly into the artistic texture. And in some plays it is elaborated in the direction of a new style. The basic opposition in *A Dream Play*, for example, is between the visionary and the practical, between the claims of the Poet and those of the Attorney, between the world of truth, where the dreams of poetry are more real than reality itself, and the world of cause and effect, where coal heavers, lawsuits and university faculties are necessary. It is suggested repeatedly, however, that precisely the world of cause and effect, in which we are miserable, is the indispensable vehicle of our true being, that only suffering can impel us toward truth; and this idea must be applied to the work's form. What we see on the stage, after all, is a poetic vision; its expressionist style emphasizes its freedom from the laws of space, time and causality. But rather than make use of its freedom in order to turn away from the world of our misery, the play does exactly the opposite; like the Daughter of Indra, who descends to earth by free choice, the play freely chooses to focus on the harsh reality of cause and effect, of senseless repetition, of imbecility in the form of strict logic. And it is this choice that is suggested to us as an ethical imperative. If we open the door and attempt to experience truth directly, we discover nothing; we must choose freely the way of suffering, the real world composed of necessities and conventions that never answer our inner needs, for only thus can we progress beyond the narrow darkness of the self. When we awaken from the theatrical "dream," we shall find ourselves in exactly the same intolerable reality that the play had depicted; and yet, as Strindberg asserts, our awakening will still somehow represent a step upwards, beyond the tormenting expressionistic fluidity of the stage vision, toward something that has become more solid and communicable by virtue of the knowledge – which we have received precisely from the vision's expressionistic quality – that it must be our free choice.

Thus the tension between expressionistic and mimetic styles, as it appears in Ibsen and even in *To Damascus*, has been left behind; but the basic ethical situation is unaltered. Strindberg is now aiming for something entirely new, but without turning his back on the complex of problems that had led him and Ibsen from a perspectivist to an impressionist and then toward an expressionist dramatic approach.

III

I shall use the term "cubism" in a relatively narrow sense, to refer to the artistic technique by which different aspects of a scene are combined into a single cohesive composition. When we observe a cubist work, we find ourselves occupying, at the same time, several different spatial points of view with respect to the same object, and I take it that this exercise is meant to reveal the true nature of our perception of space. We do not "see" space as that series of receding planes which the perspective painter constructs, but neither is there quite so much discontinuity between our actual perceptions and our awareness of space as the impressionist or the expressionist imagines. Our awareness of space, for the cubist, is simply our *knowledge* that different points of view exist with respect to the object we are observing, and this knowledge is fully integrated with our sense experience, not merely abstract; when we see an object and are aware of its being in space, then in a strong sense we actually *see* its other possible aspects. Cubist art thus makes us more conscious of a mental process we always engage in anyway. In the mere act of seeing, we repeatedly create the same kind of artistic synthesis that the cubist creates on his canvas. We do not *first* see an image and *then* infer other aspects of the object, but rather we combine the original and implied aspects into a mental composition (like the artist's physical composition) which is so thoroughly unified that we have the impression of simply "seeing" an object in space.

If these ideas are accepted as a working definition of cubism – and I make no claims concerning their validity in art history – then cubism has in common with impressionism and expressionism the recognition that space is essentially a mental construct, not a directly perceived reality. But whereas the impressionist considers space simply an illusion, and whereas the expressionist shows space as an involuntary projection of our inner life, the cubist regards space as a repeated intellectual or artistic *achievement* on our part, comparable to his own achievement in creating a unified composition our of different points of view. Thence it follows that something like cubism in drama is what both Ibsen and Strindberg ultimately require. The avoidance of expressionism in late Ibsen, and the suggestion of a counterforce in *To Damascus*, have deep poetic-ethical significance and are managed very skillfully; but neither technique is entirely satisfactory from an artistic point of view. In both cases the expressionistic is employed or suggested primarily in order that it may then be negated, and this sequence raises the question of whether it ought to have been employed in the first place. Can an element of style, which by nature belongs positively to the work's character, have negative significance in the work's meaning?

The answer to this difficulty is cubism. If a cubist drama is possible, then the negation of the expressionistic will no longer be necessary. Time will appear still as a mental creation, but no longer as a mere solipsistic mirroring of the individual; it will have the character, rather, of an objectifiable artistic achievement, and this character will satisfy the ethical imperatives of communicativeness and self-conquest which in Ibsen and Strindberg otherwise operate against the expressionistic. In any case, there is already a movement toward cubism in *A Dream Play*, where the sense of the vision as an individual's convulsive self-projection is much less pronounced than in *To Damascus*. The Daughter of Indra is less the absolute center of the vision that focuses on her than the Stranger is of his vision, and the result is an increased feeling of artistic objectivity. Or we think perhaps of the change of perspectives between Foulgut and Faircove, which suggests spatial cubism.

But if our analogy between painting and drama is valid, then the medium of dramatic cubism will be time, not space, and this leads to some problems. It seems clear that the temporal "aspects" of an object or event will include its past, present and future, and that the effect of temporal cubism will be to remind us that when we perceive something as existing in time, what we really do is create a unified artistic composition, essentially a dramatic composition, that integrates those various aspects with one another. But precisely how will a cubist style work in drama? Walter Sokel, in *The Writer in Extremis* (Stanford, 1959), suggests that the subtle overlaying of different time levels produces in some modern poetry an effect similar to that of cubism, but this alone will not necessarily satisfy the ethical demands that arise in Ibsen's and Strindberg's development. Rather than attempt an abstract answer to the question of cubism in drama, let us turn directly to Strindberg's last plays.

In *The Ghost Sonata*, as in *The Dance of Death*, the past is deliberately made obscure. When Hummel describes to Arkenholtz the complicated relations among the people in the apartment house, we naturally expect analytic drama in the manner of Ibsen's *Ghosts*, in which all the past complications are delicately coordinated and brought to bear, in a kind of crescendo, on the present action. But actually, only the fact that the Young Lady is Hummell's daughter has any direct influence on what might loosely be termed the plot. The rest of the past and present complications serve mainly as a general atmospheric explanation of why the "ghost suppers" take place, and of the Young Lady's *taedium vitae*. There are any number of strong hints about the past that are never developed: Johansson's history, for example, and the Baron's career as a jewel thief. And at the moment when Hummel is about to lay everything bare, he is sent off to the closet to die.

But in *The Dance of Death* the obscurity or uncertainty of the past is associated impressionistically with our understanding that the past is really nothing more than an idea that shapes itself differently in each person's mind; thus, even without knowing the past in detail, we still sense that the past is determining the present in a relatively logical manner (via people's evolved attitudes), just as we sense depth in an impressionist painting even without being able to compare exactly the scale of receding planes. In *The Dance of Death*, therefore, the past still exerts its influence from a position as it were behind the present, and in *The Ghost Sonata* this is no longer the case. Here the logical or chronological relation between past and present is broken – again, the details of the past that we do learn have little specific bearing on the action, but affect it only by way of atmosphere – and the past is instead simply fused with the present, as a mysterious but inexhaustible source of suffering, like the household servants in the life of the Young Lady. "I'm going now – but I am staying just the same ...," says the Cook (p. 491), and it is just so with the past, which stays even in it's going. The implied depth of impressionism, with past behind present, is replaced by an immediate fusion, as full-face and profile might be fused in a cubist painting.

The Ghost Sonata is a cubist tragedy. It has an ethical dimension that appears especially in the words of the Mummy: "But I can stop time – I can wipe out the past and undo what has been done – but not with bribery and not with threats ... but through suffering and repentance" (p. 484). Cubist style, the fusion of present and past, reminds us of our moral freedom, our ability to break the apparently unbreakable causal relation between past and present. The past is still with us, like the Milkmaid in the doorway or the ghosts around the table; and yet it has in a sense been "undone," for it is no longer a distant and unalterable determinant of the present – it is no longer out of reach, no longer simply that dread "It was" which Nietzsche's Zarathustra calls the greatest enemy of the will – but rather it has become fused with the present, thus subject to our will, our moral decisiveness, after all.

However, the ethical dimension is here not yet fully developed; the focus is upon the magnitude of suffering by which our moral freedom is purchased. If we do not live the past uninterruptedly, and suffer for it, if we shrink from the past, as Hummel shrinks from milk wagons, then the past will slip away from us, out of our control, and become again an irresistible determining force in our existence. That this, moreover, is a general law of life, not merely a result of actual guilt, is shown by the final scene between the Young Lady and the Student. Hummel has attempted to rescue his daughter from the suffering of the ghost family by rescuing her from the retributive logic of time, to which end he seeks out Arkenholtz, the Sunday's child, for whom past and future, the milkmaid and the collapsing house, are immediate realities. What Hummel does not recognize is that the state of being rescued from time, of living in the unchanging immediacy of the past, is already the very substance of his daughter's suffering, as of the Mummy's and the other ghosts'. Therefore the appearance of Arkenholtz, with his relentless candor about the true nature of human life, only makes the Young Lady's condition intolerable to the extent of destroying her. Either we live chronologically, at the mercy of time and causality and retribution – like Hummel, who does not understand that any other possibility exists – or else we achieve freedom in the immediate presence of the past, by suffering unbearably; these alternatives describe the whole of the human condition as seen in the mirror of cubist tragedy.

But tragedy as represented by *The Ghost Sonata* does not realize the full potential of cubist style; it indicates the ethical force from which dramatic cubism is born, but does not develop it. Only in *The Great Highway*, it seems to me, is Strindberg's destiny as a dramatist fulfilled. There are a number of clear points of contact between this play and *The Ghost Sonata*. The idea of controlling someone, of "taking" him or stealing his very self, by knowing about him, and especially by knowing about his past, is prominent in both works. In both there are a number of references to possible plot complications that are rooted in the past but now lead nowhere, thus producing that sense of a breakdown in the causal relation of past and present which we have discussed. Both works are basically cubist in style. But *The Great Highway* represents an important advance over *The Ghost Sonata* in that it embodies a far more solid and complete ethical justification of cubism.

At least three of the other prominent figures, first of all, are in some way identical with the Hunter, expressionist projections of him. In the case of the Wanderer – who appears significantly in response to the Hermit's question, "Who are you?" (p. 413) – this relation is obvious, especially since the Hunter later identifies himself metaphorically with the Wandering Jew. But the case of the Japanese is perhaps more interesting from our point of view, for it leads directly into the work's complex time structure. The Japanese says he has been living in Tophet for more than fifteen years, which would mean, if time operated logically, that he had been there when the Hunter had made a public spectacle of himself. Yet he seems to know nothing whatever of this event, or of the Hunter's later efforts to expose Möller; he acts as if he had never before detected a spark of true humanity in Tophet. And the Hunter, even though the spot represented on stage had been one of his haunts, and even though he remembers the other shops vividly, apparently has not the slightest recollection of the tea shop or its owner. Clearly we are meant to be puzzled by this anomaly, for the exact number of years separating the various events is mentioned no less than three times in Scene iv; and it must occur to us then that if the conversations between the Hunter and the Japanese were taking place, say, thirteen or fourteen years in the past, *before* the Hunter's crisis, the two men's unawareness of each other's existence would be no problem. But from a different point of view, these conversations are made continuous with the conversations with Möller, that belong to the present. Thus, at least on a relatively superficial level, a sense of fusion between past and present is created.

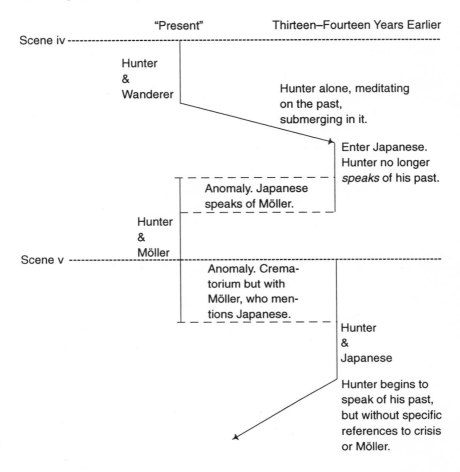

In any case, the association of the Japanese with the Hunter's past, in another way, is made by the Hunter himself when he says to Möller that he had "committed hara-kiri" twelve years ago (p. 441). If the Japanese is not a real figure from the past, then at least his ritual suicide is the reenactment of an event in the personal past of the Hunter. The Japanese *is* the Hunter at an earlier stage of his life, and the significance of this identification becomes clear when we recognize that it applies to the Wanderer as well. The Hunter himself had once been trapped into an unsatisfactory marriage; he had apparently played out the early phases of his love at exactly the spot where the Wanderer is ensnared; and at the beginning of Scene vi he implies that he, like the Wanderer, had known in advance the disastrous absurdity of the situation in which he had been involving himself. In the Wanderer, then, as in the Japanese, the Hunter encounters an epoch of his own past self, and we can therefore interpret those curious conversations between the Hunter and the Wanderer, where each repeatedly takes the words out of the other's mouth, as a depiction of the interwovenness of past and present. In our words, in our very thoughts, we are constantly forestalled by a ghostly intruder who is somehow identical with ourselves, yet also somehow alien. This, to be sure, raises a question about the similar conversation with the Girl in Scene ii, and we shall return to this question below.

But first let us note that the third figure who represents an element of the Hunter's past is Möller the Murderer. Only thus does the Hunter's tirade really make sense, in which he enumerates acts and achievements for which Möller took the credit and he the blame. Möller is that component of the self which (like Hummel, another murderer) lives chronologically, affirms its achievements, strives forward in time, attempts to leave the past behind, whereas the Hunter, like the Mummy, is that component which lives its past uninterruptedly and suffers for it, thus renewing itself and "shaking off" the "vermin" of guilt (as Möller puts it [p. 442]), but only at the price of unceasing anguish. The Wanderer, then, is the Hunter's inevitable past entanglement in the world, despite his foreknowledge of what such entanglement must lead to; Möller is the Hunter's participation in society, his attempt to fashion an identity for himself by occupying a solid position with respect to others, thus in effect using others for his own ends and so robbing them of *their* identities, as it were murdering them; and the Japanese is the Hunter's hara-kiri, his anguished crisis of self-appraisal, self-rejection and self-renewal.

At the same time, however, the Wanderer, the Japanese and Möller are also presented as individuals clearly distinguishable from the Hunter. The Hunter's past, to the extent that we learn of it, could not have happened without Möller's having functioned as a separate individual; and the reaction of the citizens of Tophet to the Hunter's question appears to confirm what he says about Möller. The Wanderer is given a specific location in the chronology of the Hunter's life by the revelation that the Waitress is the Hunter's daughter, which places a definite number of years between the Wanderer's entrapment in marriage and the Hunter's. And the Japanese is distinguished by the details of his culture and language that give clear individual contours to his being.

As with Caesar and the Tempter in *To Damascus*, we are shown figures

who are obviously expressionistic projections of the central character, yet also individuals in their own rights. But in *The Great Highway* there is none of the tension between different styles that had characterized the earlier play. In *To Damascus III* expressionist time laboriously struggles back toward mimetic time, whereas in *The Great Highway* not only the incompatibility of the Hunter's chronology with that of the Japanese, but also the chronological conflict between Scene vi and Scenes iv and v, maintains an expressionistic, strongly antimimetic quality of style to the very end. There is even an indication of temporal circularity in *The Great Highway*. The Hunter and the Wanderer have agreed on the inevitability of their meeting again, and at the end the Hunter is on his way back to the Hermit, where he had first met the Wanderer. The last scene could therefore easily be followed by the first, closing the action into an endless cycle that would correspond to the Hunter's endless quest for his true self.

In *The Great Highway*, then, mimetic style is not even a possibility, and there can be only be one reason for the prominence of those figures who hover between independent individuality and the state of mere figments. We are meant to recognize that such hovering characterizes *all* human beings as we encounter them in real life. Other people always are, at the same time, somehow both reflections of our own self and strictly distinct persons. On the one hand this idea incorporates the basic expressionist tenet that all reality is essentially a projection of the self, while on the other hand it also takes account of the Hunter's perception that communal reality, our encounter with other people, nevertheless always confuses us, that our very self is stolen from us when we deal with others, that despite all our efforts to remain spectators, we are always drawn into the stage action and in the process forget who we are. This is why the windmills are named Adam and Eve; no sooner do two human beings exist than they interfere with each other, take the wind from each other's sails. Other people, as we experience them, are always projections of ourselves, the continued presence of our own past; but they are also "other," alien, confusing, challenging.

This state of affairs – that reality, in the very process of expressing and reflecting us, also confuses us – evidently indicates the existence of a fundamental confusion or disharmony in our own being. And while this disharmony may be regarded as a defect – in the Hunter's last words, for example, about not being able to be the one he had wanted to be – it may also be regarded as a virtue, a source of human stature. The Mummy in *The Ghost Sonata* is referring to essentially the same inner state, not being the one we want to be, when she claims that she and her fellow ghosts have the *advantage*, over Hummel, of being able to experience dissatisfaction with themselves; or we think of the portrait gallery in *To Damascus III*, where the Stranger is urged to accept and affirm man's two-headedness. That other people are "other" in the very process of being images of ourselves corresponds to the capacity for suffering by which we are enabled to overcome time and live a voluntary, rather than a merely passive existence.

This point brings us back to the question of cubist style, which in *The Great Highway*, in the vision of the Hunter's constantly living in the presence of his own past, reminds us first of all that when we observe other people (as the audience observe the Hunter), we necessarily think of them as existing in time; that is, we infer and, as it were, "see" their pasts in a dramatic relation to the present (as the audience see the Hunter's past in other figures). Cubist painting, again, reminds us that we "see" an object's various aspects when we perceive it in space. But from the Hunter's actual example, from his encounter with figures hovering between identity and otherness, we learn yet more. For the essentially cubist process by which we perceive other people involves the imposition of our own thought on the object, our own interference of temporal aspects, while at the same time we relinquish our claim to that thought as *ours* and instead acknowledge its effects as *part* of the object, part of what we "see." Thus there is a natural and fairly obvious relation between this process and the combination of identity and otherness in other people for the Hunter; others are the projection of our own thought, yet disturbingly different from us. And the idea that this combination of identity and otherness, when we perceive it, reflects a human *virtue* in us, corresponds to the idea of cubist art as an achievement of the thinking and perceiving mind. But the aim of this virtue, the sense of this achievement – as becomes even clearer in the case of the Hunter than in that of the Mummy – is the organization of our own self into a cohesive unity, the integration of past with present in order to realize our moral and volitional being. It follows, therefore, the social existence, our relation to others, is a work of cubist art constantly in the making, the object of which is to create and experience our own person in a definitive form.

That social existence, in this sense, is a genuine artistic endeavor, requiring special skill and delicacy, is shown by an exactly symmetrical pattern of incidents involving the Hunter and the Wanderer. In Scene ii the Wanderer seeks to ferret out the Girl's inmost secrets, to organize and dominate her existence by knowing it, and he fails; in Scene iv he attempts exactly the opposite, to break contact with the Waitress, to have nothing to do with her, but again he fails. The point is that we may not push our relation with other people too hard, we may not approach them too closely; but neither may we arbitrarily sever our relation with them. The hovering between identity and alterity which, in characterizing other people, reveals the shape and virtue of our own humanity, is a state we must work consciously to maintain, as is shown in the contrasting scenes involving the Hunter. After the Wanderer leaves, the Hunter and the Girl do successfully approach each other, to the point of carrying on a conversation that is essentially a monologue, but they achieve this only by insisting, in what they say, on a definite distance; and the identification of the Waitress as the Hunter's daughter makes a connection with Scene vi, where the Hunter, with his daughter in another form, again keeps a precarious balance between approach and separation.

The ceaseless artistic endeavor by which we strive to lay hold of our own true self is thus also a genuine social act, not merely an exploitation of others for our own ends. For precisely by carrying out that endeavor in the way that profits us most, that brings us closest to both the whole misery and the whole merit of our condition, we also find ourselves carrying it out in such a way that it becomes a medium of communication with others, which preserves others' individuality while also making contact with it. We neither dominate nor submit, but we maintain a balance between the two that enables the other person to share at least the shape of our own experience. If we could force a strict separation between ourselves and others, this would exclude communication; and if we could force a complete incorporation of the other person into our own feeling of self, the very idea of communication would be meaningless. But when we experience other people as hovering between independent individuality and the status of mental projections of ourselves, when we experience them as something comparable to a cubist achievement – and only when this happens – community becomes possible; not in the sense that we know each other, but in the sense that we work together, or at least in the same way, toward creating human existence as a work of art by which our subjection to time is overcome, if at the price of maximum suffering. Precisely this sense of a community of distinct individuals all participating in the same artistic endeavor, moreover, is a natural part of our experience *in the theater*, where performers and spectators form an actual community united by its artistic directedness. Cubist style, in Strindberg, reminds us of *how* this community is oriented, toward the overcoming or spatializing of time; and the state of hovering that we are obligated to maintain in our experience of other people is represented by our normal relation to the stage action and images, which we know we are meant to interpret as referring to our own private existence, but which also stand at a definite distance from us by virtue of their belonging to a public ritual. Thus the character of the theater as an institution contributes directly to the work's aesthetic-ethical structure.

We are now in a position to understand the ethical message of *The Great Highway* as set forth in Scene vii. In *To Damascus* and *A Dream Play* the resistance to expressionist style arises from a mistrust of the self-investigating and self-projecting individual; somehow the individual's preoccupation with realizing his own being must be overcome in favor of a more self-mastered and outward directed attitude. But what form must a specific ethical doctrine of this sort take in order to be expressible in drama without sacrificing the important artistic and psychological insights that had led to expressionism? There is no answer to this question in abstract ethics. The answer is provided by a development in artistic form, Strindberg's gradual development toward cubism, under the guidance of the idea that living in the immediate presence of the past is a purification through suffering. For in the fully developed cubism of *The Great Highway* an entirely new ethics emerges, as a *result* of the style itself, not as a reason or an excuse for it. The doctrine of pity or compassion, the idea that we must deny ourselves in order to accept the feelings of others, is now rejected by the Hunter in his conversation with the Woman; indeed, it had already been rejected earlier, by implication, in Scenes ii and iii. No sooner do two human beings exist than they impede each other, like the windmills; but if we therefore resolve not to impede each other, if we insist on yielding to others wherever possible, the result is mere absurdity, like the society governed by the Smith in Scene iii. What we must do is not renounce our quest for self-realization, but rather prosecute that quest with yet more tenacity – we must insist on struggling with the angel, like Jacob – for then we discover that our closest approach to our own true self is also the only possible source of genuine community. This is the message contained not only in the Hunter's development, and in the hovering cubist style, and in our situation as a theater audience, but also in the work's implied circularity. Precisely by resolving to return to the Hermit, to *leave* human society in favor of the ice and snow of pure self-contemplation, the Hunter is returning to the beginning of the play, whence he will descend yet again into that precarious balance by which we are always in the process of creating, communally and artistically, a worthy human world.

There is no end to this process; we never are "the one we want to be."

And yet we must always strive uncompromisingly to achieve that state. The Tempter suggests to the Hunter that he *knowingly* live his life in a circle, by becoming Tophet's architect once again, and the Hunter drives him off by asserting a faith in the Creator, a faith which we recognize *will* lead him in a circle, down from the mountain again, in spite of himself. This is as it must be. Our existence can never be any more than an endless cycle of self-approach, dissatisfaction, and resumption of the quest; but even this cyclic process depends on our striving to go beyond it, on our faith in the absolute realizability of our true being; the process must happen *in spite* of us. For if we assent to the cycle, as the Tempter asks the Hunter to do, then our commitment to the quest for true being is no longer strong enough to produce the cycle in its essential form, to produce true human community, and we thus no longer even approach full self-realization; human existence no longer has the character of a supratemporal work of art. Hence, again, the importance of the otherness of other people. By becoming confused about ourselves, by "forgetting who we are" in society, we also repeatedly forget the impossibility of actually attaining our true self; thus we can be moved once more to commit ourselves wholeheartedly to the quest, which in turn makes social existence possible and leads us yet again into our salutary confusion, into the eternal cycle. Again, given a certain basic hunger for unified being, the individual and social aspects of our existence are revealed as natural consequences of each other, not opposites.

This ethics of maximum commitment to the quest for the true self, as I have said, is not merely expressible via cubist style, but a direct natural outgrowth of that style, and the result is an extraordinarily complete fusion of the ethical and the aesthetic, which to my mind represents Strindberg's culminating achievement. In much modern literature, especially as it is affected by the general artistic phenomenon of decadence, there is a tendency to exclude prescriptive ethics from the aesthetic realm. In earlier historical ages, it is felt, when ethical values were more widely agreed on, the ethical could be incorporated into art by a normal mimetic procedure; but the modern author, if he adopts a specific ethical position, must justify it abstractly and preach it, to the detriment of his work's artistic integrity. For both Ibsen and Strindberg, however, the ethical unsettledness of modern society is a problem, not merely a fact; neither of the two is prepared to neglect ethical considerations in determining artistic style. And in Strindberg's last works, the problem is solved in something like a definitive manner. When Shaw compares Strindberg to Shakespeare, he is actually thinking of something quite different; but it seems to me that the Shakespearean comparison is, as it were, fulfilled by the perfect fusion of ethical and aesthetic in *The Great Highway*, as well as by the gradual approach to this fusion in the other last plays. In Renaissance drama it does not occur to us, nor did it occur to the original audiences, to look for a tension between ethical and aesthetic categories; and Strindberg's aim, in essence, is to reestablish this situation in modern drama. Clearly he does not succeed, and could not, in reproducing exactly, say, the Shakespearean spirit; but that he succeeds at all, in producing even a momentary fusion of the ethical and the aesthetic in a near-Shakespearean sense, is something of a historical miracle, and is what gives his last plays the character of unsurpassable classical masterpieces, not merely that of radical formal experiments for others to build on.

NOTE

The quotations of Ibsen are from *The Lady from the Sea*, trans. Frances E. Archer, and *When We Dead Awaken*, trans. William Archer, in *The Collected Works of Henrik Ibsen*, IX and XI (New York, 1923). The quotations from *The Ghost Sonata* and *The Great Highway* are from August Strindberg, *Eight Expressionist Plays*, trans. Arvid Paulson (New York, 1965).

Strindberg's *Miss Julie* and the Legend of Salomé

BRIAN PARKER

Since Strindberg's letter to his publisher claiming *Miss Julie* (1888) as "the first Naturalistic Tragedy in Swedish Drama"[1] and the important *Foreword* which he wrote after the play was completed, it has been usual to see *Miss Julie* as an experiment in the kind of drama developed by Zola from Darwin's theories of environmental conditioning and the survival of the fittest. Thus, Martin Lamm calls the play "a strict application of Zolaesque principles" and Eric Bentley a "tragedy of the Darwinian ethos."[2] Its theme of war between the sexes has been traced partly to Strindberg's ambivalence towards his parents, as revealed in the first volume of his autobiography, *The Son of a Servant,* and partly to his stormy marriage to Siri von Essen, the aristocratic actress who created the role of Miss Julie, which he had anatomized in *The Confession of a Fool* just before he wrote the play. It is argued that he interpreted these personal experiences mainly through his reading of Schopenhauer's misogynist philosophy of "will" and Eduard von Hartmann's *Philosophie des Unbewussten* (Berlin, 1869), complicating them further by his fervent Rousseau-ist socialism at this period of his life and by his fascination with the experiments that Charcot and Bernheim were currently conducting in the treatment of hysteria by hypnosis[3] – experiments which also excited the young Sigmund Freud.

However, Strindberg's comparatively slight concern for the social, as distinct from psychological, aspects of environment was noted early (by Zola himself, among others) as distinguishing him from the main stream of Naturalism; and it has long been recognized that *Miss Julie* possesses an almost hallucinatory intensity of focus that is very unlike Naturalism in its effect[4] and that it also exploits oneiric and romantic – even fairytale[5] – elements that are literary and theatrical in origin, not social or autobiographical. Strindberg himself commented that the setting for *Miss Julie* was "a compromise with romanticism and stage decoration"[6] and, though he continued occasionally to produce such plays as *The Dance of Death,* he had effectively renounced his identification with Naturalism by 1892.

The usual way of accommodating such discrepancies is to adopt Strindberg's own later distinction between what he called the "little art" (of Naturalists such as Henri Becque) and his own "greater naturalism"[7] which concentrated exclusively on mental process, "a type of realism which has nothing to do with reality"[8] whose ruthless subjectivity is recognized as a direct inheritance from Romanticism and a forerunner of the surrealism and expressionism of Strindberg's subsequent Dream Plays.

All this is certainly to the point: *Miss Julie* is a masterwork which synthesizes many influences, anticipates much subsequent drama, and is richly various in its implications. But what has still to be explored more thoroughly is the debt of *Miss Julie* to the obsessions of the French Decadence and the techniques of contemporary Symbolism. Specifically, there has been no consideration of the play's ironic exploration of the legend of Salomé and John the Baptist, that period's central myth, which Strindberg could not help but have encountered during his stays in Paris in 1876, 1883–84, and 1885. Once the parallels between them are recognized, *Miss Julie* turns out to be far more a reaction to its time than is usually acknowledged.[9]

Before turning to the play itself, then, it will be well to sketch in this *fin de siècle* background, beginning with the intellectual and emotional attitudes which found so rich an emblem in Salomé and then considering some of the major treatments of that story around the time when Strindberg wrote his play.

II

The essence of the Decadent sensibility of the late nineteenth century, to be seen at its clearest in Baudelaire at the beginning of the period and Oscar Wilde towards the end, was the "dandy's" revolt against nature in favour of the creatively artificial. This was partly a reaction against the overwhelmingly materialist and rationalist emphasis at mid-century, which tended to marginalize both artists and an aristocracy that was losing its power and sense of purpose, creating a temporary and rather strained alliance between them. It expressed itself emotionally by a revolt against biological sex in favour of a cerebral eroticism that exalted self-sufficient androgyny (which, in practice, was often covertly homosexual, as in the case of Wilde, Proust, Jean Lorrain, and Joséphin Péladan) and devalued

women both as helpless instruments of biological instinct and as economic parasites who destroyed man's spiritual freedom by entrapping him
into the expense and social responsibilities of marriage.[10] "Woman is the
opposite of the dandy," proclaimed Baudelaire, "therefore she inspires
horror"; and both levels of criticism were sensationally exploited in
Strindberg's collection of short stories *Married*, published two years before
Miss Julie, in which the relation between men and women is presented as
an inevitable struggle for power.

This kind of paranoia produced those favourite icons of Decadent art,
woman as seductress and woman as nakedly helpless – or even dead – so
that her beauty can be admired without risk.[11] In literature it led to the
characterization of women as passive creatures of emotion and instinct or
as dangerously attractive but ruthless dolls, the grown-up sensual children
of Schopenhauer's philosophy, whose instinct is to drag men down to
their own biological level. When this predatoriness is consciously aggressive, the "*femme fatale*" results, the kind of role so much enjoyed by Sarah
Bernhardt, which, in turn, is easily associated with the "gynander" – the
unnatural woman who behaves like a man, that for Strindberg was exemplified by the "bluestocking" heroines of Ibsen.[12]

The attempt of such women to control or usurp male creativity was
emblematized by the Decadents in vampires, sphinxes, maenads, willis,
and destructive watersprites, but a particularly apt image was discovered in
the symbolic castration afforded by decapitation, or decollation.[13] This
became one of the most frequent Decadent *topoi*, exemplified not only in
the central story of Salomé – who is very often conflated with her mother,
Herodias[14] – but also by the myths of Judith, Taïs, Delilah, Turandot,
Rusalka, and the decapitated Orpheus. One of Gustav Klimt's most famous pictures, for example, is known both as *Judith I* and *Salome* (see
Dijkstra [Note 11], Plate XI, no. 24).

The characteristic Decadent stance towards women, then, was the
simultaneous urge to self-abasement and to savage domination that is
technically known as "sado-masochism." This definition was introduced
two years before *Miss Julie* appeared by Richard von Krafft-Ebing in his
Psychopathia Sexualis (1886), and was taken from the name of Leopold von
Sacher-Masoch who in 1870 had published a celebrated novel about
bondage, *Venus in Furs*, in which sex is seen not as a pleasure but as a
demonic source of pain that cries out to be disciplined. It is in relation to
this attitude that the contortions and non-naturalism of *Miss Julie*'s conclusion must finally be assessed; and the play's analogies to the Decadent
myth of Salomé will provide a convenient key to do so.

The centrality of the Salomé motif to European painting and literature from about 1860 to the outbreak of World War I is now widely accepted. Artists and writers "depict [Salomé] so often," says Phillippe Jullian, "that the little Jewish princess, who is also the heroine of LaForgue, Wilde, and Milosz, may be regarded as the goddess of the Decadence."[15] The basic story is to be found, in slightly different versions, in the gospels of *Mark* (6:14–29) and *Matthew* (14:1–2):[16] Queen Herodias, in revenge for John the Baptist's denunciation of her incestuous marriage to Herod, her brother-in-law, uses the charms of Salomé, the daughter of her previous marriage, to wheedle a gift on Herod's birthday, and when this is granted, has her daughter demand John's head. In *Mark* Herod is horrified by this request but has to keep his word; in *Matthew* he complies more readily because he wishes John dead for political reasons, and Salomé too is a more knowing accomplice. The idea that Salomé wins Herod's gift by provocative dancing was added by the Jewish historian Flavius Josephus, and subsequently elaborated by medieval commentators until Salomé became an habitual emblem for the Christian church's fight against orgiastic dancing. By 1912, it has been calculated, no fewer than 2789 French poets had written about the legend.[17]

Its renewed vogue in the second half of the nineteenth century seems to have been primed by two works, Ernest Renan's account in his celebrated *Vie de Jésus* (Berlin, 1862) and the *Atta Troll* (1847) of Heinrich Heine, a major influence on the later Symbolist writers, where Herodias's motive is changed to revenge for John's spurning of her love. Among major treatments before *Miss Julie* that were almost certainly known to Strindberg were Gustave Flaubert's quasi-historical novella *Hérodias*, in his *Trois Contes* (1877), which inspired Massenet's opera of the same name (1881); Stéphane Mallarmé's elaborate poem, also called *Hérodiade*, originally conceived as a play, which he began in 1864 and was still working on at his death in 1898, after publishing excerpts in 1869 and 1886; a long discussion of the myth in chapter five of Joris-Karl Huysmans's *A Rebours* (1884); and an interestingly ironic treatment of it by Jules LaForgue in his *Moralités Légendaires* (1886), in which Iaokanaan is a socialist from the north and Salomé accidentally kills herself while trying to throw away the prophet's decapitated head. There were also versions by a host of minor poets, with Jean Lorrain, in particular, returning to the theme obsessively – perhaps most interestingly in a poem to Herodias in *La Forêt Bleue* (1883) and in two comments on actual Parisian prostitutes and dancers, "Ballet d'automne – Salomé" in *L'Echo de Paris* (15 November 1893, under the pseudonym of "Raitif De la Bretonne") and "Petites Salomés: La Laus" in *La Revue Blanche*, 4 (1893). Four years after

Miss Julie came the most sensational version of all, Oscar Wilde's *Salomé* (written 1891–92, published in French in 1893, and in an English transla- tion ostensibly by Lord Alfred Douglas in 1894 with illustrations by Aubrey Beardsley), which inspired operas by Marrotti and, more importantly, by Richard Strauss (1906) – a masterwork that has retained its popularity.

The theme was no less frequent in the period's visual art: "the true centrepiece of male masochistic fantasies," Bram Dijkstra has recently commented, was Salomé, a "virginal adolescent with a viraginous mother, a penchant for exotic dances, and a hunger for man's holy head."[18] Again it was a subject handled by many artists, but undoubtedly the most cel- ebrated and influential treatments were two paintings exhibited at Paris by Gustave Moreau in the spring salon 1876 – in the October of which year Strindberg made his first visit to Paris and wrote articles about the new movements in French painting. The most elaborate of these canvasses is an oil painting entitled *Salomé* which depicts her, heavily jewelled and half naked in light, diaphanous robes, dancing before Herod with a large white, phallic lotus flower held erect before her; the other is a water colour called *The Apparition* which depicts her very similarly but with a vision of John's severed head floating in the air immediately before her eyes. This inspired two striking charcoal drawings by Moreau's disciple Odilon Redon, both entitled *The Apparition* and exhibited at Paris in 1882, in which Salomé's sense of guilt is emphasized by replacing the severed head with a single monstrous eye. Moreau's pictures seem also to have influenced Flaubert, Mallarmé, and Wilde, and, in particular, Huysmans's *A Rebours*, whose hero, Des Esseintes, associates them with Mallarmé's poem and masochistically exults: "[Salomé] was now revealed ... as the symbolic incarnation of world-old Vice, the goddess of immortal Hysteria, the Curse of Beauty supreme above all other beauties by the cataleptic spasm that stirs her flesh and steels her muscles – a monstrous Beast of the Apocalypse, indifferent, irresponsible, insensible, poisoning ... all who come near her, all who see her, all who touch her,"[19] Before Moreau, Henri Regnault's *Salomé* had caused similar excitement in 1870, eliciting elaborate critiques from Théophile Gautier and Paul de Saint Victor; and after Moreau's success this *topos* was taken up by scores of artists. Two that give some idea of the range of naturalistic and emblematic treatments it received are Eduard Ioudouze's 1886 painting *Salomé Triumphant* (Dijkstra, Plate XI, 20), in which she appears as a naked teenager with a cat-like, satiated stare, and an 1898 mural by Fritz Erler in which *Dance* is personi- fied as Salomé holding the bleeding head of John the Baptist between her thighs (Dijkstra, Plate XI, 26).

Interpretation of the legend naturally varies widely among so many representations. At one extreme, Mallarmé's Salomé stands for a child-like purity but also sterility in sex and art that can never be possessed; at the other extreme, she is seen as a coldly sensual, emasculating gynander (especially when conflated with Herodias); and in between come variously balanced presentations of her as a skittish adolescent, only half aware of her seductive power and innocently perverse. There are too many ramifications to treat in full, but, as we turn to consider *Miss Julie*, certain characteristic details should be borne in mind. Salomé in this period of the Decadence is essentially ambiguous, both corrupt and innocent – indeed, corrupt *because* of her innocence, destructive yet herself a victim, androgynous yet totally controlled by biological instinct; she is manipulated by a viraginous mother whose motivation is revenge; and this mother is associated (in Heine, for example, or Jean Lorrain's *La Forêt Bleue*) with the folk tradition of the "damnéd hunt," in which women who refuse traditional sexual roles – like Herodias and, significantly, Diana – ride through the night on Midsummer Eve sadistically "filling the air with great cracks of their whips."[20] Also central to the legend is, of course, the deadly seductiveness of dance: in one of his poems Arthur Symons laments:

> They dance the daughters of Herodias,
> With their eternal, white, unfaltering feet,
> And always, when they dance, for their delight,
> Always a man's head falls because of them[21]

Hofmannsthal, discussing Wilde, quotes the Persian proverb, "who knows the power of the dance, knows that love kills."[22] Hardly less important is the "somnambulism" – a state wavering between semi-lucid hallucination and dreaming proper – that Des Esseintes perceives in Moreau's Salomé and which he equates with "her unholy charm as of a great flower of concupiscence, born of a sacrilegious birth, reared in a hothouse of impiety"[23] – the seductive "fleurs du mal" of Baudelaire; and this hallucinatory hot-house atmosphere blends easily into a concern with magic and the occult on the one hand and a sickly religious desire for death, an urge to suicide, on the other. In Massenet's opera Salomé does, in fact, commit suicide; she is also punished by death in LaForgue, falling on to rocks when she tries to rid herself of the Baptist's head; in Wilde, Herod orders that she be crushed to death by the shields of his body-guard; and René Girard even reports a folk version in which she is decapitated.[24]

III

Against this grid of reference certain aspects of *Miss Julie* immediately stand out. The play takes place on the eve of June 24 and dawn of June 25, which is not only the ancient pagan fertility celebration of Midsummer but also the feast day of John the Baptist. Both associations are treated ironically. A minor Decadent theme is the association of women with their pets, and Miss Julie is represented in the play by two: the greenfinch, Serena, represents her spiritual state, while her pet dog, ironically called Diana, stands for her irrepressible sexuality. When the play begins, Diana has sneaked out and been impregnated by the lowborn pug at the lodge and, on Miss Julie's instructions, Kristen the cook is preparing a smelly concoction to abort her. Though he knows perfectly well what is going on, the valet, Jean, mischievously suggests that this is a witches' brew the two women are compounding in order to read their futures; and, ironically, after she has succumbed to her own sexuality and Midsummer "madness," Miss Julie does indeed fear that Jean may have made her pregnant. She resolves this fear by suicide, thus wiping out her father's ancient lineage and completing her mother's revenge upon him. Far from celebrating fertility, then, the play records its total annulment.

The association with the feast of John the Baptist is equally ironic. Not only is there an antagonist critical of corrupt aristocracy who is named Jean (and is never given a surname in the play, as Miss Julie points out), but the motif of decapitation is central to the action. Preparing for church, Kristen tells Jean that the lesson is to be "about the beheading of John the Baptist,"[25] then comically exemplifies this by half-choking him as she adjusts his collar and necktie, lauding pension benefits for widows and children as she does so. The motif is then picked up more seriously when Jean cuts off the head of Miss Julie's greenfinch. The bird-in-a-cage is an obvious symbol of Miss Julie's own social and psychic imprisonment (and was also a minor artistic conceit of the period[28]), and it stands in contrast to the predatory, high-flying hawks and falcons that were Jean's idealized image of aristocracy. The killing of Serena thus parallels the destruction Jean has brought to Miss Julie's peace of mind. Although she reluctantly agreed to the killing, Jean's brutality in effecting it arouses her to a furious anti-male outburst in which her kinship to Salomé is at its clearest:

Oh, how I should like to see your blood and your brains on a chopping-block! I'd like to see the whole of your sex swimming like that in a sea of blood. I think I could drink out of your skull ...   (p. 75)

And it is the delay that this episode causes which ultimately dooms their escape: "And all on account of a greenfinch," objects Jean uncomprehendingly (p. 77). The bitterest twist, however, is that it is the Salomé figure who is decapitated in this version, not the John, as Miss Julie leaves to cut her throat with Jean's razor. This takes the irony of those versions in which Salomé is punished considerably further and can be seen as Strindberg's critique of the traditional story. Like Lombroso, the phrenology expert of the period, Strindberg believed that it was only women who committed such self-destruction: "Pure, strong passion, when existing in a woman, drives her to suicide rather than to crime ... The true crime of love – if such it can be called – in a woman is suicide."[27]

June 24 is also the evening when the "damnéd hunt" rides again, to which Heine and Lorrain consigned both Herodias and Diana. Like Salomé, Miss Julie is clearly living out a scenario imposed by her mother, who raised her to enslave and destroy men. This mother is represented as a gynander, for whom there is no source in Strindberg's autobiography.[26] She preferred the stables to her husband's house, which eventually she burned; she ruined his estate by forcing the men and women who worked on it to exchange their occupations; and she raised her daughter like a boy, making her, amongst other things, labour in the stables. This upbringing gives Miss Julie, for all her rampant femininity, some of the cross-sexual characteristics so typical of the Decadence, and also contributes to a vein of sadomasochistic riding and whip references that run throughout the play. Jean admires Miss Julie's horsemanship, but tells also of her making her ex-fiancé jump over her whip in the stableyard like a performing dog, until he lost his temper, broke her whip and left; it is Kristen's vindictive warning to the groom not to let them take out horses that finally blocks the lovers' escape; and over the whole play, like Herod brooding in the backgrounds of Moreau's two pictures, looms the presence of Miss Julie's father, the Count, represented by a "big, old-fashioned bell" and speaking tube positioned centrally "above the double door" and especially by a "pair of large riding-boots with spurs," which the opening stage-direction instructs Jean to put "in a conspicuous place" (p. 61) on the set and to which there is constant reference whenever he remembers his status as a servant. Horsemanship is a traditional attribute and social distinguishing mark of the aristocracy, of course, but in this play it has also overtones of sexual dominance.

This is just one of several symbolic aspects of the set. A contrast is immediately set up between the romantic view outside and the utilitarian cul-de-sac of the kitchen with its two adjoining bedrooms, a contrast that is extrapolated in the two mimed interludes which divide the play: Kristen's work mime is tempered by her titivating and savouring of Miss Julie's scented handkerchief, while the peasants "ballet," which covers the sexual encounter of Miss Julie and Jean offstage, is equally contaminated by the fact that they use a traditional fertility rhyme about two women sleeping with the same man as a "filthy song" (in Jean's words) to mock the lovers furtively. The courtyard outside contains a fountain with a Cupid; and besides the explicit reference of its statue, fountains were a very frequent Decadent and Symbolist emblem for enclosed, self-feeding love. More generally, women were constantly connected with the shiny, unstable, devouring element of water, especially in conjunction with the moon. Hence Miss Julie's attempt to persuade Jean to risk his reputation by rowing her out on the lake to see the sunrise,[29] and Jean's later disillusioned remark that his admiration for her was merely the bedazzlement of one looking up into the "moonshine" from below.

The play's main symbol to convey midsummer fertility, however, is flowers, particularly heavy-scented lilacs: an image that is also traditionally connected with the attractiveness and fragility of women, which the Decadents saw as "fleurs du mal." Midsummer Eve, Jean says, is a time to sleep on flowers in order to make one's dreams come true – and traditionally Midsummer dreams were of future sexual mates. Outside, in the courtyard, the tops of poplar trees are visible and lilacs are in bloom, and when the peasants come in for their dance the stage direction instructs that they should have flowers in their hats and garlands of leaves around their kegs of intoxicating beer and spirits. This influence has already invaded the kitchen, moreover, before Miss Julie enters: the stove is decorated with birch twigs, the floor strewn with juniper, and, in particular, there are lilacs in an exotic Japanese spice jar on the table, a sprig of which Jean holds for Miss Julie to smell as he tells her the half-truth of his youthful worship of her; Miss Julie lets the sprig fall on that occasion, but later invites Jean to take her outside to pick more lilacs. The violet scent on Miss Julie's handkerchief is merely a synthetic equivalent of this natural perfume, with which she insists on trying to remove a mote from Jean's eye, and which Kristen sniffs briefly in her work mime, than folds neatly and decisively away. The flower image is taken further and made more explicit by Jean's memory of the church altar decorated with lilacs and by the story of his boyhood invasion of the Count's "Garden of Paradise," his first sight of Miss Julie walking as a child among the roses, the Turkish pavilion "covered with jasmine and honeysuckle" in which he thought he had found refuge, only to discover that this condemned him to crawl out through a privy. The experience caused him to attempt suicide, Jean claims, by sleeping in a chest filled with elder blossom – a flower he later changes to lilac when he admits that the incident actually happened to someone else. Switzerland, he promises Miss Julie, will be a land of perpetual evergreens and oranges; but his final use of the image is a sad comparison of her ruin to the last flower of summer now trodden into the mud.

The midsummer holiday creates a "madness" whose "spell" is only dissipated by sunrise, and Miss Julie's wild behaviour in it is explained by Kristen as partly the result of her monthly period. In his essay "On the Inferiority of Women" (1895) Strindberg cites Darwin and Herbert Spencer to argue that woman's inferiority is inevitable because "Every fourth week she finds herself caught in her menstrual period" and it is "permissible to postulate that these periodic bleedings are in part to blame for the arrest in growth and development of woman, and that indeed this anemia of necessity seems to atrophy the brain," so that the normal condition of a grown woman is that of "a sick child."[31] This opinion can also be found in Jules Bois, who describes a vengeful, infertile woman, interestingly enough, in terms of a desecrated fountain: "a fountain of life from which flows, every month, death itself ... a tide of blood which gushes forth in memory of shame and cruelty."[32]

The main symptom of this madness is Miss Julie's sexually intense dancing, which Jean several times describes as "crazy", and which is, of course, a major parallel with the legend of Salomé. At this time an insatiable urge to dance, followed quickly by exhaustion, was thought to be typical of female neurasthenia: "the movements of these wild dances," claims Harry Campbell,[33] "imperceptibly shade off into the co-ordinate movements of the hysterical fit. ... Hence it is possible that the love of dancing, so peculiarly strong among women, is the outcome of a nervous organization affording a suitable soil for hysteria" – an opinion elaborated in Havelock Ellis's *Man and Woman: A Study of Human Secondary Sexual Characters* (1894):

The reason women love dancing is very probably because it enables them to give harmonious and legitimate emotional expression to this neuro-muscular irritability which might otherwise escape in a more explosive form.[34]

Orgiastic dancing was thus associated with sexual relief and was celebrated as such by many poets and exploited in real life by dancers like Loie Fuller in turn-of-the-century Paris and, later, Isadora Duncan. Miss Julie uses dance to master Jean and take partners from other women, but the ambiguity (and pathos) of her position is revealed by her wish to avoid looking foolish by finding a partner who can *lead*.

This dancing is only one of several irrational states exploited in the play. Miss Julie oscillates between hysterical vivacity, fueled by reckless drinking (to Jean's disgust), and nervous collapses into exhaustion. She is so confused that, after sleeping with Jean, she can ask, "Was I blind drunk? Have I dreamt this whole night?" (p. 69). She tries to find relief by compulsive talking, exchanging reminiscences and confessions with Jean through which we learn about her past and his. Particularly interesting are two heavily symbolic dreams (another frequent characteristic of *fin de siècle* literature):[35] Jean's is a predatory dream of climbing to steal golden eggs from a sexual nest, Miss Julie's is quite the opposite, a masochistic wish to abase herself, to fall or jump from her social (and falsely phallic) pedestal and lie not only in the mud but *under* it, a covert death-wish that she later expresses openly. Jean's story about attempting suicide by going to sleep in a chest filled with flowers so as "to die beautifully and peacefully, without any pain" (p. 66) taps the same Decadent motif but is, of course, a lie: when Miss Julie proposes actual suicide later, he sneers, "Die? How silly! I think it would be far better to start a hotel" (p. 72).

The association of dream and death occurs again in the most mysterious and puzzling of all Miss Julie's irrational states, the lucid somnambulism into which she falls at the end of the play, in which she sees Jean suddenly as a black devil or death figure, whose burning eyes and ashy face recall both Jean's warning that she had better not "play with fire" by teasing him and the vindictive way her mother burned the family house. This final mood also has a *fin de siècle* religiosity about it, as Miss Julie ignores the ironical snobbery of Kristen's Calvinist assurance that the rich are damned and persuades herself that she will be saved among the "first" because she has made herself the "last."

In a letter to Edvard Brandes, Strindberg explains her curious state of waking dream as "completely modern, with hypnotism in a state of wakefulness,"[36] referring to Bernheim's success at hypnotising patients who were awake, but it remains nonetheless mysterious – and is certainly not Naturalistic. It is not Jean who hypnotizes Miss Julie, as Strindberg's explanation would seem to suggest, but rather Miss Julie who hypnotizes herself: when Jean objects that he cannot hypnotize her because the patient must be sleeping, Miss Julie tells him she is *already* asleep. And though she needs the impetus of Jean's command to cut her throat, her acceptance of death paradoxically reasserts her superiority over him – a shift that was even clearer in the first draft, where she is made "to snatch the razor from [his] hand with the taunt, 'You see, servant, you cannot die.'"[37] In the revision, it is Jean who takes the initiative by giving her the razor. And the fatal command does not come until after Jean's admission that, though he earlier repudiated suicide, he is so cowed by the Count's return that he would now have to cut this throat if the Count ordered it, a confession which prompts Miss Julie to instruct him to use his talent for acting and, *by imitating her father*, find the strength to give the order she requires.

This may not be very plausible psychologically (Jean's fear that Miss Julie's theft will be discovered is more credible as a motive), but it is very important thematically in terms of the contradictory impulses Strindberg has given the valet. Jean's salient characteristic is social-climbing ambition: he is unsentimental, even cynical, about sex and shrewdly pragmatic in all his personal relationships; Strindberg says in the *Foreword* that he will probably end up as the manager of a Swiss hotel.[38] This toughness in Jean is complicated, however, by elements of the dandy and sadomasochistic dreamer. From his visits to the theatre and experience as a *sommelier* in Switzerland, he has acquired certain attributes that distinguish him quite clearly from Kristen and the other peasants. Miss Julie compliments him by telling him that, out of livery and in his own clothes, he looks quite like a gentleman; he can speak French and perform the fashionable dances of the day correctly; he objects to Kristen's lack of refinement, telling her he is "sensitive"; and he is "fussy" about the quality and serving of his meals and, reflecting his training as *sommelier*, especially about the quality of his stolen wines. And as he talks about the latter, there is an interesting and significant shift of pronouns: instead of referring to the Count and his class as "they," he begins to use the pronoun "we." It is misleading to think of Jean in social reforming terms, in fact: he does not aim at individual equality but, rather, wishes to replace the Count's authority with his own. Though, in referring to the conversation of young ladies that he has overheard, he can say "Perhaps, at bottom, there isn't as much difference between people as one's led to believe" (p. 67) and can play cynically on Miss Julie's romanticism with his lie of attempted suicide, his idealization of her was quite genuine, and he grieves over her self-betrayal because, he says, "it hurts to find that what I was struggling to reach wasn't high and isn't real" (p. 70). If she comes with him to Switzerland, he promises to make enough money to buy a title so that he too can be a Count, and promises her that in his hotel she shall sit on a "throne" and summon "slaves" by ringing her bell – as now the Count summons him. When the real bell rings to announce the Count's return, Jean's confidence immediately collapses, however. His exaggerated servility has been revealed earlier whenever he referred to the Count's spurred riding boots, which silently dominate the set:

I've never been so servile to anyone as I am to him ... I've only to hear his bell and I shy like a horse. Even now, when I look at his boots, standing there so proud and stiff, I feel my back beginning to bend. (p. 68)

As he resumes his livery, there is a Brecht-like effect of costume determining character: "that devil of a lackey is bending my back again" (p. 78); he admits he is terrified of the bell and "the somebody behind it – a hand moving it – and something else moving the hand" (p. 78), which only rings more loudly in his head if he tries to stop his ears: and it is because of this fear of the bell's reiterated summons, and what it bodes, not from hatred or contempt of Miss Julie, that he gives the fatal command.

This exaggerated, non-Naturalistic dimension to Jean's servility can be clarified if one compares him to Severin, the hero of Sacher-Masoch's *Venus in Furs*. Believing that man "has only one choice, to be the tyrant or the slave of woman," but that "*One can only truly love that which stands above one*," Severin has the heroine, Wanda, whip him; but Wanda, in her turn, is dominated by a glorious Greek in his "high black boots, closely fitting breeches of white leather [and] short coat of black cloth" who, apparently, whips the two of them.[39] For Severin, it seems, Wanda has merely a surrogate dominator who had eventually to be sacrificed to true authority before an exclusively masculine relation of master and slave could be created, which he now embraces with relief. Interestingly, just such a charge of masochism was levelled at Strindberg himself in *La Revue Blanche* four years later, with a similar assumption about inevitable male dominance:

The phobia against women which has come to pervade [Strindberg's] entire creative production was set in motion by a sort of masochism, expressive of the need to suffer for the object of love's affections, with which we are all too familiar in our current literature ... They seem so flat and trivial, these women he describes to us as monsters of perversion and domination – women whom a man who is sure of himself would throw down at his feet in a single gesture of disdain.[40]

And Bram Dijkstra comments on this typical aspect of the Decadent sensibility:

Instead of directly taking the executioner's position, that of the lordly master who tramples on the world because it is his, the masochists, the Strindberg's of the late nineteenth century, needed to isolate, identify, and elevate the presumed source of their humiliation so that the destruction of their enemy – woman – would ultimately lift them to a position of parity with the imperial sadist, the godly Greek of worldly power ... The offending creature, the female predator, Salomé, must be killed outright to redeem the sacrificial male. As a result of her justifiable execution, the male would regain his masculine essence.[41]

The approach does not in itself "explain" *Miss Julie*, of course. Sado-masochism's contrast of the true and false dominator is only one aspect of the play (though a major one), and Strindberg has put so much of himself into both Jean and Miss Julie that no single response is possible: we have to admire, condemn, and pity both of them. But it does illumine the non-Naturalistic exaggeration and twists of psychology at the play's conclusion as well as its curious intensity throughout. Technically, *Miss Julie* is at least as much Symbolist as Naturalistic; and clearly it is a play very much of the Decadent period, not merely a document of Strindberg's personal life. In particular, its setting on the eve of the feast of John the Baptist, its strikingly ironic use of decollation, its emphases on the destructive influence of the heroine's gynander mother, on orgiastic dancing, and on the dangerous beauty of flowers, and its hallucinatory, dream-like quality, particularly at the conclusion, all relate it to Decadent treatments of the legend of Salomé; of which it can be seen as simultaneously an exploitation and repudiation.

NOTES

1 Martin Lamm, *August Strindberg*, trans. and ed. Harry G. Carlson (New York, 1971), p. 212.
2 Lamm, p. 214; Eric Bentley, *The Playwright as Thinker* (New York, 1946), p. 62. For one of the fullest studies, see Børge Gedsø Madsen, *Strindberg's Naturalistic Theatre: Its Relation to French Naturalism*, (Seattle, 1962).
3 See Strindberg's two essays, "The Battle of the Brains" and "Psychic Murder," both in his collection of essays entitled *Vivisections* and probably written towards the end of 1887.
4 In a letter of 1887 Strindberg wrote of his own state of mind: "It seems as if I'm walking in my sleep, as if fiction and reality were mixed together. Writing so much has made my life a life of shadows." (Quoted by Evert Sprinchorn in the introduction to his translation of *Miss Julie* [San Francisco, 1961].)
5 See Phillip Dodd, "Fairy Tales, the Unconscious and Strindberg's *Miss Julie*,"

Literature and Psychology, 28 (1978), 145–50; Edmund Napieralski, "*Miss Julie*: Strindberg's Tragic Fairy Tale," *Modern Drama*, 26 (1983), 282–89.

6 Lamm, p. 215.

7 See Strindberg, "On Modern Drama and Modern Theatre," trans. Børge Gedsø Madsen, in Toby Cole, ed. *Playwrights on Playwriting* (New York, 1960), p. 17.

8 Maurice Valency, *The Flower and the Castle* (New York, 1963), p. 267. The first person to suggest that Strindberg should be considered more of a Symbolist than a Naturalist was a contemporary French critic, René Fleury, writing in *La Revue d'Art Dramatique* for Fall 1889 (pp. 359–366) about Strindberg's "naturalist" plays and his attempt to start a Copenhagen equivalent of Antoine's Théâtre Libre. Stellan Ahlström's *Strindberg erövring av Paris* (Stockholm, 1956) does not consider his relations at this period to the Decadent and Symbolist movements; but Carl-Olof Gierow's *Documentation–Evocation: Le climat littéraire et théâtral en France des années 1880 et "Mademoiselle Julie" de Strindberg* (Stockholm, 1967), while concentrating on the play's connection to Naturalism, suggests that it also has Symbolist elements in its concern with mime and such "Wagnerian" aspects as its orchestration of non-sequential dialogue, repetition of motifs (lilac, the Count's boots) and mixture of drama, narrative, dance, and mime; Haskell M. Block's essay "Strindberg and the Symbolist Drama," *Modern Drama*, 5 (1962), 314–22, considers only Strindberg's connection with Symbolism after 1898; while in *The Flower and the Castle*, Maurice Valency speculates that Strindberg was probably influenced by French misogyny and its cult of the femme fatale, and, in discussing *The Father*, points out that Strindberg's work has a "logic of fantasy" that is closer to Symbolism than to Naturalism (pp. 267–68). Strindberg's own use of the term "Symbolism" is not a reliable guide: in a letter to Gauguin in February, 1895, recalling his fascination with French painting ten years before, he says, "At that time we did not yet possess the term, symbolism, a wretched term for a very old practice: allegory" (quoted in Block).

9 Cf. such studies as Patrick Bade, *Femme Fatale: Images of Evil and Fascinating Women* (New York, 1979); Jean Pierrot, *The Decadent Imagination, 1880–1900*, trans. Derek Coltman (Chicago, 1981); John Milner, *Symbolists and Decadents* (London, 1971); and two studies by Philippe Jullian, *Esthètes et magiciens* (Paris, 1969), and *The Symbolists* (London, 1973). Also, Roger Shattuck, *The Banquet Years: The Origins of the Avant-Garde in France, 1885 to World War I* (New York, 1961).

10 Strindberg, "De l'Infériorité de la Femme," trans. Georges Loiseau, *La Revue Blanche*, 8 (1865), 13–14.

11 See Philippe Jullian, *Dreamers of Decadence: Symbolist Painters of the 1890's* (New

York, 1971), and especially Bram Dijkstra, *Idols of Perversity: Fantasies of Feminine Evil in Fin-de-Siècle Culture* (Oxford, 1986).

12 Note: the sex struggle was thought to be especially fierce when the man was an artist, and Strindberg was influenced at this time by French novels in which male artists are destroyed by nymphets: eg. Dumas Fils's *L'Affaire Clemenceau* (Paris, 1882) especially pp. 296ff., and *Manette Salomon* and *Charles Demailly* by the brothers Edmond and Jules de Goncourt. For the man-woman figure, see Joséphin Péladan, *La Gynandre* (Paris, 1891), vol. 9 of *La Décadence Latine*, 14 vols., 1884–96. Discussing Wilde's play, Christopher Nassaar suggests a connection between this 1890s type and the myth of Cybele, who murders Attis for depriving her of virginity and is "the symbol of the aggressive, sexually perverse female whose sterile sex impulse is directed toward the subjugation and castration of the male," *Into the Demon Universe: A Literary Exploration of Oscar Wilde* (New Haven, 1974), p. 84.

13 In the 1920s Ezra Pound, commenting on Gourmont's *The Natural Philosophy of Love*, refers to man's brain as "sort of great clot of genital fluid held in suspense or reserve," *Pavannes and Divagations* (New York, 1958), p. 203.

14 In many cases the name Herodias is used when clearly it is a Salomé character that is envisaged.

15 Jullian, *Dreamers*, p. 108.

16 Helen Zagona, *The Legend of Salomé and the Principle of Art for Art's Sake* (Paris, 1960), also notes that there are classical analogues in Plutarch's *Life of Flaminius* and Cicero's *De Senectute*, XII:42. For other discussions of the Salomé myth, see: Hedwige Drweska, *Quelques Interprétations de la Légende de Salomé dans les Littératures Contemporaines* (Montpellier, 1912); Hugo Daffner, *Salomé: Ihre Gestalt in Geschichte und Kunst* (Munich, 1912); Rafael Cansinos-Assens, *Salomé en la littératura* (Madrid, 1919); also Helen O. Borowitz, "Visions of Salome," *Criticism* 14:1 (1972), 12–21; Michel Décaudin, "Une Mythe 'fin de siècle': Salomé," *Comparative Literature Studies*, 4 (1967), 109–17; and Ernst Bendz, "A propos de la *Salomé* d'Oscar Wilde," *Englische Studien*, 51 (1917–18), 48–70.

17 Claimed by Maurice Krafft, as reported in Décaudin, p. 109.

18 Dijkstra, p. 379; see also p. 385. For an extended discussion of Salomé iconography in the late nineteenth century, see pp. 379–401. Also E.W. Bredt, "Die Bilder der Salome," *Die Kunst*, 7 (1902–03), 249–54; Daffner, op. cit.; and Jullian, *Dreamers of Decadence*.

19 Joris Karl Huysmans, *Against the Grain*, trans. John Howard (New York, 1969), p. 53.

20 Jean Lorraine, *La Forêt Bleue* (Paris, 1883), p. 13 (my translation).

21 "The dance of the Daughters of Herodias," *Collected Works* (London, 1924), II,

pp. 38–9; he also has a series of Salomé and Herodias poems in *Love's Cruelty* (London, 1923), p. 19.

22 From his essay on Wilde, "Sebastian Melmoth" (1905) cited in J.E. Chamberlin, *Ripe was the Drowsy Hour: The Age of Oscar Wilde* (New York, 1977), p. 177.

23 *Against the Grain*, pp. 51–2, 56.

24 René Girard, "Scandal and the Dance: Salome in the Gospel of Mark," *New Literary History*, 15 (1984), p. 323.

25 *Miss Julie*, trans. Elizabeth Sprigge, in Samuel A. Weiss, ed. *Drama in the Modern World* (Lexington, Mass., 1964), p. 73. Subsequent references will be noted in parentheses in the text.

26 Cf. Frederick C. Frieseke's painting of women with caged birds, *The Parrakeets* [*sic*], 1908 (Dijkstra, Plate VI, 14). Strindberg's use of the dead bird as a symbol of Miss Julie's spiritual plight is the same as the clawed and battered sparrow at the feet of a guilt-stricken mistress in Holman Hunt's *The Awakening Conscience* (1853).

27 Caesar Lombroso and William Ferrero, *The Female Offender* (New York, 1958), p. 276.

28 Though Strindberg did report in a letter of October, 1888, that the play was based on "a true story ... which made a strong impression on me" about a titled young lady who seduced a stableman (Lamm, pp. 212–13).

29 The symbolism here is very like Birkin's trip with Ursula on the lake in D.H. Lawrence's *Women in Love*; while the nexus of sleep, dream, magic, moon, and water associated with the midsummer festival is, of course, explored in Shakespeare's *A Midsummer Night's Dream*.

30 Cf. the use of the hyacinth imagery associated with the soulless Adele, the Young Lady, in Strindberg's *Ghost Sonata*.

31 Strindberg, "De l'Infériorité de la Femme," trans. Georges Loiseau, *La Revue Blanche*, 8 (1895), 13–14 (my translation into English).

32 Jules Bois, "The Battle of the Sexes," *La Revue Blanche*, 9 (1896), p. 365.

33 Harry Campbell, *Differences in the Nervous Organization of Man and Woman: Physiological and Pathological* (London, 1891), p. 169.

34 Havelock Ellis, *Man and Woman: A Study of Human Secondary Sexual Characters* (London, 1894), p. 307.

35 In an essay of 1896 Strindberg says: "For many years I have taken notes of all my dreams, and have arrived at the conclusion that man leads a double life, that imagination, fancies, and dreams possess a kind of reality. So that we are all of us spiritual somnambulists. ..." (quoted in Block).

36 See Strindberg's essays on "The Battle of the Brains" and "Psychic Murder" in *Vivisections* (1887), pp. 123ff., 192ff., of vol. 22 of *Samlade Skrifter*, ed. John Landquist, 55 vols. (Stockholm, 1912–21). This is "the psychological process"

he is referring to in the "Foreword" to *Miss Julie* (in Cole, p. 178) and the psychic conflict he says drama should concentrate on in "On Modern Drama and Modern Theatre" (Cole, pp. 17–21).

37 Reported in Robert Brustein, *The Theatre of Revolt* (Boston, 1962), p. 119, n.22.

38 See "Miss Julie" (1888) in Cole, p. 177. So Strindberg cannot have intended us to believe that Jean too will be punished because Miss Julie has used his razor, as Valency suggests (p. 278).

39 See Leopold von Sacher-Masoch, *Venus in Furs*, trans. John Glassco (Burnaby, B.C., 1977), pp. 7, 26, 90–108.

40 Henri Albert, "Auguste Strindberg," *La Revue Blanche*, 7 (1894), pp. 495–96.

41 Dijkstra, p. 394.

Strindberg's *To Damascus*: Archetypal Autobiography

DIANE FILBY GILLESPIE

In August Strindberg's last play, *The Great Highway*, the Hunter, an architect, encourages the Woman to remember his buildings after his death but to forget him.[1] Such a statement seems inconsistent with Strindberg's own practice as a writer, particularly with his many frankly autobiographical prose works. In a letter to his sister dated 13 June 1882, he wrote: "creating literature does not mean inventing, finding what has never existed; literary creation means relating what one has lived. The writer's art consists in arranging his memories, impressions and experiences."[2] The artist, in other words, cannot be totally forgotten. The significant word in Strindberg's remark, however, is "arranging." Memories, impressions, and experiences are only the available materials out of which the architect designs his buildings. Not the materials themselves, but the ways they are used are most important. Possibly Strindberg's autobiographical prose works are his primary attempts to cope with personal experiences and psychological problems, while the plays, with their visual and aural dimensions, are the more consciously aesthetic arrangements or refinements of the same materials.

In several plays of his later period, Strindberg's themes are the inevitable sin and suffering in human relationships,[3] the fickleness of fame, and the contradictory nature of human experience. The plays are theodicies justifying the ways of the "Powers" to man or the ways of man to the "Powers." *To Damascus* is the most panoramic, although not necessarily the most successful, of these treatments of sin and suffering. Parts I and II, along with the autobiographical novel, *Inferno*, are the immediate products of the psychological crisis which altered the course of Strindberg's life and art. Many critics assume, therefore, that the play cannot be fully understood apart from the details of Strindberg's experiences and psychological problems during this period of upheaval.[4] The play, consequently, is read as a kind of case study or personal confession. But when we know that the Lady is a composite of Strindberg's wives, that the Mother is Mamma Uhl, the mother of his second wife, and that many of the scenes occur in and around the Uhl home, we still cannot account for any impact the play has on either reader or audience. Our emotional identification with the subject of a case study is minimal; and we are often more embarrassed than engaged by personal confession.

To Damascus, however, evidences a conscious effort to universalize personal experience. To the extent that the play "works," it does so because Strindberg touches experiences fundamental to the human condition and embodies them in symbols to which we can all respond. He is working, in other words, with what Carl Jung calls "archetypes," the "mental forms whose presence cannot be explained by anything in the individual's own life and which seem to be aboriginal, innate, and inherited shapes of the human mind."[5] These mental forms are represented or repressed in various ways according to cultural and individual differences, but the fundamental patterns and many of the symbols remain constant. Because Strindberg's psychological idiosyncrasies have received so much attention, an attempt to read at least one of his plays archetypally helps to achieve a more balanced critical perspective.

A Stranger in *To Damascus* is on a pilgrimage which is life. He quests after various secular grails which, when found, prove to be brass rather than gold. The Lady tells him, however, that he searches for the wrong things: "But why haven't you desired things that transcend this life, that can never be sullied?" (Pt. I, i, p. 28). So his pilgrimage has a decided spiritual dimension as well. He travels the same road as Shakespeare's characters and Goethe's Faust, a road of physical and spiritual birth, death, and rebirth. Strindberg's comments in *Open Letters to the Intimate Theatre* indicate his preoccupation with this basic pattern in the human experience. To Strindberg, Shakespeare's characters are projections of Shakespeare himself at various stages in his life cycle and, more generally, representations of Man. "Who is Hamlet?" Strindberg asks.

He is Shakespeare; he is man when he leaves childhood, enters life, and finds that everything is quite different from what he had imagined it. Hamlet is the awakened youngster, who discovers that the world is out of joint and feels called upon to set it right and becomes desperate when he puts his shoulder to the stone and finds it immovable.[6]

Similarly, we know that the Stranger had set to be the Emancipator, to free humanity from bondage. When he is frustrated he becomes the Destroyer, bent upon using his ability to make gold to destroy humanity. The pattern is pervasive: enchantment gives way to disenchantment, idealism to disillusionment in endless alternation. Strindberg continues:

Hamlet is the tragedy of man, written when Shakespeare was about forty, the psychically critical age in a man's life. Luther says a man is a child until he is forty. He means that a man lives like an unreflecting sleepwalker, dependent, working by means of other people's thoughts and ideas which he learned as a child and imagines are his own. Then he awakens, his eyes open, he sees through the deception and the illusions, rages about having been fooled, and has to revise his whole philosophy. It is a sort of measles at forty – a closing of accounts that prepares for the coming of age and wisdom.[7]

Appropriately, the Stranger is about forty in Strindberg's play: he has been waiting for happiness, he says, for forty years (Pt. I, i, p. 25); the Landlord defines his precise age as thirty-eight (Pt. I, i, p. 38). Moreover, he is often referred to as a child, questioning everything and everybody but himself. He is a sleepwalker in a dream play, living according to the law of revenge of the Old Testament which he learned as a child (Pt. I, i, p. 29). "If you ever awake from your dream," says the Mother to him in Part II, "you'll find a reality of which you've never been able to dream" (Pt. II, Act II, i, p. 135). But the awakening is slow and painful. Throughout most of the trilogy, permeated as it is with Old Testament trappings and allusions, the Stranger is raging against and revising those teachings. Perhaps the awakening is never complete. Measles at forty are considerably more serious than measles at four. Recovery may be apparent, but side effects may do permanent damage.

Hamlet, according to Strindberg, is the product of Shakespeare's third period, characterized by "doubt and suffering" as well as by his "most powerful" plays. Shakespeare's fourth period, however, "shows how a person broken by misfortunes or crimes attains harmony through suffering. ..."[8] The three parts of To Damascus encompass this process of transition from third to fourth period. The Stranger is something like Hamlet, but ultimately like Goethe's Faust, as Strindberg's own comments again make clear. Hamlet, according to Strindberg, is a "prototype of Faust; a thinker who tries to get at the very basis of the simplest of matters. ..."

[Hamlet] wants to know what one is not permitted to know; and because of arrogantly wanting to know God's secrets which has a right to remain secrets, Hamlet is punished by the kind of madness called skepticism, which leads to absolute uncertainty, and out of which the individual can be saved only by faith: childish faith which through the sacrifice called obedience one gets as a sort of Christmas-gift wisdom, the absolute certainty that surpasses understanding.

Goethe's Faust, in Part II of that play, attains this certainty as Hamlet does not.[9] Strindberg's Stranger likewise is an arrogant and impudent questioner, and his madness is the kind called skepticism. Often he is rebuked for trying to fathom the unfathomable and for lacking faith. The Lady particularly reproaches him, and her view ultimately opposes that of the Tempter. Part III revolves around a struggle between Lady and Tempter, faith and doubt. The Tempter is the last to leave the Stranger, but the Lady wins. In the monastery, even the language with which questions are asked is transcended.

Strindberg reads Shakespeare's *The Tempest* as a "final confession, view of life, farewell, thanks, and prayer." He quotes the famous passage, "'We are such stuff / As dreams are made on, and our little life / Is rounded with a sleep ...'" and affirms its truth, especially "when one gets on in life; if one looks back at what one has lived through, it is so terrible one hardly believes it is real, and the best that had a sort of reality slowly dissolves as if it were smoke. Is it strange if one begins to doubt the reality of reality?" Strindberg then notes that Shakespeare in *The Tempest* "has in several places emphasized that life is a dream and has tried to dramatize this Buddhist idea. ..."[10]

A difference exists, however, between a "dream" and a "dream play."[11] Because the dream play is meant to be understood, the artist paradoxically must order an apparently chaotic experience. Yet he must communicate the feeling of chaos. Strindberg points out that the consciousness of the dreamer accepts and relates what happens. That acceptance aids the audience's acceptance. But more than that, as Jungian psychology reveals, dreams often do tap the archetypal: thus a kind of order is inherent in them; the author of a dream play can emphasize that order to give form to his work. The reader and audience of a dream play, therefore, need be less cautious about interpreting the productions of the artistic dreamer than about interpreting those of the actual dreamer, since the former exercises conscious control which invites us to exercise our own. Poems are "waking dreams," says the Daughter of Indra in *A Dream Play*. The author was awake when he wrote; we are awake when we perceive.[12]

Strindberg's comments on Shakespeare's plays and his comments elsewhere, especially in his Preface to *A Dream Play*, suggest that the physical head is unable to hold the mind or to define its boundaries. Strindberg literally turns the Stranger's head inside out, then sets him, and us, in the middle.[13] Consequently, various facets of his personality are outside the Stranger's physical head as we see or imagine it on stage. He has more trouble than we do in recognizing these facets as belonging to him, mainly because he does not want to do so. Most of the time he struggles with a feeling of disconcerting familiarity and frustration. Insight or understanding, then, is presented in terms of physical sight. "Once I merely saw objects and events, forms and colours," the Stranger says, "whilst now I perceive ideas and meanings" (Pt. I, i, p. 27). The irony of the statement is that it is truer than he knows. He tells the Lady, too, that he would like to see her thoughts. "But you've heard them," she replied. "That's nothing ... ," he returns, "I want to see them! ... What one says is mostly worthless" (Pt. III, Act III, iii, p. 253). Conversely, "people" are inside the Stranger. The Doctor says he is in the Stranger's blood (Pt. II, Act I, p. 132). And the Stranger talks of "someone" within him whose life he can destroy only by destroying his own (Pt. II, Act II, i, p. 142).

Not only all the scenes are set within the Stranger's mind, but visual symbols of the brain within this staged "brain" emphasize its predominance. Throughout most of Part I, for example, the Lady crochets. At one point, the Stranger looks at her work and says: "It looks like a network of nerves and knots on which you've fixed your thoughts. The brain must look like that – from within" (Pt. I, iv, p. 55). This idea undergoes subtle and complex developments. The Stranger compares the Lady at her work to one of the Fates; she weaves, in this case, the life of the mind. When she finishes the "useless work," the Stranger suggests that, since it is soiled, she dye it rose-red. He further remarks that it looks like a roll of manuscript on which is inscribed their story (Pt. I, xv, pp. 102–103).[14] The Lady's crochet work, then, is connected with the recurrent rose-room setting, as well as with another series of visual representations of the brain – churches, chapels, and monasteries.

The Stranger is just as hesitant about entering such buildings as he is about acknowledging various characters in the play as his own creations. The understanding and acceptance of all aspects of his personality are connected throughout with religion, although in a general rather than an orthodox sense. The Gothic church, along with a café and post office, appears in the first and last scenes of Part I. In the first scene, the Lady is in and out of the church trying to persuade the Stranger to enter. The church has a colored rose window which darkens at the end of the scene when the Stranger attributes his evil thoughts to the Lady and misinterprets her kiss. The fact that, in the final scene of Part I, the Stranger is still writing in the sand and thinking about the letter he is to pick up at the post office, which he then picks up, suggests that he has dreamed the intervening scenes during a lapse in activity or conversation, that the rose window has become the rose room, a deeper penetration into the life of the mind. At the end of the last scene, the Lady again tries to lead him to the church, and we see him go as far as the door. Much intervenes, however, before we find him at the monastery, a kind of Jungian "collective unconscious" containing all of Western culture and knowledge. Gradually the Stranger will learn to unlock the doors of this endless edifice and to understand not only his own personality, but also the basic forms of the human psyche reflected there.

A comment recurrent in the trilogy is "So you know that too," or "So you've discovered that," or some other variation. The Stranger continually is disconcerted by repetitions in his experience and recognitions of himself in others. The Beggar he meets in Part I, for example, echoes what the Stranger has just said to the Lady about having everything but remaining dissatisfied. The Beggar also has a scar on his forehead given him by a near relation, something the Stranger has just explained about himself. The Stranger, frightened and skeptical like Thomas in the New Testament, wants to touch the Beggar to make sure he is real (Part I, i, pp. 31–33). Of course he is, since he is a humourous caricature of the Stranger's own pretentiousness, pomposity, and false pride. By scene v, the Stranger himself has become a Beggar. The Beggar is back in Part II, however, to mock the Stranger's speech at the "honorary" banquet, to counsel him in prison, and to haunt him at various other times in the remainder of the trilogy.

We are introduced immediately to other personality parts. The Dead Man "mourned" at the beginning of Part I has the same attributes as the Stranger (wife-deserter, drinker, good-for-nothing); the Stranger is described in the same way shortly afterwards by a Landlord he does not know. The "dead" Stranger is accounted for by the Mother's charge that the Stranger is spiritually dead (Pt. I, xi, p. 92). Caesar, the madman, is also like the Stranger. The doctor named the madman "Caesar" after a schoolfellow who had had that nickname. We discover, not surprisingly, that Caesar had been the Stranger's nickname (Pt. I, ii, p. 48). The madman, Caesar, is a manifestation of the Stranger's superman complex, complete with laurel wreath and the ability to rearrange creation by growing Christmas roses in the summer. Like the Beggar, the madman appears at the honorary banquet to mock the Stranger and at several other points in the trilogy besides. The Doctor, too, is like the Stranger, a caricature of his preoccupation with death and madness, and of his isolation. The two exchange wives and have the same in-laws. The Doctor, we find out "sinned" against the Confessor by taking the Lady away, just as the Stranger sinned against the Doctor by doing the same. Moreover, both of them defy the "Powers." The Doctor has a woodpile, a mundane Tower of Babel, which he builds high just to dare lightning to strike it. When the Stranger's defiance is broken somewhat by his stay in the convent in the middle of Part I, he returns to find the woodpile diminished. "... I've got rid of my woodpile," the Doctor says. "I want no thunder in my home. And I shall play no more with the lightning" (Pt. I, xvi, p. 107).

The Stranger seems more aware of his role in creating the Lady than he is of his relation to any of these others. He names her Eve and gives her an age and a character. The Mother keeps pointing out his responsibility in this respect: "by means of this Eve, that you yourself had made, you intended to destroy the whole sex!" she exclaims (Pt. I, vii, p. 69). When the Stranger turns the Lady into an avenging Fury, the Mother again points out that he has made her what he calls her (Pt. II, Act I, p. 121). In an interesting reversal of the Genesis story, the Stranger's book is the apple of the knowledge of good and evil, and the Mother tempts the Lady to break her vow and read it. As the Stranger sums up the situation at the end, "she absorbed my evil and I her good" (Pt. III, Act III, iii, p. 259). The Lady, however, is more than a foil for the male aspect of the Stranger's personality, as Carl Dahlström suggests. She and he are two sides of the same archetypal coin.

The aspects of the Stranger's personality which Dahlström finds represented in *To Damascus* are three: Male, Intellectual, and Failure. The Male he describes as that portion which must be fulfilled both biologically and socially. The Stranger is therefore lover, husband, and father, subdivisions of the Male which are not always in accord. The Male aspect, Dahlström says, is revealed through dialogue and not externalized in any of the characters in the play; the Lady is merely its foil.[15] I suggest, on the contrary, that the Lady is another aspect of the Stranger's personality, a feminine aspect he does not want to acknowledge.[16] The second aspect, the Intellectual, is not embodied as a character in the play until Part III, when the Tempter appears. This aspect of personality includes the "Emancipator" or "Liberator," who tries to instruct and free mankind from bondage. It also includes the "Destroyer," who, frustrated in the former effort, desires to annihilate the world by making gold.[17] Male and Intellectual are constantly at war. As Emancipator, the Stranger wishes to free the Lady; as Male, he wishes to bind her. Or, if we see her as a portion of the

Stranger's personality, as I suggest, Male and Intellectual are both in opposition to her, but for different reasons. To the Male, she suggests weakness and passivity, to the Intellectual, faith; whereas the Male is associated with strength and activity, the Intellectual, with questioning and ultimately cynicism and doubt.

Dahlström labels "Failure" that aspect of the Stranger's personality revealed in such characters as the Beggar, Caesar, the Beggar-Confessor-Dominican. they suggest mockery, negation, and finally, annihilation of the Stranger's self. Dahlström dubs them "Failure" primarily because he does not read the end of Part II positively. The only way the Stranger can resolve the conflict between Male and Intellectual is to annihilate his personality altogether, something he does unwillingly, without triumph. He yields, according to Dahlström, as a tragic last resort forced upon him by a social order in which man cannot develop "to his highest form, or indeed ... even maintain integrity and rationality."[18] The development of the play thus becomes a series of leave-takings of various aspects of the personality until, after the Tempter is left behind, the Stranger has none.

While I do not read the ending positively either, I think it is inherently more complex. The Stranger is resigned and certainly untriumphant. Nevertheless, the process of the play seems to be one of self-discovery and self-acceptance as much as one of self-annihilation. More simply, the Stranger annihilates a limited notion of self in favor of an archetypal self. He changes from a man who sees evil everywhere and is shied away from as if he were the Devil to one who sees, in the person of Old Maia, that good as well as evil "comes back." From a man determined not to be made a fool of by life, the Stranger, continually made the fool, becomes a "wise fool." "You must let yourself be fooled, more or less, to live at all," counsels the Lady early in the play (Pt. I, i, p. 27). An obstinately proud, defiant man, concerned with worldly fame, the Stranger is set upon the road to humility and obedience; on it he learns that guilt is universal and forgiveness essential. In the two-headed portrait gallery, affirmation versus negation gives way to comprehension, and "either" versus "or" becomes "not only – but also" (Pt. III, Act IV, ii, p. 283). Oppositions in conflict give way to oppositions accepted and comprehended. What is disturbing about the end of the play are the implications of this overly neat thesis-antithesis-synthesis resolution. Does the end of Part III depict the symbolic death of the Stranger's old, limited self, or can the resolution be achieved only in actual death?[19] Just as the boundaries between the inner life of the mind and the external world become blurred in this play, so do the boundaries between life and death.

Additional insight can be derived from a book which mentions neither *To Damascus* nor August Strindberg: Maud Bodkin's *Archetypal Patterns in Poetry: Psychological Studies of Imagination.* All of the patterns explored in this basically Jungian book not only find expression in Strindberg's play, but are emphasized in it. I have already mentioned the pilgrimage and life cycle. More interesting in the case of this play are the archetypes based on contradictions. What is most consistent about the Stranger's character, in all of its manifestations, is his inconsistency. Bodkin's discussion of the conflicts in literature between Heaven and Hell, God and Satan, and the positive and negative manifestations of Woman reveals that these apparent contradictions are really only interrelated parts of the same whole. The implication is that in the author, in the work he or she creates, and in the person responding to that work, all the oppositions exist, latent or dominant as the case may be. In *To Damascus*, Strindberg explores these fundamental oppositions and dramatizes them in ways that reveal their presence within us.

Of all the literary examples Bodkin discusses in her book, Milton's *Paradise Lost* best illustrates her point. Many critics have noted the ambiguity in the reader's response to the "characters" of Satan and God. Satan, striving against oppression, asserting his indomitable will, preferring to rule in Hell than to serve in Heaven, strikes us as heroic, a positive force. God is correspondingly the oppressor: stuffy, inflexible, and repressive. Yet Satan is arrogant and destructive, in which case God's punishment becomes just and beneficial. As one takes on positive qualities, the other takes on negative, and vice versa.[20] The same is true of Milton's Eve, who, at various points in *Paradise Lost*, is Eternal Mother, Goddess, and Temptress; and our view of Adam's character shifts correspondingly.[21] Bodkin suggests that in human experience, man can be exalted in his attraction to woman, in which case she takes on the positive qualities just mentioned; or he can fear that attraction, in which case she is a negative force.[22] The same ambivalence is true in women's attitudes toward men, although less evidence is available in male-dominated Western art.[23]

Similarly, in *To Damascus*, the Stranger vacillates between self-condemnation and self-justification, and we vacillate with him. When he blames himself, in his own character or as one of his self-projections, then the Powers are just and woman redemptive. In contrast, when he defends himself, takes pride in his suffering, and defies the Powers in a heroic and Satanic way, then the Powers are unjust and oppressive; in these instances, woman is one of them. One moment he is Job, the upright man unjustly punished; the next he is Job, the self-righteous man justly punished and better for his suffering. Because of these fundamental contradictions, the play becomes a complex series of ironies. People want love, get it, then do not want it. The farther the Stranger is from the Lady, the nearer he feels himself to be, and the nearer the farther. When they meet, they wish to part; when they part, they wish to meet. Ariel is Caliban and Caliban is Ariel. People who accuse each other of sin and crime turn out to be sinful and criminal themselves. The oppressed, in their turn, are oppressors. Idylls in the forest are witches' caldrons; freedom is bondage; fame is infamy. All are two sides of the coin which is human experience. Man has a will, yet he is determined; he loves, yet he hates. When we see one side of the coin, we soon see the other, as if the coin was spinning on its edge. As the Stranger finally says, anticipating the drama of the Existentialists: "What a joke life is, if you take it seriously. And how serious, if you take it as a joke!" (Pt. III, Act III, iii, p. 255).

To communicate these contradictions, Strindberg uses verbal, visual, and aural images and symbols. He shows a preference for symbols in the Jungian sense, those drawn out of the racial memory of man or at least out of Western culture; he avoids symbols meaningful only within the context of the work, although these are present too.[24] Universal symbols, along with the almost continual presence of the Stranger, the appearance and reappearance of the various characters who represent aspects of his personality, repeated scenes, seasonal and life cycles, foreshadowings, recapitulations, recollections, and recurring themes, give the play unity and coherent structure. The most obvious example is the ravine and mountain symbolism which appears throughout Western art as suggestive of Hell and Heaven, the "dark night of the soul," and redemption, despair, and aspiration. The Stranger travels from ravines and various hellish settings, like the banquet hall of Part II, to the mountains of Part III.

Also fairly obvious in Strindberg's choice of traditional color symbolism. Not so obvious is the way he uses it to underscore the fundamental contradictions which are the subject of the play. The rose is traditionally ambivalent, sacred and secular. Flower and color are associated throughout the trilogy with women in both their redemptive and their destructive roles. Green is similarly ambivalent. The Lady's green dress and coat appear in several scenes in Part II, either worn by her or hanging up in the room. The green clothing hangs up and she wears white when she holds her new baby. The Stranger in this scene refers to her "green witch's dress" (Pt. II, Act IV, iii, p. 181), which she wore at their first meeting, and in the pocket of which she hid letters from him after their marriage. But the Stranger's Alpine hat is also green, a fact that associates him with her.

Green here has its traditional connotations of the evil, jealous spirit: the two people torment each other, are suspicious of each other, each fearful of the other's power and the other's past. Green, however, is also the color of rebirth and growth, of spring and summer. Strindberg sets his association in opposition to the other. When the Lady is redeemer again in Part III, her little room is "as bright green as a summer meadow" and "fresh green like hope" (Pt. III, Act III, iii, pp. 251–252).

Most important in this respect is the symbolism of black and white, and, it is sufficient merely to note, the parallel dark-and-light symbolism. In Strindberg's play, black and white suggest the ultimate extremes, the reduction to the most basic of human experiences: death and life, evil and good, sin and purity. In *To Damascus*, the Stranger confronts all that is traditionally connoted by black and white until he finally comprehends these confrontations, at least in part, and wears the colors himself. Throughout the trilogy, black and white serve as reminders of the nature of the journey he undertakes: the smithy and his wife whom the Stranger meets on his journey in Part I are black with soot and white with flour respectively; similarly, the Mother's house has white walls and a soot-blackened ceiling, a setting which must communicate oppressiveness or impending doom or evil in addition to the "not only – but also" perspective the Stranger has not yet achieved. That the religious figures have achieved such a perspective is suggested by their black-and-white costumes. The Augustinian nuns in the birth scene in Part II, for example, are dressed that way. So is the Mother. In this scene, birth and death coexist, although the Lady lives after all. The Lady wears white when she cares for her newborn child and black to mourn its death.

To the Stranger, however, black signifies the evil he sees everywhere. When he sees the Lady in mourning, he says: "So black! So black and so evil." The Lady replies: "No longer evil. I'm in mourning ..." (Pt. III, Act I, p. 205). Even when he appears in Part III in black-and-white clothing, he still sees the white house pointed out by the Confessor as black. The Confessor tells him: "You still *are* black, but you'll grow white, quite white!" (Pt. III, Act IV, i, p. 268). And in the final scene, the Stranger is dressed in white, then wrapped in a black biercloth. Because black and white suggest physical death and life, spiritual death and life, as well as evil and good, exactly what transpires in this final scene remains unresolved. Presumably, black is associated no longer with evil, but rather with the finality of death to the temporal world and rebirth into spiritual life, or merely with the final oblivion of physical death. We cannot be certain. What is certain is the reduction of the Stranger to the elemental situation where he confronts death and life, evil and good, and accepts both as parts of himself and the general human experience. We feel uncomfortable with the ending because the archetypal contradiction is still at work within us: we regret that the Stranger has stopped raging and defying; we are glad to see him at peace, no longer a stranger to himself.

Since the Bible is one of the primary Western representatives of the creation-fall-redemption-apocalypse pattern in human experience, Strindberg's many allusions to it in this play are another good example of his emphasis on the archetypal. The obvious allusion is contained in the title, "The Road to Damascus" or simply "To Damascus." As the title suggests, the Stranger is a kind of Saul, the New Testament persecutor of the Christians who in Acts ix journeys to Damascus to bring Christians bound to Jerusalem. On the way, a light and a voice cause him to fall to his knees. "Saul, Saul, why persecutest thou me," says the voice of Christ. Saul is instructed to continue to Damascus, where he will be told what to do. When he arises, he is blind and can neither see nor eat for three days. In Damascus, Saul's sight is restored through the agency of Ananias, who also sees that he is fed and baptized. Saul then begins to preach for Christ, suffering some of the same persecutions he had inflicted upon others. Strindberg does not follow the New Testament story step by step. The play contains several references, in addition to the title, to the road to Damascus, which, for the Stranger, is a circular, winding, and arduous road upon which he wanders with the rage, self-pity, and arrogance which keep in abeyance the other aspects of his personality. Like Saul, he undergoes a crisis, and that crisis blinds him, although he has intimations of some meaning and significance. Only at the very end of the trilogy does he begin to comprehend what he is to do. Significantly, the title is not simply "Damascus" but "*To* Damascus." Strindberg's emphasis is on the journey and the crisis. About the aftermath, he is uncertain.

The Bible, however, contains two Sauls, one in the Old Testament as well as one in the New. The differences between the two Sauls, both of whom the play suggests, again parallel contradictions in the Stranger's personality and in the human experience in general. The New Testament title is fixed upon a play permeated by the Old Testament. The Stranger indicates that he was brought up according to the Old Testament law of revenge. That most of the play should bear the Old Testament mark, then, is natural; the Stranger is comfortable in that milieu. But although revenge is the only law he knows, like the wicked judge in Strindberg's *Advent*, revenge is not meant to be the only law. The progress of the play is toward Damascus, a crucifix with Christ upon it suffering in the Stranger's place, and forgiveness: primarily, in the Stranger's case, self-forgiveness. Whether the Stranger can ever eradicate the Old Testament mark from his brow is another matter. Nevertheless, he is saved from becoming entirely the Saul of the Old Testament by undergoing some of the experiences of the New Testament Saul.

The Old Testament figure, anointed the first King of Israel, helps to unite his people by fighting successfully against the Philistines and other enemies. But Saul is jealous, moody, and quarrelsome, possessed by periods of madness during which he fights with everyone close to him. During these spells, David calms him with his harp and songs. Saul disobeys God on one occasion: he gives the wishes of his people precedence over God's commands. Out of favor, he finally dies by falling on his own sword to prevent being killed by his enemies. While the parallels with the Stranger are not exact, they are illuminating nonetheless. The Stranger, too, has unstable, quarrelsome periods. Appropriately, in Part II, the Corpus Christi pageant passes the Stranger and the Confessor to the accompaniment of one of David's Psalms. Like King Saul, also, the Stranger is overly concerned with public opinion. He wants fame and recognition; he repeatedly asks people if they know who he is. Ultimately, one of the conditions of his entry into the monastery is a denial of all concern with earthly fame. The Stranger, however, does not die in the manner of King Saul. In Part I, the Stranger, during a contented moment with the Lady, wants her to die with him. She refuses, and he must continue to confront his enemies as King Saul did not. Death is too easy. The mad, proud King Saul and the Saul who persecuted the Christians join hands and, in the person of the Stranger, trudge toward Damascus.

In the Biblical world of the play, the Stranger also is the righteous Job and the self-righteous Job. He is God creating Eve; and he is Satan from whom people shrink. He is the Tempter of the Lady and, by the Lady, tempted. He is Cain, bearing the mark of sin against his fellow man; but he is also Abel, sinned against. Although he is an enraged Christ driving the money-changers from the Temple and a suffering Christ crucified, his world is mostly the Old Testament world in which the curse of Deuteronomy is read; the sins of the fathers are visited upon the children of succeeding generations; the children of Israel are led by a pillar of cloud and punished, like Lot's wife, who became a pillar of salt; and the priests of Baal and the builders of the Tower of Babel defy God. In this world, Adam and Eve are driven out of the Garden of Eden. "We've been driven from the garden," says the Stranger to the Lady, "and must wander over stones and thistles. And when our hands and feet are bruised, we feel we must rub salt in the wounds of the ... other one" (Pt. I, xiv, p. 98). But although Strindberg seems less comfortable with this idea and less emphatic in his suggestion of it, the Stranger's world is also that of the "fortunate fall."

In the monastery at the end of Part III, the Stranger is finally on the way to seeing himself as part of a grand stream of contradictory human experience. Consequently, a good many of the allusions in the play associate him with mythological, historical, and literary figures of all kinds. The two-headed portrait gallery includes many of these, but the earlier portions of the play contains them as well. The Lady is not only Eve, but Pandora, one of the Furies, one of the Fates, Ariel, and Caliban. The Stranger and the Lady are Orpheus and Eurydice when they are reunited in Part III. The Stranger is Bluebeard as well as Polycrates. He is Faust, Caesar, Lear, Prometheus, Hercules. He is all of the forces opposing these heroes as well. He is human aspiration and repression in modern dress. He is the "archetypal hero-figure" who, as Bodkin says, "stands poised between height and depth, between the Divine and the Devilish, swung forward and upward in reflection of imagination's universal range, hurled back and downward in expression of individual limitation and the restraining censure of the whole upon the part."[25]

To Damascus, then, is an archetypal autobiography, a work in which Strindberg draws attention to the elements in his personal life which are the fundamental patterns of human experience as a whole: the pilgrimage of life through the stages of birth, middle-age crisis, death, and physical and spiritual rebirth, as well as the contradictory Hell-Heaven, Satan-God Temptress-Goddess sides of the ever-spinning psychic coin. In this context, Strindberg's play acquires new life, and the state of mind he describes, some of its traditional dignity and resonance.

NOTES

1 August Strindberg, *The Great Highway*, in *Eight Expressionist Plays*, trans. Arvid Paulson (New York, 1972), p. 453.

2 As quoted in Gunnar Ollén, "Strindberg 1962," *World Theatre*, 11 (Spring 1962), 14.

3 For a general discussion of this theme is Strindberg's later plays, see Einar I. Haugen, "Strindberg the Regenerated," *JEGP*, 29 (April 1930), 257–270.

4 Gunnar Ollén, in his Introduction (trans. Esther Johanson) to *The Road to Damascus: A Trilogy*, trans. Graham Rawson (New York, 1960), takes this position. Ollén's whole discussion, however, is one of statement and qualifica-

tion. For instance, after drawing the parallel between the Lady and Frida Uhl, Ollén says: "On the other hand, the chief female character of the drama does not correspond to her real-life counterpart in that she is supposed to have been married to a doctor before eloping with THE STRANGER, Strindberg" (p. 14); and, "Even minor characters, such as CAESAR and THE BEGGAR, have their counterparts in real life, even though in the main they are fantastic creations of his imagination" (p. 16). All references to the play in my text are to Rawson's translation.

5 Carl G. Jung, "Approaching the Unconcscious," in *Man and His Symbols*, ed. Carl G. Jung and M.-L. von Franz (Garden City, N.Y., 1964), p. 67. Evert Sprinchorn in "'The Zola of the Occult': Strindberg's Experimental Method," *Modern Drama*, 17 (September 1974), 251–266, associates *To Damascus* with Jung's emphasis on synchronicity (256). Sprinchorn's main concern, however, is to place Strindberg's work in the context of writers on both natural science and psychic phenomena whom he had read.

6 August Strindberg, *Open Letters to the Intimate Theatre*, trans. Walter Johnson (Seattle, 1966), p. 98.

7 Ibid., p. 101.

8 Ibid.

9 Ibid., pp. 101–102.

10 Ibid., pp. 203–204.

11 Jung emphasizes the need for caution in applying symbols whose associations are fixed to individual dreams. He stresses the importance of the psychological makeup of the individual dreamer which is responsible entirely for some symbols and may represent the archetypal patterns in individualized ways ("Approaching the Unconscious," pp. 53, 92). Maurice Valency, however, in *"A Dream Play*: The Flower and the Castle," excerpted from *The Flower and the Castle* (New York, 1963), pp. 326–342; rpt. in *Modern Drama*, ed. Anthony Caputi (New York, 1966), pp. 428–429, notes that dreams, unlike dream plays, are governed by no conscious artistic aims.

12 August Strindberg, *A Dream Play*, trans. Elizabeth Sprigge, in *Modern Drama*, ed. Caputi, p. 213.

13 This aspect of Strindberg's work is discussed by, among others, Sprinchorn; Sam E. Davidson, "The 'Stream-of Consciousness' Drama," *Poet Lore*, 42 (Spring 1933), 71–80; and Gerald Parker, "The Spectator Seized by the Theatre: Strindberg's *The Ghost Sonata*," *Modern Drama*, 14 (February 1972), 373–386.

14 Compare the shawl which is the story of torment in *A Dream Play*.

15 Carl E.W.L. Dahlström, "Situation and character in *Till Damaskus*," *PMLA*, 53 (September 1938), 886–902.

16 Robert Brustein, "Male and Female in August Strindberg," in *Modern Drama*, ed. Travis Bogard and William I. Oliver (London, 1965), p. 341, makes this point in a more general way. Consider, too, Maud Bodkin's comment in *Archetypal Patterns in Poetry: Psychological Studies of Imagination* (London, 1963), p. 203:

> The poet who, like Virgil, by his poetic gift possesses those delicate intuitions and sympathies with all forms of life that are commonly thought of as constituting femine sensibility, and who yet accepts as inevitable a system of "masculine" thought and morality, ignoring all such sympathies, holds a part of himself unrealized. It will cry out upon him, alienated and suffering like Dido. It will move upward toward the light, like Eurydice, through the power of his song, then plunge back into the gloom, as he turns from poetry to actual life. In the experience of those readers of the poems who share in any degree such thwarted imaginative sensibility, the same inward drama will find expression.

17 One could also make a case for putting the Doctor in this category.
18 Dahlström, 902.
19 Compare Robert Brustein's reading of *A Dream Play* in "August Strindberg: *A Dream Play*," excerpted from *The Theatre of Revolt* (Boston, 1964), pp. 126–133); rpt. in *Modern Drama*, ed. Caputi, p. 445. Consider also Jung's comment in "Approaching the Unconscious," p. 85:

> The sad truth is that man's real life consists of a complex of inexorable opposites – day and night, birth and death, happiness and misery, good and evil. We are not even sure that one will prevail against the other, that good will overcome evil, or joy defeat pain. Life is a battleground. It always has been, and always will be; and if it were not so, existence would come to an end.

20 Bodkin, pp. 246, 269.
21 Ibid., pp. 165–170.
22 Ibid., pp. 172–173.
23 Ibid., pp. 299–307 on Virginia Woolf's *Orlando* and Emily Brontë's *Wuthering Heights*.
24 Many sounds and objects accumulate meanings within the context of the play, although sometimes the line between such symbols and the archetypal ones is difficult to draw. The funeral march, for example, pursues the Stranger and emphasizes the basic physical and spiritual life-and-death problems with which he grapples. The mill grinding and the sound of water and the waterfall are heard and referred to until they become elaborate extended meta-

phors. The mill grinds the sins of the past and continually shows them forth in new yet disconcertingly familiar forms. The poorhouse from which a demented woman beckons occurs in several scenes from the Mother's house and from the rose room within that house. The Lady's crochet work is another example. It becomes connected, however, with the archetyal rose symbol. Much of the visual, aural, and verbal imagery is ominous – like the stuffed bird of prey on the table in the Mother's house and the surgical instruments which the Doctor cleans, as well as the painting in the convent of the Archangel Michael killing the Fiend, a painting before which the Stranger lowers his eyes. The hunting sounds and objects walk the line between contextual and archetypal symbols. On the one hand, they underscore the quest upon which we find the Stranger, and we recall that the main character in *The Great Highway* is actually called the Hunter. On the other hand, the Stranger is hunted, persecuted, pursued. The ambivalence is summed up nicely in the constellation Orion, which appears in the sky of Part II. Orion was a mythological hunter accidentally killed by Diana, who loved him and placed him in the stars. The book the Stranger tore as a child is related. Appropriately, it was *The Swiss Family Robinson.* Ever since childhood, the Stranger has suffered from his inability to see good in and to make a new life out of catastrophe and isolation. Letters, newspapers, the Stranger's book about his first marriage, flowers of various kinds, all appear and reappear in complex counterpoint on various levels of significance. Everything is mysterious, but comprehensible within the logic of the dream play.

25 Bodkin, p. 245.

Pirandello's Mirror

MARVIN ROSENBERG

In a time when great questions had to be asked in the drama, Pirandello seemed to be ready to ask the right ones, brilliantly. He was the proper child of a questioning age, nourished on two great revolutionary movements: a revolt of the arts against all conventional forms that obscured experience, and a parallel revolution in psychology that stripped away conventional ideas of behavior to get at the nuclear process. Pirandello seemed ideally to combine the means of the new art with the probe of the new psychology, in that exploration of the self that has always been one of the chief provinces of drama. Unlike contemporaries following the same paths who were pasting the insights of Freud and Jung upon their drama, he seemed to have made his own many secrets of the psyche: he understood, with the first psychoanalysts and Gestaltists, that each man perceives life in a context determined by his needs and wants, that men seldom break out of this narrow personal world in which, instead of "seeing," they project on the screen of life the meanings they want to find there. So his drama asked the crucial questions : What is the self, if indeed there is one? What is its morality? Its conscience? Its goal? What is the responsibility of the artist who deals with it, of his audience?

Two things matter here: how well did Pirandello put the questions? How did he answer them? On the first count, he deserves very high marks, for the daring and scope of his dramatic visions. Out of the very conditions of felt life discovered by the psychologists – the dilemma of mutually exclusive contexts, the defense mechanisms of projection, of self-deception, of regression – he made his major plot devices. The dissolution of dramatic personality begun by Strindberg is extended: Pirandello dramatizes the absurdity of identity. If he admits an ego, it is usually only to show its transience under the centrifugal and centripetal forces of experience.

Diego, the *raissoneur* of *Each in His Own Way*, speaks explicitly the play-wright's brilliant, terrible insights into the mind, with its burden of shames, and guilts, its petty thoughts, its imagined crimes, its unspeakable desires, the numberless little sins of man's many souls that are "rejected and buried in the depths of our being, and from which thoughts and actions are born – actions and thoughts which we refuse to recognize, but which, when we are forced to it, we adopt or legitimize ... with appropriate adaptations, reserves, and cautions." The mind – the self – is a restlessness:

All our ideas, in short, change in the restless turmoil we call life. We think we catch a glimpse of the situation. But ... impressions change from hour to hour: A word is often sufficient or even just the manner in which it is said – to change our minds completely! And then besides, quite without our knowledge, images of hundreds and hundreds of things are flitting through our minds, suddenly causing our tempers to vary in the strangest way!

In all his best self-questioning plays, Pirandello's characters find that the firm selves they believe they own are in fact made up of evanescent hopes, impulses, wishes, fears, social pressures, the instincts of the animal inheri-tance. They are driven deeper: Pirandello tried to make them express – explicitly, in his *Six Characters* – "as their own living passion and torment the passion and torment which for so many years have been the pangs of my spirit: the deceit of mutual understanding irremediably founded on the empty abstraction of words, the multiple personality of everyone corresponding to the possibilities of being found in each of us, and finally the inherent tragic conflict between life (which is always moving and changing) and form (which fixes it, immovable)."

Hence his characters usually wander as in a hall of mirrors, thinking they look for reality, while, in fact, they desperately try to find safe illusions – "ideals" – to live by. When, for a moment, they seem "real" to an audience, their non-realism is often suddenly declared: they turn out to be in a play-within-a-play, as in *Each in His Own Way*. Here the make-believe of life and theater are intermingled; in fact the entertaining illusion of the stage is as nothing compared to the indispensable illusions that permit troubled, living men to exist. Rocca and Delia have deceived each other and them-selves as to their motives toward each other; in the end, seeing through illusion, they feel bound to "drown together" in the blood of the man whose death was caused by their passion; but this is only the fiction of a play-within-a-play; for in the next dimension the "real" Delia and her lover, in the audience, are confronted with this illusion of their own lives, and likewise storm out to "drown in blood," while the actors and the stage audience are left to wonder – as the actual audience watches. What is real? When do dimensions end? In *Right You Are* the characters, to make life workable, settle for the impossible illusion that a woman may have two irreconcilable identities. The Pretender-king in *Henry IV* can at first find life only tolerable – then, after the murder, only possible – by playing mad, thus living the ultimate illusion. The heroine of *The Life I Gave You* must deceive herself to accept a son's death; the heroine of *Naked* must deceive herself even to bring herself to commit suicide. In *The Rules of the Game*, Leone protects himself from experience by the enforced illusion of life as gamesmanship. Identity is impossible for the Unknown of *As You Desire Me:* she must be what is demanded of her. So must the poet of *When Someone is Someone.*

Against the power of illusion, Pirandello's characters are almost helpless. Society's moral code, instead of giving them support, only encourages them to greater ironies. The lawbreaker in *The Pleasure of Honesty* is more "moral" than his "proper" associates. In *Liola,* the heroine – the unhappy wife of an impotent old man – learns that her husband thinks his mistress is bearing him a son (who is actually the child of the gay seducer Liola); in revenge, the wife also arranges to beget a child by Liola, whom she used to love – but she "morally" remains the old husband's wife, and lets him think the child is his. In *The New Colony*, the whole result of the system of law seems to be breed lawlessness.

The traditional moral safeguard of the troubled character was an inner stability, usually called a conscience; to the usual tentative selves in Pirandello, it is only another social projection. In the extensive treatment of it in *Each in His Own Way*, it turns out to be the tendency people have to act as others expect them to. It is either a self-constructed image to live safely by, a defense against threatening inroads of the instinct, or it is derived frankly from social pressure. The characters live through an experience of ultimate disillusionment when they prove that, in terms of "reason," they are nothing except what is thought they should be – sometimes mere projections of their acquaintances. Those who champion one thing in one context find themselves on the other side in another one; their "morals" – self-deceptions – change as they see themselves from others' eyes. And these are the characters in the inner play; the "real" people watching the drama take their cue from this, and are obliged to do as the fictional characters do. The guidance of instinct, an alternative that Pirandello seemed to have had some trust for in his earlier writings, not only does not serve in his drama as a substitute for conscience, but it drives his characters to wild and ludicrous acts.

To this questioning playwright, the world becomes endlessly ironic. Whenever a seeking character seems to find a frame of reference for life, he discovers a larger context that mocks his limited vision. His impulses, his ideals, his facts, even his self often turn out to be illusory, or relative. This incisive, incessant questioning is often brilliantly done; but, incessant as it is, it raises a further question that brings us to the second part of our equation: from what stance do all these questions come? Is there any center? Any focus? Is there any meaning in this questioning of meaning?

Pirandello has been called a pessimist. Well, an artist is entitled to pessimism if, seeing something of the wholeness of life, with some soundness, he can find only despair in it; if his pessimism is the voice of a spirit that has plumbed experience selflessly, and must cry out a dark truth. The playwright is certainly not obligated to use drama to preach hope: Pirandello wrote justly to his actress friend Marta Abba, "Since art belongs to the realm of disinterested feeling, one must choose between the objectives of art and those of propaganda. The two cannot be practiced together." But: "disinterested feeling." Could this artist really function as an impersonal prism, focussing the drama of life onto the stage without any personal bias? Pirandello seemed to feel he had achieved such a neutral, refractive method: interviewed in London, he reiterated his favorite description of his technique:

I have had the audacity of placing a mirror in the very center of the stage. It is the mirror of intelligence. Man, while alive, lives but does not see himself. Sentiment, by itself, is blind; I have therefore so managed that this blind man at a certain moment should open his eyes and should see himself in that mirror and should stand as if frozen by the unthought-of image of his own life.

But Pirandello's way of "reflecting" life, as he noted in his *Six Characters* preface, was to let his characters act out his own torments. Is he holding the mirror up to himself? Then how disinterested is his own response to life? Do his personal involvements affect the truth of what he sees in his looking glass?

Particularly revealing here are Pirandello's occasional affirmations. They seem to have no real place in the dark mirror into which he is staring, but rather to be dragged in as a deliberate attempt to lighten the gloom. Even so, he does not exploit those usual symbolic triumphs of fertility over decay, love and marriage; in Pirandello these are almost always insubstantial, usually lost in irony, turning out to be products of illusion, or passing impulse, or social pressure, or of destructive passion. When Pirandello brings himself to think positively, he reaches for miraculous assurance beyond the savage reflections of life he normally recognizes. And, inevitably, as even Vittorini, the playwright's over-fond champion observes, the more Pirandello tries to deal with constructive thought, the poorer his play. In *Lazarus*, in defiance of his other questionings, the playwright accepts a self, a soul, a personal entity that is changed not by circumstances, projection, or restless inner life, but by a miracle-making God. The play begins with the usual Pirandello verbal and character ironies, but they are swallowed up in an encompassing divine intervention. Diego, a crusty monster of repression, dies and is brought back to life by a scientist. At first he suffers a brainstorm at this denial of the conventional order he believes in; but then, when his little daughter, his sweet, touching, crippled heroic little daughter, is miraculously cured and able to walk again, the stage is bathed in tears and exaltation, even the most cynical recognize divinity at work, "And all the others too, dumbfounded with joy, stand there, their lips shaping the word: 'Miracle.'"

This is the kind of sentiment that Pirandello normally recognized as the most dangerous kind of illusion; in *Lazarus*, he seems to be released to an orgy of repressed fantasies. Thus he finds another refuge in a theme that he usually mutes, or contradicts: the pastoral idyll, the lost life of the country paradise where man can live naturally and happily. So Diego's wife, having left him, lives simply and joyfully with her lover and their two natural children in Arcadian simplicity on the land. According to the young would-be priest, Lucio, their "good, natural life" puts them beyond the law, and Diego's resentment.

This sentimental "positive" view of the pastoral is a sharp contrast to the author's more usual, hard-headed view of rural life. The early Pirandello rather favored the earthy, animal satisfactions of the country; so his Liola is a swaggering rooster in a henyard, who triumphs over the old cuckold in a way reminiscent of the *commedia*, and there is nothing sentimental about the gossipy, shrewish life of the country women. It is as hard and bitter as townlife. In *The New Colony*, the play where Pirandello comes to grips with men as part of a social organization, there seems at first to be the promise that "natural" life on an isolated island may even change the brutalized life of waterfront scum into something sweet and good. But the hopes of the men, once they flee the mainland for their lonely island colony, are doomed by their humanity. Their happiness soon subsides, faced down by competition, suspicion, illness, discouragement. Once laws inevitably reappear to control passion, they provoke the old passions to break them. Projections grow up about the leader; might and right find common ground: the idyll is destroyed. Nature is no savior.

In the one survivor of the Colony we may see another of Pirandello's rare, favorite positive sentiments. La Spera, the dockside whore, has been one of the moving forces in the colony. She is about to have a baby, and she wants it to grow in a better place than the old one. She is the only one who genuinely breaks out of the narrow prison of her own wishes and projections: she urges the others to "refuse to think of oneself. ... When you hold out your hands to grasp something, it always eludes you. But if you stretch them out in giving, then you will gather everything that comes your way, and the lives of others will become your own." This is an idealism that Pirandello does not cancel out with irony; and significantly, it represents the ideal of the mother. When the father of La Spera's son, to strengthen his own sense of power, tries to take the boy from her, she says "No! If you take him, the earth will tremble." He tries to take the boy, sure enough the earth trembles, and the whole island is swallowed by the sea, along with all the islanders – except La Spera and her son alone on a promontory on the waters, perhaps the seed of a new society.

The power of mother love is not always so magical in Pirandello, but it remains one of the strongest of passions, and often gives meaning to character. Thus, to Lucia, the mother in *The Life I Gave You*, her son Fulvio is enough to give meaning both to her life and death; the young married woman who is adulterously bearing Fulvio's child – note that mother love and illicit love often entwine[1] – seeks her only hope of joy in this act of begetting. In *The Pleasure of Honesty*, the mother, grieved at the spinsterhood of her daughter, condones the daughter's affair with a lover; the daughter, Agata, grows strong enough through her pregnancy to cast off her lover for the convenient "rascal" whom the lover and her mother made her marry to cover her shame. Thus a rare[2] kind of happy ending is managed between the "sinful" woman and the "rascal" – again on unmotivated affirmation, since nothing in the given relationship of the two prepares for it.

Woman herself is rarely strong enough to provide a positive stance for Pirandello, though where he seems to be taking as his model Marta Abba, he comes closest. Thus, in *The Wives' Friend*, one of the plays dedicated to the actress, he presents a kind of Ideal in his heroine, named Marta: she is so good and beautiful and sensitive and intelligent that no man dares think of her as a bride, so all her men friends mismarry and need her wisdom and compassion.

What is most important about Pirandello's affirmations is that they dangle: they affirm without in any way meeting or solving the important questions raised by his drama. The miraculous rebirth and cure; the miraculous saving of the reformed whore-mother and her baby: these are, like the deed of a whimsical god in a machine, unrelated to the central agony – the central irony – which informs Pirandello's dramatic actions: that man is an ever-changing thing in an ever-changing context, that he cannot fix for long on truth, or certainty, or any permanent relationship. The evasive miracles seem in fact to be symbolic of Pirandello's dream of escape from this ironic world that he does not – cannot – confront. Now is the time to recall his wish in *Six Characters:* to express his own torments, particularly "the inherent tragic conflict between life (which is always moving and changing) and form (which fixes it, immovable)." There is no *inherent, tragic* conflict here – except to the mind that rejects the conditions of existence, and clings to the infant, megalomaniac dream of omnipotence, that wants to have everything. On a high enough level – of the hero who would be god, of the god-man revolting against the godfather, of the striver who would sell his soul for magic power – there is, in this regressive impulse, a theme of tragic size; but Pirandello's people do not strive so much, they hardly strive at all. "There is not one noble or heroic figure in the roster of his characters," Landor MacClintock observes, "not one who, herolike, struggles against his fate, not one generous soul, not one who asserts his dignity as a man; there are only victims rebelling against destiny in black desperation, lamenting the fact that they do not understand the plan of the universe, nor their own place in it."

Life in Pirandello's plays is often pervaded by ugliness – rarely physical, as in the slum life of *The New Colony*, but rather spiritual; characters complain about the filth, the degradation, in which they live. In comparison with life, art is generally made to seem much better: it offers escape from the wild confusion of existence into a timeless, fixed world. *Six Characters* plays this out. The "real" life of actors and director in the theater turns out to be shoddy, shrill, trivial; the dignity of the agonized Characters is in comparison majestic. The Characters are vital, alive; the "real" people move in their shadow. In somewhat the same way, the "real" lovers of *Each in His Own Way* find they must rise to the dignity of what their acted counterparts did on the stage: the "Spectator Who Understands" observes, "They saw themselves there, as in a mirror, forced into the situation that has the eternity of art."

In *Tonight We Improvise*, another play that laughs at the theater's shortcomings in the face of art, the playwright's personal motif is even more clearly stated. In this play involving an acting company about to put on a Pirandello play, the actors – except when drawn into the story of the "eternal" characters – are all stereotypes of vanity and superficiality, directed by the bumbling, loquacious Dr. Hinkfuss. Hinkfuss, in his extended philosophical monologues to the audience, often speaks Pirandello's central philosophy. He argues that every man tries to create a timeless self, but must fail, because the self is transient, utilitarian, and always in danger of being "thwarted, perverted, and deformed" by life. What Hinkfuss then says is most revealing the Pirandello's own view: "Art, in a certain sense, is a revenge on life." *Revenge on life* – this sounds a theme that echoes again in Pirandello's drama – and also in his personal correspondence, as we shall see. Thus, in *As You Desire Me*, the Unknown One, deriding Salter's claims to being a serious writer, offers this proof: that he never had "felt compelled – because of a real torment, a real despair – to take *revenge on life* as it is, as it has been made for you by other people and through circumstances. ..." The verb in both cases is *vendicare*, which means revenge in the strongest sense – getting even for an offense suffered. One who thinks often of revenge is *vendicativo* – revengeful.

Much of Pirandello's drama, it begins to appear, has been a revenge on life – and on the theater and its audience, which never, it seemed to him, fully appreciated his excellence. Well, they would be sorry. In naked letters to Marta Abba, recently published, he complained bitterly of Italy's failure to accept his ideas for a national theater, Italy's failure to applaud all his work. Of the unfavorable reception of *Lazarus*, he cried out, with adolescent self-pity:

What can I do about it? I cannot think of anything I have done to bring out this ill-feeling against me. I have worked. In one year I contributed four plays to the dramatic literature of my country. Time will tell if they are alive and vital: they will survive. And my country will have to live down the shame of having misunderstood them and of having treated me unjustly. But by now I am used to being insulted and it no longer hurts me.

When *Tonight We Improvise* opened in Berlin, part of the audience was violently against it – "the black envy of a gang of rascals, egged on by my ex-translator." Pirandello reports that most Germans thought the play wonderful; but he broods, sees himself the enduring, misunderstood hero:

You see how right I had been to feel worried. ... Last night I thought I was back in Italy. Everywhere I am pursued by hatred. Perhaps it is only right that this should be so, that I should die this way, annihilated by the hatred of triumphant cowards, by the incomprehension of idiots. After all they are the majority. The catcalls of idiots and of my enemies would not hurt me if my spirit were still what it used to be. But I have lost the pride of my isolation, the love of my disconsolate sadness. ... My two staring eyes remain inexorably fixed, despairing, proud, tired, heavy-lidded with a pain that no one will ever be able to understand or know. A great absolute immobility.

To the end of his life he was working out his revenge on a world that treated him so. In his last year, he wrote Marta Abba, "Mankind does not deserve anything, stubborn as it is in its constantly growing stupidity, in its brutal quarrelsomeness." So the play he was writing when he died, *The Mountain Giants*, was to tell "the tragedy of poetry forced to exist in the midst of the brutal modern world." It is, in fact, a shadowy, symbolic allegory of the betrayal of a great poet-playwright's art by lesser beings. The poet has died because of this unrequited love for a Countess, a beautiful woman, married, an actress. She is now inspired to spread his drama widely, to ensure him his deserved immortality. She comes, with her husband and her acting company, to a strange way station: a place where, in a kind of half-light of fantasy, a colony lives "on the border of life": its people, headed by a magician, Cotrone, seem to be able to escape into the timeless world of imagination. They "invent the truth." Their very dreams come to life, and their life turns into dreams. The only reality is spiritual; the world is illusion; the body only a mask of constantly changing identity; "Woe unto him who sees himself in his own body and with his own name." Cotrone tries to persuade the Countess that the only place where the poet's art can be eternal is in this timeless, unreal place. But she insists on an audience, and he finds her one.

It will be the Giants of the Mountain, the dwellers in the highest places. If the play is fit for the Gods, the Gods must see it. But the artist can expect no such luck in this world. At the last moment, the Giants decide to send their servants instead. The Countess and Cotrone find themselves giving a subtle message to noisy workmen who want only their usual riotous entertainment. These uncouth spectators, exasperated by the beauty they cannot understand, destroy the Countess and tear her defenders to pieces. It is not the poet who has failed, but the actors and the audience: the first, the "slaves of art," have not known how to communicate it to the second, the "slaves of life"; have not yet prepared them for spiritual things. The poet has no chance unless he is served better.

The escape of the poet from the unappreciating world into a dream retreat like Cotrone's was an old yearning of Pirandello's; in 1929, when he was first beginning to think out his revengeful *Giants*, he wrote a starkly revealing letter to Marta Abba:

Never have I wished for insanity as much as I do now. Only insanity can give what fate has denied. Riches, happiness, ... For the insane, the possession of wealth is not an illusion, nor is the fulfillment of their wishes unreal. They have achieved happiness. The "child" that a poor mad mother is nursing may be made of common rags. What does it matter? From that rag she really receives all the joys of mother-hood, and woe to him who takes it from her! It would be the most cruel of cruelties to say to her: "Wake up, you are dreaming!" When we sleep, all of us are insane. But in the insane the state of sleep continues even when their senses are awake.

I don't know why, as I am sitting here, musing, these thoughts have come to me. ... Perhaps because these days – I don't know what it depends on – I am experiencing something rare for me: the pleasure and anguish of dreaming. How wonderful it is *to take one's revenge* [my italics], while asleep, on the feelings of shame and on the sense of logic that plague one during the day.

Revenge, again. Why did Pirandello dream so warmly of getting even with life, why fondle, so often, the joys of madness?[3] How much of his dark mood can be blamed on his heritage – on the somber climate of feudal-ism, feudism, and violence of his Sicilian birthplace? How much of it was the product merely of the Italian fashion of moody, grotesque drama that Pirandello had inherited, and was exploiting? How much of his anger at life came from his own suffering? Surely he had had his share of troubles: He had been thrust from prosperity into poverty when the family business failed; his wife went mad, was hysterically jealous, and yet he kept her with him for years (While he felt how much envy? How much guilt?). When he became successful as a writer he was not invariably successful, and the critics sometimes handled him roughly. He could see with a painful clarity the hypocrisy and self-deception of man; he was agonizedly aware of the inner buffetings of impulse, of passion, of shame, of hate for the "logic" of sanity. But he himself insisted, in his *Six Characters* preface, that the personal torment he was expressing "had nothing to do with the drama of my personal experience." And certainly other artists have suffered as much from life: have been poor, have had mad wives or endured other family disasters, have been attacked by critics, have seen man and them-selves too close. Probably others have used art for revenge, too, though it is more likely that the purpose was not consciously known: for the fanta-sies of art, like those of dream work, may only help covertly to manage the anguish experienced by the unconscious. What distinguishes Pirandello is that, sensitive as he was to the revenge motif, he could not get a perspec-tive on his own experience of it, or of his own relationship with life. Consider some of his contemporaries in the drama, other troubled men facing the problem of man's self-deception: Ibsen, dealing with characters who must live by a "life-lie"; Shaw, with his "onslaught on idealism" – on the phony, lip-service ideals men devise to disguise reality; O'Neill, the poet of the "pipe-dream." For these artists, the limited contexts in which men move were not unassailable: there is the sense that a wider context might be discerned, if man would struggle for it.

This is still a remove from the tragic drama of the ultimate context; where a God, or fate, or some other absolute force defines the limits of man's knowing, and he strives futilely against a barrier of power or darkness. Once given the notion that no absolute barrier exists, that man, imperfectly knowing, can yet know a little more, a little more, and there is no end to the struggle, even if it is doomed to failure. The "new" psychology that presented Pirandello with his questions also supplied the answer – if the Gestalt is confused and changing, if the psyche turns on itself and others out of ignorance of malformation, a passion for understanding may clarify figure and ground, may bring a perception of the self-defeating, distorting mechanisms. There is still room here for the strife and scope of tragedy: the enemy of the not-yet-known can be as worthy an opponent as the fated, and a tragic error in this unremitting battle as fateful. A struggle for conscious understanding is irrelevant for Expressionist – or extreme Absurdist – dramas, which are concerned with reflecting inward confusion and turbulence, and which indeed regard consciousness – the attempt to impose order on inwardness – as the ultimate absurdity; but the form and content of Pirandello's drama lead directly to a challenge to conscious effort to resist the irrational. Where the anti-naturalistic forms necessarily turned inward from realism, to suggest felt like symbolically, Pirandello held almost always to a drama of hard, realistic life, in which subconscious torments were consciously perceived; he achieved his great ironies precisely by showing how consciousness is endangered by illusion – the illusion of self-deception, of projection, of social fashion, of the theater. But he never gave consciousness a chance to engage on its own terms. In the outer life of the world Pirandello had been most wronged; and in the pursuit of his vendetta it was this life which he had to demean, sometimes by comparing it unfavorably with art, sometimes with madness.

The effect was a shortcoming in the art as well as the man. Consider, as an example, the unsatisfying *Right You Are*. The two sets of "truth" about the identity of Signora Ponza – is she wife or daughter? – are cleverly paraded, but the dilemma is of course not as unsolvable as Pirandello wishes it to seem. In the audience, the human passion for closure – for completing an unfinished Gestalt by finding and filling in the pertinent, missing details – demands a test of the dilemma by "reality." But the playwright won't have this: and to avoid it, he must diminish his play. The ambiguous Signora Ponza, like Pirandello's other heroines who are content to accept their identity from others' projections, *is*, as she proclaims, a *nobody* – a nobody as a dramatic character and also a nobody as a reflection of human personality because she has forfeited the search for an ego which, however uncertain, is man's eternal task. She is in fact engaged in a charade of madness with the other two: Pirandello's joke that it is the "normal" people who do not understand her double identity begins to wear thin as this motif is clearly seen. We do not understand because the conspirators in her "illusion" are abetting *insanity*. They are refusing the responsibility of conscious reason. And when, at the curtain, Laudisi, Pirandello's spokesman for his madness, prevents any disclosure, and "With a look of derisive defiance at them all ... bursts out laughing," there is a momentary, terrible perception that this play is indeed the product of a mind that could consider preferring madness to the hard struggle for understanding.

Since Pirandello's overruling irony demands that his characters in these "who-am-I" plays forsake the search for their own egos, and submit to the identities impressed on them, there is almost never a showdown, the dramatic struggle simply evaporates. Unless there is a miracle, the characters who tentatively seek individuality must give up, and return to their given personalities – as The Unknown in *As You Desire Me* goes back to her soiled life with Salter. Perhaps the most significant of these surrenders is that of the author-hero of the late play *When Someone Is Someone*. This is probably the most explicit of Pirandello's revenges on life. This hero is so depersonalized an image of fame that his name is given simply as three asterisks: ***. Presumably he is a great poet. In his maturity, he has discovered a new creative identity, and, from the inspiration of a beautiful young woman (perhaps another disguise for Marta Abba) is writing, under a pseudonym, vigorous young verse that has excited and rallied the new generation. But before his double identity can be revealed, family, friends, publisher, the state join to make him deny the radical new poetry. Can the old poet break loose from his pattern, and affirm growth and change? Here, if ever, the struggle for identity might assume cosmic dimensions: even if the poetic spirit is doomed in this prison-world, it can at least beat against the bars. But there is no struggle at all: the artist peevishly accepts the social jail he finds himself inhabiting. "I can't be 'myself'! I mustn't be 'myself'!" Again, this is a hero who is really a "nobody" – he has no "self" either as a character or a person. He has allowed himself to be encapsulated in an image of a great poet as if – Pirandello suggests – this is inevitable; of course it is not. Examine this "great poet" of Pirandello's: he does not, in fact, seem to have poetry in him, he has himself chosen this stuffy wife, raised this conventional family, submitted to this conformist social environment; he has chosen to hide his new poetry under an assumed name; and as he lives without distinctive grace and dignity – and without striving – he accepts the living death of a socially conferred identity. "Look what life did to me," he seems to say, as he lies in the bed he has made for himself.

Pirandello exploits the revenge theme in reverse in *Diana and Tuda*. Here the playwright's spokesman, Giuncano, feels so guilty about shaping experience in the fixed form of sculpture that he "revenges" life by destroying his statues (again the verb is *vendicare*). He exults in a kind of animal "madness" that has freed him from the labor of art. But, as he is growing old, he knows he will soon be trapped anyway in the fixity of death. There is no way out. He too wants everything – not as a vast dreamer or striver wants them, but as does a frustrated dabbler in wish fulfillment.

Because Pirandello is so powerful a playwright, his drama sometimes has betrayed his philosophy. Thus in *Six Characters*, the contrast, so important to him, of the immortality of the Characters as against the transience of the "real" people – the actors – dissolves in the heat of the play. Once the Characters are in action, they are not perceived as eternals, but as if, like most other persons of drama, they are "real" people involved in terrible human problems. They are once seem more "real" than the actors, because only they are engaged in an intense, determined struggle for identity. It is the actors who turn out not to have the "reality" of being; while the Characters, in their urgency, and in the sense – as soon as their flashbacks begin – of their struggling in the present, absorb audiences in an experience of a continuing life action; and this experience accumulates up to the climactic shooting at the end. The attempt by Pirandello to cancel out with irony this mounting linear crisis fails because the Characters are too "life-like"; the audience, attuned to the transience of existence, understands too well how decisive the deeds of men can be, and it feels the Characters' crucial moments to be fateful. This is the more so because of the shallow stereotypes of the presumably "real" actors: and this leads to the perception of how very crudely Pirandello stacks his cards against these "real" stage people in all his "theatre-versus-life" plays. It is the "actors" who always become, in fact, the "eternal" stock types of hack art, in their superficial, almost caricatured outlines. As in *Six Characters*, so, in other plays, they are *nobodies,* no more than their labels: "Actors and actresses" in *Each in His Own Way,* "The old character man," "The character woman," etc. in *Tonight We Improvise.*[4] In these latter plays, too, the "characters" take on the dimensions of life in action, become "real" people, force the audience to share in the urgency of their search for identity, in the significance of their struggles of existence. Their "lifelikeness" gives them meaning. So life resists Pirandello's revenge.

The persistence of the feud in the playwright's mature period is most significant. Recall that in *Six Characters* the Father in particular, Pirandello said, expressed his own torment. The essential fact about the Father is his eternal reliving of an ugly experience that commands endless remorse. Again and again, the agony of this experience is to be repeated. This is a dramatic parable of the obsessive neurosis at work: the compulsive return to a fixated experience by a mind that cannot free itself for new experience. This explains, I think, the repetitiveness in Pirandello's work, the failure to advance in concept and vision, that has troubled his warmest admirers. He returned again and again to prod a psychic sore.

The limitations of Pirandello's conceptions of art were also apparent in his conception of living. He was not simply pessimistic; he bore a grudge against the human condition. There was not enough homage in life for him: ergo, this was life's fault; he took it as a personal insult. "My country will have to live down the shame ... of having treated me unjustly" – because it did not admire one of his poorer plays. It first here that Pirandello, who could speak so arrogantly of the "brutality" of man (that is, of his enemies) could also – alone among contemporary artists near the first rank – publicly adore the bully Mussolini, and openly champion Fascism, that terrible war by organized brutality against the free spirit. It was Pirandello who offered his Nobel Prize to be melted into weapons for Mussolini's spectacular brutality against Ethiopia. Pirandello complained privately against Fascism – only because it did not admire him enough. "Mankind does not deserve anything ..." he wrote, as if he could abdicate membership – and all the while he was looking at mankind in a mirror: his "fixed, despairing, proud, tried, heavy-lidded" eyes stared into the dark part of himself. He could have found a better reflection in that Pirandello who, despite the torments of life, struggled on like other men and did indeed impose a pattern of both life and art; who, by showing man the jungle of illusion, opened a way to find paths in it. But self-pity is a great distorter of perception. The ultimate irony is that this artist, who seemed to understand so keenly how man's perspectives can be limited by illusion, how projections and self-involvement distort personality, how men defend themselves against reality, should himself be unable to see clearly in his mirror.

NOTES

1 The "soiled woman" ennobled by childbirth – and ennobling others – also motivates *Either of One or No One* and *Better than Before*.

2 A similar magic transformation of a mock marriage into a real one occurs in *It Is Only in Jest*. In *Other People's Point of View* a marriage is held together when the barren wife takes her husband's mistress's child; in *Grafting* when the husband accepts the child begotten on his wife by a rapist.

3 As in *Henry IV* and *As You Desire Me*.

4 The irony beyond Pirandello's irony is that in the final reality the "real" characters and the "unreal" actors are both represented by the professional actors, who as artists made it possible for him to achieve both kinds of effects he aimed at.

Each in His Own Way – Ciascuno a suo modo
Six Characters in Search of an Author – Sei personaggi in cerca d'autore
Right You Are If You Think You Are – Cosi è (se vi pare)
Henry IV – Enrico Quarto
The Life I Gave You – La vita che ti diedi
Naked – Vestire gli ignudi
The Rules of the Game – Il gioco delle parti
As You Desire Me – Come tu mi vuoi
When Someone Is Someone – Quando si è qualcuno
The Pleasure of Honesty – Il piacere dell' onesta
Liola – Liolà
The New Colony – La nuova colonia
Lazarus – Lazzaro
The Wife's Friend – L'amici delle mogli
Either of One or No One – O di uno o di nessuno
As Well as Before. Better than Before – Come prima, meglio di prima
It is only in Jest – Ma non è un cosa seria
Other Peoples' Point of View – La ragione degli altri
Grafting – L'Innesto
Tonight we Improvise – Questa sera si recita a soggetto
The Mountain Giants – I giganti della montagna
Diana and Tuda – Diana e la Tuda

Pirandellian Theatre Games:
Spectator as Victim

J.L. STYAN

Pirandello has a good deal in common with Molière: his results are so thought-provoking that he is discussed first as a philosopher when he is very much of a *farceur*.[1] I have chosen the word carefully, and use it in the sense of "practical joker."[2] And his methods seem to encourage directors to take liberties of their own. Those interested in the story of his success on the stage point to the sensational production of *Six Characters in Search of an Author* when it was directed by Georges Pitoëff at the Théâtre des Champs-Élysées in 1923. By that time the Paris audience was moderately accustomed to the shocks and surprises of a symbolist and surrealist drama. 1917 had seen Apollinaire's *The Breasts of Tiresias*, in which the rebellious feminist wore red and blue balloons for bosoms, and let them fly on strings before exploding them. 1921 saw Cocteau's *The Wedding on the Eiffel Tower*, also at the Théâtre des Champs-Élysées, a play flaunting two music-hall compères dressed as gramophones and a set like a camera: on the command, "Watch the birdie!", an ostrich stepped out.

But in 1923, the actors in *Six Characters* did worse yet: they entered in their everyday clothes and walked through the auditorium. They had invaded the province of the audience, breaking the comfortable rule of nineteenth-century theatre that actors should know their place. And when they climbed on the stage, there was nothing on it. Neither Apollinaire nor Cocteau had thought of being as surrealistic as *that*. Then came the sensation. When it was the moment for the six Characters to enter, they were flooded with a green light and lowered to the stage in an old cage-lift, a stage elevator previously used for scenery. Pitoëff had had a bright idea, Paris went wild, and Pirandello was honored by the French government.

This remarkable event could be viewed in different ways. Was it simply a stunt, another touch of Dada, and therefore too irrational to warrant explanation? Were characters to be regarded as pieces of scenery? Was there some profound philosophical implication that the imagination had forsaken standards of objective reality? It was certainly not symbolism, which Pirandello hated: he believed that the mechanical shape imposed on a symbolist play could destroy its spontaneity, and in 1925 he wrote to the *Virginia Quarterly Review* insisting that *Six Characters* was conceived in a moment of untrammelled illumination.[3] Nor was the director trying to suggest that the Characters were descending from supernatural spheres – in any case, the creaking machinery would have ruined any etherial quality.

There was absolutely no illusion about their entrance at all, and in her recent book Anne Paolucci has argued persuasively that the trick made a complete breach in theatre tradition.[4] Well, it was a time for complete breaches, and attempts had been made before to burst out of the dramatic frame and abolish the conventions of the proscenium arch. Max Reinhardt had alarmed the London audiences watching his *Oedipus Rex* in 1912 by having his huge crowd of supers, made up of battalions of drama students and boy scouts, surge through the auditorium, up the aisles and over a gangway built over the seats. If Greek decorum was somewhat forgotten, the audience was quite overwhelmed, and *Punch* had a delicious drawing of the terrible predicament which awaited the unfortunate spectator who arrived late and was swept down the aisle by a forest of Theban spears.

Nevertheless, the required response to seeing some actors lowered in an old stage elevator was, "Look, they're lowering some actors in an old stage elevator." The effect was a disarming way of saying at the outset that here was a play which was not going to deal in illusion, but simply *investigate* it, without trying to deceive the audience. This of course is more easily said than done, as Brecht was to discover. For an audience likes nothing so much as to be deceived and to believe what it sees. I once produced *Waiting for Godot*, and when it came time for the moon to rise over Beckett's virtually empty set, I lowered a round piece of cardboard on a piece of very obvious string – a very non-illusory moon indeed. The audience was upset that I had spoiled the illusion, even though any was of its own making. But in no time at all the audience accepted my cardboard moon, and damned illusion set in again. Now Pirandello considered that his play was "a sustained satire" on all such romanticism.

Pirandellian drama was working a fresh vein of theatre, one which would nowadays be explained as "metatheatre": theatre which makes its audience conscious of the theatre's own element in order to work. In

L'umorismo Pirandello had insisted that comedy must make us "perceive the opposite," and that humor must make us "*feel* the opposite."[5] But in that provocative essay he was writing as a theorist. The problem for Pirandello the practical theatre artist was to find a way to *make* us perceive and feel the opposite. There is all the difference in the world between reading a recipe for *spaghetti bolognais* and actually eating it. It is precisely the difference between the philosopher and the *farceur*. Pirandello's plays may investigate the act of artistic creation, or the human personality, or the existence of the individual will, or the incidence of truth and reality, but his achievement as a playwright turns on his ability to make an audience *experience* these good things.

To make each member of his audience a Pirandellian humorist, he contrived to make us see that the other side of tragedy is farce, that when you have peeled an onion there is nothing left but tears, that a life of chance is a terrifying thing. If Cleopatra's nose had been larger, he wondered, who knows what might have happened to the history of the world? That little "if" became part of Pirandello's stage practice. It had nothing to do with Stanislavsky's "magic if." Pirandello's theatrical "if" was used like a question mark, Stanislavsky's like a commandment. Pirandello's "if" inspired the conflicting accounts of sanity and insanity in *It Is So! (If You Think So)* in 1916 – they deceive the audience as much as the towns-people. It inspired his masterpieces, *Six Characters* written in three weeks in 1921, *Henry IV* written in two in 1922. In his remarkable preface to *Six Characters*, written long after the play had proved itself on the interna-tional stage, Pirandello thought of his imagination as a "nimble little maidservant called Fantasy," a creature who was a little puckish and malicious. He claimed that she had unloaded on him a whole family who would not go away. She was his way of stretching his audience's perception of the human condition.

To make a point about the "if" in *Henry IV*: I strongly suspect that any performance of this play should make us suffer the same fluctuations of belief and disbelief about Henry's sanity as the on-stage audience suffers. But most productions and nearly all accounts of the play imply that the audience soon learns that he has recovered his senses after twelve years, and that he has devoted the rest of the time to teasing his servants and visitors for his own pleasure. So it was in the first production of the play in New York at the Forty-fourth street Theatre in 1924, when Henry was played by Arnold Korff with laryngitis and a strong Viennese accent (known in the trade as "slurred delicatessen"). The *New York Times* reported: "Throughout the long first act and a large part of the second, the simple reality of the situation in hand is hidden from the audience, and indeed from all the people on the stage with the exception of this 'Henry IV' himself. The result is a tedium of meaningless situations and seemingly superfluous disquisition. Surely the interest of the evening can only gain by disclosing the central, significant *fact*."[6] Clearly, the reviewer was in no doubt that Henry was sane. The *Tribune* speculated whether Henry was cured or merely convalescent, even if it did not much care which: "It is disclosed that the gorgeous imbecile regards himself as of sound mind, whether he is or not. ... At the end he kills [the man] responsible for his accident. Since that character seemed last night to be the most lucid in the cast, his judgment may be taken as authoritative. As they dragged him, dying, from the throne-room, he shouted, 'He is not mad! He is not mad!'" This review at least leaves the case for insanity open. The assumption that Henry is really sane implies that the role of the audience is merely that of *voyeur*, watching him getting up to his tricks, an assumption which distorts the performance. But this is to deny Pirandello the extraordinary achievement in this play of matching the action on the stage with the secret doubts of the audience, the very technique which creates the dialectic by which our feelings must contradict themselves. If we believe Henry to be sane, the play is effectively over for us.

And why should we believe that Henry is sane? Only because he says so. Is then a madman sane because he says he is? – no more than a sane man is mad because *he* says so. Especially if he is only a *character*. This is the familiar conundrum of "All statements in this square are false," or of "Brothers and sisters have I none, but this man's father is my father's son."

Here is the line by which Henry apparently announces to his servants that he is sane: "Can't you see how I handle them, how I fool them, make them appear before me just as I wish?" But when they laugh at this, he brings them to their knees with a voice of thunder, the emperor's voice, the voice of a madman. I suggest that not even Henry's clever servants are sure he is sane, for what is the dividing line between anger and insanity? He certainly *looks* insane with his grotesque white face and the clown-like red spots on his cheeks, his pathetic attempts to restrain the ravages of time. And he doubts his grip on reality in that terrifying moment in the half-light when Frieda speaks his name from the frame of her mother's portrait: "Henry! ... " The voice should not, of course, sound like that of a suburban housewife calling her husband. When Henry kills Belcredi at the end, it surely is the act of a madman, an act committed when he has lost control. So that when Henry finally announces to the world that he is trapped for the rest of time, the audience is simultaneously being told that, however many times it goes to the play, it will never know whether Henry was sane or not.

The effect is that of the familiar Pirandellian curtain laugh, that of Laudisi and the Step-daughter. By being forced to sustain such doubts, we are ourselves to know a little of what it is like to be prisoners of the mind and victims of time.[7] Forty years later, Samuel Beckett was to take up the analogous theme of the compulsion of birth and death, that we neither want to come into the world, nor want to leave it once we are here. In Richard Coe's words, we are never free, unless it is the freedom to crawl east on a boat travelling west.

Like any *farceur*, Pirandello works hard to manipulate the responses of his audience by tricks and surprises. His most successful moments are those when the stage succeeds in asserting total control. In *Six Characters*, one of his concerns is to startle us with the suggestion (later picked up by Harold Pinter) that only creatures of fiction are likely to know what they are. Other people are like Pirandello himself when he noted in horror that "Someone is living my life, and I don't know a thing about him." So he tries to bring his audience to a belief that fictional characters can be more real than live actors, even when the actors apparently belong to our world.

The achievements of the milliner's shop scene lies in that. The fictional Father and Step-daughter are to perform with all Ibsenite earnestness, on the most profound level of realism the players are capable of. Then, "without seeming false in any way," as Pirandello's direction insists, the Leading Man and the Leading Lady are simply to repeat their words. A brilliant device! No matter how well they act, they must *always* seem false. The plain fact is that when you imitate someone, it always sounds as if you are putting him down. And even if the difference is only slight, to perceive it is to be convinced that the copy is wrong. Such inevitability was another of Pirandello's tricks, and the pain of the Father and the Step-daughter had inevitably to give way to laughter.

To top this, Pirandello makes devilish use of the customary prompter of the period, as the revised version of 1925 insists. The prompter presumably reads all the lines in a high-pitched monotone as if from his box downstage center. The Actors come in a fraction of a second behind him, giving the unreal effect of an echo, thus: "Good afternoon, Miss / afternoon, Miss." Then the Actors say the wretched lines yet again, till all feeling is drained from them. Clearly knowing what he was doing, Pirandello went one better than this, and had the Director himself jump up to demonstrate how to speak the lines in that over-emphatic way teachers adopt when they are trying to get a point across – the method travellers use abroad when they do not know the language: the rule is to say it again, only louder. This bit of business was expanded in 1925, so that the audience hears the lines of the milliner's shop scene spoken in four different tones, each sounding worse than the last. Criticism of the art of the theatre is built into the arrangement, and the audience is forced to conclude – not consciously, of course – that the Actors are of little account.

We should look again at the deception with which the play begins. The audience comes into the theatre, and seeing a rehearsal in progress, is to assume it is still in the real world it has just left outside the theatre. The tactic was apparently so successful in Rome in 1921, and after Kommissarjevsky tried it in London in 1922, and Brock Pemberton in New York the same year, and Pitoëff in Paris in 1923, and Reinhardt in Berlin in 1924, that the author continued to introduce new devices. The changes he wrote into the final version of 1925 were, however, not superficial gimmicks, but fundamental structural improvements chosen to manipulate the audience. Because of the virtual monopoly in America of Edward Storer's ill-written 1921 version,[8] the one enshrined in Eric Bentley's *Naked Masks*, many non-Italian commentators seem unaware of the changes made.

The revision begins with the hammering of nails into wood as the stage crew goes about its work. There is nothing more mundane than the sound of a hammer. It quite dispels any magic we associate with an evening in the theatre and it positively blunts the edge of our anticipation. Then not only do the Actors enter casually from the back of the house, the world of the audience itself, but after the play seems to have got under way, the Leading Lady enters down the aisle with her pet dog. By 1925, the Characters also enter from the house, led in by the Doorman, and whereas in the first version they stand in a "tenuous light" to suggest their origin in fantasy, in 1925 Pirandello recommended that they wear light masks. This device is never seen nowadays because, as I believe, it inhibits the audience's subsequent ability to believe in the reality of the Characters. When the play was given John Houseman's television treatment,[9] with the Characters popping up on a screen-within-a-screen, I felt that any hope of distinguishing between real and unreal was pretty slim.

The moment when Mme Pace enters unannounced as the seventh Character afforded another chance to develop the teasing. The Actors no longer stood back stupefied, but in fear rushed wildly off the stage into the auditorium, so by physical association encouraging the audience's own uncertainty. All this suggests that Pirandello was aware, well ahead of his time, that to break out of the proscenium arch was to induce a new level of dramatic experience. When playing the Emperor Charlemagne, Artaud once alarmed his teacher Charles Dullin by approaching his throne on all fours. Dullin tried to hint that the performance was a shade too stylized, whereupon Artaud reared up crying, "Oh, so it's realism you want!" Artaud went on to produce Vitrac's *The Mysteries of Love* in 1927 by starting the performance in a stage box to encourage audience participation, and he fired a gun at the audience as Pitoëff had done in *Six Characters*. Like Pirandello, Artaud wanted to engulf his audience.

Soon after this, Erwin Piscator was turning his loudspeakers and searchlights on his audience. He thought of his theatre as a "play-machine," and his promptbook was like a manual for engineers. "The playhouse itself," Piscator wrote, "is made to dissolve into the shifting, illusory space of the imagination." This was heady stuff, but the intoxicating point is that all those years ago Pirandello was making his contribution to the current theatre of the environmentalists.

The greatest trick in the *Six Characters* of 1925 was to extend the shock ending. In the revision, Pirandello did not disclose the fate of the two children until the last possible moment. In this way, the drowning of the little Girl and the suicide of the Boy came as a complete surprise, so that their unreality was left far more in question. When the Director called for lights, Pirandello did not allow the curtain to fall. He calculated that at such a moment, when an audience was on the point of returning to its familiar reality, at a moment of total ambivalence, the play had it most in its grip. The theatre was immediately flooded with light as if some supernatural hand had suddenly pulled the switch. No gentle raising of the lights to ease us back into reality, but, still using the element of theatre, a plunge into another reality. The device was repeated when the Director called yet again for the lights to be switched off: the sudden and immediate blackout was shocking and uncanny.

When the Director was finally given some light, it was an unexpected green flood which made the Characters into bizarre silhouettes. But only *four* of the six. The Girl and the Boy were dead, and now they were missing, as if they were really dead. At this point, the four Characters advanced to the front of the stage (like the inmates of Charenton) and stopped. But not the Step-daughter. She burst into strident laughter and ran up the aisle through the audience. At the back of the house she paused, turned and laughed again. Finally, she swept through the foyer and out into the street beyond, laughing all the way. Only then did Pirandello allow his audience to leave. Unfortunately, the audience was obliged to go out the same way.

We talk a little glibly about metatheatre, perhaps – Lionel Abel's notion[10] that Hamlet was the first character to know that someone was writing a play about him, although, of course, the Prince was rather anxious about the way the plot would turn out. As the audience in a metadrama, we however tend to be one jump ahead. Now Pirandello spoiled all that. He showed us that illusion is not only inseparable from the reality, but often *is* the reality. So it is that at the center of life we find fantasy, and so it is that all the world's a stage. We may well wonder whether metaplaywrights like Jean Genêt and Tom Stoppard, indeed the whole metacritical industry, could have got under way without Pirandello. As we know, *Six Characters* was at first criticized because at the end the Characters seemed more real than the Actors, fiction more real than life, and it appeared that chaos reigned. But Pirandello's claim was that his insights were "the very opposite of chaotic":[11] to be able to shake up his audience and his critics represented a triumph of art over life, and of the playwright over his chosen art.

NOTES

1 This paper was read to the Pirandello Society at the convention of the Modern Language Association of America, San Francisco, December 28, 1979.

2 One thinks of Molière's *L'Impromptu de Versailles* as his Pirandellian play.

3 "Pirandello Confesses ... Why and How He Wrote *Six Characters in Search of an Author*," trans. Leo Ongley, *Virginia Quarterly Review*, 1 (April 1925): "I hate symbolic art, for it makes a mechanical structure" (38); "The play was conceived in one of those moments of illumination when the imagination acts with untrammelled spontaneity" (43).

4 *Pirandello's Theatre: The Recovery of the Modern Stage for Dramatic Art* (Carbondale, Ill., 1974), p. 2.

5 See Pirandello, *On Humor*, trans. Antonio Illiano and Daniel P. Testa (Chapel Hill, N.C., 1974).

6 January 22, 1924, p. 15.

7 A few years later, the theatrical devilry of *Tonight We Improvise* proved that Pirandello was capable of trying to deceive his audience totally.

8 First published in *Three Plays* in 1923. Frederick May's translation of the 1925 version was published in London in 1954 but not made available in the United States. This version was reprinted in my collection *The Challenge of the Theatre* (Encino, California, 1972), now out of print.

9 Adapted Paul Avila Mayer, produced Norman Lloyd, directed Stacy Keach for the Hollywood Television Theatre, 1976. We may wonder whether this is "metatelevision."

10 *Metatheatre: A New View of Dramatic Form* (New York, 1963), p. 58.

11 *Virginia Quarterly Review, op. cit.,* 51.

An Author in Search of Characters: Pirandello and Commedia dell'arte

JAMES FISHER

We Italians "enjoyed" the industrial revolution after a long time-lag. So we are not yet a sufficiently modern nation to have forgotten the ancient feeling for satire. That is why we can still laugh, with a degree of cynicism, at the macabre dance which power and the civilisation that goes with it performs daily, without waiting for carnival.[1]

Commedia dell'arte was the rarest of theatrical forms – a non-literary theatre that emphasized the skill of the improvising actor. Commedia actors transformed human frailty into incisive satire as they literally created a play before the audience's eyes from a simple scenario. The popularity of commedia grew over the centuries as the forms and characters it inspired evolved, supplying diverse and delightful entertainments throughout Europe's theatres. In many cultures, these commedic forms offered a style of ritualized carnival – a popular street theatre that served not only as communal fun, but also as a political instrument through its ever present satire and mockery of the powerful. This seemingly casual and lowly form of theatre became a distinctly powerful *lingua franca* of the imagination, connecting cultures and artists throughout Europe. Like the best and rarest forms of theatre, commedia was both spiritual and intellectual. It proved to be universally malleable and national, adapting in each country where it appeared to the needs of that culture's artists and audiences.

Although some nineteenth century dramatists, artists, composers, and writers had been drawn to commedia characters and images, at the beginning of the twentieth century, almost simultaneously, a diverse group of playwrights, actors, directors, and designers rediscovered commedia in ways that would permanently change the direction of the modern theatre.

Edward Gordon Craig, Vsevolod Meyerhold, Max Reinhardt, and Jacques Copeau, among many others, sought liberation from the pervasiveness of Realism, as well as from the stale remnants of elaborate spectacles, over-wrought melodramas, and stilted acting styles of the preceding century. Perhaps due to the lack of concrete literary and performance evidence, these artists had highly individual and, at times, distinctly contradictory notions about commedia. Their understanding of its spirit and traditions permitted their rich imaginations wide scope as they attempted to define commedia. Most of them viewed it as an amalgam of elements from traditional Italian commedia, as well as its many commedic antecedents and derivatives: classical comedy, medieval jesters and farces, the comedies of Molière, the Venetian plays of Goldoni, the *fiabe* of Gozzi, Pierrot[2] in the tradition of Deburau, pantomimes, music hall, circus, carnival, street entertainments of all kinds, and the variety stage. Significantly, they redis-covered improvisation, masks, stereotypical characters, and movement through their understanding of commedia. They also noted the centrality of the commedia actor who, aided by masks, could rise above realistic illusion to create larger-than-life and universal human symbols. The improvisatory commedia style, with its buoyant energy and direct assault on the senses of its audience, had virtually no parallel in modern theatre.

These twentieth century iconoclasts share the view that commedia is theatrical art at its pinnacle of expressiveness and creativity. Many of them were drawn toward a kind of archetypal Jungian vision which reduced and also transformed life into a handful of simple plots and stereotypical figures that confront us with spiritual and intellectual glimpses of our deepest beings. The characters of commedia thus became the expression of the universally human; to the modern mind the characters' magic was powerful because it was a kind of street psychology, revealing directly who we humans are. Particularly in the character of Arlecchino, the leading *zanni* of commedia, modern theatre found a model in which to embody an absurdly lyrical vision of contemporary humanity, leading ultimately to such varied creations as Charlie Chaplin's "Little Tramp," Beckett's and Ionesco's existential clowns, Handke's Kaspar, and the explosion of post-modern clowns and new vaudevillians in recent years.

The rediscovery of commedia by Craig, Meyerhold, Reinhardt, Copeau, and their similarly inclined contemporaries, energized a new theatri-cal revolution, moving the theatre away from Realism toward a new Theatricalism. More to the point, modern theatre seems to be in a state of perpetual revolution between various kinds of formal, controlled dialecti-cal drama and newer, increasingly theatricalized movements.

One of the leaders of this theatrical revolution was Italy's Luigi Pirandello, a playwright born of the very culture from which commedia had emerged. His earliest plays are written in dialect, and seem mostly inspired by Sicilian folk traditions; his final plays are highly symbolic, and untied to any particular traditions. His philosophical plays, written between 1917 and 1924, are his most acclaimed and are, among other things, his most commedia-inspired works. In these plays, he examines the contradictory, paradoxical, and absurd aspects of life, through a mixture of comic and tragic elements, emphasizing conflicts between appearance and reality, and between the comic mask and the tragic face hidden by it. In every seemingly real situation or statement that he makes, Pirandello plays out its opposite possibilities as well. Illusion and reality, madness and sanity are perceived by his characters and audiences to exist within the same space and time. In a sense, he was an Absurdist dramatist, viewing human beings as tragically ridiculous creatures making their way in a world of shadowy realities and values. The action in his plays often escalates a normal state of affairs onto a plane of intensified farce where truth and reality are illusive and incomprehensible at best.

Many scholars have touched on the influence of commedia dell'arte on Pirandello's earliest works, but few have given much credence to the notion that the traditions of improvised comedy had any truly significant impact on Pirandello's major plays. Recently, two scholars have published examinations of the relationship of commedia to Pirandello's plays. Antonio Alessio's "Pirandello and the commedia dell'arte," published in *The Science of Buffoonery: Theory and History of the Commedia dell'Arte* (1989), and Jennifer Lorch's "Pirandello, Commedia dell'Arte and Improvisation," published in *The Commedia dell'Arte from the Renaissance to Dario Fo* (1989), similarly argue that although Pirandello "was clearly fascinated by ideas about improvisation,"[3] he ultimately took "a totally opposite road to that of the *commedia dell'arte.*"[4] Lorch and Alessio note the pervasiveness of interest in commedia in early twentieth century European theatres, but both tend to limit most of their examination to how Pirandello used, or, more to the point, did not use improvisation. Alessio particularly rejects commedia as having any true significance in understanding Pirandello's plays. However, as suggested earlier, Pirandello's contemporaries, including Craig, Meyerhold, Reinhardt, and Copeau, among others, each began with uniquely contradictory notions of what commedia was and how it might be useful to the modern stage. Each was inspired as well by various later forms that had been, to varying degrees, spawned by commedia. Pirandello's view of commedia was, it seems, also highly individual, based less on a scholarly knowledge of commedia's history than on a basic and profoundly intuitive understanding of its characters, scenarios, and acting style. Placing extraordinary characters in absurd and densely complex situations with impossible resolutions delighted Pirandello. His plays, as commedia scenarios do, create surprising and fantastic situations that seem too complex to unravel. He manages a return to the ordinary through his magical ability to resolve the complicated contradictions and through flights into commedia-style farce. Pirandello's finest works are mature and polished *literary* achievements, not rough spontaneous commedia scenarios, yet he depends heavily on the skill of the athletic and improvisatory actor and an illusion of spontaneity, in true commedia fashion. *Right You Are, If You Think You Are* (1917), *Six Characters in Search of an Author* (1921), *Henry IV* (1922), and *Tonight We Improvise* (1929), will fall as flat as any uninspired commedia scenario in the hands of uninventive actors.

Pirandello hoped to introduce new methods of theatrical production in Italy similar to those he had discovered in other European cultures. He was fascinated by puppets, having been familiar with traditional Sicilian puppets since boyhood. He also advocated the use of actual masks, but, more often, employed stylized make-up and lighting effects instead of actual masks in his productions. The mask supplied him with a tangible symbol for the conflict between illusion and reality, the issue at the core of his plays. Masks were both protective and destructive to him, and they served as metaphors, as well as theatrical devices in his plays. To Pirandello, the mask was a disguise, a way of hiding or obscuring truth and creating a shifting sense of reality. Reality did not necessarily hide behind a single mask, for to Pirandello everything was masked: "Masks, they are all masks, a puff and they are gone, to make room for others masks."[5]

He admired such fellow commedists as "Reinhardt in Germany and Craig in England,"[6] but was less disposed toward the new scenic innovations of the day "which more or less overwhelms a work of art rather than defining it or realizing it completely."[7] He focused on a reform of acting that included experimentation with commedia performance techniques, especially improvisation. He saw the author, rather than the actor, as the true theatrical creator, despite his belief that "many bad plays have become excellent by what the actors have created and thus triumphed on stage!"[8] As Russian dramatist Nikolai Evreinov had, Pirandello developed a philosophy of theatricality which suggested that "it was not the actors who had invented the improvisations of the *Commedia dell'arte*, but it was the playwrights who had become actors, who had lost all their artistic ambitions and had become attracted by 'momentaneous' life."[9]

Pirandello strove to create an illusion of spontaneity and improvisation in the plays that he crafted with extreme care. He recognized, however, that "theater, before it is a traditional form of literature, is a natural expression of life,"[10] a grotesque carnival expressing both the madness and mystery of life. Looking to carnival traditions for inspiration, he observed the "many sad things"[11] the songs of the carnival "say to those who know how to read into them!"[12] His plays presented, in his own view, "new problems to be resolved,"[13] and were "built entirely upon live impressions, which have flashed before my imagination as an artist."[14]

In addition to these "live impressions," it seems that Pirandello, like other Italian theatrical artists, found commedia a potent resource. In 1908, he published his lengthy essay, "Humor," an early explication of this aesthetic principles, and of the diverse literary influences on his work. Noting that "Caricature, extravagant farce, and the grotesque are often mistaken for authentic humor,"[15] he examines the ironies, contradictions, and rhetoric of humor, along with a survey of Italian and international "humorists." Humor was not merely "a play of contrasts between the poet's ideal and reality,"[16] although

a great deal depends on the poet's temperament and that his ideal, confronted by reality, may react with indignation, or laughter, or compromise; but an ideal that compromises does not really show that it is sure of itself and profoundly rooted. And is this limitation of the ideal all that humor consists of? Not at all. The limitation of the ideal, if anything, would be not the cause but rather the result of the particular psychological process which is called humor.[17]

As the twentieth century's most philosophical commedist, Pirandello did not wish to confuse "comic spirit, irony, or satire with humor,"[18] but described humor as "an *eccentricity of style*."[19] In what may well be an allusion to the inherent humor of commedia, he explains that humor

originates out of a special state of mind, which can, to some degree, spread. When an artistic expression succeeds in dominating the attention of the public, the latter immediately begins to think, speak, and write in accordance with the impressions it has received; thus, such an expression, originating from the particular intuition of a writer, soon penetrates into the public and is then variously transformed and regulated by it.[20]

He cites an example of an old woman, whose face is grotesquely made-up and whose clothes are absurdly out of fashion. The old woman, a commedic pretender to youth, is *comic* in her belief that she can create an impossible illusion, but Pirandello finds *humor* in a *"perception of the opposite,"*[21] that the old woman may indeed be distressed by her appearance, shifting the observer's reaction to one of pity. Basically, he is interested in the character's complex and contradictory inner emotions which exist, often in conflict, with the outer appearance. This suggests one reason why commedia, with its masked characters (a comic mask hiding a character inside who is also doubled in perception), was of great significance to him.

Pirandello hardly mentions comic theatre or commedia itself in "Humor." Later, in his introduction to Silvio D'Amico's *The Italian Theatre,* commedia figures prominently in his essay, and he clearly identifies it as a significant force in his own drama, as well as that of his predecessors and contemporaries. Commedia, he writes, was born out of authors, like Ruzzante (Angelo Beolco), who "indulged their own personal tastes and ambitions,"[22] yet were acquainted with literary works. These authors were "so deeply involved in the Theater, in the life of the Theater, as to become, in fact, actors; who begin by writing the comedies they later perform, comedies at once more theatrical because not written in the isolated study of the man of letters,"[23] but in front of an actual audience. For Pirandello, it seemed absurd to imagine this as merely an accidental discovery of actors. The authors thus "lost all their serious artistic pretensions: the transitory, impassioned life of the Theater must have taken such full possession of them that the only interest left to them was that of the spectacle itself – a complete absorption in the quality of the performance and communication with the audience."[24] No longer an author, or even an actor, the figure onstage became a type, with a vivid stage life of its own. In essence, what remained in these characters for Pirandello "was their sheer movement."[25] They required order in his view, and each was assigned specific tasks with distinguishing dress and dialect, leading toward "some sort of intrigue within a more or less logical pattern of development which the classical forms, long emptied of their content, easily provided."[26]

Pirandello saw commedia as an inheritance of Roman comedy, as part of a tradition, and not as a national naive form as so many more sentimental commentators have seen it. By the time commedia had reached its peak, it had developed as "a quicker and more prudent way, certainly a more decisive way, of profiting from all the material of classical comedy,"[27] from the ancients through Ruzzante and his contemporaries. Commedia provided internationally acclaimed entertainment because the Italian theatre had, above all others, "drained the recovered classical world of all that it had to offer."[28] Pirandello claimed that the triumph of theatre throughout Europe during the Renaissance was a direct result of the influence of Italian theatre, especially commedia. Craig had credited the Italians with supplying the theatre with its true spirit, and Pirandello concurred, emphasizing that the plays of Shakespeare, Molière, Lope de Vega, and others, were outgrowths of

the Italian matrix. Molière alone was frank enough to admit: "*je prends mon bien où je le trouve*," in answer to those who remarked that perhaps he had gone too far in appropriating not only situations and characters but entire scenes from our *commedia dell'arte*; and he was right in shrugging off such remarks, considering the narrow point of view reflected in them. The truth is that all these great authors, these originators of the European Theater, had appropriated – without being aware of it – something quite different: the very spirit of our Theatre.[29]

He felt that literary history generally overlooked the importance of Italian Renaissance theatre and drama, undoubtedly due to the lack of traditional literary evidence, and he regretted "that the Italian theater, having reached at last the possibility of bringing forth a great author, should have given us, with Goldoni, simply a minor version of Molière."[30]

Yet, Pirandello did have considerable admiration for the plays of Goldoni, who he acknowledged was rightly recognized "for having relaxed the rigidity of the masks in their strained and artificial laughter and for having reanimated the now flexible muscles of the human face with the natural laughter of a life caught in the midst of the most vivacious and, at the same time, most exquisite and incomparably graceful activity."[31] Pirandello saw his own shattering of nineteenth century rigidities as similar to Goldoni's. Thus he shared Craig's view that although "Molière is purer Commedia dell'arte,' more genuine theatre of the grand and traditional manner, Goldoni is pure Italian comedy and of a little kind which has never been equalled: it is the best of its kind."[32]

Goldoni's most significant achievement, according to Pirandello, was more than just enlivening the fading characters of traditional commedia. Goldoni created new figures and transcended the old ones, "with an unapproachable facility, with an astounding lightness of touch,"[33] bringing to them "all the volubility, the fluidity, the contradiction, the spontaneity of life"[34] necessary to pave the way for the emergence of the contemporary theatre. He saw himself as a kindred spirit with Goldoni and commedia actors. Commedia had broken through the formality of Renaissance art forms, and Pirandello similarly attempted to break through the narrow bounds of the late nineteenth century stage. "Modernizing" theatrical traditions seemed appropriate to Pirandello, for whom theatre should never be archaeology but an ever renewing form in which "a work of art is no longer the work of the writer (which, after all, can always be preserved in some other way), but an act of life, realized on the stage from one moment to the next, with the cooperation of an audience that must find satisfaction in it."[35] Here Pirandello seems to empower the actor, the creator of the act, as in commedia tradition.

Pirandello believed that the contemporary Italian theatre succeeded where even the greatest of Europe's modern theatre had not, "in their greater realism and their greater fidelity to life"[36] and in the emergence "as in the *Commedia dell'arte*"[37] of "regional characters and forms of expression."[38] In a sense, the Italian theatre, through commedia, had rediscovered a "vast virgin world of the unexplored life of human personality,"[39] transforming the *maschere* of commedia into *maschere nude*, human characters minus the trappings of civilized behavior and social pretensions.

Pirandello's early plays most obviously demonstrate the influence of commedia and Italian folk traditions on his work. Most of these, including *Liolá* (1916), *Think It Over, Giacomino!* (1916), and *Cap and Bells* (1917), feature simple, stock comic situations with occasional elements of fantasy, and characters who are clearly inspired by commedia's masks (in *Liolá*, for example, Uncle Simone, the old man bragging of his potency, is an obvious variation of commedia's Pantalone). More important, they introduce themes developed later in his most sophisticated works: the relationship and duality of masks, sanity and madness, illusion versus reality, and the need for compassion in all human matters.

Cap and Bells is set in a realistic drawing room where Pirandello has combined aspects of Pantalone and Arlecchino in the character Ciampa, who is both a scheming servant (in this case, a bank employee) and a deceived elderly husband. Ciampa's wife is having an affair with his boss, Cavalier Fiorica, but Ciampa allows it to continue for the sake of keeping his job, as long as he and his wife can maintain an illusion of respectability. When the boss's wife, Beatrice, publicly reveals the affair, Ciampa has to stop the tidal wave of gossip her revelation starts in their small Sicilian town. He convinces his wife and her lover that since Beatrice's jealousy has caused a public embarrassment, the only way to rectify it is for Beatrice to be declared insane. The mask of madness works, and Ciampa, his wife, and Fiorica are able to resume their "normal" lives. This Machiavellian little play owes much to commedia in its stereotypical characters. Ciampa, for example, sees humans as merely puppets:

I am a puppet, you are a puppet, we are all puppets. Is it enough, do you think, to be born a puppet by divine will? No, Signor! Each can make himself the puppet he wants, the puppet he can be or that he believes himself to be. And this is where the insanity begins, Signora! Because each puppet wishes to be respected, not only for what he has inside himself, but for the mask he wears to the world. Not one of the puppets is contented with his role, each would like to stand before his own puppet and spit in its face.[40]

Actor Angelo Musco (1872–1937), who had begun his career with a Sicilian marionette theatre and in the company of Giovanni Grasso, had significant impact on Pirandello's earliest plays. With his own company, Musco had popular successes with *Think It Over, Giacomo!*, *Liolá*, and *The Jug* (1917), playing the *brillante* (another stock character, one that "sparkles" like a diamond). Critics applauded his infectious comic skill, and even Craig described him as one of the great actors of the day. Other critics, such as Silvio D'Amico, were offended by his flagrant improvisations and willingness to depart from the written text. Musco's obvious strength was his ability to act in response to the reactions of his audience. Like commedia actors, he moved freely within the loose confines of the scenario, nimble enough to seize a comic moment and play it to the hilt.

It is unclear why Pirandello tolerated Musco's flamboyant disregard for his dialogue, but he was undoubtedly as attracted to the actor's skill as he was repelled by the liberties Musco took with his plays. Once Pirandello was outraged at a dress rehearsal for *Liolá* when he realized that Musco's actors had not properly learned their parts. Refusing Musco permission to use his text, he grabbed his script and left in a fury, telling Musco in no uncertain terms that the performance was called off. Musco ran after him, insisting that he needed no script, his cast would improvise the play anyway. Actors like Musco, who continued to perform as commedia actors, were a rare breed. Most Italian actors of the day had long abandoned the improvisatory and natural style in favor of a formal declamatory style, presumably to add weightiness to the literary dramas of the day. Pirandello, who found this type of theatre pretentious and its actors stiff, preferred a spontaneity typical of commedia, yet at the same time controlled by the structure and language of his polished scripts. Given the choice between Musco's liberties and the lifelessness of most Italian players of his time, Pirandello chose to endure, and event to admire, Musco's improvisations.

Pirandello's first important full-length play, *Right You Are, If You Think You Are* (1917), appears to be as loosely constructed as a commedia scenario: thus creating the illusion of improvisation. Eric Bentley, who has translated the play, describes the play's central character, Lamberto Laudisi, a *brillante*, as "Harlequin in modern dress, a Harlequin who has invaded the realm of philosophy, and who behaves there as he had behaved elsewhere."[41]

Laudisi is the cynical observer who watches Councillor Agazzi and his family pry into the personal life of Signor Ponza, secretary to Agazzi. Mysteriously, Ponza's wife and her mother (Signora Frola) have never been seen together. Signora Frola claims to live alone to avoid interfering in her daughter's life, but Ponza insists that she has been isolated because she is insane. His first wife (Signora Frola's daughter), he says, was killed some years before in an earthquake that conveniently destroyed any written evidence of the marriage. Signora Frola turns the tables by insisting that it is Ponza who is insane; she claims that his present wife is her daughter. Ponza responds by saying that he pretends insanity to humor Signora Frola, and he is distressed to become the "target of insufferable persecution."[42] Finally, Agazzi demands that Ponza's wife appear. She does, dressed in mourning with a thick veil, and announces that she is Signora Frola's daughter and the second wife of Ponza. She continues: "to myself I am no one. No one."[43] This is met with protestations from the others, but she concludes, "I am the one that each of you thinks I am."[44] Laudisi, laughing derisively at the "truth-seekers," proclaims that Signora Ponza has spoken with "the voice of truth!"[45] Pirandello's notion of *maschere nude* causes him to people *Right You Are* with stock characters recognizable as commedia types. Using the psychological language common in the early twentieth century, Stark Young suggests, "Mental Habits, Characteristic Human Emotions, Thematic Ideas"[46] are the stock characters of *Right You Are*. Undoubtedly, Pirandello would have preferred to think that he had put commedia-inspired characters on the stage rather than "Mental Habits."

Along with his translation of *Right You Are*, Bentley includes some production notes suggesting that a director

remember that actors – especially the actors of the *commedia dell'arte* whose skill Pirandello wished to revive – once were, and can be again, the main part of the show. Tell your actors to let go. Have them shout, swagger, gesticulate – at least in the earlier rehearsals. For you have to get them to act and talk instead of strolling and muttering like mannequins with a pin loose. And if they perform their roles from outside instead of pretending to *be* the people who are not people, Pirandello would be better served.[47]

Six Characters in Search of an Author (1921) gained international celebrity for Pirandello through its exposition of both the illusion and reality inherent to theatre and to life. In it, a Producer has assembled his acting company to prepare a production of a play by Pirandello (in an early bit, the Producer furiously derides Pirandello's plays: "And if you can understand them you must be very clever. He writes them on purpose so nobody enjoys them, neither actors nor critics nor audience"[48]). The rehearsal is interrupted by the appearance of a Father, a Mother, a Stepdaughter, a Young Boy, and a Baby Girl. The Family explains that they are characters from an unfinished play and they plead for permission to recreate a crucial moment in their lives, claiming that they would supply the director and his company with a scene from which they may construct a finished drama. The Producer and his actors are skeptical, but the Father proceeds to explain that his wife had fallen in love with another man and he has stepped aside, permitting her to live with the other man, by whom she has had three illegitimate children. He has also arranged for a legitimate child, a Son, to live in the country. The Mother contests the Father's account, claiming that he had tired of her and pushed her into the arms of another man, separating her from her Son. The Father continues to explain that some time later he failed to recognize the Stepdaughter in Madame Pace's bordello and only the appearance of the Mother at the crucial moment prevented him from dishonor. The Father convinces the Producer to improvise the scene with his actors. They resist, however, through an allusion to commedia:

Leading Actor. Is he serious? What's he going to do?
Young Actor. I think he's gone round the bend.
Another Actor. Does he expect to make up a play in five minutes?
Young Actor. Yes, like the old actors in the commedia del'arte!
Leading Actress. Well if he thinks I'm going to appear in that sort of nonsense ....
Young Actor. Nor me.
Fourth Actor. I should like to know who they are.
Third Actor. Who do you think? They's probably escaped lunatics – or crooks.
Young Actor. Is he taking them seriously?
Young Actress. It's vanity. The vanity of seeing himself as an author.
Leading Actor. I've never heard of such a thing! If the theatre, ladies and gentlemen, is reduced to this ...
Fifth Actor. I'm enjoying it!
Third Actor. Really? We shall have to wait and see what happens next I suppose.[49]

The actors finally do attempt to play the roles of the Father and the

Stepdaughter in this scene, but the characters, especially the Stepdaughter, protest the actors' vulgarized treatment of the scene. She insists that the scene be played truthfully, leading to a debate with the Producer which raises the idea that truth may be an impossibility in a theatre as well as in life. In this madcap philosophical scene, Pirandello grinds to dust the sentimentalizing excesses of the contemporary Italian theatre:

> *Producer.* The truth! Do me a favour will you? This is the theatre you know! Truth's all very well up to a point but ...
> *Stepdaughter.* What do you want to do then?
> *Producer.* You'll see! You'll see! Leave it all to me.
> *Stepdaughter.* No. No I won't. I know what you want to do! Out of my feeling of revulsion, out of all the vile and sordid reasons why I am what I am, you want to make a sugary little sentimental romance. You want him to ask me why I'm in mourning and you want me to reply with the tears running down my face that it is only two months since my father died. No. No. I won't have it! He must say to me what he really did say. 'Well then, let's take it off, we'll take it off at once, shall we, your little black dress.' And I, with my heart still grieving for my father's death only two months before, I went behind there, do you see? Behind that screen and with my fingers trembling with shame and loathing I took off the dress, unfastened my bra. ...
> *Producer.* (*his head in his hands*) For God's sake? What are you saying!
> *Stepdaughter.* (*shouting excitedly*) The truth! I'm telling you the truth!
> *Producer.* All right then. Now listen to me. I'm not denying it's the truth. Right. And believe me I understand your horror, but you must see that we can't really put a scene like that on the stage.[50]

The Father defensively explains that having found the Mother and her children destitute, he took them in with himself and the Son. The Stepdaughter continues despite this to blame the Father for her shame and the Son rejects them all. Requested to enact the scene in which he rejects the Mother, the Son refuses and exits to a garden, when he finds the Young Boy beside a fountain staring in horror at the drowned body of the Baby Girl. Before this news can be fully grasped, a shot is heard. The Young Boy has killed himself, sending the characters into shock, and causing the observing actors to protest hysterically that "It's all make-believe."[51] The Father, however, protests: "What do you mean, make-believe? It's real! It's real, ladies and gentlemen! It's reality!"[52] The Producer, perplexed by his inability to comprehend the clash between real life and theatrical illusion, finally dismisses them all: "Make-believe?! Reality?! Oh, go to hell the lot of you! Lights! Lights! Lights!"[53]

Depending on his experience as a playwright and director, combined with his despairing but compassionate view of human nature and art, Pirandello makes use of his understanding of commedia-style improvisation to create and recreate the complex relationships of his emblematic characters. Caught up in the complex tangles of life, his "actors" and "characters" are ordinary people he uses as types, but like the characters of commedia they seem to have free expressions and movements that even their author did not give them. They also suggest commedia masks: the Stepdaughter is the *inamorata*, the Father is Pantalone, and the Actors and Actresses are *zanni*. Pirandello succeeds at the unlikely task of combining Realism and nearly pure commedia in a single play. By using theatre as a metaphor he exposes his characters' tragedies, by breaking through the illusion of the theatre with the illusion of improvisation. In this remarkable achievement, Pirandello reveals the complex and ever-changing realities that always lurk beneath the mask of Realism:

the result was what it had to be: a mixture of tragic and comic, fantastic and realistic, in a humorous situation that was quite new and infinitely complex, a drama which is conveyed by means of the characters, who carry it within them and suffer it, a drama, breathing, speaking, self-propelled, which seeks at all costs to find the means of its own presentation; and the comedy of the vain attempt at an improvised realization of the drama on stage.[54]

In less than a year after *Six Characters*, Pirandello completed another masterwork, *Henry IV* (1922). This play explores the tragedy of a middle-aged Italian nobleman who, after a fall from a horse at a carnival, lives with the delusion that he is Emperor Henry IV. Twenty years of tailoring his life to suit his madness leads five individuals, Matilde Spina (a former lover who had jilted him), Belcredi (her current lover), Frida (her daughter), Frida's fiancé (who is also the madman's nephew), and a doctor, to attempt to cure him. Henry is furious at their intrusions, since he has used his madness as a protective mask against reality. After he reveals to his attendants that he is actually sane, they inform Matilde, who refuses to believe them. Henry's emotions are stirred by seeing Frida, who reminds him of the youthful Matilde, and he admits that he regained his sanity some years before, but continues to find his particular masquerade as good as any other. In Act Three, he grabs hold of his costume and explains that "This ... for me this is an obvious, deliberate caricature of that other masquerade which goes on all the time, in which we're all involuntary clowns without knowing it ... (*Indicating* BELCREDI.) ... when we dress up as who we think we are. You have to forgive them, because they still don't see that clothes ... habits ... are the same as personality itself."[55]

In a climactic moment, Henry insists that his fall at the carnival was a result of Belcredi's dirty work. Henry stabs Belcredi, who is carried away dying and insisting of Henry, "You're not mad! He's not mad! Not mad at all!"[56] Henry realizes, however, that to escape the consequences of his act he and his lackeys must continue his masquerade: "Yes ... no choice now ... (*He calls them round him, as if for protection.*) Here together ... here together ... and for always!"[57]

In *Henry IV*, Pirandello's characters are again inspired by the masks of commedia. Frida and the nephew are the *inamorati*, Belcredi is the jealous lover, and the doctor is a semi-comic quack, resembling commedia's Dottore. Henry himself is a commedia clown, an Arlecchino, impersonating a madman. In a sense, he improvises his way through his masquerade and through his life, but finally, and tragically, he is permanently trapped behind his mask of madness.

Each in His Own Way (1924) also depends on commedia elements, and is similar in many ways to *Six Characters in Search of an Author*. Basing the play on an actual newspaper account of a young artist's suicide over his lover's betrayal, Pirandello mixed the reactions of his audience with the drama itself. In the first part of the play, Doro Palegari defends the dead artist's lover, Delia, blaming her new lover, Michele, for the tragedy. Francesco Savio, however, takes the opposing view, and they quarrel. The next day they meet and both attempt to apologize, but they fall into a quarrel again, having now taken each other's former opinion. Delia appears herself and, after learning of the two versions of the story, she is confused over which is correct. During a supposed intermission, and with Delia and Michele angrily watching, the "theatre lobby" is shown and the "audience" visible in it argue about the play, which they generally consider a joke on them.

At the beginning of the second act, preparations are proceeding for a duel between Doro and Francesco, but Michele, wishing to defend his own honor, follows Delia to Francesco's house. A violent confrontation between Delia and Michele, born of a passion that has turned to hatred, makes it clear that neither Francesco's nor Doro's version of the tragedy is true. During the final intermission, the "real life" Delia and Michele appear to attack the director and the actors of the play, proclaiming that the version of their lives shown is ridiculous. They re-enact the scene, to

the anger of the "actors," and the play concludes as the theatre manage-
ment apologizes to the "audience." In *Each in His Own Way*, Pirandello
merges the illusiveness of reality with his self-contradicting commedia-
style characters. As he himself wrote, "life, as I said, is unstable. What I
have attempted to do is capture the instability of life and fix it in dramatic
form."[58]

In 1925, Pirandello established his own theatre company in Rome, the
Teatro D'Arte, subsidized by grants from Mussolini's government. The
troupe toured widely in Europe and America, and Pirandello himself
performed on many occasions, often taking roles in his own plays. During
this time, his plays had become popular with international audiences and
were often produced abroad. Oddly, some early international directors of
Pirandello's plays, particularly Max Reinhardt,[59] tended to overlook their
commedia aspects, making them more elaborate and soberly realistic than
Pirandello had intended. When he directed, Pirandello used simple settings and strove for lightness and spontaneity in the acting. He staged
many of his own works as well as plays by Italian and European dramatists
he admired. Among the productions during the troupe's first season
at Teatro D'Arte was Evreinov's commedia-style one-act, *A Merry Death*.
Pirandello made experiments with commedia techniques, and especially
encouraged his company to improvise in rehearsals. He typically rehearsed
for several days, and then had his actors improvise around a specific
theme, aiming for the spontaneity he believed must be at the heart of
theatre.

With his own play, *Tonight We Improvise* (1929), which he produced in
1930, Pirandello presents, as he did in *Six Characters in Search of an Author*
and *Each in His Own Way*, an examination of how theatre is created,
emphasizing the idea that theatre comes alive when it is tied directly to the
imagination of the actor. The stage directions for the play confirm his
conviction that critics and audiences were unwilling to accept a play that
emphasizes improvisation. In *Tonight We Improvise*, a director, Hinkfuss (a
broad caricature of Reinhardt), urges his actors toward commedia-style
improvisation of their roles from a simple scenario. In his stage directions,
Pirandello indicates that

Much curiosity has been aroused by the advertisement, in the newspapers and on the playbills,
of an unusual sort of improvised show. The dramatic critics of the town are the only ones who
have not thought it worth their while to come, feeling it will be easy enough the next morning to
say what a hodge-podge the thing was. (Good Lord, you know, one of those hoary old commedia
dell'arte things; but where will you find, in these days, actors who are capable of improvising

like those funny devils of the real commedia dell'arte, who, so far as that goes, were helped out not a little by their traditional mask and other trappings, as well as by their repertory?) To tell the truth, they are a little put out by the fact that the name of the writer who has provided stage manager and actors of the evening with their scenario does not appear on the playbills or anywhere else; accordingly, deprived of any hint that might conveniently enable them to fall back upon a ready-made opinion, they are in dread of contradicting themselves.[60]

After a noisy fracas backstage that alarms members of the "audience," Hinkfuss comes forward to try to prepare them for the "unusual perform-ance,"[61] and to confess that the author of the "scenario" to be performed is, in fact, Pirandello. This is greeted with some distress from planted actors in the audience, and Hinkfuss acknowledges that

He's played the same trick twice, on a couple of colleagues of mine, sending one of them Six lost Characters in Search of an Author, which created a riot on the stage and upset everybody very much, while on the other one he palmed off a trick comedy that caused the audience to rise up and stop the show; but it's different this time; there's no chance of his doing that to me.[62]

Following some further explanation of how the play-within-the-play will be performed, Hinkfuss sets the scene in Sicily where four beautiful young women, Mommina, Totina, Dorina, and Nené, encouraged by their lib-eral mother, entertain several aviators. One conservative young man in the group, Verri, is attracted to Mommina, but resents her free-wheeling manner with the other men. He fights the other men off and proposes marriage to Mommina. When Hinkfuss attempts to interrupt the flow of the "improvised" story, he fails, and the play proceeds on its own without him. Mommina's father has been killed in a café brawl, and feeling she has no choice, she marries Verri.

In the last act of the "improvised" play, Mommina has had two daugh-ters by Verri, but her life with him has been a living hell, due to his intense jealousy and brutality. Suffering from a weak heart and Verri's roughness, Mommina drifts away from sanity into memories of her parents and sisters, and her love of music. Images from her past float by her as she tells her daughters of the happiness she might have had if she had not married Verri. Singing her favorite aria, she dies, leaving Hinkfuss protesting the artificiality of the play and its author. The actors counter by proclaiming the artificiality of the director and the significance of the author. Despite the conflicts, Pirandello proves the necessity of theatre – and its unique ability to capture the conflicting and shifting emotions of life as they seem actually to occur.

Tonight We Improvise, like *Six Characters in Search of an Author* and *Each in His Own Way*, resembles commedia in its character transformations, the sudden changes of direction in the action, the conflict between the play and the play-within-the-play, and what Pirandello described as the "'aggressive vitality' of the *commedia*."[63] He also makes it clear in his plays, as in commedia, that the emphasis is on the illusion of the actors' creativity, not on any realistic happening. A feeling of urgency and spontaneity is created by the playwright, as in commedia, despite the fact that the actors work from a complete and carefully constructed script with finished dialogue. It was necessary for an actor in a Pirandello play, as A. Richard Sogliuzzo writes, to "function skillfully within these various levels of reality while appearing to be confused as to the distinctions between fact and fiction, art and life, and his identity as character or actor."[64]

Imbued with a love of theatre, a theatre that supplied characters as symbols for ever-changing and contradictory human emotions, and with his despairing, ironic, and finally compassionate view of the human condition, Pirandello concluded that "All that remains to me is a great pity for humanity, forced to live out its allotted span upon this cruel earth."[65] Using the characters, techniques, and spirit of commedia, he brilliantly illuminated humanity's struggle on this "cruel earth."

NOTES

1 Dario Fo, "Author's Note," *Accidental Death of an Anarchist*. Adapted by Gavin Richards from a translation by Gillian Hanna. Introduced by Stuart Hood (London, 1987), p. xviii.

2 French commedia character derived from Italy's Pedrolino, a *zanni* role first played by Giovanni Pellesini (c. 1526–1612). The character incorporated elements of Pulcinella, but is best known in the variation made famous by Jean-Gaspard Deburau in which the character became a gentle mime pining away for a lost or unrequited love.

3 Jennifer Lorch, "Pirandello, Commedia dell'Arte and Improvisation," *The Commedia dell'Arte from the Renaissance to Dario Fo*. Ed. Christopher Cairns (Lewiston, 1989), p. 301.

4 Antonio Alessio, "Pirandello and the commedia dell'arte," *The Science of Buffoonery: Theory and History of the Commedia dell'Arte*. Ed. Domenico Pietropaolo (Ottawa, 1989), p. 299.

168   James Fisher

5 Cited in Jana O'Keefe Bazzoni, "The Carnival Motif in Pirandello's Drama," *Modern Drama*, 30 (1987), 421.
6 Cited in A. Richard Sogliuzzo, *Luigi Pirandello, Director: The Playwright in the Theatre* (Metuchen, NJ, and London, 1982), p. 77.
7 Idem.
8 Cited in Eric Bentley, ed., "Pirandello and Performance," *Theatre Three*, 3 (Fall 1987), 70.
9 Oscar Büdel, *Pirandello* (New York, 1966), p. 97.
10 Cited in Bentley, ed., 69.
11 Cited in Bazzoni, 414.
12 Idem.
13 Cited in Sogliuzzo, p. 77.
14 Ibid., p. 244.
15 Luigi Pirandello, *On Humor*. Introduced, Translated, and Annotated by Antonio Illiano and Daniel P. Testa (Chapel Hill, NC, 1974), p. 5.
16 Ibid., p. 93.
17 Idem.
18 Ibid., p. 103.
19 Idem.
20 Idem.
21 Ibid., p. 113.
22 Luigi Pirandello, "Introduction to The Italian Theatre," trans. Anne Paolucci. *The Genius of the Italian Theatre*, Ed. Eric Bentley (New York, 1964), p. 23.
23 Ibid., p. 24.
24 Idem.
25 Ibid., pp. 24–25.
26 Ibid., p. 25.
27 Idem.
28 Idem.
29 Ibid., p. 21.
30 Ibid., p. 26.
31 Ibid., pp. 26–27.
32 E. Gordon Craig, "Introduction," *The Liar. A Comedy in Three Acts*. By Carlo Goldoni. Trans. Grace Lovat Fraser (London, 1922), p. 7.
33 Pirandello, "Introduction to The Italian Theatre," p. 27.
34 Idem.
35 Ibid., p. 28.
36 Idem.
37 Idem.
38 Idem.

39 Ibid., p. 29.
40 Luigi Pirandello, *Sicilian Comedies: Cap and Bells; Man, Beast and Virtue.* Trans. Norman A. Bailey and Roger W. Oliver (New York, 1983), pp. 27–28.
41 Eric Bentley, *The Pirandello Commentaries* (Evanston, IL, 1984), p. 29.
42 Luigi Pirandello, *Right You Are.* A Stage Version with an Introduction and Notes by Eric Bentley (New York, 1954), p. 115.
43 Ibid., p. 130.
44 Idem.
45 Idem.
46 Stark Young, *Immortal Shadows* (New York, 1948), p. 86.
47 Bentley, *The Pirandello Commentaries*, p. 7.
48 Luigi Pirandello, *Three Plays: The Rules of the Game, Six Characters in Search of an Author, Henry IV.* Trans. Robert Rietty and Noel Creegan, John Linstrum, Julian Mitchell (London, 1985), p. 74.
49 Ibid., p. 96.
50 Ibid., p. 115.
51 Ibid., p. 133.
52 Idem.
53 Idem.
54 Luigi Pirandello, "Preface to *Six Characters in Search of an Author*," *Naked Masks.* Ed. Eric Bentley (New York, 1952), p. 366.
55 Pirandello, *Three Plays: The Rules of the Game, Six Characters in Search of an Author, Henry IV,* p. 197.
56 Ibid., p. 200.
57 Idem.
58 Cited in Sogliuzzo, p. 43.
59 In a characteristic gesture of his admiration for *Six Characters in Search of an Author*, Reinhardt practically took it apart structurally and made many changes.
60 Luigi Pirandello, *Tonight We Improvise.* Trans. Samuel Putnam (New York, 1932), p. 18.
61 Ibid., p. 25.
62 Ibid., pp. 25–26.
63 Cited in Sogliuzzo, p. 42.
64 Ibid., p. 43.
65 Cited in F.L. Lucas, *The Drama of Chekhov, Synge, Yeats, and Pirandello* (London, 1963), p. 357.

Sicilian Themes and the Restructured Stage: The Dialectic of Fiction and Drama in the Work of Luigi Pirandello

ANNE PAOLUCCI

When, in 1923, at the age of 56, Luigi Pirandello won European acclaim with the Pitoëff production of *Six Characters in Search of an Author* (the same play that had been booed and had caused a riot at its premiere in Rome two years earlier), the Italian writer had already published six of his seven novels, several scattered volumes of short stories, and four volumes of poetry. His reputation as a writer of fiction was already established when he turned to drama; and although he never gave up writing novels and short stories (and was to convert many of these into plays in the years that followed), Pirandello had clearly shifted his sights and direction by 1923. For the rest of his life his artistic priorities were to be focused on theater.

It was in 1916 that Pirandello finally awoke to his potential as a dramatist with the recognition he received in Italy for two plays written in Sicilian dialect – *Pensaci, Giacomino! (Think it Over, Giacomino!)* and the genial *Liolà* – both written for the renowned Sicilian actor Angelo Musco. These early plays reflect the "verismo" of his already mature fiction; later plays and short stories will continue to depict in a variety of ways the realism made popular in Italy at the time by other Sicilian writers like Giovani Verga and Antonio Fogazzaro – a deep-rooted interest in the closed society of southern Italy, where rigorous conventions cannot be subverted without risking one's life and loved ones, where all is subordinated to "real" values (property, land, dowries) which shape the life of the community and all those in it, where women cannot break out of a "no exit" situation without dishonouring themselves and their families, where marriage is an economic necessity first and foremost. For Pirandello, the oppressive poverty and inescapable destinies of the poor, the bonds that trap the rich, the silent suffering of women who must succumb to the dictates of the external values that will insure their pitiful existence, the ostracized rebels who cannot escape their fate even away from the source of their troubles – the entire spectrum of Sicilian attitudes and values is depicted in all its aspects and always with awe and compassion for the frailty of the human condition. Even in the "theater" plays that made him an international avant-garde sensation as a playwright, Pirandello insists on a core narrative of intense existential confrontations: women trapped by their passion and driven to destruction by their unfulfilled ambitions and guilt; exiled and ostracized women who carry their jealousies and resentments into more cosmopolitan settings without succeeding in divesting themselves of those emotions or their consequences; men and women driven to death by the irreversible, inescapable events dictated by a closed society which haunts them even far from home.

In depicting the erosion of the soul within the Sicilian setting which he loved and felt oppressed by, Pirandello displayed – both in fiction and drama – the kind of genial combination of "strong local colour" and "unconscious universality" which (according to T.S. Eliot) is the mark of greatness in literature.[1] Pirandello's fiction and much of his drama are rooted in this paradox. As a playwright, however, Pirandello soon hit on a new and powerful theme, perhaps the inevitable result of focusing on the barren lives of people living in a barren place, where nature itself is hostile and the individual a victim without reprieve. His earliest plays as well as his novels and short stories examined the effect of such an existence in the most detailed way; but by 1921, with *Six Characters*, he turned with even greater fascination to exploring *personality* in its conscious and deliberate effort to come to terms with the environment. We see in *Six Characters* a new obsession translated powerfully into a stage language itself new and overwhelming. The Sicilian story is there, still, but only as motive for examining the experience *outside* itself, outside its local habitation, against the conventions and prejudices of another kind of life and commitment. The stage itself becomes a living character in this extraordinary confrontation; and the actors move in and out of "real" and "stage" roles in a telescopic oscillation that forever destroyed the notion of stage and audience as distinct and mutually exclusive realities. With the "theater" plays, Pirandello found the medium and language of redemption for the damned souls of his closed society. In exploring the maze of its own consciousness, personality could free itself from the bonds of external necessity; the process – regardless of the result – was in itself liberating. The struggle for identity defines one's limits and therefore one's potential.

The "theater" plays announce this new and exciting direction in the most vivid terms; and they make clear at the same time that the search for identity was a most promising subject for the new drama of existential emotions and avant-garde techniques. As Robert Brustein insists, Pirandello hit on something truly extraordinary, for his example served to instruct just about every important playwright of our time.[2] In a rush of inspiration, Pirandello wrote in a short span of four years three of the four plays that were to revolutionize the European and world theater and set it on a new, totally unexpected course for decades to come. In *Six Characters, Enrico IV*, and *Each in His Own Way*, Pirandello discovered not only his own potential as a playwright but in the process also rediscovered the full potential of theater. Drama, he made stunningly clear, was a *continuum*, a constant *becoming*. He used telescopic techniques to destroy the passive notion of static "illusion" on stage, superimposing action, moving actors in and out of their "formal" roles, juxtaposing "real" events with stage plot, creating a dialectic spiraling of roles within roles, settings within settings, realities within realities. In the fragmentation that resulted, a new force was unleashed that was to revitalize both drama and fiction in the years that followed.

The first large indication of Pirandello's growing interest in exploring the inner world of personality as it seeks organic identity is to be found in the early novel *Il Fu Mattia Pascal (The Late Mattia Pascal)*, written in 1904. The work has puzzled some critics who would like to see a straight-line development from such early but fully worked-out statements of Pirandello's major theme to later works, especially the "theater" plays. Writers like Renato Barilli reflect a tendency to see *Il Fu Mattia Pascal* out of sequence, for the next novel, in 1909, *I Vecchi e i giovani (The Old and the Young)*, seems to revert to the heavy Sicilian inspiration of earlier works like *L'Esclusa (The Outcast)*, all of which, as I have indicated, draw richly from the realistic regional novels of Verga, Fogazzaro and – in the case of *L'Esclusa* – Luigi Capuana.[3] Barilli in fact reviews *I Vecchi e i giovani* out of sequence in his own critical analysis of Pirandello's narrative writings. Yet there is even in this large historical panorama of the effects of the unification of Italy on Sicily and the entire Italian South a consistency of interests and an unwavering focus that deserve to be noted. The Sicily that is forgotten, betrayed, abandoned, left to its grim future by the politicians in Rome, who are intoxicated with their new power as leaders of the latecomer to the family of European nations, is itself a character waiting to be redefined, rediscovered, restructured, redeemed. In drawing a rich, complex canvas not unlike that of Lampedusa's *Il Gattopardo (The Leopard)* later, Pirandello also has occasion to exercise his extraordinary gift for tracing complex motivations and intentions. The people he draws for us are caught in political realities not very different from the Camus-like trap in which Mattia Pascal or the mad emperor Enrico IV find themselves. Even "out of sequence," *I Vecchi e i giovani* is surprisingly consistent with Pirandello's later works in depicting the struggle between oppression and freedom, the search for identity, the existential frustrations and despair in the face of unrelenting hostile forces.

It is indeed in the strange story of Mattia Pascal, however, that Pirandello's exploration of the stages of consciousness and the search for identity is given unexpectedly mature form at a very early date. Escape and return here become a spiraling dialectic, the end circling back to the beginning in a tragic-ironic-humorous conclusion. The protagonist of this early novel has been called "a fugitive from life"[4] but he is more properly a magician creating his own illusions and, as always in Pirandello, rejecting those illusions in the end. The story contains elements of gross improbability, but Pirandello somehow makes it believable. Mattia Pascal, seeking an opportunity to vacation alone and escape his wife's nagging, goes to Monte Carlo, where he wins a great deal of money. On his way home, he reads an account of his "death" – a suicide by drowning, the body identified as his by his wife and others. He accepts this grotesque turn of events as a sign, an opportunity to start a new life. Under the assumed name of Adriano Meis, he proceeds to travel throughout northern Italy; but in time he is once again caught in the familiar web of personal relationships and social commitments and thus realizes that he cannot really ever escape. The new life he has given himself is not only similar to the old but adds to his difficulties, since his new identity cannot be legally recognized. With the realization that he has in fact created a new trap for himself, he stages a second "suicide" – leaving his hat, cane, and a signed note on a parapet of a bridge along the Tiber – and returns to his home in Sicily. There he finds his "widow" married again and with a new family. Not fazed by the problems created by his return (not the least of which is the illegitimate status of his former wife's child by her new husband), he returns to his job as town librarian and dedicates himself to writing about his experience.

Almost two decades later, the novel still seemed far-fetched to many serious readers. For the 1921 Mondadori edition, Pirandello included an appendix in which he explained the contradictions "between reality and imagination" and cited a notice which had appeared in one of the leading Italian papers some months earlier about a man "who had visited his own grave."[5] This is the very year when audiences and critics booed *Six Characters* for its implausible core story of incest and the strange new stage language of the play. In spite of its difficult twists, however, the novel won recognition for Pirandello when published in book form by the firm of Treves. This was indeed an achievement at a time when Verga was still unappreciated and D'Annunzio was the great literary light of Italy. According to Douglas Radcliff-Umstead, the success of *Il Fu Mattia Pascal* was due in large part to Pirandello's "effort to move beyond the Veristic preoccupation with the problems of life in a closed provincial world." The novel "represented precisely the desire to escape enslavement within society through the construction of a wholly original personality."[6] Gaspare Giudice goes even further:

It was probably in the very writing of *Il Fu Mattia Pascal* that Pirandellian fiction, until then searching for objective correlatives, works its way with greater assurance into the conscience, becomes introspective, making careful distinctions within the context of a special kind of subjective humor .... One finds in it what amounts to an enjoyment of misery, a flash of intuition that takes sour delight in feeling out a new-found wound that has not yet begun to fester.[7]

Clearly, then, *Il Fu Mattia Pascal* was the first direct statement of a theme rooted in a pessimistic view of man trapped by hostile forces but rising out of that condition by a slowly evolving consciousness of freedom – a theme richly suggesting a cyclical return to a basically unchanged beginning, which is to say, the dialectic of escape and return with all its ironic suggestivity, roles within roles, ironic parallels often superimposed (the first accidental "suicide" and the deliberately staged "suicide"), a special brand of humor (the perverse decision at the end not to cancel the "death certificate"), paradoxes (committing "suicide" in order to be restored to life), multi-layered self-evaluations and self-analyses, restructuring past events according to one's ideal vision or deliberate re-interpretation or some master plan (including the writing of the experience after settling back in), etc.

With *Six Characters* the focus shifts: the core story becomes a distant motif, an echo, a reminder that all experience must pass through the mirror of the self and must be evaluated in terms of that mirror image. The shift can surely be attributed to some extent to the demands of the stage, which – for Pirandello – was the ideal medium for bringing together the illusion of life and the reality of the self. In this play "escape" also becomes freedom from the predictable connection between intentions and deeds: freedom from stage conventions, dramatic action and resolution, familiar dialogue and internal communications. There is nothing uncertain about this first "theater" play; it too is a fully mature product, an incredible tour-de-force, an experiment that could not have been foreseen but would never be forgotten. It marks the beginning of the contemporary theater with all its fragmented attitudes, states of mind, contradictory emotions, Hamlet-like irrelevancies; but little of what follows in other parts of the world will match the totality of the Pirandello experiment. Pirandello himself, from this time on, will deliberately extend and expand his new vision of theater, incorporating into the later plays in an organic evolution all that had gone before, while exploring the intriguing dramatic potential of personality through paradoxical postures that reduce facts, relationships, documents – all that we usually take for granted – to provocative questions.

Pirandello himself acknowledged the new direction he had taken in 1917 (four years before *Six Characters*), with *Cosí è (se vi pare)* (*It Is So! [If You Think So]*), in a letter to his son in which he shares his own excitement about the play: " ... it's a grand piece of demonic mischief ... bursting with originality" (" ... è una gran diavoleria ... d'una originalità che gridà").[8] The work was adapted from one of his own short stories; the flavor of *Il Fu Mattia Pascal* is still pervasive. The plot relies heavily on familiar elements of the grotesque and the implausible. In a relentless stripping of all "proofs" of identity, all the routine "evidence" we take for granted in asserting ourselves and our relationships with others, Pirandello undermines the certainty of our innermost convictions and forces us to new definitions.

The plot is ingenious: Signora Ponza's true identity is in question because of the paradoxical and contradictory assertions made by her husband and by Signora Frola, ostensibly her mother. Ponza, when forced to explain the strange living arrangements (his mother-in-law has been set up in an expensive flat next to that of his employer, while his wife lives across town in an inexpensive walk-up), explains that he keeps the two women apart because Signora Frola believes her daughter to be still alive when in fact she has died and he, Ponza, has remarried. Signora Frola has a totally different story to tell: it is Ponza who suffered a breakdown when his wife was taken ill and placed in a nursing home; but when she was restored to him he refused to believe that it was his wife. A second "marriage" had to be performed to resolve the situation. Both stories, as they are separately told, are convincing; but under the determined questioning of Laudisi (the eternal skeptic) the others begin the doubt everything, and the search for "facts" begins. The evidence, however, proves most ambiguous since the small town from which the newcomers had moved was destroyed by an earthquake and nothing can be checked out. Finally, the woman herself is brought in to speak for herself, but all she says to the assembled company is: "I am the daughter of Signora Frola ... and the second wife of Signor Ponza ..."

Cosí è (se vi pare) is the brilliant prelude to the "theater" plays, the first Eisensteinian superimposition of identities. The transformations described in the earlier *Il Fu Mattia Pascal*, within a narrative structure, here are given immediacy on stage as shifting images. Laudisi, the probing skeptic who turns everything into doubt, serves as a catalyst for the process of dismantling "reality" – but he is by no means the spokesman for Pirandello's conclusions about the world. By questioning everything, Laudisi forces us to turn inward, to struggle with the reflection of self, to destroy the dichotomy of consciousness and self-consciousness. He himself retains a double image, however; he is an aborted experience. To confound him with Pirandello's view of things is patently absurd. The insistence of a simplistic notion of "reality vs. illusion" as the large Pirandellian theme, to regard Pirandello as a relativist (granted he had met Einstein!), is utterly misleading. Reality is something each of us must define and redefine – not in solipsistic terms but as a shared experience, a conviction that others will recognize and accept from within, with certainty, as Signor Ponza and Signora Frola succeeded in doing, in spite of their seemingly contradictory assertions.

The mirror image in this play is the symbol of the moment of contradiction which is the beginning of self-awareness, or reality. Laudisi, looking at himself in the mirror and humorously addressing his reflection with " ... who is mad, you or I? ... Of course, I understand! I say it's you, and you say it's me" (p. 101), dramatizes for us the unbridgeable distance between external reality and self-conscious certainty. He is the moment of negation in the Pirandellian equation. With *Cosí è (se vi pare)* Pirandello grasps once and for all the power of the stage and the full potential of his grand theme. He realizes, moreover, that the stage is for him the perfect medium in which to depict that theme in all its variety.

The "theater" plays are proof of the symbiosis achieved. *Six Characters* is a moving stage image of shifting roles in the process of definition: actors playing "real" people, actors playing "actors" in rehearsal; actors creating a new script given to them by the "real" people; life drama measured against the written script of a play; the illusion of improvisation on stage; the core story of passionate and unacceptable emotions narrated by the "real" people who are looking for the perfect "script" in which to relate that story (a story that, in what will become typical Pirandellian fashion, will be truncated by an unexpected event and not brought to traditional dramatic resolution). In this work, Pirandello transforms the stage itself into a multi-layered experience, pushing the dramatic action into the background as he probes the intricate nuances of the role/character relationship and the difficulty of communicating life as drama. The play in fact is a forceful statement of what will become for theater of the "Absurd" one of its most provocative features: theater pushed to the edge of non-theater as its lines of communication break down under the exacting scrutiny of the dramatist-analyst.

Enrico IV (1922) follows closely upon *Six Characters* and appears long before the second and third plays of this "theater" series (*Each in His Own Way* [1924]; *Tonight We Improvise* [1930]), but it is in many ways the powerful resolution of the theater/life dichotomy explored in the three other plays. In it the six characters find their author, director, star actor. Enrico IV is not mad in any ordinary sense but retains the mask of madness for his own eccentric purposes, continuing to play his role as someone embedded in past suffering, permanent amnesia. He is in fact the lucid director who rewrites the script in his own image. He is the star actor forcing the others to play the roles as he has written and dictated them. The many-layered textures are rich and striking, especially the emperor 20 years older seen as a young man again in the person of his nephew Carlo Di Nolli dressed in the emperor's costume and these images superimposed on that of a portrait depicting the emperor at Di Nolli's age dressed in the same costume, etc. This play is a pyrotechnic display of Pirandello's agile dramatic skill; nowhere is there a loose or half-baked experimental notion. The mirror image has become a series of infinite pulsating reflections. What we witness is a living experience of superimposed awareness, realized in the context of a truncated stage action that, as expected, is not resolved in the traditional way.

Pirandello must have been working during this time on his last novel, the ingenious *Uno, nessuno, e centomila* (*One, No one, and a Hundred Thousand*), which was completed by 1924–5. The exploration of "madness" as an excessive sensibility that will not rest in the routine acceptance of things – the theme that had emerged as early as *Il Fu Mattia Pascal* and had found powerful expression in *Enrico IV* – is given full play in this work, in which Pirandello's notion of *humor* finds its most elaborate expression as well. The technique is very Joycean and avant-garde, in keeping with Pirandello's already established dialectical idiom of reversals, inversions, non-communicable experiences, esoteric postures that verge on madness, all that he had so deftly developed both in fiction and drama. In that novel, Pirandello finally abandons the "Other" of *Il Fu Mattia Pascal* and introduces the "I" in the mirror if identity. By this time he has also abandoned all residue of social commentary and gives himself up totally to depicting the humor of a situation in which the protagonist, Fausto Bandini, obsessively tries to capture his "real" self, finally "fleeing commonplace troubles for the oblivion of a divine insanity."[10]

The novel is humorous in the sense that Pirandello took such pains to elucidate in his treatise on the subject, *L'Umorismo*. The humor he defines and so skillfully draws for us in many of his works and especially in this last novel is a special kind of release – again reminiscent of what has become familiar to us through the works of such later dramatists as Ionesco, Beckett, and Edward Albee – humor that is itself an essential moment of self-awareness, the kind of humor that recognizes the paradox in things, the comic and mad as one, the essential and organic fusion of these contradictory postures, what is called "il sentimento del contrario" by Pirandello (not simple *perception* but a *feeling* for the profounder contradictions of a situation which may well include tragic self-delusion that appears on the surface comic, even ludicrous).[11] The hero of the novel begins by trying to catch his reflection in store windows and mirrors to find out if his nose is really somewhat crooked. This comic situation is pushed to its limits with obsessive clarity and detail, ending with Bandini's admission that he prefers to give up the world he knows and spend the rest of his days in an insane asylum where he can pursue his quest for identity without interruption, in peace.

Rarely has there been such a rich and varied body of major literary works exploring such an intriguing theme. From his earliest fiction to his last great novel, in all his plays – but especially in those in which the theater itself becomes the stage for the reconstructed personality – even in such works as *L'Umorismo*, Pirandello shows himself a master of literary forms and expression. In his late "myth" plays – *La Nuova colonia* (*The New Colony* [1928]); *Lazzaro* (*Lazarus* [1929]); *I Giganti della montagna* (*The Mountain Giants* [1936, unfinished]) – he introduces yet a new dimension. Emotional and psychological immediacy and dramatic complexity are there woven into transparent allegories reminiscent of Spenser's world in its details and Dante's in its artistic yearning for completeness. Those remarkable "fable" plays deserve attention not only as an even more complex examination of the identity crisis and dissolution of personality depicted in Pirandello's earlier works (approached in the myth plays as a search for *social, religious,* and *artistic* identity) but also as the ultimate expression of the paradox of non-communicability, of "art transcending itself" as art in its search for the terror in us all, charting the depths of personality in its darkest and most sublime expression.

NOTES

1 T.S. Eliot, "American Literature and the American Language," *To Criticize the Critic* (New York, 1965), p. 54.
2 Robert Brustein, "Pirandello's Drama of Revolt," in *Pirandello: A Collection of Critical Essays*, ed. Glauco Cambon (Englewood Cliffs, NJ, 1967), p. 133.
3 Renato Barilli, *La Linea Svevo-Pirandello* (Milano, 1977), pp. 153, 186.
4 Douglas Radcliff-Umstead, *The Mirror of Our Anguish: A Study of Luigi Pirandello's Narrative Writings* (Cranbury, NJ and London, 1978), p. 162.
5 Ibid., pp. 166–67.
6 Ibid., p. 163.
7 Gaspare Giudice, *Luigi Pirandello* (Torino, 1963), p. 179. My translation.
8 Ibid., p. 319.
9 Pirandello, *It Is So!! (If You Think So)*, tr. Arthur Livingston, in *Naked Masks*, ed. Eric Bentley (New York, 1952), p. 138. All further page references will be cited in the text. See my discussion of the play in Anne Paolucci, *Pirandello's Theater: The Recovery of the Modern Stage for Dramatic Art* (Carbondale, IL and London, 1974), pp. 64–88.
10 Radcliff-Umstead, p. 192.
11 See Pirandello, *On Humor* [*L'Umorismo*], tr. Antonio Illiano and Daniel P. Testa (Chapel Hill, NC, 1974), pp. 131–32, 145. The entire book is excellent reading and most important in any discussion of Pirandello's humor and how it influenced later playwrights of the "Absurd." See also p. 113, where Pirandello illustrates the levels of perception involved in his definition of "il sentimento del contrario" with a colorful description of "an old lady whose hair is dyed and completely smeared with some kind of horrible ointment; she is all made-up in a clumsy and awkward fashion and is all dolled-up like a young girl. I begin to laugh. I *perceive* that she is the *opposite* of what a respectable old lady should be. ... [T]he comic consists precisely of this *perception of the opposite*. But if, at this point, reflection interferes in me to suggest that perhaps this old lady finds no pleasure in dressing up like an exotic parrot, and that perhaps she is distressed by it and does it only because she pitifully deceives herself into believing that, by making herself up like that and by concealing her wrinkles and gray hair, she may be able to hold the love of her much younger husband – if reflection comes to suggest all this, then I can no longer laugh at her as I did at first, exactly because the inner working of reflection has made me go beyond, or rather enter deeper into the initial

stage of awareness: from the beginning *perception of the opposite*, reflection has made me shift to a *feeling of the opposite*. And herein lies the precise difference between the comic and humor." *L'Umorismo* was written in 1908 and revised in 1920: the playwright surely must have recalled this and similar passages from the work when he described the Marchesa in *Enrico IV*. She too dyes her hair and tries to look younger for her lover – one of many postures which make up her multi-faceted "portrait." (See also in this connection my discussion in *Pirandello's Theater* of "The Creative Madness of Henry IV," particularly pp. 95–97.)

Six Characters: Pirandello's Last Tape

ANDREW K. KENNEDY

I

There can be little doubt that Pirandello's *Six Characters in Search of an Author* owes its continued hold on our imagination – and its power as theatre – to the successful fusion of two orders of experience: the pain of role-playing in any life, and the painful limitations of dramatic art, particularly the crisis of post-Ibsen naturalism.

The way Pirandello achieves this fusion is familiar enough and can be restated as follows. The imagined but prematurely abandoned "characters," who come to claim performance on the stage, feel themselves caught in the false fixity of a few moments of action; so they hope to be shown, to be re-created in the precise sense, through a different and compensating fixity: the Grecian urn perfectedness of art. But the completion and rehearsal of an unfinished play is not at all like the Grecian urn; on the contrary, it brings back the flux of life and inchoate creation, and the characters have to suffer again an awareness that exceeds their role. In effect, they react to this openness by wanting to choose the *kind* of play that suits them. And the two most articulate characters – the Father and the Stepmother – are torn by a desire for seemingly conflicting types of play: they want absolute fidelity to every naturalistic detail (the yellow plush of Madame Pace's sofa) while also wanting to go beyond this reduced play to express their essential inwardness: they want to be chorus, and they want to *mean* more than their fixed actions and words.

To put it another way, *Six Characters* embodies not only the paradox of art against life, fixity, and happening. It also presents the tension between a play of abundant verbal expression and one that is reduced to a photographic fragment. In what follows I want to examine this tension – in terms of form, action and language. And it is language, what the play can tell us about the crisis of dramatic speech, that will be my main concern; I believe it is a theme that has received little attention so far.

II

Before taking a closer look at the text, I should like to recall that Pirandello, with all his theatrical inventiveness, was a literary dramatist in several senses. Like Shaw and Beckett, in their different ways, he was a prolific writer outside the theatre; and when he turned to drama he not only insisted on the importance of the "book," the text, but he was caught, like many of the moderns, in the intolerable wrestle with words. It seems to have been a case of a rich prose writer needing to count every dramatic coin, a touch of late-nineteenth-century verboseness struggling to find its own economy. And it is revealing to see, from a characteristically wordy definition in an early essay on drama, that the economy he admired was that of Ibsen – what he called *azione parlata*:

it is necessary for the dramatist to find the word that shall be the *action itself spoken*, the living word that can move, the immediate expression, connatural with the act ...[1]

Now it is clear that in *Six Characters* we find something like a parody of this wonderful economy where word and situation are one. What we have instead is a split between these two, the words are incommensurable, there are too many or too few, they sprout in luxuriance or else wither away. All this is carefully controlled by Pirandello and the tension in the dialogue follows from the open form around the closed scene.[2] Nevertheless, the classic proportions of modern realism are disrupted. We grasp this most directly through the grotesque disproportion of the lines given to the father inside the fixed situation – *The Scene* – and what I shall call the open situation outside it. In his *Scene* the Father is tied to a mumbling minimal utterance, as in re-enacting the high-class brothel meeting with the Step-daughter:

Then ... well ... it shouldn't any longer be so ... May I take off your hat?[3]

Contrast with this any of the Father's prolix set speeches in the open situation – instances of soul-white-washing on one level – as when he states the pathos of words being irredeemably private:

But can't you see that here we have the cause of all the trouble! In the use of words! Each one of us has a whole world of things inside him. ... And each one of us has his own particular world. How can we understand each other if into the words which I speak I put the sense and the value of things as I understand them within myself. ... While at the same time whoever is listening to them inevitably assumes them to have the sense and value that they have for him. ... The sense and value that they have in the world that he has within him?[4]

And so on, with variations. I think this disproportion of the word goes right through the texture of the play.

It is as if (to extend Pirandello's metaphor) the Author came to his characters aware of their desire for potentially infinite self-expression; but the fictive play-in-the-making not only reduces the expressible to the minimum, it is the first *record* of the decline of spoken action in modern drama.

III

The fictive unwritten play – the central invention in the play – exists as a text; at least, it can be reconstructed. All we have to do is to read the script from the prompter's sheets, and as we do so we may read certain portents in that text.

It is a lucky find, that prompter who can take down the character's lines, as they are spoken, in shorthand. The producer, representing narrow naturalism, is obviously delighted: the prompter's copy supplies the need for a text, or rather a script – recording exactly what was said in the supposed original off-stage event.[5] It thus anticipates the tape-recorder. As spoken dialogue it should stand out, in gesture and voice, both from the actors' imitation and from the characters' parabeses and interruptions. If it stands out less immediately on the printed page, in diction and rhythm, that shows the relative uniformity of speech levels available for modern drama even within Pirandello's multi-level play. At all events the resulting script is short enough to be played back within a single performance – again like tape-recorded material and the scene-plays of Beckett. The play-back technique is, incidentally, related to that moving-static sense of an eternal recurrence which is part of the play's interest; but here I want to look at the content of that reconstructed script.

To begin with, there would be much more stage direction than dialogue: all the lively shuffling action around Madame Pace's sofa and hatstand would end up in italics. The outline for the script – "got up," we may recall, in the twenty-minute interval in the Producer's office – allows for two "acts,"̈ in fact two short scenes: the foiled prostitution in Madame Pace's dress shop and the final violence in the garden. They represent the two fixed – and crucial – events in the lives of the Characters. If the producer had his way, all the action would be combined into *one* "continuous well-knit scene," or, literally, a closed action.[6] For, several years before Brecht, the alternative open stage is ridiculed: "You do understand that we can hardly stick up notices telling the audience what the scene is. ... Or change the set three or four times in one act."[7]

The striking thing is that the narrow naturalism of the producer points to a structure found congenial by the conventions of "absurd drama" at a later date, though for different reasons. In fact the two conventions might well agree on several of the despairing demands made by the Producer, as on this one: ... "and yet in that small fragment we have to be able to hint at all the rest of the secret life of the character."[8]

One may observe in passing that the point here discussed is related to a more general question. Lukács has argued, with the novel in mind, that modernism is nothing but an extension of naturalism.[9] If we wanted to see whether this argument is valid – and valid in modern drama – we might set our Pirandello fragment-play against, say, Konstantin's "advanced" play in *The Seagull* at one end of the scale, and against *Krapp's Last Tape* at the other. I think it could be shown that the fragmented lyricism in Konstantin's play ("It is cold, cold, cold. ... It is deserted, deserted, deserted") remains, in the context of the whole play, a satire on what Chekhov presents as failed art, however sympathetically. Pirandello's method is much more problematic, in that what was in part intended as a satire on the impoverished theatre is so closely tied up with the radical tragi-comic questioning – of time, identity *and* language – in the texture of the whole play. By the time we come to Beckett the fragmented play-back not only becomes the whole play, but the scene-play is an attempt to create – out of the accepted break-down of time, identity and language – a timeless pattern *through* language. ("Shadows of the opus ... magnum." – "Nothing to say ... not a squeak.")

What dialogue remains in the prompter's script seems to amount to this: a few murmured speech fragments surrounded by silence (Father-Stepdaughter) and two "heartrending" screams (the Mother). Five out of the six characters voice – or do not voice – the fictive author's reluctance "to find the *word* that shall be the action itself spoken." So the script can be read as a play of minimal speech.

IV

For a start, the two child-characters are non-speaking – "they can no longer speak"[10] according to the mother, they are only there as presences to keep her torment alive; and in his 1925 Preface to the play Pirandello underlines this by playing with the idea of inchoate creatures of the imagination, at once insubstantial and inert. In short, they are stage images, and in terms of dramatic invention they can be regarded as instances of the retreat from the world.[11]

The Son is also silent within his scene, though outside it he is articulate enough to insist on his right to non-action and non-speech – in keeping with the wishes of the Author.[12] Moreover, when bullied by the Producer who is determined to get something, a few lines, a sketchy scene, out of him, the Son reiterates that he rushed out of his room the moment his Mother entered it, on the eve of the family catastrophe, without saying a word (senza dir *nulla*). And when pressed to say what he did after leaving the room he says:

[*everybody's attention is on him; amidst the anguished silence he takes a step or two towards the front of the stage*]:

Nothing ... As I was crossing the garden ...

[*He breaks off and becomes gloomy and absorbed.*][13]

So a third Character is well on the way to study a long silence, and the word "nothing" (*nulla* is repeated three times at this point in the Italian text) is a kind of key here. For one can see the Son not only as a reluctant Character,[14] but as a symptom of a new imaginative reluctance to create more than a very few "externalised" speaking parts. And the fictive Author, who would like to have consigned the Son to a speechless limbo, is a recognisable figure who is getting tired of stories and phrases.[15] True, outside his scene the Son goes on to give a horrifying account of how he found the little girl drowned in the fountain and they boy "with madness in his eyes" before suicide. But as this violent conclusion is mimed, one may suppose that the "eye-witness account" would become yet another stage direction in the prompter's script, and the Son would, finally, be allowed to retreat into silence.

When we come to think about the Mother, it is clear that she too is an image-character, the suffering mother, a village Mater Dolorosa; and much of her effectiveness is visual. (In a direction usually ignored, Pirandello describes a mask of sorrow for her with "wax tears fixed in the corners of the eyes and coursing down the cheeks.") Nevertheless, she speaks; and her speech is essentially a cry. Within the two scenes of our reconstructed prompter's script she utters nothing but two screams, and little more than "My daughter ... she's my daughter!" or "Oh my son! My son!" can be distinguished in performance.[16] The first scream comes when the Mother rushes in between Father and Stepdaughter to prevent the consummation of an act felt as incest; the other marks the horror of the Boy's suicide. It is easy to dismiss this as melodrama. For me it seems more significant that these scenes work like the climaxes in Italian opera and some "neo-realismo" films: piercing voice and violent movement. The reason why these scenes move us – why Pirandello's original satiric intent cannot extend to these climaxes – is not only because human suffering is barely distanced here, let alone mocked. One may also see in these scenes of violence, apart from the obviously denatured remnants of Romantic drama, the pitting of image and noise *against* sustained chunks of rational-ised dialogue. It points to another form of minimally verbal drama: the counterpart of the quiet fragment-play.

If, within the fixed situation, the mother's speech is a kind of cry, in the open situation almost everything she says is a protest against action. There is her reluctance to have the veil lifted from her face, the oft-repeated plea to stop the re-enactment of her scenes, and the trick-scene with Madame Pace – where she appears *in absentia* – only to try and nullify that act, that dialogue. Her key-line might be:

No, no! My God! Stop it please![17]

Existentially, this embodies the naive pathos of a suffering person wanting to undo the fixity of action (as in the apocryphal story of the woman spectator in the box who called out to Othello: "Stop it, can't you see she loves you!"). But in terms of dramatic art, we see a fourth character on the way towards minimal action and speech. Like the Son, the Mother was conceived by Pirandello as a half-abandoned creation of the mind, mid-way between the articulate Father-Stepdaughter and the silent children. But in this fiction we can now see the ascetic imagination withdrawing from more and more – until only two characters are left with the desire to articulate, to find in words the meaning of action.

The main interest of the Stepdaughter in the present context is that she is – like the Father – articulate, but, unlike him, eager to speak her lines, reenact her scenes. From her point of view, the *Scene* is the old "obligatory scene" of the well-made play; and she feels she must speak her lines because they seem to justify her – while the Father needs all the resources of an inward gloss to extend (and extenuate) the fixed speech that condemns him. In short, the Stepdaughter is a relatively solid and naturalistic left-over from the old drama. Where the others are silent or reluctant performers, she has enough exhibitionism – the histrionic desire to be seen and heard – to want to add to the prompter's text words *not* her own:

Well, then, let's take off this little frock at once, shall we?[18]

I have already said that the Father's articulateness in the open situation marks a central disproportion: an excess of words trying to eke out what he feels as a constricting pittance of words in his fixed scene. An essential link must now be added: the link between the Father's acute word-consciousness and his constant questioning of his own identity. The speech already quoted is, alone, sufficient to establish the link; for in that jump from the "use of words" to "Each one of us has a whole world of things inside him,"[19] we connect a sense of isolation through language with what one of the moral-bias critics of the play has called "the dissolution of the ego."[20] Certainly, the Father is represented as both isolated and as "many persons ... many persons ... according to all the possibilities of being that there are within us. ..."[21] I would say that if the Father's whole part exemplifies more than anything in the play the "dissolution" of character, then the few words he is allowed within the fixed scene can be seen as the fossilised fragments of that dissolution. Hence the tragi-comic contradiction of wanting to preserve each syllable of speech fragment intact, while insisting that the whole speech-sequence is untrue to the self. To correct the actor and pedantically recall the question-tag actually spoken:

Not "hope" – "will it?," "will it?"[22]

is to provide the divided character with the kind of prop the preservation of an exact record sometimes promises to shaken identity. Meanwhile, there remains the furious objection, all that inwardness, which knows that this fossil speech of the fixed scene is not enough; and Pirandello shares the predicament. So he creates in the Father an impoverished naturalistic Hamlet: with all that shopworn, manic near-soliloquising. Still tied, in a one-minute scene, to the last relatively solid character – the Stepdaughter – he is about to loosen this link, to be left to his own subjectivity. And the logical extension of the Father is the solitary character, surrounded by a deep solipsistic silence through which the fragmented record of a fixed yet timeless moment is played back again and again. That is why I see in the Father an early Krapp.

In sum, the prompter's copy points towards the act-play or the scene-play with one or two characters; – and the dialogue within it towards that extreme naturalism that ends by transcending itself: where minimal language is used in a new way. The "word that is action itself spoken" is being reduced to brief snatches, single words, cries or silence, and the resulting fragment is "played back" and so organised that it is felt to represent not a slice-of-life but a timeless moment. If there is something static about this, if the words are too limited for the "emotions embalmed alive"[23] in them, then what is static and limited becomes the stuff of drama.

V

I am conscious that, for the purposes of discussion, I have isolated what is only one element in the play. To see this element is, I hope, revealing; but it would be perverse not to see around it. I have already suggested that Pirandello stands between Chekhov and Beckett in his ambivalent use of the fragment-play.[24] On the one hand there is the firmly placed satire on the naturalistic stage, on the other hand the move towards solipsism. There is the break with the solid perspective of realism, and yet much of the dialogue in the full play – all that explanation to the explanation-hungry producer – presents firm clues to motive, time past and consequence; and even the Father expresses his sense of the fragility of words in remarkably robust-looking rhetoric. The play is made up of this tension of opposites.

This tension is related to Pirandello's artistic aims as stated in the 1930 Preface to the play. Clearly, Pirandello's main intention was to go beyond the mere story to express a "deeper spiritual need." The Preface is, among other things, a kind of manifesto of aesthetic idealism: like Dante's Francesca the half-abandoned "characters" will return, always living and new, in the work of art which lives for ever as form. Francis Fergusson quotes the Preface[25] and makes it central to his distinguished study of the play, seeing the play as the fulfillment of the stated intention: "he lifted the action, as it were, from the realm of fact and sensation, of eavesdropping and the curious intrigue, to the more disinterested realm of contemplation." And this realm is reached (I summarise) by letting the characters contemplate the crucial moments in their lives played over "as though for the first time."[26]

I can accept this, but only by stressing once more the wishful compensatory quality in this Grecian urn view of art – and it is not, in the end, altogether compelling. I have used Keats's image precisely to underline the ambivalence – tragic life is breaking in, and, in the present instance, the resources of dramatic art are breaking down. In so far as Pirandello's idealistic view of life and art does compensate, the Characters do find the author they seek, in spite of these two agents of diminishment: the fictive author's reluctant imagination and the producer's narrow convention. Dissolving identity and fragmented speech are eked out by ideal art.

But hindsight and repeated personal response to the play make one understand the line of progression – both historical and psychological – from the idealistic view of art to a certain creative nihilism. The art-play after Pirandello (in Beckett and others) appears, as if in fulfillment of the wishes of Pirandello's fictive author, as a beautiful small structure, the perfect compensatory image for meaninglessness. Then the remaining scaffolding goes. And the resulting play will be found related to the one contained within Pirandello's *Six Characters*: short, timelessly played back, static-spontaneous; the characters isolated; and the dialogue – in its fusion of inwardness and exact recording – the action itself *barely* spoken.

NOTES

1 *L'azione parlata* (1899), from Eric Bentley; *The Life of the Drama* (London, 1965), p. 98, also *Theory of the Modern Stage*, ed. Eric Bentley, New York, 1968.
2 The production of the play by the *Compagnia dei Giovani*, directed by Giorgia di Lullo (London, Aldwych Theatre, March 31–April 6, 1966), was exceptionally clear in presenting this tension: a swirling play of compensatory self-expression was being enacted around the fixed *Scene* – as if two opposed conventions of drama had come into collision.
3 *Six Characters*, translated by Frederick May (London, 1954), p. 43.
4 Ibid., p. 17; compare: Prefazione (Mondadori, 1954), p. 11: "the deception of (mutual) understanding based, irremediably, on the empty abstraction of words;" (My translation).
5 This need for exact recording may also explain why the Producer does not take up the Juvenile Lead's invitation to improvise in the manner of the commedia dell' arte.
6 Op. cit., p. 60. Cf. "un' azione simultanea e serrata," Mondadori ed., p. 84.

7   To which the Leading Man replies – it has some irony in the present context – "They used to in the good old days."

8   Op. cit., p. 50.

9   George Lukács, *The Meaning of Contemporary Realism*, London. 1962, p. 34 in particular, but throughout the chapter, "Ideology of Modernism."

10 Op. cit., p. 52.

11 George Steiner, *The Retreat from the Word*, "The Listener," July 14 and 21, 1960. These articles only touch on drama incidentally; but the context is relevant.

12 Op. cit., p. 67.

13 Ibid.

14 "Reluctant" is Pirandello's word. Prefazione, ed. cit., p. 10.

15 Cf. "for me it was never enough to represent the figure of a man or a woman ... to tell a story ... for the mere pleasure of telling it." – Prefazione, p. 8, and "How tired I am of stories, how tired I am of phrases that come down with all their feet on the ground! ... I begin to long for some little language ... broken words, inarticulate words ..." Virginia Woolf, *The Waves* (London, 1955), p. 169.

16 Op. cit., p. 53 and p. 68. In the original this effect is even stronger.

17 Op. cit., p. 13.

18 Op. cit., p. 49.

19 Cf. above: p. 3.

20 Joseph Wood Krutch, *Modernism in Modern Drama* (Cornell, 1953). Incidentally, Krutch predicts, "somewhat light-mindedly," that this is a play to end all plays.

21 Op. cit., p. 46.

22 Op. cit., p. 46.

23 For the context of this Pirandello phrase see: Lander MacLintock, *The Age of Pirandello*, Indiana University Studies, 1951, quoted by Bamber Gascoigne, *Twentieth Century Drama*, London 1962, p. 107.

24 Cf. above, p. 1.

25 Francis Fergusson, *The Idea of a Theater* (New York, 1954), pp. 201–202. The passages from the Preface, quoted by Francis Fergusson without reference, come from two different sections of the Preface.

26 Ibid.

Godotology:
There's Lots of Time in *Godot*

RICHARD SCHECHNER

Two duets and a false solo, that's *Waiting for Godot*. Its structure is more musical than dramatic, more theatrical than literary. The mode is pure performance: song and dance, music-hall routine, games. And the form is a spinning away, a centrifugal wheel in which the center – Time – can barely hold the parts, Gogo and Didi, Pozzo and Lucky, the Boy(s). The characters arrive and depart in pairs, and when they are alone they are afraid: half of them is gone. The Boy isn't really by himself, though one actor plays the role(s). "It wasn't you came yesterday," states Vladimir in act two. "No Sir," the Boy says. "This is your first time." "Yes sir." Only Godot is alone, at the center of the play and all outside it at once. "What does he do, Mr. Godot? ... He does nothing, Sir." But even Godot is linked to Gogo/Didi. "To Godot? Tied to Godot! What an idea! No question of it. (*Pause.*) For the moment." Godot is also linked to the Boy(s), who tend his sheep and goats, who are his messengers. Nor can we forget that Godot cares enough for Gogo/Didi to send someone each night to tell them the appointment will not be kept. What exquisite politeness.

Pozzo (and we must assume, Lucky) has never heard of Godot, although the promised meeting is to take place on his land. Pozzo is insulted that *his* name means nothing to Gogo/Didi. "We're not from these parts," Estragon says in apology, and Pozzo deigns, "You are human beings none the less." Pozzo/Lucky have no appointment to keep. Despite the cracking whip and Pozzo's air of big business on the make, their movements are random, to and fro across the land, burdens in hand, rope in place: there is always time to stop and proclaim. In Act One, after many adieus, Pozzo says, "I don't seem to be able ... (*long hesitation*) ... to depart." And when he does move, he confesses, "I need a running start." In Act Two, remembering nothing about "yesterday," Pozzo replies to Vladimir's question, "Where do you go from here" with a simple "On." It is Pozzo's last word.

The Pozzo/Lucky duet is made of improvised movements and set speeches (Lucky's has run down). The Gogo/Didi duet is made of set movements (they must be at this place each night at dusk to wait for Godot to come or night to fall) and improvised routines spun out of long-ago learned habits. Pozzo who starts in no place is worried only about Time; he ends without time but with a desperate need to move. Gogo/Didi are "tied" to this place and want only for time to pass. Thus, part way through the first act the basic scenic rhythm of *Godot* is established by the strategic arrangement of characters: Gogo/Didi (and later the Boy) have definite appointments, a rendezvous they *must* keep. Pozzo/Lucky are free agents, aimless, not tied to anything but each other. For this reason, Pozzo's watch is very important to him. Having nowhere to go, his only relation to the world is in knowing "the time." The play is a confrontation between the rhythms of place and time. Ultimately they are coordinates of the same function.

Of course, Pozzo's freedom is illusory. He is tied to Lucky – and vice-versa – as tightly as the others are tied to Godot and the land. In the scenic calculus of the play, rope = appointment. As one coordinate weakens, the other tightens. Thus, when Pozzo/Lucky lose their sense of time, there is a corresponding increase in their need to cover space. Lucky's speech is imperfect memory, an uncontrollable stream of un-consciousness, while Pozzo's talk is all *tirade*, a series of set speeches, learned long ago, and slowly deserting the master actor, just as the things which define his identity – watch, pipe, atomizer – desert him. I am reminded of Yeats' *Circus Animals' Desertion* where images fail the old poet who is finally forced to "lie down where all the ladders start/ In the foul rag-and-bone shop of the heart." Here, too, Pozzo will find himself (Lucky is already there). Thus we see these two in their respective penultimate phases, comforted only by broken bursts of eloquence, laments for that last lost love, clock time.

The pairing of characters – those duets – links time and space, presents them as discontinuous coordinates. Gogo/Didi are not sure whether the place in Act Two is the same as that in Act One; Pozzo cannot remember yesterday; Gogo/Didi do not recall what they did yesterday. "We should have thought of it [suicide] a million years ago, in the nineties." Gogo either forgets at once, or he never forgets. This peculiar sense of time and place is not centered *in* the characters, but *between* them. Just as it takes two lines to fix a point in space, so it takes two characters to *unfix* our normal expectations of time, place, and being. This pairing is not unique to *Waiting for Godot*; it is a favorite device of contemporary playwrights. The Pupil and the Professor in *The Lesson,* Claire and Solange in *The Maids,* Peter and Jerry in *The Zoo Story:* these are of the same species as *Godot.* What might these duets mean or be? Each of them suggests a precarious existence, of sense of self and self-in-the-world so dependent on "the other" as to be inextricably bound up in the other's physical presence. In these plays "experience" is not "had" by a single character, but "shared" between them. It is not a question of fulfillment – of why Romeo wants Juliet – but of existence. By casting the characters homosexually, the author removes the "romantic" element: these couples are not joined because of some biological urge but because of some metaphysical necessity. The drama that emerges from such pairing is intense and locked-in – a drama whose focus is internal without being "psychological." Internalization without psychology is naked drama, theater unmediated by character. That is why, in these plays, the generic structure of their elements – farce, melodrama, vaudeville – is so unmistakably clear. There is no way (or need) to hide structure: that's all there is. But still, in *Godot,* there are meaningful differences between Vladimir and Estragon, Pozzo and Lucky; but even these shadings of individuation are seen only through the couple: to know one character, you have to know both.

In Aristotelian terms drama is made of the linked chain: action > plot > character > thought. Connections run efficiently in either direction, although for the most part one seeks the heart of a play in its action (as Fergusson uses that term). These same elements are in *Godot,* but the links are broken. The discontinuity of time is reflected on this more abstract level of structure. Thus what Gogo and Didi do is not what they are thinking; nor can we understand their characters by adding and relating events to thoughts. And the action of the play – waiting – is not what they are after but what they want most to avoid. What, after all, are their games for? They wish to "fill time" in such a way that the vessel "containing" their activities is unnoticed amid the activities themselves. Whenever there is nothing "to do" they remember why they are here: To wait for Godot. That memory, that direct confrontation with Time, is painful. They play, invent, move, sing to avoid the sense of waiting. Their *activities* are therefore keeping them from a consciousness of the *action* of the play. Although there is a real change in Vladimir's understanding of his experience (he learns precisely what "nothing to be done" means) and in Pozzo's life, these changes and insights do not emerge from the plot (as Lear's "wheel of fire" does), but stand outside of what's happened. Vladimir has his epiphany while Estragon sleeps – in a real way his perception is a function of the sleeping Gogo. Pozzo's understanding, like the man himself, is blind. Structurally as well as thematically, *Godot* is an "incompleted" play; and its openness is not at the end (as *The Lesson* is open-ended) but in many places throughout: it is a play of gaps and pauses, of broken-off dialogue, of speech and action turning into time-avoiding games and routines. Unlike Beckett's perfectly modulated *Molloy*, *Waiting for Godot* is designed off-balance. It is the very opposite of *Oedipus*. In *Godot* we do not have the meshed ironies of experience, but that special anxiety associated with question marks preceded and followed by nothing.

What then holds *Godot* together? Time, habit, memory, and games form the texture of the play and provide both its literary and theatrical interest. In *Proust*, Beckett speaks of habit and memory in a way that helps us understand *Godot*:

The laws of memory are subject to the more general laws of habit. Habit is a compromise effected between the individual and his environment, or between the individual and his own organic eccentricities, the guarantee of a dull inviolability, the lightening-conductor of his existence. Habit is the ballast that chains the dog to his vomit. ... Life is a succession of habits, since the individual is a succession of individuals. ... The creation of the world did not take place once and for all, but takes place every day.

The other side of "dull inviolability" is "knowing," and it is this that Gogo/ Didi must avoid if they are to continue. But knowledge is precisely what Didi has near the end of the play. It ruins everything for him:

Was I sleeping, while the others suffered? Am I sleeping now? To-morrow, when I wake, or think I do, what shall I say of to-day? That with Estragon my friend, at this place, until the fall of night, I waited for Godot? That Pozzo passed, with his carrier, and that he spoke to us? Probably. But in all that what truth will there be? [*Looking at Estragon*] He'll know nothing. He'll tell me about the blows he received and I'll give him a carrot.

Then, paraphrasing Pozzo, Didi continues:

Astride a grave and a difficult birth. Down in the hold, lingeringly, the grave-digger puts on the forceps. We have time to grow old. The air is full of our cries. (*He listens.*) But habit is a great deadener. (*He looks again at Estragon.*) At me too someone is looking, of me too someone is saying, He is sleeping, he knows nothing, let him sleep on. (*Pause.*) I can't go on! (*Pause.*) What have I said?

In realizing that he knows nothing, in seeing that habit is the great deadener – in achieving an ironic point of view towards himself, Didi knows everything, and wishes he did not. For him Pozzo's single instant has become "lingeringly." For Pozzo "the same day, the same second" is enough to enfold all human experience; Didi realizes that there is "time to grow old." But habit will rescue him. Having shouted his anger, frustration, helplessness ("I can't go on!"), Didi is no longer certain of what he said. Dull inviolability has been violated, but only for an instant: one instant is enough for insight, and we have a lifetime to forget. The Boy enters. Unlike the first act, Didi asks him no questions. Instead Didi makes statements. "He won't come this evening. ... But he'll come to-morrow." For the first time, Didi asks the Boy about Godot. "What does he do, Mr. Godot? ... Has he a beard, Mr. Godot??" The Boy answers: Godot does nothing, the beard is probably white. Didi says – after a silence – "Christ have mercy on us!" But both thieves will not be saved, and now that the game is up, Vladimir seeks to protect himself:

Tell him ... (*he hesitates*) ... tell him you saw me and that ... (*he hesitates*) ... that you saw me [...] (*With sudden violence.*) You're sure you saw me, you won't come and tell me to-morrow that you never saw me!

The "us" of the first act is the "me" of the second. Habits break, old friends are abandoned, Gogo – for the moment – is cast into the pit. When Gogo awakens, Didi is standing with his head bowed. Didi does not tell his friend of his conversation with the Boy nor of his insight or sadness. Gogo asks, "What's wrong with you," and Didi answers, "Nothing." Didi tells Estragon that they must return the following evening to keep their appointment once again. But for him the routine is meaningless: Godot will not come. There is something more than irony in his reply to Gogo's question, "And if we dropped him?" "He'd punish us," Didi says. But the punishment is already apparent to Didi: the pointless execution of orders without hope of fulfillment. Never coming; for Didi, Godot has come ... and gone.

But Didi alone sees behind his old habits and even he, in his ironic musing, senses someone else watching him sleep just as he watches Gogo: he learns that all awareness is relative. Pozzo is no relativist, but a strict naturalist. In the first act he describes the setting of the sun with meticulous hand gestures, twice consulting his watch so as to be precise. Pozzo knows his "degrees" and the subtle shadings of time's passing. He also senses that when night comes it "will burst upon us pop! like that! just when we least expect it." And for Pozzo, once it is night there is no more time, for he measures that commodity by the sun. Going blind, Pozzo too has an epiphany – the exact opposite of Didi's:

Have you not done tormenting me with your accursed time! It's abominable! When! When! One day, is that not enough for you, one day he went dumb, one day I went blind, one day we'll go deaf, one day we were born, one day we shall die, the same day, the same second, is that not enough for you!

Of the light gleaming an instant astride the grave, Pozzo has only a dim memory. He has found a new habit to accommodate his new blindness; his epiphany is false. The experience of the play indeed shows us that there is plenty of time, too much: waiting means more time than things to fill it.

Pozzo/Lucky play a special role in this passing of time that is *Waiting for Godot*'s action. Things have changed for them by Act Two. Pozzo is blind and helpless, Lucky is dumb. Their "career" is nearly over. Like more conventional theatrical characters, they have passed from bad times to worse. The rope, whip, and valise remain: all else is gone – Lear and the Fool on the heath, that is what this strange pair suggests to me. But if they are that *in themselves*, they are something different to Gogo/Didi. In the first act, Gogo/Didi suspect that Pozzo may be Godot. Discovering that he is not, they are curious about him and Lucky. They circle around their new acquaintances, listen to Pozzo's speeches, taunt Lucky, and so on. Partly afraid, somewhat uncertainly, they integrate Pozzo/Lucky into their world of waiting: they make out of the visitors a way of passing time. And they exploit the *persons* of Pozzo/Lucky, taking food and playing games. (In the Free Southern Theatre production, Gogo and Didi pick-pocket Pozzo, stealing his watch, pipe, and atomizer – no doubt to hock them for necessary food. This interpretation has advantages: it grounds the play in an acceptable reality; it establishes a first act relationship of double exploitation – Pozzo uses them as audience and they use him as income.) In the second act this exploitation process is even clearer. Pozzo no longer seeks an audience. Gogo/Didi no longer think that Pozzo may be Godot (Gogo, briefly, goes through this routine). Gogo/Didi try to detain Pozzo/Lucky as long as possible. They play rather cruel games with them, postponing assistance. It would be intolerable to Gogo/Didi for this "diversion" to pass quickly, just as it is intolerable for an audience to watch it go on so long. What "should" be a momentary encounter is converted into a prolonged affair. Vladimir sermonizes on their responsibilities. "It is not everyday that we are needed." The talk continues without action. Then, trying to pull Pozzo up, Vladimir falls on top of him. Estragon does likewise. Obviously, they can pull Pozzo up (just as they can get up themselves). But instead they remain prone. "Won't you play with us?" they seem to be asking. But Pozzo is in no playing mood. Despite his protests, Gogo/Didi continue their game. It is, as Gogo says, "child's play." They get up, help Pozzo and Lucky up, and the play proceeds. When they are gone, Estragon goes to sleep. Vladimir shakes him awake. "I was lonely." And speaking of Pozzo/Lucky, "That passed the time." For them, perhaps; but for the audience? It is an ironic scene – the entire cast sprawled on the floor, hard to see, not much action. It makes an audience aware that the time is not passing fast enough.

This game with Pozzo/Lucky is one of many. In fact, the gamesmanship of *Waiting for Godot* is extraordinary. Most of the play is taken up by a series of word games, play acting, body games, routines. Each of these units is distinct, usually cued in by memories of *why* Gogo/Didi are where they are. Unable simply to consider the ramifications of "waiting", unfit, that is, for pure speculation (as Lucky was once fit), they fall back onto their games: how many thieves were saved, how many leaves on the tree, calling each other names, how can we hang ourselves, and so on. These games are not thematically meaningless, they feed into the rich image-texture of the play; but they are meaningless in terms of the play's action: they lead nowhere, they contribute to the non-plot. Even when Godot is discussed, the talk quickly becomes routinized. At one time Vladimir spoke to Godot. "What exactly did we ask him for?" Estragon asks. Vladimir replies, "Were you not there?" "I can't have been listening." But it is Gogo who supplies the information that Didi confirms: That their request was "a kind of prayer ... a vague supplication." And it is both of them, in contrapuntal chorus, who confirm that Godot would have to "think it over ... in the quiet of his home ... consult his family ... his friends ... his agents ... his correspondents ... his books ... his bank account ... before taking a decision."

This kind of conversation populates *Godot*. A discussion or argument is transformed into routinized counterpoint. Much has been said about the beauty of Beckett's prose in this play. More needs to be said about its routine qualities. Clichés are converted into game/rituals by dividing the lines between Gogo and Didi, by arbitrarily assigning one phrase to each. Thus we have a sense of their "pairdom," while we are entranced by the rhythm of their language. Beckett's genius in dialogue in his *scoring*, not his "book." This scoring pertains not only to language but to events as well. Whatever there is to do, is done in duets. By using these, Gogo/Didi are able to convert anxiety into habit. Gogo is more successful at this than Didi. For Gogo things are either forgotten at once or never forgotten. There is no "time-span" for him, only a kaleidoscopic present in which everything that is there is forever in focus. It takes Didi to remind Gogo of Godot, and these reminders always bring Gogo pain, his exasperated "Ah." For Didi the problem is more complex. Gogo says "no use wriggling" to which Didi replies, "the essential doesn't change." These are opposite contentions; that's why they harmonize so well.

A few words about Time. If waiting is the play's action, Time is its subject. Godot is not Time, but he is associated with it – the one who makes but does not keep appointments. (An impish thought occurs: Perhaps Godot passes time with Gogo/Didi just as they pass it with him. Within this scheme, Godot has nothing to do [as the Boy tells Didi in Act Two] and uses the *whole play* as a diversion in his day. Thus the "big game" is a strict analogy of the many "small games" that make the play.) The basic rhythm of the play is habit interrupted by memory, memory obliterated by games. Why do Gogo/Didi play? In order to deaden their sense of waiting. Waiting is a "waiting *for*" and it is precisely this that they wish to forget. One may say that "waiting" is the larger context within which "passing time" by playing games is a sub-system, protecting them from the sense that they are waiting. They confront Time (i.e., are conscious of Godot) only when there is a break in the games and they "know" and "feel" that they are waiting.

In conventional drama all details converge on the center of action. We may call this kind of structure centripetal. In *Godot* the action is centrifugal. Gogo/Didi do their best to shield themselves from a direct consciousness that they are at the appointed place at the prescribed time. If the center of the play is Time, dozens of activities and capers fling Gogo/Didi away from this center. But events at the periphery force them back inwards: try as they will, they are not able to forget. We may illustrate the structure thus:

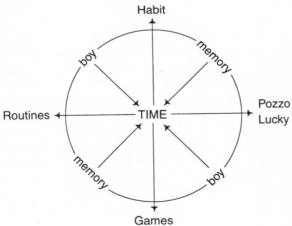

Caught on the hub of this wheel, driven by "re-minders" toward the center, Gogo/Didi literally have no where to go outside of this tight scheme. The scenic counterpart is the time-bracket "dusk-darkness" – that portion of the day when they must be at the appointed place. But even when night falls, and they are free to go, our last glimpse of them in each act is:

> *Estragon.* Well, shall we go?
> *Vladimir.* Yes, let's go.
>   *They do not move.*

As if to underline the duet-nature of this ending, Beckett reverses the line assignments in Act Two.

What emerges is a strange solitude, again foreshadowed by Beckett in his *Proust.* "The artistic tendency is not expansive but a contraction. And art is the apotheosis of solitude." In spinning out from the center, Gogo/Didi do not go anywhere, "they do not move." Yet their best theatrical moments are all motion, a running helter-skelter, a panic. Only at the end of each act, when it is all over for the day, are they quiet. The unmoved mover is Time, that dead identicality of instant and eternity. Once each for Didi and Pozzo, everything is contracted to that sense of Time where consciousness is possible, but nothing else. To wait and not know *how* to wait is to experience Time. To be freed from waiting (as Gogo/Didi are at the end of each act) is to permit the moon to rise more rapidly than it can (as it does on *Godot*'s stage), almost as if nature were illegally celebrating its release from its own clock. Let loose from Time, night comes all of a sudden. After intermission, there is the next day – and tomorrow, another performance.

There are two time rhythms in *Godot*, one of the play and one of the stage. Theatrically, the exit of the Boy and the sudden night are strong cues for the act (and the play) to end. We, the audience, are relieved – it's almost over for us. They, the actors, do not move – even when the Godot-game is over, the theater-game keeps them in their place: tomorrow they must return to enact identical routines. Underlying the play (all of it, not just the final scene of each act) is the theater, and this is exactly what the script insinuates – a nightly appointment performed for people the characters will never meet. *Waiting for Godot* powerfully injects the mechanics of the theater into the mysteries of the play.

Action and Play in Beckett's Theater

JOHN FLETCHER

Comedy was gesture before ever it was words. In all ages the movements and gestures of the actors have been of prime importance in the theater, especially in the popular theater. From the banal mountebank and juggler of the public square, to the rigid, conventional action of the Peking opera, the theatrical phenomenon has always been characterized by an important active element.

Clownery, in particular, is a dramatic form that is at once very popular and immediately comprehensible. The clown has only to appear for a child to burst into laughter; after this first elementary apparition, the ritual gestures, carefully rehearsed in advance, carry the spectator's hilarity to its paroxysm. The contrast between the latter's glee and the clown's seriousness is striking: the spectator is lost in delight and the clown is concentrating on accomplishing correctly the falls and "accidents" he has prepared so minutely. For his is a difficult art, since it seeks to reproduce voluntarily the clumsy and absurd actions that others commit involuntarily. Like Shakespeare's wise fools, he is ridiculous by trade, imitating to the point of caricature (but not quite) what makes men silly, to such a degree that he becomes a kind of laughter-provoking mechanism; and like all mechanisms, he works best when in proper trim. The clown, in fact, instinctively follows Bergson's dictum: "the attitudes, gestures and movements of the human body are laughable in direct proportion to the degree in which this body reminds us of a simple machine."

Music hall is another popular form, and an essentially varied one, consisting of comic turns interspersed with song. The typical music hall comedian tells his jokes and ends his turn with a sentimental song. Sometimes he is joined by a partner, and they indulge in cross-talk; one of the men will embody "common sense," and the other obtuseness. Their misunderstandings give rise to laughter. This, too, requires careful rehearsal if the comedians are to attain the rapidity of reflex which most closely imitates the spontaneity of absurdity in everyday life. Here again, therefore, seriousness on the part of the actors is the necessary condition of laughter on the part of the spectators; and here again, it is the mechanical that provokes hilarity, but whereas clownery is mostly action, music hall comedy is mostly words.

A third popular form is mime. This has been a vital element in drama ever since the Greeks. An action as simple as that of tearing at one's hair and raising one's eyes to the sky is fully sufficient to convey the idea of grief and despair. The possibilities of universally understood gestures are exploited in grand opera, for instance, and mime can exist as an art form in its own right in the hands of a performer like Marcel Marceau, who is able, without recourse to words, to render a remarkably wide range of emotion, and tell a surprisingly large number of stories.

The three basic forms of action: circus clownery, music hall cross-talk, and dramatic mime, are all found in Beckett's theater, and serve to enrich it. This is appropriate, since his drama illustrates man's many attempts to fill life's emptiness, and so accords an important role to action in its varied forms. The Beckettian hero is a sort of clown who uses words and performs gestures that are intended to be amusing, in order to pass the time. But unlike a real clown, he seeks not to amuse others, but to cheat his own boredom; he is acting, but for himself.

Of all Beckett's plays, it is in *Waiting for Godot* that circus games are the most in evidence. Estragon, for example, pulls and tugs demonstratively at his boot; inadvertently lets his trousers drop about his feet when untying the string that serves as his belt, and fails to understand at once his companion's admonition to pull them up again; and drops off to sleep, only to wake up again a moment later with a start. As for Vladimir, he walks with his legs wide apart, because of his affliction, and frequently rushes to the wings, impelled by an urgent desire to urinate. In Act II, all the characters tumble on the floor; and Vladimir and Estragon do their gymnastic exercises clumsily, and stagger about the stage as Valdimir tries to inspect the wound on his friend's leg. The two argue, fall out, kiss and make up, only to recoil in disgust at the other's smell. Vladimir keeps tapping on the crown of his bowler to dislodge a flea that is troubling him, and eventually adopts Lucky's hat in desperation; Clov, too, is troubled by fleas, and shakes insecticide powder into his trousers to destroy them.

Pozzo's actions, all somewhat caricatured, are intended to indicate that he is a kind of ring-master (Lucky being his performing animal), and also to reveal the sort of complacent and unthinkingly callous man he is. He eats noisily, pulls on his wine-bottle, burps contentedly, fills his pipe, sprays the back of his throat with his vaporizer, "clears his throat, spits," all of this with a satisfied air. Lucky, on the other hand, reveals his nervous and unstable temperament by his panting and trembling, just as he shows the latent viciousness of the persecuted underdog in giving Estragon a violent kick in the shins.

In Beckett's drama, action is explored to the limit of the normally admissible, and beyond: the smallest acts of existence are re-enacted boringly and monotonously, as if to emphasize the derisory nature of our everyday mechanical gestures. Thus Winnie, in *Happy Days*, brushes her teeth, paints her lips, adjusts her hat, puts on and takes off her glasses, all the more earnestly since these actions fill her "day." It is, indeed, in this play that action, in the Beckettian sense of the word, is most important; together with Winnie's soliloquies, it forms almost the whole matter of the play.

In *Endgame*, Clov spends the time hanging on his hands, in moving the step-ladder about the stage. These irritating actions, interspersed with five brief laughs, announce the play's theme, even before a single word has been spoken, a theme summed up as "Old endgame lost of old, play and lose and have done with losing." In his first words, spoken with yawns, Hamm declares the active element will be uppermost in the play: "Me – to play." He wakes up without prompting; but in *Act Without Words II* the characters are wakened by a prod from a goad mounted on a wheel, and Winnie's sleep is broken by a piercing bell. All these characters, once aroused, carry out the gestures that remain possible for them. Hamm betrays his general anxiety in getting Clov to push him about in his arm-chair on castors, and in his neurotic need to be assured that he is "right in the center" of the room. At a loss, he cries out, "Think of something!" The dustbin-lids lift, to reveal Nagg and Nell, and the dustbin-lids are clamped down again; in between, Nagg tells his story, grimacing and white-faced like a clown, about the Englishman and his tailor, but he knows his gag no longer comes off: "I never told it worse. I tell this story worse and worse." A little later, the telescope slips from Clov's hands: "I did it on purpose," he says, killing time by the most pointless actions. Pozzo begs Estragon, who has invited him to sit down, to "ask [him] again;" similarly, Hamm requires Clov to ask him about the progress of his "story:"

> *Hamm.* ... I've got on with my story. I've got on with it well. Ask me where I've got to.
> *Clov.* Oh, by the way, your story.

Hamm. What story?

Clov. The one you've been telling yourself all your ... days.

Hamm. Ah you mean my chronicle?

Clov. That's the one.

Hamm. Keep going, can't you, keep going!

Clov. You've got on with it, I hope.

Hamm. Oh not very far, not very far. There are days like that, one isn't inspired.

This sort of dialogue is typical of Beckett's theater. It is in *Waiting for Godot*, however, that cross-talk is exploited to the full. More than eight times in that play Estragon and Vladimir exchange music hall-type lines:

Estragon. And what did he reply?

Vladimir. That he'd see.

Estragon. That he couldn't promise anything.

Vladimir. That he'd have to think it over.

Estragon. In the quiet of his home.

Vladimir. Consult his family.

Estragon. His friends.

Vladimir. His agents.

Estragon. His correspondents.

Vladimir. His books.

Estragon. His bank account.

Vladimir. Before taking a decision.

Estragon. It's the normal thing.

Vladimir. Is it not?

Estragon. I think it is.

Vladimir. I think so too.

    Silence

The direction "silence" is significant here, for it suggests that all this is the dialogue of two comedians facing each other on a music hall stage and pausing here for laughter. But it is that, and more: these exchanges often are tinged with poetry, as in the exchange about "All the dead voices," while remaining rooted firmly in traditional music hall:

Estragon. Que voulez-vous?

Vladimir. I beg your pardon?

Estragon. Que voulez-vous?

Vladimir. Ah, que voulez-vous? Exactly.

And as in the circus too, where one of the clowns will imitate the antics of another, mirroring in a comic manner his colleague's farcical behaviour, Beckett's characters ape each other, so that the spectator may know the absurd things happening off-stage:

Exit Vladimir hurriedly. Estragon gets up and follows him as far as the limit of the stage. Gestures of Estragon like those of spectator encouraging a pugilist.

The action often turns to cruelty and persecution: Pozzo torments Lucky, Estragon kicks Lucky to avenge himself, Vladimir strikes Pozzo to make him be silent, Hamm nags at Clov, who hits him with the toy dog, and insults his father ("Accursed progenitor!"). Sometimes the action can be almost gratuitous, as in the very fast exchange of three hats between Estragon and Vladimir in Act II of *Waiting for Godot,* which is pure Laurel and Hardy. Nevertheless, even this juggling has a point: Vladimir ends up wearing, not his own hat, but Lucky's, inheriting with it Lucky's gift of the gab. Significantly, when Lucky returns, he is dumb. Moreover, the play on boots has a theological interpretation, revealed to Harold Hobson by the author: namely, that one of Estragon's feet is blessed, and the other damned; the boot will not go on the foot that is damned, but it will go on the foot that is blessed, just as one of the thieves was saved. This is the reason why Estragon cries out with pain when he tries to walk in a boot on the foot that is damned, as at the end of Act II.

Krapp's Last Tape shares several of the characteristics I have been examining. Krapp's walk is laborious; he tipples and coughs and splutters, and nearly slips on a banana-skin: the hoariest of gags are calmly performed in Beckett's theater. He cups his ear with his hand to listen to the tape, sweeps boxes and ledger on to the floor, looks up a word in the dictionary, switches his tape-recorder on and off, and staggers a little after drinking backstage. All this is deliberately clownish.

In the radio plays, sound fills auricular space in much the same way as action fills visual space in the stage plays. The sound of a bicycle-bell and the squeak of brakes herald Mr. Tyler's arrival, or more precisely *constitute* his arrival, and the purring of a motor brings Mr. Slocum on to the scene. Similarly, gears grind, hens squawk, and the train "pulls up with [a] great hissing of stream and clashing of couplings." It is by these and by similar sounds that the action, which is of great importance in the stage plays, finds its radiophonic equivalent.

It is hardly surprising that Beckett should have written texts for mime, the *Acts Without Words,* in which nothing intervenes to affect the pure simplicity of action, since the whole is plain gesture. In the first of these, a man is "flung backwards on stage" from the right, tries to go out right again, but is "immediately flung back on stage." The only guide to his character is a "familiar gesture," not translated in the English version, that of "folding and unfolding his handkerchief." He soon learns to bow to the requirements of his obscure punishment and to respect the rules of the game: he reacts to the whistle which conveys his orders to him, and covets the carafe which descends from the flies to tease him. Then, finding the water impossible to reach, he attempts suicide, and then gives up and "looks at his hands," just as Belacqua did at the end of Beckett's 1934 short story, "A Wet Night."

Act Without Words II has two characters: a thin, slow, and clumsy man A, and a stout and active man B, living in two separate sacks. They are obliged to come out, each in turn, and carry out a number of banal gestures, such as teeth-brushing, hair-combing, praying, and so on. The two men never meet: each plays alone. Their two sacks shift, after each turn, a little further towards the spectator's left. There are three such turns, A's, B's, and the beginning of A's second.

These mimes are not of great interest in themselves, but they do throw light on the other plays. Beckett has said in conversation with Charles Marowitz that his interest is "not so much in Mime but in the stratum of movement which underlies the written word," and he went on to amplify his meaning in these words:

Producers don't seem to have any sense of form in movement. The kind of form one finds in music, for instance, where themes keep recurring. When, in a text, actions are repeated, they ought to be made unusual the first time, so that when they happen again – in exactly the same way – an audience will recognize them from before. In the revival of *Godot* (in Paris) I tried to get at something of that stylized movement that's in the play.[1]

This statement is about the only one Beckett has ever made about his dramatic technique, and it reveals the importance that attaches to mime in his plays.

The whistle recurs fourteen times in *Act Without Words I*; in *Godot* Valdimir knocks several times on the crown of his hat to dislodge the flea, and Estragon devotes himself even more frequently to the boots that give him so much trouble. But the most famous *leitmotiv* of that play is, of course, the line "We're waiting for Godot" and its inevitable corollary, "Ah!" (*C'est vrai*, in the French – a phrase Beckett says he found impossible to translate adequately). Similarly, Vladimir twice wonders whether night will ever fall, and then, when it does, sighs "At last!" The spectator who has been following attentively would not fail to notice this echo of a point made previously. This is a characteristic phenomenon: the expression "Nothing to be done" recurs four times in the play, Estragon's dreams which Vladimir refuses to hear about three times, and the carrot issue twice – at least once in each act, since doubling is a frequent device in Beckett's works, especially in the novel *Molloy*. In *Godot* it plays a vital part: Pozzo is conceited in the first act, blind in the second, Lucky the "thinker" goes dumb, but "the essential doesn't change," as Vladimir says, since the two men keep on waiting in vain for Godot to come, and the boy (if it is the same boy) brings the same message each time. Each time, too, Vladimir and Estragon plan half-heartedly to hang themselves the next day, and the two acts end in exactly the same way, except that the roles are reversed:

> *Estragon.* Well, shall we go?
> *Vladimir.* Yes, let's go.
>   *They do not move.*
> *Vladimir.* Well? Shall we go?
> *Estragon.* Yes, let's go.
>   *They do not move.*

The slight alteration brought about by such a reversal of roles is characteristic; it is Estragon who, at the end of the first act, hopes that they will be able to hang themselves the next day, but at the end of the second act it is Vladimir who says, "We'll hang ourselves tomorrow," adding, since he is an optimist, "Unless Godot comes." There are numerous other examples of such doubling in the play, especially in a slightly modified form, so much so that it gives the play that asymmetrical structure which accounts for much of its power. A fair proportion of the echoes are undoubtedly picked up by most spectators even on first acquaintance with the work, and the aesthetic satisfaction they engender no doubt accounts for the fact that despite its lack of traditional development and suspense, the play works with the most diverse audiences. Another factor lies in the tension created in a good performance that respects Beckett's stage-directions, especially those relating to pauses and silences. In the recent London Royal Court Theater production, supervised by the author, the actors maintained during pauses the stance and attitude which they had adopted as the last words were being uttered: they did not fidget or budge, but stared before them, until the time allowed for the pause had elapsed. Not only was the tension palpable, but the play's characteristic rhythm was preserved: a burst of activity followed a still silence, in regular alternation. When this is correctly done, *Waiting for Godot* exerts an almost uncanny force on the spectator, revealing to him its uncommon beauty.

In *Endgame*, which has a similar, if more sombre power, the guiding thread is provided by the allusions to playing, losing, telling, and joking. Clov asks a question Nell has already asked Nagg, "Why this farce, day after day?" and says three times, "Something is taking its course." Hamm, in particular, consciously *acts* a part: he quotes Baudelaire grandiloquently in his final speech ("a little poetry ...") and twists Shakespeare ("My kingdom for a nightman!" and, later on, "Our revels now are ended ..."); he tells himself a "story" made up of his guilty memories, playing out his life like the ham actor he is. Beckett's characters never forget that they are present at their own spectacle:

Vladimir. Charming evening we're having.
Estragon. Unforgettable.
Vladimir. And it's not over.
Estragon. Apparently not.
Vladimir. It's only beginning.
Estragon. It's awful.
Vladimir. Worse than the pantomime.
Estragon. The circus.
Vladimir. The music-hall.
Estragon. The circus.

And when Vladimir "hastens towards the wings," Estragon calls after him, "End of the corridor, on the left," and he answers, "Keep my seat." In *Endgame*, Clov asks, "What is there to keep me here?" to which Hamm replies: "The dialogue." Beckett's people know they are actors, and they agree to take parts in which they do not believe, but they do it with disgust and are not taken in by their own game.

In *All That Fall* the local races are the object of repeated allusions, such as "Nice day for the races," or "Divine day for the meeting." In *Happy Days* the *leitmotiv* is the expression "to speak in the old style," underlining the present meaninglessness for Winnie of such terms as "day," "yesterday," and so on: there are no longer any days in her universe, only intervals between two bells, bathed in harsh light.

208 John Fletcher

It is striking that Beckett does not hesitate to use the most extreme artifices of style in his drama: he even borrows from the conventions of oriental theater, as for example in makeup; he ordains a "very red face" for Hamm and for Clov, and a "very white face" for Nagg, Nell, and Krapp. He does not respect the moral attributes attaching to these colors (red is good and white evil), but it is nevertheless possible that he has adopted them from the East, unless he is merely thinking of the traditional makeup of clowns, with their simple extremes of coloring. On the other hand, he never orders masks for his characters, and even insists, in *Play*, "But no masks."

He may well, indeed, have adopted the slow pace that is characteristic of his plays from eastern drama. During a London rehearsal of *Godot*, Beckett is alleged to have told one of the actors that he was not *boring* the spectators enough. A slow, majestic development is essential to a Beckett play, which cannot be rushed through, for laughs or for any other reason: the only gags are told in such a way as to be deliberately unfunny (like Nagg's about the tailor), and the humor, which is very real, lies rather in the meandering of the dialogue than in any particular joke or situation. Properly produced, these plays should not bore in the usual sense, although they cannot fail to be tedious to anyone expecting thrills and excitement in the theater. But the fact that the inmates of a California penitentiary were able to respond profoundly to *Godot* is enough to show that the average first-nighter is not necessarily a good judge of true theater.

It is nevertheless true that Beckett's plays – like his novels – tend towards a more and more barren simplicity. The first, the unpublished and unperformed *Eleuthéria*, had three acts and seventeen characters on a stage divided into two halves, of which one represented the hotel room occupied by Victor Krap, and the other the middle-class home of the Krap family, who try to bring about the return of the prodigal. Mime was already an important element in this complicated play, but it tended to become submerged under other elements. In the latest pieces, *Happy Days* and *Play*, there is hardly any plot left; light is the most active element, pinpointing the three characters of *Play* and forcing each to speak individually and in ignorance of the utterances of the others, just as it glares down mercilessly on Winnie, forcing her to play, to say, in her mound, "day" after "day," each time with a little more difficulty, a little more deeply embedded in the earth. *Play* is potentially endless, able to be repeated *ad infinitum* with only slight modifications, a punishment as hellish as that imagined by Sartre in *Huis clos*. Oppressed by strange tyrants, Beckett's characters nevertheless maintain their courage somehow, and their defiance; more than ever, therefore, their watchword remains the proud, terrible, and provoking reply of Hamm's:

> *Clov.* (*imploringly*) Let's stop playing!
> *Hamm.* Never!

NOTE

1 *Encore* (March/April 1962), p. 44.

Acting for Beckett

RUBY COHN

Samuel Beckett's absorption in the performing arts has been profound and sustained. In Dublin, he went to the Abbey, in London to the music-hall, in Paris to the little theaters. Today, a friend of theater people, he sees their work where he lives or visits. His poem, *Whoroscope*, is a dramatic monologue. After writing his first novel, *Murphy*, he took copious notes for a play about the Dr. Johnson–Mrs. Thrale relationship, which, however, he did not write. After World War II, Beckett turned almost simultaneously to fiction and drama – in French. *Eleutheria*, unpublished and unproduced, precedes the *Godot* which made him famous, and which involved him directly in theatrical production. At first a silent observer during rehearsals, he has now directed *Godot* and *Endgame* in English, *Play* in French, and *Eh Joe* in German. Early this year, his sixtieth, he wrote me that he had been busy with "14 weeks nonstop theatre cinema and TV." To this day, then, the performing arts continue to fascinate him even though he views them as a gregarious game, an evasion of the lone exploration of fiction.

Through the years, Beckett's fiction has pared away narrative garb to zero in on man narrating. Similarly, Beckett's drama is concentrated down to man acting, even as the different plays emphasize by examining the building-blocks of drama – entrances, exits, monologues, dialogues, tableaux, movements, and stillness. Beckett's conflicts are basic oppositions: Gogo and Didi cannot leave the Board, while Pozzo and Lucky cannot stay. Hamm cannot stand, while Clov cannot sit. The radio plays cannot be seen, whereas the mime plays (including *Film*) cannot be heard. *Krapp's Last Tape* separates a man from his taped voice; *Words and Music* separates language from melody; *Eh Joe* separates the filmed actor from the recorded voice. In *Happy Days* and *Play*, the characters are cued into the action by which they exist.

Aristotelian drama, which imitates an action, is crystallized by Beckett to the acting which is all we know of living. Beckett's drama draws us to its root: *dran* – to do, to perform; through radicalizing all aspects of performance, Beckett underlines and undermines his problematic opening: "Nothing to be done."

Beckett as Director:
The Manuscript Production Notebooks and Critical Interpretation

JAMES KNOWLSON

This essay does not attempt to capture the extraordinary fascination, the atmosphere of keen concentration and the unusual "feel" of rehearsals when Samuel Beckett is directing his own plays. It seeks rather to provide an over-view of some of the ways in which Beckett's directorial notes can occasionally initiate, but, more often, assist or confirm critical interpretation. It also sets out to consider how these notes pose some rather taxing problems for the critic who is seeking to make significant use of them.

First of all, for those unfamiliar with this material – which is after all for the most part still unpublished[1] – what are these manuscript notebooks? They are notes prepared by Beckett when he is about to direct his own plays; they are consulted by him prior to, but not normally in the course of, actual rehearsals and they are sometimes (though not always) corrected by him in the light of rehearsal changes. They figure, of course, only as a part, although a major one, of the material that is available to anyone working on the topic of Beckett as director of his own plays.

The notebooks are numerous, very detailed and, as one would expect, extremely meticulous: "practically Cartesian in [their] organization of information and insight" wrote Alan Schneider.[2] There are twelve separate notebooks in Reading University Library's Beckett Archive relating to Beckett's own productions of seven different stage plays[3] (plus one, *Come and Go* in Berlin,[4] when Beckett advised the director, Walter Asmus), and of the television play *He Joe* (*Eh Joe*) and the televised version of *Was Wo* (*What Where*) for Süddeutscher Rundfunk.[5] In addition, at last count there were, in the same collection, eleven texts annotated by Beckett with his various cuts, changes, notes and queries, and guides to himself as director. Of the four plays with which I shall primarily be dealing, Beckett has directed *Endgame, Krapp's Last Tape* and *Happy Days* several times, but

Waiting for Godot only once, until his recent "supervision" of the San Quentin Drama Workshop production, directed initially by Walter Asmus, then rehearsed jointly by Beckett and Asmus in London for performance in Australia and Europe.[6] In critical writing about Beckett's theatre, the notebooks have so far been used by a mere handful of scholars.[7]

Beckett's director's notebooks are, first and foremost, practical, working notebooks. They deal frequently with precise, immediate problems of staging: the various positions of Estragon and Vladimir in *Waiting for Godot* *vis à vis* each other, the tree and (in the Schiller Theater and San Quentin productions) the stone; how Pozzo and Lucky should lie when they fall from the vertical; how many paces Clov should take in *Endgame* when he is "having an idea," or May when she is "revolving it all" in her "poor mind" in *Footfalls*; and so on. They also identify specific problems for the director, the actors, the lighting engineer or the stage manager: should Clov's response to Hamm's whistle be "instantaneous like jinni to Aladdin or time lag?"[8] (answer: instantaneous); should the song in *Endgame* or the hymn in *Krapp's Last Tape* be cut? (answer: recently, yes on both occasions); should the discarding of the mirror be removed from *Happy Days*? (answer: no); how will the cuts that Beckett wants to make in the parasol text of the same play synchronise with the slow consuming of the canopy? (answer: try it and see). These are a few of the questions that Beckett poses in the pages of the various notebooks and mostly (though again not always) manages to solve after further consideration or following practical trials on stage.

But after working very closely on most of these notebooks myself – and after reading with profit two excellent chapters on *Waiting for Godot* and *Happy Days* in Dougald McMillan and Martha Fehsenfeld's forthcoming book *Beckett at Work in the Theatre* – it seems to me that the distinction between practical staging (what has been called "the local situation")[9] and issues of vision, theme and structure is a purely artificial one that for much of the directorial material simply cannot be sustained. The notion of the writer-director translating one sign system into another is not, of course, entirely appropriate here, since Beckett's plays were written specifically with the possibilities and the constraints of the medium for which they were intended very much in mind. However, Beckett himself maintains that the early plays were not "seen" clearly enough in stage terms and, in production, he has changed numerous details of the later plays, which so evidently were. The fact that so many differences exist between the text on the printed page and the work as it appears on the stage should, I think, both encourage analysis of the nature of the relationship between the two

and, at the same time, discourage naive "intentionalism" on the part of the critic.

For the position is a relatively complex one. From being, to use Beckett's own image, "the worm at the core of the apple," the writer necessarily places himself outside it when he becomes the director of his own work, not, as so often happened with Eugène Ionesco, in order to discuss it critically but to translate it into scenic images, concrete figures in space, and patterns of movement and sound.

At a rehearsal of *Glückliche Tage* (*Happy Days*) in Berlin, Beckett stated that, when he came to direct his own work in the theatre, he studied the text as if it had been written by someone else, adding that perhaps it did come from someone else, since it had been written so long ago.[10] For the writer is, in William Golding's phrase, a "moving target";[11] in the interval between writing a particular play and directing it, perhaps ten, fifteen or even twenty years later, Beckett's own experience as a director as well as a writer who has advanced much further along his own path – not to speak of his own experience as a human being himself subject to the modifications of the "cancer" Time – may have modified the view that he takes of his own work or helped him to reappraise the technical means of realising it on stage.

There are several examples where Beckett's experience in directing one play seems materially to have affected his work on another: the emphasis on the rhythm and the quality of sound of Krapp's pacing with the banana, for instance, or Clov's walk back and forth to his kitchen in the San Quentin Drama Workshop productions of *Krapp's Last Tape* and *Endgame* almost certainly arose out of his earlier work at the Royal Court on *Footfalls*; the use of different lighting levels in *That Time* and *Footfalls* probably emerged from his early experiments with lighting with Jean Marie Serreau and George Devine on *Play* in the 1960s. Even the fact that the most recent San Quentin production of *Waiting for Godot* saw Estragon and Vladimir most poignantly and humanly holding hands may have some connection with the relationship between the old man and the child in Beckett's most recent prose work, *Worstward Ho*,[12] or with an image in the television play *Nacht und Träume*.[13]

In a number of cases too, it seems clear that Beckett's own attitude towards one of his plays has in itself evolved. It would be rather surprising, indeed, if this had not occurred. It is difficult to believe, for example, that the Beckett of 1979, who insisted on the lack of awareness, unheroic nature, and almost manic quality of Winnie in *Happy Days*, would have admired so much the courage and the lyricism displayed in Madeleine

Renaud's performance in the same role in 1963, which many spectators still prefer. Similarly, the rigour and the ruthlessness that Beckett brought to bear on his own text when he came to direct *Godot* in Berlin in 1975 (the play was "messy," he told Ruby Cohn)[14] will have come as no surprise to anyone who had experienced his previous intense concern as a director with theatrical shape ("form in movement,"[15] to use Beckett's well-known phrase), balance, rhythm and economy of movement in his earlier German productions of *Endgame*, *Krapp's Last Tape* and *Happy Days*.

As anyone who has directed in the theatre will appreciate, however, there is another major factor which a director may experience either as restricting or as liberating, sometimes even as both. This centres primarily on the voice, the physical appearance, the personality and the degree of technical expertise of the actors who are cast in a particular production. *Happy Days*, for instance, could never be the same with Billie Whitelaw as with Madeleine Renaud; *Krapp's Last Tape* would always be different with Patrick Magee, Pierre Chabert, or Rick Cluchey as Krapp. And, of course, it is one of the truisms of experience that a play transforms itself like chameleon so that it is rarely precisely the same at the end of the month or the run as it had been at the beginning, even changing from night to night. The limitations that are imposed by the presence of flesh-and-blood figures with their personalities, voices, mannerisms, and gestures apply also to the limits imposed by the stage itself and the technical resources available – one may think of the difficulties that were encountered in lighting *Play* or, with more radical results, the problems that were experienced in lighting Auditor satisfactorily in *Not I* at the Royal Court Theatre in 1976.

The levels of immediacy proliferate, then, somewhat bewilderingly as one surveys the gap between the writer-director "seeing" the play in his mind's eye and the play as it eventually comes to be staged. "Do it any way you like, Alan"[16] is certainly not Beckett's formula as a director to his actors, but he does find himself spending considerable time coping with the inescapable choices and compromises that the theatre inevitably imposes – whether it be crawling himself over the barren terrain of the *Happy Days* set at the Royal Court to see how the particular actor playing Willie, Leonard Fenton, can crawl or sprawl with his particular physique on that particular mound, so changing Willie's only front-of-stage appearance; or, more recently, in the San Quentin *Godot*, finding ways in which Estragon and Vladimir can come together for one of their dance or walking routines, or in which Pozzo can deliver his monologue on "twilight" as Beckett's Pozzo but also as Rick Cluchey playing Pozzo. Yet, at this stage, we perhaps need to remind ourselves both how rarely Beckett departs from certain fundamental concepts that underlie his productions and also how relatively early the preparation of his notebooks comes in the staging of his plays.

Although these theoretical questions may appear very intriguing, they seem to me to be much less interesting than the practical questions that they raise. What can these directorial notebooks bring to an understanding of the plays? Do Beckett's notes on staging (in which he has, incidentally, shown himself to be flexible as well as ingenious) illuminate certain fundamental themes or dominant structures of the play? Do they point to others that critics may still have dealt with very little? These are a few of the questions to which the existence of the notebooks gives rise. Theatre, or, more precisely, performance scholarship – even more directly than textual scholarship – can here assist criticism, but only if the essential complexity of the situation upon which I have touched briefly is kept firmly in the forefront of our minds.

Some of the notebooks seem to offer the critic relatively little, while others supply far more. It requires, for instance, no directorial notebook to stress the importance in *Endgame* of the "grain upon grain" theme of time: "Finished, it's finished, nearly finished, it must be nearly finished."[17] Yet even here the Schiller 1967 and the San Quentin 1980 notebooks and the associated annotated copy of the latter production[18] help to focus on the way in which this theme is articulated structurally throughout the work. While "something is taking its course,"[19] stage time is structured by a combination of Clov's refrain "I'll leave you," repeated ten times and at regular intervals, and of Hamm's question "is it not time for my painkiller?" reiterated six times, again at regular intervals. As Beckett's notes make clear, however, the "running out" process does not proceed regularly, but occurs in minute grains with a deadly slowness. The San Quentin notebook suggests that Beckett sees one of these changes as having occurred before the play begins. His note on the beginning of the play reads "C[lov] perplexed. All seemingly in order, yet a change. Fatal grain added to form impossible heap. *Ratio ruentis acervi.* Last straw."[20] Within a matter of moments from the opening of the play, Hamm and Nagg are told that there are no more bicycle wheels, no more pap, no more nature. Yet it is, in the English text, another twenty-five pages before Clov announces in, for this play, rapid succession that there are no more tide, navigators, rugs, painkiller and coffins. Yet another grain, or grains, seems then to have been added, although, since the informant is always Clov, we cannot be absolutely certain that he is telling the truth.

For one of the important changes that Beckett made in the 1980 San Quentin production of *Endgame* was to add further deliberate deceitfulness to Clov's relations with Hamm. This deceit also emanates from Clov's desire to move about the refuge as little as possible, since he finds movement acutely painful. He is, writes Beckett in the San Quentin notes, "stiff, sore at knees / waist. When still tries to straighten, restoops ... moving painful as economical as possible."[21] As a consequence, instead of moving to the back wall after "Then move" and instead of climbing up the ladder first to open and then to close the window, he stays "sur place" (on the spot), pretending to walk by performing a brief tramp-tramp on the stage (2 steps loud, 2 less loud),[22] or again pretending to climb the steps by knocking on them.[23] This is echoed by the crescendo of thumps that Beckett suggests Clov should give to Hamm's chair, instead of moving it, when the tyrant wants it put "Bang in the centre."[24] "It's a lie! Why do you lie to me?" Hamm had just asked. And as Hamm goes on bullying, so Clov continues to deceive.

"There are no accidents in *Endgame*; everything is built on analogy and repetition,"[25] was Beckett's by now familiar remark to his Schiller Theater cast. And the notebooks (and performances) contribute significantly to an appreciation of the use of parallels or analogies in the pairings of the characters, in the actions, and in the numerous verbal or sound echoes that are found in the play. Nagg's voice and attitude in his "tailor" story should echo Hamm's in his narration; Clov's reaction to Hamm's "In my house" should parallel Hamm's reaction to Nagg's "It's natural. After all I'm your father"; Hamm should wilt from Nagg's "Yes, I hope I'll live till then" speech and this should correspond to Clov's response to Hamm's "Yes, one day you'll know what it is, you'll be like me."[26] But, on another level, the knocks on the bin should also echo those on the wall. There is evidence of little real change in Beckett's attitude to parallelism between his two productions in 1967 and 1980 except perhaps in his even more meticulous attention to detail. What is clear, however, from a study of both directorial notebooks is the way in which Beckett's direction clarifies the cruelly symbiotic relationship which lies at the hub of this play and also how he translates a theme such as "the difficulty of ending" into the minutiae of acting detail.

Beckett's 1969 Schiller Theater production of *Krapp's Last Tape* and subsequent publication of his director's notes, along with his verbal advice to Martin Held on this and subsequent productions,[27] have probably been largely responsible for the depth of our present critical understanding of this rich little play. The remarkable pages of the 1969 *Regiebuch* that

Endgame production notebook 1980: R.U.L. Ms. 1975.

All illustrations are reproduced courtesy of the estate of Samuel Beckett and Reading University Library's Beckett Archive.

Beckett devoted to the light and dark emblems and his comments on Manichean divisions deeply embedded within the text or in its setting[28] helped to reveal how the intellectual infra-structure is built upon separation and attempted reconciliation and how closely Krapp's obsession with a woman's eyes was related to it.[29] But the publication of the *Regiebuch*, Pierre Chabert's article after Beckett's 1975 Paris production, and the

Bethanien (i.e., San Quentin Drama Workshop) *Krapp* notes[30] stressed other aspects of the play that are almost as important both to its thematic content and its dramatic impact: e.g., the oppositions between brooding silence and immobility, on the one hand, and sharp sounds and rapid purposeful movement, on the other (Beckett wrote in the notebook that he had cut "Tout ce qui gêne passage abrupt de l'immobilité au mouvement on qui ralentit celui-ci");[31] the association of the darkness surrounding Krapp with death through the "Hain," as he looks behind him for "Old Nick";[32] and the way in which the tape recorder, as the sole companion of Krapp's solitude, has come to be identified with whatever the taped voice was saying – hence, at times, the "masturbatory element."[33] Even the constant use of repetition in the direction – Krapp's return to a "listening pose," pacing to and fro at his table, opening and closing his eyes, raising and lowering the head, laughing, cursing, grunting and so on – is related to the thematic centre of the play, since the power of instant recall leads only to an experience of discontinuity and disillusionment rather than to the harmony and the integration to which as a young writer Krapp had once aspired. And the repetition of the tape with the girl in the punt fascinates him but also leads him inexorably back to that sense of loss and failure in which the play is steeped. Looking at the play from the outside in order to direct it brought Beckett to focus much more clearly than any critic had previously done on themes that widened the resonance of the play and to incorporate details into his direction that both removed what was inessential and highlighted the central theme of separation or reconciliation.

Throughout his four productions of this play, however, Beckett has been very wary of the dangers both of over-stylisation and of the over-explicit. So, while the light-dark oppositions have been increased in the setting, they have been reduced in Krapp's costume and hymn singing. And it is crucial to stress that because the playwright has worked from the dual position of what he feels works best on stage and what is truest to his understanding of the sense and the shape of the play, the post-1969 production version of the play functions dramatically far more successfully than does that of 1958.

Beckett's own two productions of *Happy Days* in 1971 and 1979[34] highlighted aspects of the play which have rarely been grasped by critics. I shall confine myself to two points only relating to the notebook which Beckett prepared for the 1979 London production.[35] First is the elemental nature of the world that Winnie inhabits, torn between the air to which her nature assigns her and the earth which progressively engulfs and threatens to devour her. In the margin of the copy annotated by Beckett for the Royal Court production, Beckett cited, as one of the two quotations that Winnie had forgotten, the following line from *Childe Harold's Pilgrimage*: "Soft eyes looked love to eyes that spake again."[36] Winnie has indeed much of the Childe Harold about her, who "Droop'd as a wild falcon with clipt wing / To whom the boundless air alone were home."[37] Beckett commented to his Berlin Winnie "She is a weightless being, being devoured by a cruel earth"[38] and said to Martha Fehsenfeld that "she was a bird with oil on its feathers." She also fears being consumed by fire in the shape of the fierce heat which dries up everything, burns the parasol and extracts all moisture, even perspiration, from the earth ball and its inhabitants: "the heat is much greater, the perspiration much less"[39] says Winnie.

These elemental divisions are reflected not merely in the separate natures of the bird, Winnie, or the turtle, Willie.[40] They find their way into most of Winnie's movements and into many of her utterances or verbal tones. In the recent Royal Court production, the contrast between aspiration upwards and movement downwards, between lightness and optimism, on the one hand, and heaviness and sorrow, on the other hand, operated on both a literal and a metaphorical level, informing both Winnie's busy chatter and the most ordinary of her gestures. The would-be cheerfulness of her first act "usual voice" was often pierced by darker tones, as sorrow "keeps breaking in." And as the section of the notebook entitled "+ ... −" (i.e., positive/negative oppositions) shows,[41] sadness intruded into words and phrases that are not overtly scored that way. As Martha Fehsenfeld has pointed out,[42] the contrast between expansion and contraction was echoed in Winnie's own movements, as her gesture towards prayer was halted and her bird-like swooping movements were arrested as she reached into the bag.

Secondly, Beckett's notebook draws attention to the way in which props, objects in Winnie's barren world, suffer from an atrophy of the primary element and an abnormal development or hypertrophy of the secondary element,[43] (e.g., a parasol has too small a canopy for it to perform the function for which it was intended and too long a handle, or the toothbrush has "scant setae" and again an elongated secondary element). For although "things have their life," they constantly intrude upon the comfort and bearable nature of Winnie's own existence. The parasol will not protect Winnie from the fierce heat of the sun; the bag is there in Act II but, as with the parasol, she is unable to use it. So objects and persons participate in a world characterized by displacement, disunity, fragmentation and disarray. If Winnie tries to domesticate the harshness of her cruel

Props   53

Order of appearance :

Bag, parasol, toothbrush, tube, mirror,
glasses/case, handkerchief, revolver, bottle,
lipstick, hat, ~~━━━━~~ mag. glass,
mus. box, nailfile

Bag: massive pothike black presence in
general bleachedness. Cabas. Stiffened.
anchored. ~~loose handles~~ drooped overt
+ garden. yawning ~~━━━~~ maw.

Parasol : telescopic (not indispensable), ◆
~~exaggeratedly long handle~~, ~~beak or knob~~,
small canopy, ~~━━━━━━━━━━━━━━~~
~~━━━━~~ pink ?

Toothbrush : long yellow handle, scant setae.

Tube : long, flat, bare.

mirror long silver handle, small round glass.

Glasses/case old fashioned plain steel frame,
~~small oval~~ lenses, branches once open fixed
for on/off one hand (h). case soft ~~━━~~ black
open sheath for easy out/in.

Handkerchief : lacy, small.

Revolver : black, long muzzle.

Bottle : long, rect., long neck, cap, worn
~~label upper half~~, dreg of red liquid.

Lipstick : long silver holder, screw system,
end of rouge.

Hat : flimsy, brimless, collapsible, mangy
~~━━~~ limp feather. Colour ? - ~~Black~~.

Mag. glass. ~~Same style as mirror~~. Rect.
glass.

Mus. box : small for concealment. Black.
~~Loud~~ weird.

Nailfile : long, narrow, silver.

Gen. principle : hypertrophy ~~━━━~~ secondary,
atrophy primary.

Happy Days production notebook 1979: R.U.L. Ms. 1730.

world by her own mixture of habit and apparent unawareness, the force of the play surely lies in the ironies that arise from applying her brand of "profound frivolity" with its instinctive compulsion to "look on the bright side" to a situation composed of such abject circumstances. It is not that critics have not recognized certain of these features. It is that Beckett's *Happy Days* notebooks draw together apparently disparate features of the play to form a much clearer, sharper perception of the vision that lies behind the work.

In the case of *Waiting for Godot*, it would be rather surprising if, after all this time, Beckett's notebooks were to throw much new light on this most studied of plays. Yet they do provide striking evidence of how the author regards some of the play's most fundamental themes a quarter of a century after its composition. They show, for instance, how important crucifixion images are to Beckett's Berlin production. There are cruciform patterns formed by moves across stage on the upstage horizontal line and back down the vertical centre line on a raked stage; the bodies of Pozzo and Lucky after their fall from the vertical lie in the shape of yet another cross; there are several tableaux of Pozzo or Lucky supported between the two friends, recalling, in Ruby Cohn's words, "the many paintings of a crucified Christ between two thieves";[44] Estragon and Vladimir often stand on either side of the tree; and Estragon in particular stretches out his arms, in John Donne's words, "mine owne Crosse to be."[45] In the recent San Quentin production supervised by Beckett,[46] where the same cruciform images prevail, the production sets them in the context of a long drawn-out martyrdom where the painful waiting is relieved by fewer and less animated "little canters" than in Beckett's production of nine years earlier. Balletic vaudeville numbers have become a few tired "wriggles" as the nails go in.

The second important feature of both the Schiller Theater and the San Quentin productions was that the central themes of desire for fulfilment and unity, yet experience of incompletion and separateness meet in the organised patterning of movements into semi-circles, arcs, and chords (and, in the San Quentin production, triangles). So Estragon and Vladimir move in opposed patterns of curved paths and straight lines; in McMillan and Fehsenfeld's words, "like a geometric arc and chord [they] connect cardinal points and define the boundaries of a closed circular world."[47]

The image of circularity has understandably tended to dominate critical discussion of both the shape of the play and the view of human existence that is portrayed within it. The Schiller notebooks suggest another image which is, I believe, just as important. In discussing Estragon and Vladimir's

Waiting for Godot production notebook 1975: R.U.L. Ms. 1396/4/3.

movements, Beckett writes there that the "gen[eral] effect of moves esp[ecially] V's though apparently motivated that of those in a cage"[48] and at one moment he even contemplated having the "[f]aint shadow of bars on stage floor,"[49] in the end deciding against this degree of "explicitation." In the red notebook, he writes "Thus establish at outset 2 caged dynamics, E sluggish, V restless + perpetual separation and reunion of V/E."[50] For Beckett's man is, as Lucky's dance suggests, imprisoned in a net, able only to move around the strands of the mesh in the particular compartment which the two friends find themselves to be occupying. On occasion, they sketch out circles, but these circles are traced within the spatial delineation of a larger net or mesh. When, in Beckett's production, Vladimir and Estragon go off stage, they are merely beating their wings like birds trapped by the strands of the net, bouncing back as if on elastic into the stage space to which they are inextricably tied. The theme of incarceration is one which pervades all of Beckett's theatre. Beckett wrote to Rick Cluchey of his part as Krapp, "make the thing your own in terms of incarceration, for example. Incarceration in self. He escapes from the trap of the other only to be trapped in self,"[51] and he told Hildegard Schmahl that May in *Footfalls* was also totally encapsulated within herself ("being for herself," in Beckett's own words).[52]

Such apparently revealing insights from the author-director occur from time to time in Beckett's directorial notebooks and understandably tend to be pounced upon and developed gratefully, sometimes perhaps a trifle naively, by the critic. They need, of course, to be treated with much caution, emanating as they do from "a moving target." The dilemma is, of course, that the movements of that target are difficult, sometimes indeed impossible to trace, let alone fully explain. The task of the critic seems here to become one of balancing curiosity and caution, handling the evidence provided by Beckett's production notebooks with an awareness of the dangers of what could so easily become yet another form of critical reductionism.

NOTES

1 Beckett's manuscript production notebook prepared for the production of *Happy Days* at the Royal Court Theatre, London in June 1979, edited by James Knowlson, was published by Faber and Faber, London and Grove Press, New York, 1985. The other directorial notebooks are to appear with the same publishers, edited by James Knowlson, S.E. Gontarski, and Dougald McMillan, in 1988.

2 Alan Schneider, "Working with Beckett," in *Samuel Beckett: The Art of Rhetoric*, eds. Morot-Sir, Harper, and McMillan, North Carolina Studies in the Romance Languages and Literatures, 5 (Chapel Hill, 1976), p. 280. Also printed in *Theatre Quarterly*, 5 (No. 19, 1975), 32.

3 The notebooks relate to the following plays directed by Beckett: *Endgame* (Berlin, 1967 and London, 1980), *Krapp's Last Tape* (Berlin, 1969), *Happy Days* (Berlin, 1971 and London, 1979), *Waiting for Godot* (Berlin, 1975 and, with Walter Asmus, Adelaide, 1984), *Footfalls* (London, 1976 and Berlin, 1976), *That Time* (Berlin, 1976), *Play* (Berlin, 1978).

4 *Kommen und Gehen* (*Come and Go*), directed by Walter Asmus, advised by Beckett, was premièred with Beckett's own production of *Spiel* (*Play*) at the Schiller Theater Werkstatt on 6 October 1978. See Ruby Cohn, *Just Play: Beckett's Theater* (Princeton, 1980), pp. 235–236 and *Theater Heute*, 12 (December 1978), 6–10.

5 *He Joe* (*Eh Joe*) was directed by Beckett for the Stuttgart television station, Süddeutscher Rundfunk, January 1979, with Heinz Bennent as Joe. *Was Wo* was broadcast on Beckett's eightieth birthday, 13 April 1986.

6 *Waiting for Godot*, San Quentin Drama Workshop production directed by Walter Asmus, under the supervision of Samuel Beckett. Rehearsed at Riverside Studios, London, from 20 to 29 February for the opening performance at the Adelaide Festival, Australia on 13 March 1984.

7 Ruby Cohn, *Just Play*, pp. 230–279; Samuel Beckett, *Happy Days. Oh les beaux jours*, ed. James Knowlson (London and Boston, 1978); James Knowlson, "*Krapp's Last Tape*: the evolution of a play, 1958–1975," *Journal of Beckett Studies*, 1 (Winter 1976), 50–65; Dougald McMillan and Martha Fehsenfeld, *Beckett at Work in the Theatre* (London and New York, 1988).

8 Quotation taken from Beckett's manuscript notebook prepared for the San Quentin Drama Workshop production of *Endgame* in May 1980, Reading University Library Ms. 1975.

9 Schneider, p. 282.

10 Alfred Hübner, *Samuel Beckett inszeniert* Glückliche Tage (Frankfurt, 1976), p. 10.

11 William Golding, *A Moving Target* (London, 1982). The phrase is the title of an address given by Golding to Les Anglicistes in Rouen, 16 May 1976.

12 "Hand in hand with equal plod they go. ... Joined by held holding hands. Plod on as one." *Worstward Ho* (London, 1983), p. 13.

13 See *Nacht und Träume* in *Collected Shorter Plays of Samuel Beckett* (London and Boston, 1984).

14 Cohn, p. 258.

15 See Charles Marowitz, "Paris Log," *Encore* (March 1962), 44.

16 Schneider, p. 278.

17 *Endgame* (London, rpt. 1976), p. 12 (the edition used by Beckett for the 1980 production).

18 Schiller Theater Werkstatt production, directed by Beckett, 26 September 1967, and San Quentin Drama Workshop production, also directed by Beckett, in May 1980 at the Riverside Studios, London. Both notebooks are in Reading University Library, Ms. 1396/4/5 and Ms. 1975. The 1980 annotated copy is in the same library's Beckett collection, Ms. 1974. The Schiller Theater Werkstatt notebook has been discussed by Ruby Cohn in *Just Play*, pp. 237–245, so I concentrate here on the later San Quentin production.

19 The phrase is repeated three times, on the third occasion Hamm saying "I'm taking my course." *Endgame*, pp. 17, 26, 31.

20 Reading Unversity Library (subsequently R.U.L.) Ms. 1975. The Latin quotation is from Horace's Second Book of *Epistles*, i, 47. The actual text of Horace is "ratione ruentis acervi," i.e., "by the argument of the diminishing heap," the sophist argument that was outlined by Cicero in the *De Divinatione*, II, ii.

21 R.U.L. Ms. 1975.

22 *Endgame*, p. 14.

23 *Endgame*, p. 43.

24 *Endgame*, p. 24.

25 Michael Haerdter, *Materialen zu Beckett's* Endspiel (Frankfurt, 1968), p. 54.

26 R.U.L. Ms. 1975.

27 See *Samuel Beckett* Das letzte Band. *Regiebuch der Berliner Inszenierungz*, ed. Volker Canaris (Frankfurt, 1970); *Samuel Beckett:* Krapp's Last Tape. *Theatre Workbook no. 1*, ed. James Knowlson (London, 1980).

28 These pages are reproduced in facsimile in James Knowlson, *Light and Darkness in the Theatre of Samuel Beckett* (London, 1972).

29 See James Knowlson and John Pilling, *Frescoes of the Skull: The Later Prose and Drama of Samuel Beckett* (London and New York, 1979), pp. 81–92. See also Eugene Webb, *The Plays of Samuel Beckett* (Seattle and London, 1972).

30 These are assembled in *Samuel Beckett: Krapp's Last Tape, Theatre Workbook no. 1.*

31 R.U.L. Ms. 1396/4/16, p. 13.

32 Krapp looks behind him into the darkness stage left, because, as Beckett has made clear on a number of occasions, he senses the presence of death lurking close at hand. Beckett has regularly referred to this look as a "Hain," following the eighteenth-century German writer, Matthias Claudius, for whom the "Hain" was a death figure, though a comforting one. In rehearsals and to the author, Beckett alluded to Claudius's poem "Death and the Maiden," which Schubert set to music both as a song (D531) and as a string quartet (D810). In

the poem, Death says to the Maiden "I am a friend and do not come to punish. Be of good courage. I am not wild. You should sleep softly in my arms." But Dougald McMillan and Martha Fehsenfeld have suggested plausibly in *Beckett at Work in the Theatre* that the figure of death may be seen as being closer to Claudius's explanation of the opening engraving in his collected works showing the skeletal figure of "Freund Hain" leaning on his scythe.

33 R.U.L. Ms. 1396/4/16, p. 67. The tape recorder is referred to there as an "agent masturbateur."

34 Beckett directed *Happy Days* at the Schiller Theater Werkstatt, Berlin, in September 1971 and, again, at the Royal Court Theatre, London, in June 1979.

35 Beckett's directorial notes for the Royal Court production are in R.U.L. Ms. 1730.

36 Byron, *Childe Harold's Pilgrimage*, Canto III, stanza xxi.

37 *Childe Harold's Pilgrimage*, Canto III, stanza xv.

38 Hübner, pp. 38–39.

39 *Happy Days* (London, 1966), pp. 27–28.

40 The words applied to Winnie and Willie are Beckett's own. See Hübner, pp. 43–44.

41 R.U.L. Ms. 1730, p. 10.

42 In *Beckett at Work in the Theatre*.

43 R.U.L. Ms. 1730, p. 53.

44 Cohn, p. 260.

45 John Donne, "The Crosse," *The Divine Poems of John Donne*, ed. Helen Gardner (Oxford, 1952), p. 26.

46 Two performances, considered as final dress rehearsals, were given at the Riverside Studios in London on 1 and 2 March 1984, prior to the opening of this production at the Adelaide Festival on 13 March.

47 Fehsenfeld and McMillan, *Beckett at Work in the Theatre*.

48 R.U.L. Ms. 1396/4/3, facing p. 1 (Beckett's pagination).

49 R.U.L. Ms. 1396/4/3, facing p. 1 (Beckett's pagination).

50 R.U.L. Ms. 1396/4/4, p. 5.

51 *Samuel Beckett*: Krapp's Last Tape. *Theatre Workbook no. 1*, p. 127.

52 See Walter Asmus, "Practical aspects of theatre, radio and television: Rehearsal notes for the German première of Beckett's *That Time* and *Footfalls* at the Schiller Theater Werkstatt, Berlin," *Journal of Beckett Studies*, 2 (Summer 1977), p. 91.

Being and Non-Being:
Samuel Beckett's *Not I*

HERSH ZEIFMAN

When the curtain rises on *Not I*, Samuel Beckett's most recent work for the stage, the first thing we are aware of is a disembodied human mouth, seemingly suspended eight feet in the air, trapped in the harsh glare of a spotlight amid the surrounding darkness. The long line of partially disembodied characters in Beckett's drama makes its first appearance with Nagg and Nell in *Endgame*;[1] having crashed on their tandem in the Ardennes and lost their shanks, the two now inhabit dustbins. Whatever else they may represent, the ashbins (or dustbins) are clearly death images, symbolically apt containers of decaying human flesh, linked with the grave via such traditional Biblical images as "dust thou art, and unto dust shalt thou return" (Genesis 3.19). In *Happy Days*, the process of disembodiment has gone one step further. At the beginning of Act I, Winnie is discovered interred in a mound of sand up to her waist; by the second act, however, the mound has reached her neck, thus obliterating her entire body except for her head. This mound of sand is, once again, a brilliantly conceived icon of death-in-life; figuratively and literally, Winnie has *both* feet in the grave, and the rest of her must inevitably follow.[2] The three characters of *Play* are likewise imprisoned up to their necks, in vases which Beckett specifically labels "*urns*," thereby evoking both the ashes of cremation and the tomb. All that remains of their bodies are their faces – "*Faces so lost to age and aspect*," Beckett directs, "*as to seem almost part of urns.*" And in *Not I*, there is no longer even the entire face, but simply a mouth, chattering compulsively. By now we know full well what disembodiment signifies in Beckett's drama; there is no longer the need for an implicitly coffin-like receptacle.

Like so many of Beckett's characters, fictional and dramatic, the Mouth proceeds to tell us a story. And like any good storyteller, she begins at the beginning – with birth. As the torrent of words issuing from the Mouth continues, we gradually realize that we are hearing not fiction but autobiography, that the Mouth is in reality relating the details of her own life, describing to us her own present situation, a fact she tries desperately to disguise by narrating in the third person. And the details of their life are succinctly summed up in approximately a dozen lines: she was born prematurely, into a "godforsaken hole" (the ironic literalness here is a recurrent Beckettian technique); she was abandoned at birth by her parents; she received no love either as a child or "at any subsequent stage." "So typical affair," the Mouth concludes.

These are all the facts of her life the Mouth considers noteworthy, until that moment when, coming up to seventy and wandering in a field looking aimlessly for cowslips, she suddenly felt all the early April morning light gradually disappearing, she suddenly found herself becoming insensible. The death images here are subtle and striking. "Coming up to seventy" reminds us of the Biblical life span of three-score years and ten (Psalms 90.10); we may think of the sixty-nine-year-old Krapp, and recall that the tape we hear him making is, ominously, his "last" one. And the image of picking flowers in a field evokes Psalm 103.15–16, a passage Beckett has referred to frequently in his writings. In *Endgame*, for example, Hamm remarks that the dead Mother Pegg "was bonny once, like a flower of the field"; her fate is thus the Mouth's fate as well, the fate of all mankind, as the Biblical simile implies: "As for man, his days are as grass: as a flower of the field, so he flourisheth. for the wind passeth over it, and it is gone; and the place thereof shall know it no more."

As the light surrounding the Mouth gradually fades and disappears, so too does sound: "all silent as the grave [...]," the Mouth notes; "all dead still ... sweet silent as the grave." And yet, this is not quite true, for the Mouth experiences neither complete darkness nor complete silence. The silence is broken by the sound of "buzzing ... so-called ... in the ears ... though of course actually ... not in the ears at all ... in the skull ... dull roar in the skull." The Mouth is not the only Beckett dramatic character to hear sounds, the sounds of suffering and death. In *Happy Days*, for example, Winnie admits: "My head was always full of cries. [...] Faint confused cries." And in *Waiting for Godot*, the skulls of Gogo and Didi vibrate with the muffled cry of dead voices: "They make a noise like wings. / Like leaves. / Like sand. / Like leaves." The darkness is similarly broken, by a ray of light which, the Mouth informs us, "came and went ... came and went ... such as the moon might cast [...] flickering on and off [...] like moonbeam [...]" For Beckett, as for Dante in Canto XX of the *Inferno*, the moon is invariably identified with the exiled Cain, branded for life and doomed to suffer. As Belacqua Shuah, the protagonist of Beckett's short story "Dante and the Lobster," comments: "The spots [in the moon] were Cain with his truss of thorns, dispossessed, cursed from the earth, fugitive and vagabond." This image of "the branded moon" occurs repeatedly in Beckett's work, a paradigm of divine punishment and rejection.

It is hardly surprising then, that the Mouth interprets the sound of buzzing and the beam of light as "all part of the same wish to ... torment ...," that her initial thought is that she is being punished for her sins. As Beckett wrote in his 1931 book on Proust: "The tragic figure represents the expiation of original sin, of the original and eternal sin of him and all of his 'socii malorum,' the sin of having been born." The statement is explicit enough: man's ultimate transgression is birth itself, an act over which he has no control, yet paradoxically one for which he must continually atone. Thus the title character of Beckett's novel *Malone Dies* comments: "So long as it is what is called a living being you can't go wrong, you have the guilty one," a conclusion likewise reached by the protagonist of one of Beckett's *Texts for Nothing*: "to be is to be guilty."

And yet, reasons the Mouth, how can God be punishing her for sins, for her Sin, if she is not physically suffering? For, surprisingly, she feels, at the moment, no pain. Unless, of course, she is *meant* to be suffering, *thought* to be suffering. Perhaps, then, she should groan, *pretend* to be suffering, if it is suffering that is indeed required. ("Vain reasonings," she concludes.) Woman 1 in *Play*, in a similar situation, advances a similar argument:

Is it something I should do with my face, other than utter?
Weep? [...]
Bite off my tongue and swallow it? Spit it out? Would that placate you? How the mind works still to be sure!

But though the Mouth's spirit is willing, the flesh is weak – a Cartesian split between mind and body which affects so many of Beckett's characters. For her body, that disreputable "machine" – however much of it exists, that is – will not follow her bidding:

the machine ... so disconnected ... never got the message ... so powerless to respond ... like numbed ... couldn't make the sound ...

This paralysis is relatively short-lived, however, for the Mouth gradually discovers that words are being spoken and, incredibly, they are issuing from her:

mouth on fire ... stream of words ... in her ear ... practically in her ear ... not catching the half ... not the quarter ... no idea what she's saying ... imagine! ... no idea what she's saying ... and can't stop ... no stopping it ... she who but a moment before ... but a moment! ... could not make a sound ... no sound of any kind ... now can't stop ... imagine! ... can't stop the stream ... and the whole brain begging ... something begging in the brain ... begging the mouth to stop ... pause a moment ... if only for a moment ... and no response ... as if it hadn't heard ... or couldn't ... couldn't pause a second ... like maddened ...

The sense of terror here is almost palpable, for this "maddened" stream of words appears to have a will of its own, lying totally outside the Mouth's control. And what is the point of it all? The Mouth can only rationalize that there must be something she has to tell, some "truth" about her life that, once spoken, will allow the words to stop, will grant her absolution:

something she had to tell ... could that be it? ... something that would tell ... how it was [...] how she had lived ... lived on and on ... guilty or not [...] something she didn't know herself ... wouldn't know if she heard ... then forgiven ... God is love ... tender mercies ... new every morning ... back in the field ...

What the Mouth is seeking is thus, essentially, salvation, as the Biblical images she employs clearly imply. "God is love," the Mouth reminds us, echoing 1 John 4.8; and it is to that God of "tender mercies ... new every morning," the God of Psalms 79.8 ("O remember not against us former iniquities: let thy tender mercies speedily prevent us") and of Lamentations 3.23 ("[The Lord's mercies] are new every morning,") that she launches her appeal. For if she somehow manages to come up with that truth, that magic formula for atonement, she will be "forgiven," her sins "purged" away – she will be "back in the field," the field of Paradise, an image Beckett used once before in his early poem "Enueg I":

Then because a field on the left went up in a sudden blaze
of shouting and urgent whistling and scarlet and blue ganzies
I stopped and climbed the bank to see the game.
A child fidgeting at the gate called up:
"Would we be let in Mister?"

"Certainly" I said "you would."
But, afraid, he set off down the road.
"Well" I called after him "why wouldn't you go on in?"
"Oh" he said, knowingly,
"I was in that field before and I got put out."

The Mouth is in much the same position as the three characters in *Play*, sifting through the detritus of their past lives in order to discover that one magic key that will free them from their chains of suffering and grant them redemption. As Woman I comments: "Is it that I do not tell the truth, is that it, and that some day somehow I may tell the truth at last [...]?" It is the position, too, of Dante's Belacqua, the Ante-purgatory figure described by Beckett in *Murphy* as "immune from expiation until he should have dreamed [his life on earth] all through again, with the downright dreaming of an infant, from the spermarium to the cremato-rium [...] before the toil uphill to Paradise." The one significant differ-ence, however, is that Beckett's cosmography lacks a Paradise.

In Dante's *Divina Commedia*, there is no real physical difference between Purgatory and Hell. The torments suffered by the denizens of *Purgatorio* are every bit as horrible as those suffered in *Inferno*; indeed, if one were to pick up the *Purgatorio* and read a passage at random, the severity of the punishment meted out to the characters might just as easily convince one that he was reading the *Inferno*. The difference is rather a psychological one, a theological one. The pain in *Purgatorio* is as intense as in *Inferno*, but it is not eternal. The unfortunates in *Purgatorio* know that eventually their torments will cease, that eventually they will be allowed to enter the bliss of *Paradiso*. If this hope were proved illusory, if Paradise were exposed as a cruel hoax, then Purgatory would not differ in the slightest from Hell. And it is precisely this hoax that Beckett's drama exposes so relentlessly. The characters of *Play* repeat the details of their earthly lives, like Belacqua, but they do so *endlessly*; for them, there is no possibility of "expiation," of divine salvation. Thus, at the end of *Play*, Beckett directs "*Repeat play exactly*," and the curtain finally falls on the beginning of yet another repetition.

Not I ends similarly, with the Mouth still desperately trying to discover the right words, the right formula, even as the curtain descends:

all right [...] try something else ... think of something else [...] so on ... hit on it in the end ... think everything keep on long enough ... then forgiven [...] keep on ...

not knowing what [...] what she was trying ... what to try ... no matter ... keep on ... (*curtain starts down*) ... hit on it in the end ... then back ... God is love ... tender mercies ... new every morning ... back in the field ... [etc.]

The play ends essentially where it began; and movement that is circular is, in fact, stasis. The Mouth will never cease searching for a salvation that will never materialize; the circle, by definition, defies completion.

It is this repeated sense of frustration, this continual denial of consummation, that Beckett's plot patterning invariably emphasizes. The traditional kind of plot development is linear. Movement in a straight line suggests that one is going *somewhere*, that the point towards which one is moving is at least capable of being attained. In Beckett's plays, on the other hand, development is circular, precisely because the goal is always beyond reach. Thus, nothing ever "happens" in Beckett's drama because nothing *can* happen, because life is a futile, endless pattern of repetition without renewal, of desire without consummation, of suffering without transcendence. The same cycle continues eternally: one is born, one suffers, one dies, *da capo*. The myth of divine salvation is one of life's most persistent, and most tragic, illusions.

It is not only the play's pattern of circularity that implies that the Mouth's quest for salvation is doomed to failure. For one thing, the very concept of a "merciful" God is seriously called into question, and by the Mouth herself. For while the words she uses may express faith in a God of mercy, the manner in which those words are delivered undercuts that faith: the phrase "merciful God" is punctuated by the Mouth with two laughs, the first brief, the second prolonged. In his novel *Watt*, Beckett distinguished three different kinds of laugh, all similar in being "strictly speaking [...] not laughs, but modes of ululation": the bitter, the hollow, and the mirthless. Beckett's plays provide lavish illustration for this thesis, since none of Beckett's dramatic characters ever laughs out of genuine delight or happiness. Their laughs are invariably sardonic comments on the heights of metaphysial absurdity or the depths of human anguish, eloquent testimony to the pervasiveness of divine malice. Think, for instance, of Winnie's single laugh in *Happy Days*. After Willie explains that the little white ball Winnie has seen in the emmet's arms is an egg and thus a symbol of "Fornication," Winnie murmurs "God," joins Willie in laughter, and comments "How can one better magnify the Almighty than by sniggering with him at his little jokes, particularly the poorer ones?" The bestowal of life is thus one of god's "poorer jokes"; as Robert Frost succinctly phrased it, "Forgive, O Lord, my little jokes on Thee / And I'll forgive Thy great big one on me."[3]

In my analysis of *Not I* up to this point, I have given the impression that the Mouth is the only character on stage, that Beckett has finally written a true monodrama. For, interestingly enough, although he has consistently toyed with the form, Beckett has never actually produced pure monodrama. It is true that *Act Without Words I*, for example, is specifically labelled by Beckett "*A Mime for one Player.*" But while, on the surface, only one player appears to be involved, in reality there are two. When the player is repeatedly flung onto the stage, someone must be doing the flinging; similarly, when various objects descend from the flies, someone must be sending them down. This "someone" is represented in the text by the sound of a whistle. Like the bell in *Happy Days*, like the spotlight in *Play*, the whistle transcends its classification as a stage property and becomes a "character" – indeed, the antagonist – in the play: a divine surrogate whose purpose it is to prod and torment its victim.

Eh Joe, Beckett's television play, likewise has only one character on view – Joe himself. But even if we ignore for the moment that character whom we hear but do not see – the woman's voice within Joe's head – there is still another character involved: the television camera. Just as Beckett used the very mechanisms of theatre – sound effects, lighting, props – to suggest antagonistic "characters" in his stage plays, he now similarly exploits the mechanics of television. As the Voice forces Joe to recall painful scenes from his past, as each repeated "Eh Joe?" cuts like a knife through the protective barriers he has erected and exposes the raw hurt at his core, the camera, perfectly synchronized with the Voice's stages of attack, physically stalks him, gradually zeroing in for the kill until, at the end of the play, Joe's anguished face is trapped in "maximum closeup."

In *Krapp's Last Tape*, it is the tape recordings of Krapp at earlier periods of his life which rob the play of true monodrama status. For the earlier Krapps are, in a sense, *different* Krapps, and so different characters. There is thus a tension, for example, between the incarnation of Krapp at thirty-nine, exultant with the "fire" he feels within him, and the present, final reality, the Krapp at sixty-nine: the dark, dead ash of a dejected, weary old man, trembling on the brink of death.

And there is likewise a tension in *Not I*, for the Mouth is *not* alone on stage, as no Beckett character is ever truly alone on stage. Hers may be the only words in the play, but it is not the only presence. For listening to her every word is the mysterious figure of the Auditor: a "*tall standing figure, sex undeterminable, enveloped from head to foot in loose black djellaba with hood* [...]"

And not merely listening, for it gradually becomes clear that the Auditor, too, has "lines" in this play, although we cannot hear them. The Mouth, however, does; and we can infer from her words precisely what those lines must be, and the moments at which they are delivered.[4] The Auditor's function seems to be to correct or add information to the Mouth's account of her situation. The Mouth accepts every correction she is offered – usually willingly, at times grudgingly, particularly as the nature of what she must accept becomes more painful and distressing:

pick it up there ... get on with it from there ... another few – ... what? ... not that? ... nothing to do with that? .. nothing she could tell? ... all right ... nothing she could tell ... try something else ... think of something else ...

Or rather, she accepts every correction except one: the ultimate correction, the one truth she is unable to face – that the story she is telling is in fact her own story, that the "she" constantly referred to should really be "I." Five times she is required to accept this; five times she vehemently refuses: "what? ... who? ... no! ... she! ... After each refusal, the Auditor raises his arms from his sides and lets them fall back, a gesture Beckett describes as one of "helpless compassion." The movement lessens with each recurrence, until by the fifth and most vehement denial of all ("what? ... who? ... no! ... she! ... SHE! ... "), it has ceased altogether. A second later, the curtain begins to descend; the Auditor has tried his best, and has conceded defeat.

This refusal to acknowledge directly the truth of one's existence, the truth of its pain and terror, is a recurrent theme in Beckett's plays. We see it dramatized most clearly, perhaps, in *Happy Days*, in which Winnie likewise distances herself from her own misery by displacing it, by attributing it to a fictional creation: in this case, a girl called Mildred. It is only through the guise of a different persona that Winnie can express the suffering she in fact feels but is unable to articulate directly. Ostensibly, Winnie's story concerns Mildred's fright at seeing a mouse:

Suddenly a mouse ran up her little thigh and Mildred, dropping Dolly in her fright, began to scream – (*Winnie gives a sudden piercing scream*) – and screamed and screamed – (*Winnie screams twice*) – screamed and screamed and screamed till all came running [...] to see what was the matter [...] what on earth could possibly be the matter.

Needless to say, the story is not really about the fright of a girl named

Mildred; it is rather a pretext which permits Winnie, through the persona of Mildred, to scream, to express her pent-up emotions of fear and horror and dismay in the only way she can.

The Mouth in *Not I* follows precisely the same procedure, even down to the screams. For when the Mouth screams twice in the middle of her monologue, she can claim that it is not really she who is screaming (what reason does she have to scream?); she is simply illustrating how the woman in her story was unable to scream. The Mouth's refusal to relinquish the third person is thus essentially a refusal to see herself for what she really is. As Beckett commented in an interview with John Gruen: "Somewhere [man] must know that self-perception is the most frightening of all human observations. He must know that when man faces himself, he is looking into the abyss".[5] "Esse est percipi," decreed Bishop Berkeley – to be is to be perceived.[6] Beckett agrees – indeed, has written an entire film script, called simply *Film*, illustrating precisely that point – except that he has added a hideously cruel twist. For the perceiver is no longer external, Berkeley's benevolent and reassuring "eye of God," but internal, and its gaze is far from comforting – to be is to be perceived by oneself as suffering.

And more than that, it is ultimately to acknowledge that there is no salvation from that suffering, that Godot, in effect, will never come. For Beckett's characters, the prospect is simply too frightening. They prefer not to perceive, to remain drugged and oblivious – like Estragon, to escape, if only metaphorically, into the unconsciousness of sleep. Thus, when the Boy begins delivering his message that Godot will not come, Estragon literally falls asleep;[7] in order to continue living with the comforting illusion of hope, he must deliberately make himself insensible (as Malone comments: "Coma is for the living.") For if Beckett's characters ceased hoping, they would have to acknowledge that their entire existence consisted merely of the futile attempt to wrest meaning out of the very heart of meaninglessness, and this they are unprepared to do.

This the Mouth is unprepared to do. By clinging so tenaciously to the third person, she makes herself doubly unconscious – if it is not she who is suffering, then it is not she who must be brought face to face with the knowledge that there is nothing to tell, nothing to think, no release from the suffering. The compassion the Auditor feels for her is genuine – in stark contrast with the usual transcendent figure in Beckett's plays, he is both human and humane. It is as if he were saying to her: "Look, start by acknowledging that it is *you* you are talking about, that it is *your* terror, *your* suffering. And then admit that redemption from that suffering is impossible; perhaps in that very admission there is a kind of redemption, the only redemption man is capable of achieving." The Mouth, however, refuses to listen. Thus, salvation is shown to be unattainable in Beckett's plays, not simply because it doesn't exist, but because the characters won't admit that it doesn't exist, and are therefore denied the only kind of "salvation" possible to them: the "peace" that comes from finally accepting that there can be no real peace.

The action of *Not I* is a metaphor of the search for a non-existent salvation not simply on the metaphysical level, but on the artistic, as well. The play thus presents essentially a double focus. On the one hand, the Mouth's dilemma is a dramatic statement of *man's* dilemma, a metaphysical endgame from which there is no escape. And on the other hand, it is a statement of *Beckett's* dilemma, an artistic endgame equally futile. For Beckett, too, is "coming up to seventy"; he too is engaged in displacing his own pain by telling stories about fictional characters. (When the Mouth thus cries out "what? ... who? ... no! ... she! ...,: it is, in one sense at least, Beckett crying out as well – it is not his own pain he is describing, but the pain of a "character." And note Beckett's cunning in making the protagonist of *Not I* specifically a woman, thus increasing the distance between author and persona.) And Beckett, too, is hoping for a kind of salvation, the peace that will be attained when the right story is finally told.

Beckett is clearly aware of these parallels, and of the ultimate futility of his quest. As the Unnamable comments: "Strange notion in any case, and eminently open to suspicion, that of a task to be performed, before one can be at rest. Strange task, which consists in speaking of oneself. Strange hope, turned towards silence and peace." Indeed, Beckett frequently dramatizes the futility of this quest, as his portrait of the artist in his radio play *Cascando* clearly demonstrates:

story ... if you could finish it ... you could rest ... sleep ... not before ... oh I know ... the ones I've finished ... thousands and one ... all I ever did ... in my life ... with my life ... saying to myself ... finish this one ... it's the right one ... then rest ... sleep ... no more stories ... no more words ... and finished it ... and not the right one ... couldn't rest ... straight away another ...

But the awareness that the stories are pointless, that the salvation is unattainable, coincides with the *need* to tell stories. So Estragon and Vladimir will continue to wait for Godot even though they know he will never come; so the Mouth will continue to talk about "she" searching for the "right" words to say even though there is nothing to say; so Beckett will continue to write, spilling words into the void. I quote the final lines of *The Unnamable*:

you must say words, as long as there are any, until they find me, until they say me, strange pain, strange sin, you must go on, perhaps it's done already, perhaps they have said me already, perhaps they have carried me to the threshold of my story, [...] you must go on, I can't go on, I can't go on, I'll go on.

The effect of *Not I* on a theatre audience is, almost literally, stunning.[8] One spends the first few minutes of the play in a kind of furious concentration, straining to hear and make sense of that torrent of words gushing forth in a mad, frenzied rush, the Mouth's desperate attempt either to *elude* silence ("One way of looking at speech," Harold Pinter has remarked, "is to say it is a constant stratagem to cover nakedness,")[9] or else somehow to *attain* it (in Susan Sontag's opinion, Beckett's writing expresses the subliminal idea "that it might be possible to out-talk language, [...] to talk oneself into silence.")[10] So intense is one's concentration, indeed, so hypnotic is the effect of that one central focus of light, that it may be several moments before one is even aware of the presence of the Auditor. Despite this concentration, however, it is almost impossible to catch, let alone immediately make sense of, every word the Mouth utters. Instead, one is left with a more general impression: a sense of terror, of suffering, of almost ineffable sadness. *Not I* is a frightening experience in the theatre – not simply because we sympathize with the Mouth's terror, but because we are made to feel it directly. We listen so intently to the feverish stream of words that, after a while, they start to bore into our skulls, they start physically to hurt. We look so intently at the immobile spotlight that, after a while, it appears to change shape and position, to dance in front of our eyes. We are being, in effect, viscerally assaulted, we are experiencing what the Mouth is experiencing, and the compassion we feel for her is equally a compassion we feel for ourselves.

Not I takes perhaps fifteen minutes to act, and while it is not so brief a play as the two that preceded it – *Come and Go*, which Beckett specifically labelled a "dramaticule," and *Breath* – it is nevertheless brief enough as theatre pieces go, even one-acters. Yet, despite its relative shortness, *Not I* is anything but a "dramaticule," a theatrical snippet. *Come and Go*, in contrast, is not only short, it is fairly slight. A haunting threnody on the inescapability of death, *Come and Go* can make a powerful theatrical impression, but it is clearly a minor work in the Beckett canon. And the same is true of *Breath*, a play which lasts roughly thirty seconds and has neither dialogue nor characters (although Kenneth Tynan managed to scatter a few nude bodies around when he included the play as the prologue to *Oh! Calcutta!*). *Breath* is essentially a brief gloss on *Waiting for Godot*, a striking dramatization of Pozzo's chilling metaphor: "They give birth astride of a grave, the light gleams an instant, then it's night once more." With *Not I*, however, we are on totally different ground: the ground of a minor masterwork. "Rather difficult and elliptic," as Beckett once observed of *Endgame*, "mostly depending on the power of the text to claw ...,"[11] *Not I* is almost a compendium of those themes and images which have obsessed Beckett throughout his now lengthy writing career, and merits consideration, its brevity notwithstanding, as one of his finest, most complex dramatic achievements.

NOTES

1 It is true, of course, that the characters in Beckett's radio plays are disembodied in a rather different sense, but I am here referring specifically to stage characters who are physically in a state of disintegration.

2 The English description of Winnie's burial in the mound, "stuck up to her diddies in the bleeding ground," was, interestingly enough, translated by Beckett into French as "fourrée jusqu'aux nénés – dans le pissenlit," adding a level of irony absent in the English. In French slang, "manger le pissenlit par la racine" means "to push up daisies"; there is a further implication, then, that Winnie's mound is in point of fact a grave.

3 "Forgive, O Lord," in *In The Clearing* (New York, 1962), p. 39.

4 I do not mean to imply that the Mouth is consciously aware of the Auditor's presence, that she literally "hears" his "words"; or, indeed, that the "words" necessarily stem from him. Nevertheless, it is clear that the Mouth's monologue is subject to some kind of corrective process, internal or external, and it seems to me that the Auditor comes to represent, for the audience, the visual symbol of that corrective process – the attempt to make the Mouth admit the truth about herself – as well as being a witness to its failure.

5 "Samuel Beckett talks about Beckett," *Vogue* (December 1969), 210.

6 See *Principles of Human Knowledge*, IX, in *A New Theory of Vision and Other Writings*, ed. A.D. Lindsay (London, 1910), p. 117.

7 At any rate in the second act of the play. But even in the first act, though technically awake, he still remains essentially unheeding:

Vladimir. Did you not hear what the child said?
Estragon. No.

8 I have seen Alan Schneider's excellent production of *Not I* on two separate occasions, in New York and Toronto, the Mouth brilliantly played on both occasions by Jessica Tandy.

9 Quoted in Ronald Hayman, *Harold Pinter* (London, 1968), p. 79.

10 "The Aesthetics of Silence," in *Styles of Radical Will* (New York, 1970), p. 27.

11 "Beckett's letters on *Endgame*," *The Village Voice*, 19 March 1958, 8.

Samuel Beckett's Media Plays

LINDA BEN-ZVI

The recently released Faber and Grove Press editions of the collected shorter plays of Samuel Beckett contain twenty-nine works. Of that number nearly half are plays written for a medium other than the stage: seven for radio, five for television, and one for film. The high number may surprise those who think of Beckett primarily as a dramatist of the theatre; it may also surprise those who read Beckett criticism, since names like *Cascando* and *Eh Joe* rarely appear except as items in some general overview of Beckett's writing. For example, individual media plays are identified by title in only six of the seventy-four Beckett entries in the 1981 PMLA bibliography, in only three of the sixty-four entries in the 1982 edition. When media plays are discussed, it has become almost a given to preface the analyses – as Clas Zilliacus and Martin Esslin do in their seminal studies of the radio dramas – with regrets about the lack of attention the works usually receive.[1]

The most obvious reason for the critical neglect of such a large portion of the Beckett canon is inaccessibility: inaccessibility of the texts because of inaccessibility of performances. The radio dramas are rarely produced; and although tapes of the original broadcasts can still be located in the BBC archives, few go to the trouble required to hear them. Beckett's one film, *Film*, has also received a limited distribution; outside of Beckett meetings it is not often shown in either of its two versions.[2] And while most of the television plays have been produced in more than one language and have had a wider dissemination than the radio plays because of the availability of videotapes of the originals, they too have reached a small audience.

Unable to experience the media plays in the forms in which they were intended, the Beckett critic has had to approach the works solely through the text – a severe limitation. Even a brief glance at the printed script of *Film* reveals the problem: discussing a work that consists of a series of camera angles and actor positions, with the only auditory sign "ssh!". Similarly, how does one grasp the power of the television play *Ghost Trio* when music supplements the specified positions of the camera and the stylized gestures of the actor, or when music becomes a character – as in *Words and Music* – interacting with another character named Words. Even the most sensitive reader will be at a loss to imagine the resulting harmonies and cacophonies.

Perhaps because of such obstacles, evaluations of Beckett's media works have varied more widely than assessments of his fictions and theatre pieces. While John Fletcher describes *Words and Music* as "the weakest of the radio plays,"[3] Hugh Kenner and Vivian Mercier praise it, Kenner calling it "the most original use to which Beckett has put radio, and one is tempted to say as original and moving a use as any to which radio has been put."[4] Mercier goes even further and calls both *Words and Music* and *Cascando* "two of his [Beckett's] most moving works."[5] Both critics, however, indicate that they are basing their appraisals on a reading of the text, since neither has heard the original. "I regret that I have only an intuitive base for this judgment," (p. 169) Kenner says; "I do not feel I have understood it fully on the basis of the words alone," Mercier writes (p. 153).

Both critics might well have reached the same evaluations of the plays after experiencing them in performance, but what they based their critiques on was a form deprived of its essential element: the shaping presence of the medium itself. This loss is far greater in media plays than it is in theatre works. Unlike the stage that provides audiences the freedom a spatial form allows – the possibilities of scanning the scenes at will, fixing on gestures, props, and stage business – the media plays are temporal, coming to audiences sequentially, through the means of a mechanical device that imposes restrictions on the work and on the listeners or viewers. If the means is banished from the process of transmission, as it is when these plays are read, the loss is far greater than when the live theatre actor is reduced to a fictional presence on a printed page.

Certain writers may create plays without anchoring them to particular forms, but Beckett is not such a writer. In each case he writes with a specific medium in mind. Those who have worked with him on these projects – Martin Esslin and Donald McWhinnie on the radio dramas, and Alan Schneider on the film – have commented on Beckett's acute sense of the problems and possibilities of the form in question.[6] Beckett, himself, has repeatedly indicated the careful wedding of medium and play in his works, and has therefore been adamant about any transference of a play from one medium to another.[7] In a letter that Clas Zilliacus uses as the frontispiece for his book *Beckett and Broadcasting*, Beckett explains to his American publisher his refusal to allow *All That Fall* to be transferred to the stage. "*All That Fall* is a specifically radio play, or rather radio text, for voices, not bodies," he begins. "Even the reduced visual dimension it will receive from the simplest and most static of readings ... will be destructive of whatever quality it may have and which depends on the whole thing's *coming out of the dark.*" Beckett continues with the same injunction against the transference of *Act Without Words* to film: "If we can't keep our genres more or less distinct, or extricate them from the confusion that has them where they are, we might as well go home and lie down."[8]

Essential, then, to any appraisal of Beckett's writing – fiction, drama or media plays – is an awareness of the specific form in which Beckett conceived the work, since for him, more than for most writers, the work not only is predicated on the form but invariably becomes a critique of its form. This tendency can be seen in Beckett's earliest writing, the aborted *Dream of Fair to Middling Women*, where his persona/writer indicates that his theme is the process of fiction as well as the progress of his character, and his goal is to expose the shortcomings of what usually passes for fiction: the "clockwork cabbage stories" exemplified by the works of Balzac.[9] Instead of assuming omniscience, this storyteller commits himself to revealing the paucity of his means. Whenever his story is well launched and promises a logical progression to some sort of conclusion, the hand of the storyteller quickly appears to stop the action, destroy the narrative, and fragment the characters, as they are fragmented in life. The narrator in *Dream* thus becomes a kind of instructor, pointer in hand, reminding the reader that "The only unity in the story is, please God, an involuntary unity" (p. 118) or "The fact of the matter is we do not quite know where we are in this story" (p. 7), or, after a particularly long digression, "Perhaps the pen ran away, don't for a moment imagine Belacqua is down the drain" (p. 65).

When he turns to drama, Beckett engages in the same self-conscious comment on dramatic form. Hamm in *Endgame* may be a modern Hamlet, but he is also a ham actor aware of the eviscerated genre in which he must play, attempting through his deprecatory comments on soliloquies, asides, complications and underplots to resurrect the form by stripping away its incrusted conventions and revealing the artifice that passes for reality. Even more consistently, Beckett calls into question the very definition of drama – the imitation of an action – by having his characters talk rather than move, or talk about moving while they remain frozen in place. Progressively over the years, Beckett's stage plays have jettisoned almost all physical movement until, in works like *That Time* and *A Piece of Monologue*, near stasis is achieved. In the process, however, Beckett has salvaged an entire area that had never before been considered fodder for drama: the action of a mind in turmoil, actively engaged in a struggle with an inert physical body that listens to its own words.

Beckett's radio, film, and television works follow the practices the writer has established in his fictions and theatre writings. They take as their starting points the traditional conventions of the form; but rather than using them as means to an end, to tell a story, Beckett foregrounds the devices – radio sound effects, film and video camera positions – and forces the audience to acknowledge the presence of these usually hidden shapers of texts, just as he has previously forced readers to witness the hesitant acts of composition and the fitful attempts at action. In his media work, Beckett also follows a pattern he has established in fiction and stage drama, and pares down each new piece, simplifying, eliminating extraneous elements, ever working toward some pure coalescence of material and form. The busy landscape of *All That Fall* gives way to the tripartite arguments of *Cascando*; the nine camera positions of *Eh Joe* become the three angles of *Ghost Trio*; the logorrhea of *Embers* is reduced to the visual image and dream of *Nacht und Träume*. Each work becomes an outpost established on the borders of the unexplored world of that medium. From the new position, Beckett sends forth his story: the familiar tale of a world where words fail, the past fades, the future is uncertain, nature is cruel, god is absent, and people go on.

Because the metaphysical situation is consistent in almost all Beckett's works, it is possible to read a media play and recognize themes presented in other forms, respond to their handling in the new work, and even – as Mercier does – argue for the power of a work that is not "fully understood" in relation to a particular medium. However, to take Beckett at his word, it is important to see how specific works – like the following selected radio, film, and television plays – not only reinforce or rearticulate familiar themes, but explore the limitations and possibilities of a specific medium.

All That Fall

In June 1956, the BBC Third Programme approached Beckett about writing a play specifically for radio.[10] In a letter to his friend Nancy

Cunard, written one month later, Beckett reported: "Never thought about Radio play technique but in the dead of t'other night got a nice gruesome idea full of cartwheels and dragging of feet and puffing and panting which may or may not lead to something."[11] On July 18, John Morris, controller of the Third Programme, described a meeting with Beckett: "I got the impression that he has a very sound idea of the problems of writing for radio and I expect something pretty good."[12] By September, the play *All That Fall* was completed, and it was first aired on January 13, 1957, produced by Donald McWhinnie and starring Mary O'Farrell and J.G. Devlin as the Rooneys with Patrick Magee as Mr. Slocum and Jack MacGowran as Tommy.

If he had not thought about the specific techniques of radio before 1956, Beckett had already laid the groundwork for the depiction of a world "coming out of the dark" much earlier. In his fictions of the 1940s and 1950s – *Watt*, the trilogy, *Texts for Nothing*, and *How It Is* – he had repeatedly equated life with speech. "I'm a big talking ball, talking about things that do not exist, or that exist perhaps, impossible to know, beside the point,"[13] the Unnamable says, describing himself and by extension all Beckett personae.

Trapped in language, but desiring a certainty that words cannot supply, the characters share a common dilemma – "I have no voice and must speak, that is all I know" (p. 307) – and a common realization – "There is nothing but what is said. Beyond what is said there is nothing."[14] Those familiar with Beckett's work are aware of the double-edged implications of the phrases, which echo the last words of Wittgenstein's *Tractatus*. All that can be known is what the words say, and yet they say little, never penetrating the "nothing" that lies beyond, in the silence. Building upon this impasse and upon the Democritus quotation – "Nothing is more real than nothing" – Beckett balances language and silence in an attempt to delineate the "somethings" from the "nothing."

Radio, a medium that consists entirely of sounds and silences emanating from an unseen source, received by an unseen presence, is particularly suited for exploring such dichotomies. In *All That Fall*, all the people and objects that Maddy Rooney encounters are first heard as faint noises that grow in intensity and diminish into silence. The pattern reinforces and replicates the central pattern of life in Beckett's works: from void to life to void, from silence to speech to silence: "birth astride of a grave."[15] "Are you going in my direction," Mr. Slocum asks her, and she replies, "I am Mr. Slocum. We all are."[16] The sound pattern marks this direction, a movement from nothing, toward nothing.

Sounds eke out a world from the silence. The first sounds that open the play are those Beckett calls "Rural sounds. Sheep, bird, cow, cock, severally, and then together" (p. 12). They designate a pastoral setting; they also designate nature, the specific nature of the Boghill world. At first bucolic, it slowly becomes more threatening: bleats give way to wind and rain, and finally to "tempest of wind and rain," the last words of the play (p. 39). Inscribed in this natural cycle is the human cycle of goings and comings, marked in the text by the dragging feet of Maddy and Dan, their assorted puffings and pantings, and Dan's cane. The longer they walk, the more difficult the way because of the impediments of nature and their own exhaustion and decay. Mrs. Rooney's encounters on her walk to and from the station provide further examples of the same state of human decay and natural calamity. She greets each passer-by with inquiries about loved ones and learns that Christy's wife is "No better," his daughter "No worse" (p. 12); that Tyler's daughter has had "the whole ... er ... bag of tricks" removed, leaving him "grandchildless" (p. 14); that Mr. Slocum's mother is "out of pain" (p. 17); that Mr. Barrell's father is dead. Tommy is an orphan; Jerry is alone. The inhabitants of Boghill seem literally bogged down, impeded.

Decline, however, is not limited to people. Each conveyance that approaches is more complex but equally flawed. Christy's hinny, a hybrid ass, so anxious to continue suddenly stops short. My. Tyler's bicycle wheel recently pumped hard is now flat. Mr. Slocum's car dies. The train is late. Language also weakens and alters. In Grimm's Law, as Dan points out, sounds move from voiced to voiceless. Words lose their meanings and become archaic; phrases are no longer remembered, or only half remembered. Languages even die; Gaelic, for example, Maddy notes. Other human sign systems do not fare much better. Counting, "one of the few satisfactions in life!" (p. 30) for Dan, leads to faulty conclusions, as it does for most of Beckett's counters.

A possible buffer against this pain is religion – the force that should uplift. It does not. Besides the title, several images from the 145th Psalm reverberate ironically through the play. "Tender mercies" shown to Mrs. Rooney are all regretted since the offerer receives no praise or recompense; the "eyes of all [who] wait for thee" become the blind gropings of Dan Rooney; and instead of the prophecy "One generation shall laud thy works to another," one generation passes its maladies and human suffering to the next. In fact, the only prophecy that is fulfilled in the play is the one offered by the unnamed mother to her daughter Dolly, "one can be sucked under" (p. 25), an image fulfilled when Jerry describes the child's death "under the wheels"(p. 39).

Rather than being uplifted, Maddy and her husband are bent over. This dichotomy between vertical and horizontal is represented by the late train. Due to arrive at twelve thirty, a time when the hands of the clock would be in a straight vertical line, it arrives, instead, at twelve forty-five, when the vertical is cut by the horizontal at a right angle. The clock becomes an icon for the world of Boghill: the plodding walk of the inhabitants at right angles to the desired "flying up" or salvation.

These themes are familiar ones in Beckett's works; what is significant about *All That Fall* is the aural transcription the themes receive. "Going on," the motto for all Beckett personae, is beaten out by the sounds of feet, cartwheels, bicycles, cars, and trains albeit late. These sounds are set in contrapuntal fashion to the forces that impede them: nature, the sudden capricious changes in the weather, and fate or chance or human intervention that places children under the wheels of trains. These numerous sounds turn Boghill into an aural equivalent of King Lear's heath. Lear's brandishing his fist to the elements and imprecating nature become in the radio drama Maddy Rooney's persistent panting and plodding against the blasts of rain and wind.

Beckett is fond of building his compositions on triads, and in *All That Fall* he adds to natural, human, and mechanical sounds the sounds of music: Schubert's *Death and the Maiden*. Music, which Beckett had briefly introduced in *Godot* and which would become progressively more dominant in later plays, is used in this work for several purposes. First, it sets the perimeters of the landscape over which Maddy walks; the strains of the work are heard as she embarks, and heard again as she and Dan return at the end of the day. Second, each refrain brings forth a comment, the first becoming the opening words in the play: "Poor woman. All alone in that ruinous old house" (p. 12); the second marking the end of the journey: "All day the same old record. All alone in that great empty house" (p. 37). In true Beckettian fashion, even language has become enervated along the way; one of the two adjectives preceding *house* is shorter, having lost a syllable en route.[17] The phrases remind the listener of the loci of the play: the walking woman and the stationary woman subject to the same condition. As Maddy says, "It is suicide to be abroad. But what is it to be at home ... ?" (p. 15) Both alternatives bring the same "lingering dissolution" (p. 15). While Pozzo and Lucky must physically intersect the point where Vladimir and Estragon stand, the two women in the radio drama can become coordinates through the sounds of music and moving feet, the temporal medium allowing the two to meet and meet again by a repetition of the aural confluence. Third, the music serves to reinforce the themes of death and decay expressed by Maddy in her exchanges with her Boghill neighbors and with her husband as they make their way home from the station. Finally, the music calls forth the image of the old woman in the old house by use of a traditional device of radio drama where a sound effect or music is used to identify some person, object, or situation.

The technique of associating sound with image is one Beckett repeatedly uses in his play. Following the sound of cartwheels, Maddy identifies the source – Christy; after a bell, Mr. Tyler makes known his presence. The sound of a slap becomes a sign of wasps; the sound of a shout indicates a woman being beaten by her husband. Since the entire world of the play is a predicated on sound, the use of sound/object identification is central to the creation of an aural verisimilitude of some sensate, material world. However, Beckett intersperses these devices with others that tend to undermine the carefully crafted Boghill environs. He has Maddy think again and again that she hears sounds the radio audience do not hear, particularly the sounds of the approaching mail train. At other times, Beckett forces his audience to fill in the silence as they choose. For example, Mr. Tyler's efforts to balance on his bicycle and doff his hat must be imagined without the prompting of accompanying sounds; so too his position after Connelly's truck passes. Maddy's "Ah there you are!" (p. 15) is purposely vague. By so doing, Beckett reveals the arbitrariness of the world he has created and hints at the presence of another world, one unheard and beyond the listener's ken, a world that exists within the skull of Maddy Rooney, at an even further remove than the aural transcriptions to which the audience is privy.

The most elaborate and extended sound sequence gives rise to the funniest image in the play: Maddy's arduous struggle into and out of the front seat of Mr. Slocum's car, an aural vaudeville, hilarious in its use of grunts, pants, and creaks that accompany the sexual puns of the wordplay. It is also the sequence that most undermines the aural verisimilitude. When Maddy attempts to reverse the movement, exiting from the car, Tommy the station boy suddenly says, "Mind your feather, Ma'am" (p. 19). "What feather?" the listener must ask, because there has been no mention of a feather earlier. Thus, the picture of Maddy must be altered to accommodate this new piece of information. What had previously been vivid and concrete gives way to yet another picture, this one topped with a feather.

Yet to ask "What feather?" is to open the way for the more disturbing and central question that underlies the play: "What Maddy?" Maddy is – like all Beckett's personae – a character made of words, others' words. The words constantly change, slip, fail to specify all possible situations and attitudes, and fail to enumerate details such as feathers. By this deft sleight of word – the weight of a feather – Beckett suddenly points to the fragility of his Boghill construction, the fragility of a world predicated on language, and points to the "nothing" that exists beyond the world of words, in the silence of the past and future.

To indicate that the rupture caused by the feather is not accidental, Beckett immediately follows the unsettling experience with the introduction of Miss Fitt, the appropriately named "dark lady," who explains that her failure to recognize Maddy comes from the fact that "I am not there, Mrs. Rooney, just not really there at all. I see, hear, smell, and so on, I go through the usual motions, but my heart is not in it" (p. 23). Nonbeing, or being that lies outside of the physical world, is again suggested near the end of the play when Maddy tells her husband the story of a girl who "had never really been born!" (p. 36) – a story Beckett first heard in a lecture delivered by Carl Jung in London in 1935. Like the play *Footfalls*, the Beckett work it most closely resembles, *All That Fall* explores the possibility of verifying self through physical means, particularly sounds: the sounds of a world coming over the radio waves, or the sounds of feet hitting a bare floor. In both works the central character fades in and out of focus – figuratively in the radio drama, literally on the stage.

Having built a form and then destroyed its foundation, Beckett goes even further and strikes at the very heart of the format of radio drama: a suspended period of time in which an imaginary world is temporarily created by sound clues, and in which an audience patiently follows image after image in order to reach some point, usually the answer to such questions as "what happened?" or "who did it?".

As Maddy returns home, completing her journey, there should be a conclusion commensurate to the imaginative trip the radio audience has made. Listeners, used to having mysteries solved in the last minutes of a program, expect to be told who killed the child. Beckett's sudden revelation of the death, his hints about Dan's culpability, and his refusal to identify Dan's part in the event may be purposely contrived, not so much to raise metaphysical questions or to fulfill words uttered within the play – "Did you ever wish to kill a child?" (p. 31) – as to thwart the conventional form of radio, in much the same way that Beckett frustrates the conventional desires of a theatre audience to know if Clov leaves and if Willie caresses or kills Winnie. Beckett, like Ibsen in *Ghosts*, leaves his play unfinished in order to indicate the artificiality of forms that tie together all loose pieces, and to suggest that true verisimilitude would demand that some questions go unresolved. Such adherence to actual experience would provide a basis upon which to build a new radio form – or theatre – that approximates the mysteries of life, yet does not always seek in the last five minutes to solve them.

Film

Beckett's one film is appropriately entitled *Film*, because it does not tell a story as much as it displays the nature of the medium. His radio plays were aural exchanges emanating from the dark; his film and subsequent television plays are ocular exchanges between object and camera, with the audience a duplicating force, seeing as the camera sees, just as before they were a validating presence for the speaking self, hearing him or her be.

Beckett makes this camera control the theme of *Film*. Using as its motto a phrase from the philosopher Berkeley, "*Esse est percipi*" (To be is to be perceived), the work presents two angles of vision, represented by two cameras. The first, and dominant, angle is called E for Eye. It is the perceiver as pursuer. Beckett's general introductory notes make clear that until the end of the film, the audience is not to know who or what the "pursuing perceiver" is.[18] Established from the beginning, however, is the horror that E causes those who come under its gaze. Beckett's early notes for the project indicate: "Those who look at Eye [on] street stairs turn horrified away."[19] What they see is themselves as objects. It is the second camera, designated O for Object, that represents the perceived as pursued. To differentiate between these two angles of vision is important. Since the central object O is a man with one eye, his vision is blurred. Therefore in the first two sections of the film – on the street and in the vestibule – O's vision is introduced, so that when E and O are alone in the room in the third section, it will be apparent who is perceiving the objects within the room. Such distinctions are technically difficult, and Beckett recognized the constraints under which he was working. "We're trying to find," he told the production crew, "a ... cinematic equivalent for visual appetite and visual distaste ... a reluctant ... a disgusted vision [O's] and a ferociously ... voracious one [E's]."[20]

The technical interplay between the two "visions" becomes the central dilemma for the film makers, compounded because the film is silent except for a "ssh!" which ironically serves to underline its arbitrary, non-verbal state. In his production notes accompanying the printed script, Beckett indicates that his original model for the work was the silent slapstick films of the 1920s. "Climate of film comic and unreal. O should invite laughter throughout by his way of moving" (p. 12), Beckett writes.

Thus described, the film is a variation on the old Keystone Kops chase, except that the pursuer is the one eye – I – that will not be eluded. By using a familiar cinematic form, Beckett once more is able to play against a tradition, here the vaudeville chase epics of early Hollywood, and he is able to reinforce the connection by using one of the actors most closely associated with the form: Buster Keaton, deadpan comedian of so many silent film chases.

Keaton is the object E follows through the three parts of the film: down a street, into a vestibule, and up to a room. The printed script calls for the street scene to include people, all in couples, walking to work in a "small factory district" (p. 12) However, in filming, this scene proved too difficult to do, and instead the film opens with a close-up of Keaton's hawklike eye, peering directly into the camera, a kind of icon for the ocular chase to follow. The substituted introduction reflects the original title of the work, *The Eye.*

Throughout most of the picture it is the stalking vision of E that fills the screen: the vision through which the audience must perceive the action. As long as E stands at an angle not exceeding forty-five degrees behind O, O does not experience "anguish of perceivedness" (p. 11), as Beckett says in his notes. Exceeding this angle, as E does on the street, in the stairwell, and in the room, O cringes, hides his face, and attempts to elude his pursuer. Whetting the audience's curiosity and preparing for what he labels the "investment" – the final confrontation between E and O – Beckett has E momentarily focus on the couple with whom O collides and an old flower seller descending the stairs in the vestibule. Each exhibits the same facial reaction: mouth open, eyes wide in horror. These early confrontations become preface to the climactic one in the room.

In section three, the longest part of the film, O goes through a ritual of ridding the sanctum of all possible eyes. Windows, doors, parrot cage, and fishbowl are covered; dog and cat – after a long vaudeville-inspired routine – are ejected; a print of "the face of God the Father" (p. 32) on the wall is torn into four pieces. A manila envelope whose circles seem to resemble eyes is turned to dispel the illusion. The seven pictures it holds – pictures in which peering eyes look at O in various stages of life – are ritualistically torn in two. Having finished, O lapses into sleep, as the rocking chair comes to rest. It is then that E moves, circling the room, confronting O twice, once retreating, and then, rousing him from sleep, in Beckett's words, "investing" him with self-perception. O's look of recognition repeats that of the couple and flower seller: open mouth, eyes wide. Now the gaze finally reveals the pursuer. O is shown staring in horror into the face of the perceiving self, himself, whose look is "impossible to describe, neither severity nor benignity, but rather acute *intentness* (p. 47). Next to the head of E, a big nail is visible. At the sight, O raises his hands, covers his eyes, and after glimpsing E once more, slowly drops his head, as the rocking motion of the chair subsides again.

In his focus on the eye of the perceiver, Beckett creates a film about film, depicting the unique property of the form. The audience are not, as in conventional films, lulled into forgetting the manipulation of the controlling camera eye; here the audience become allied with the camera, since they must see, at this severely restricted angle, what E sees, while all the time in doubt about who or what E is. The final investment thus becomes a shared one: O unable to avoid self-recognition, the audience unable to avoid the imposition of the camera. Just as in radio, where he plays familiar expectations against stylized form, subverting the traditional last-minute revelations and final closure, in his cinema experiment Beckett once more explodes a conventional format. Chase movies are built upon the audience identification with either the pursuer or the pursued, with the kops/cops or the rubes/robbers. Beckett forces the viewers to suspend this usual alignment, since he withholds the reason for the quest, the nature of the pursuer, and the motivations of the pursued. All that remains is the inexorable presence of the camera against which they are powerless to do anything but avert their gazes. Beckett foregrounds the experience of perception and indicates how subjective and fragmented – one-eyed – human sight may be, shaped as it is by a flight from self-awareness that renders it partial.

Beckett also plays with the convention of the silent film, not silent at all as E's "ssh!" indicates. By refusing to use words to explain images, Beckett forces audiences to respond directly to what they see and think about how they see. He also implies that words would not change anything, since the duality of self is experienced beyond language. *Film* allows Beckett to *show* this duality rather than talk about the perpetual fight over possession of the first person pronoun. On the screen, both selves can be offered as discrete angles of vision, a concretization of what the unnamed narrator says in *Fizzle 6*: "I've seen you, it was me, with my other's ravening eyes" (p. 43).

Ghost Trio

Beckett's involvement with television began in 1966, two years after *Film*. The play *Eh Joe* was written for the English actor Jack MacGowran and produced by BBC television on July 4, 1966. In it Beckett again makes use of the camera, but this time it is single; and it is limited to nine demarcated positions, moving four inches closer to the lone figure, Joe, at intervals between speeches, until it stand peering into his eyes. Joe's movements at the beginning resemble those of the furtive O in *Film*, checking and securing window, door, cupboard, and bed, all outsized and clearly not realistic. Convinced that he is undetected, Joe sits on the edge of the bed as the television dolly showly moves in for the first shot, stopping as a voice begins. It is not the voice of Joe, however, but that of an unseen woman, whose words appear to emanate from within Joe, who sits silently, listening. As the camera moves inexorably closer, the voice sketches Joe's loveless life.

Obviously unlike the motion picture screen, the television screen is small; therefore when the face of Joe fills it, his suffering becomes intimate and personal. As the camera hovers only a few inches from his eyes, the features become a mask of sorrow, moving in their details. In the German version with Deryk Mendel that Beckett directed, the furrow over the bridge of the actor's nose mesmerizes the viewer, becoming an eloquent counterpoint to the sordid story the head contains. Again, as in *Film* and *All That Fall*, the power of the medium shapes the work. Read, the play is among Beckett's most banal. Seen, the banality of the life is etched dramatically on the face of the man who has lived it, and the work gains power because of the visualization of waste, the effect achieved without any word from Joe.

Ten years separate *Eh Joe* from Beckett's next television drama, *Ghost Trio*. Several important developments occurred in the interim that may help to explain the differences between the two works. First, Beckett's stage dramas in the decade had grown progressively more visual or image-centered. *Not I, Footfalls,* and *That Time* rely on the impact of images: a gaping, moving mouth; a pacing, draped form; a staring face. Second, the works had become more insistently repetitive, playing with slight permutations of movements, sounds, and words, slight shifts in a formal schema, offering possible freedom accorded within a circumscribed world or dramatic pattern. Although the tendency toward repetition and variation can be seen as early as the play *Play* and the fiction piece *Lessness*, it becomes the dominant mode of the theatre pieces from *Not I* on. When he returned to television with *Ghost Trio*, therefore, Beckett created a work less traditionally narrative than *Eh Joe* and more concerned with both visual depiction and repetitive movements.

In *Ghost Trio*, a white-haired figure dressed in a long greatcoat is seated in a room, "the familiar chamber,"[21] a female voice says. The voice, labeled V, is not that of a loved one, as in *Eh Joe*; rather, it is the depersonalized voice of a narrator, directed to the television audience, describing room, objects, and figure in the same flat tones. "Good evening. Mine is a faint voice. Kindly tune accordingly" (p. 248), she says twice. She calls the viewer's attention to the room, first in general terms, "Look," then in more detail, "Now look closer" (p. 248). Each item is isolated, a segment of it representing the whole. Floor, wall, door, window, and pallet are described in that order, and then flashed on the screen in reverse order, after which the voice says, "Look again" (p. 248). Only then is the inert figure at right mentioned in a sentence that places him last: "Sole sign of life a seated figure" (p. 249) called F.

The play is divided into three parts, designated I Pre-action, II Action, and III Re-action, each consisting of numbers indicating camera shots: I – 35 shots, II – 38 shots, and III – 41 shots.[22] In Part I, all of the objects in the room are displayed from angle A, the farthest remove of the camera; and then from close up, while the figure is approached from three angles of the camera, A, B, and C; and finally, in a close-up. Only at B does music sound, emanating from a small hand-held tape recorder his fingers clutch, left hand in a clawlike position, right hand with four fingers straight, the thumb hidden. The segment ends with the camera returning to a general view of the room.

Part II, called "Action," follows F on his rounds in his room. Twice the voice indicates, "He will now think he hears her" (p. 250). With each anticipation, F's left hand is abruptly raised, his head turned toward the door. After the second motion, F stands, goes to the door, listens, slowly opens it, bending down almost in half to peer outside, then returns to the upright position as the door slowly closes and the third "No one" (p. 250) is spoken by V. From the door, he moves to the window, opens it, and repeats the same movement while V repeats, "No one" (p. 250). From there he moves counterclockwise to the pallet and the mirror, staring into the latter as V records his surprise with an "Ah!" (p. 251) rising in intensity. The circuit again brings F to his stool, where he takes up the recorder, begins to listen, and once more thinks "he hears her" (p. 251). After the second futile search and return, the music becomes audible at A. The section ends with V commanding "Stop" and "Repeat" (p. 251).

Part III, "Re-action," is a repetition, or nearly, of Part II, except that this time there are two angles of camera, reminiscent of the dual angles in *Film*: one from the camera observing at a remove of C; and the other from the vantage point of F, indicating for the first time what F sees as he peers

out door, window, and in mirror. The only other added views are those of
the recorder on the stool and the mirror, presented from neither perspective. As F opens the door, the rectangular shape of the hallway against the
walls is visible; as he looks out the window, he sees a steady downpour of
rain; and as he looks into the mirror, he sees himself – long, white,
mangled hair, tired eyes. Finally, when he rises a second time to open the
door, he responds not to his imagination, but to actual footsteps and an
actual knock. In the hall is a small boy who has come in out of the rain,
wearing a rubber hat and coat. The child says nothing, but closes his eyes
and shakes his head from center to left, and repeats the slight action
before turning and moving slowly down the hall into darkness, his feet
echoing as he moves. Returning once more to his position on the stool, F
begins the music once again, and it plays on till the end. This time,
however, the hands that have remained in the same position since Part I
shift: both hands now clasp the recorder with clawlike ferocity and continue to do so until the end, when the head slowly rises and a look, not
indicated in the text – almost a smile – graces the countenance. At that,
the camera retreats to A and the figure remains inert; the hands, however,
are now crossed, with fingers straight in a visual indication of finality, no
longer anticipatory or clutching.

This brief description indicates that the play offers certain familiar
Beckettian themes: waiting for someone or something that never arrives; a
messenger sent to indicate the absence of the desired one; and a figure
alone in a bare room, like Molloy, Moran, O in *Film*, and Joe. Again, the
reader of the piece, despite the numbered camera directions and the
dearth of words, can recognize the situation as one presented in other
Beckett writings. Once more, however, it is in the production of the work
that the themes take shape. For as much as the play is about the anticipation of a loved one, it is also about the act of seeing.

V in Part I trains the viewer's attention on sections of the room,
signaling the recurrent rectangles, the dominant form in *Ghost Trio*.[23]
Each rectangular shape is seen against a still larger rectangle: the window
against the wall, the door against the wall, the pallet against the floor, even
the tape recorder against the stool. The horizontal rectangle of floor that
opens the first section of the play is balanced by the horizontal rectangle
of the pallet that closes the initial visual tour. Providing further symmetry
within the play, Beckett has the horizontal stool balanced by the vertical
position of the recorder when F puts it down, and the pattern is repeated
by the horizontal pallet seen against the vertical of the pillow upon it. All
these rectangles, of course, are subsumed in the framing rectangle of the

television screen, possibly being viewed in the rectangle of "the familiar room" of the viewer: world within world ever expanding – or receding.

Once she has taught the viewer how to see, V teaches the viewer how to perceive movement around these rectangular shapes. In highly stylized, nonrealistic, balletic fashion, F glides, ghostlike to the strains of Beethoven's *Fifth Piano Trio* (*The Ghost*), touching the now familiar objects, viewing them in search of the illusive loved one. Having gone through the ritual once – a trial run – under the directorial instructions of V, F moves silently again, and the audience is shown the now doubly familiar room from yet another perspective: that of F, both object in it and subject viewing it.

Yet there are still two other hovering presences in "the familiar room," both represented by different angles of vision. The first is the music, made visible by the image of the rectangular tape recorder. In III.12, the camera directions read: "Cut to close-up from above of cassette on stool, small grey rectangle on larger rectangle of seat" (p. 252). The description resembles the rectangles upon rectangles in Part I, "shades of the color grey" (p. 248). Placed in a section that in almost all respects repeats the actions and angles of Part II, however, the image seems jarring, out of place. But it does call attention to the presence of the music as a discrete element, heard but not visually noted earlier. By introducing a close-up shot of the recorder in III, Beckett seems to be exposing the artifice of background music, a muted adjunct in most television dramas, but one that affects visual responses albeit unacknowledged by the audience. In *Ghost Trio*, rather than having the music function as an ancillary agent in the play, Beckett creates a work that offers a visualization of the music.

The other image not accounted for in Part II, but shown in III.24, is the mirror. The directions read: "Cut to close-up of mirror reflecting nothing. Small grey rectangle (same dimensions as cassette) against larger rectangle of wall" (p. 253). The description of the shape and of the grey color parallels that of the recorder, and of the physical confines of the room and its objects in Part I. Why Beckett chooses to show the mirror with the cassette at this point in the play, and not earlier with floor, walls, door, window, and pallet, is not certain. One possibility is that only in Part III, "Re-action," is the mirror capable of showing F as both subject and object, who has been made whole by the dual angles of the camera and the progression of the play. Another possibility may be that the mirror which reflects what is in the room – giving back the image of the one who gazes in it – differs from the other objects, at least from the window and door that open to the outside, to the macrocosm. The mirror alone, like music, reflects the self. It is appropriate, then, that only in Part III are the mirror and the music accorded an individual camera shot, not subsumed into either of the established angles in the work – what the viewer sees through the primary camera or what F sees as he looks out. They are offered as independent elements that the viewer must acknowledge as part of "the familiar chamber" of the play. Like Maddy's feather, they are new facts that force the viewer to reconstruct the image of the play.

Ghost Trio is one of Beckett's most powerful visualizations of the agony of waiting and the pain of solitude. Read, however, the work conveys little of this power: neither its stark balletic movements nor its confluence of music and gesture. Seen, it concretizes the situation, and in so doing offers a critique on the act of seeing – in life and on the television screen that seeks to reflect it. Like the art that makes Watt's pot less familiar the more it is described, Beckett's rectangular television world explodes "the familiar room" of F and the viewer, revealing both as series of shapes and patterns that render them new and unsettling. Beckett's accomplishment in this work – and in most of his media plays – is to point to the possibilities of new uses for the all too "familiar" media. Revealing the conventions of sound and shape, Beckett clears the way for their uses in a form that takes as its subject the limitations of sound and sight in perceiving the world. On the page, as Kenner indicated, Beckett's movements toward these ends can only be intuited.

NOTES

1 Clas Zilliacus, *Beckett and Broadcasting* (Åbo, 1976), and Martin Esslin, "Samuel Beckett and the Art of Broadcasting," *Encounter*, 45 (September 1975), 38–46.

2 The first version of *Film*, commissioned for Evergreen Theatre, was directed by the late Alan Schneider. Samuel Beckett was present during the shooting, in New York, in July 1964. The original film was in black and white; a second version, in color, was made in 1979 by David Clark, for the BBC Film Institute. The version restores the originally intended opening scene – even extending it – and includes sound effects, not specified in Beckett's script.

3 John Fletcher, as quoted in John Fletcher and John Spurling, *Beckett: A Study of His Plays* (New York, 1972), p. 101.

4 Hugh Kenner, *A Reader's Guide to Samuel Beckett* (New York, 1973), p. 169. Further reference will appear in the text.

5 Vivian Mercier, *Beckett/Beckett* (New York, 1977), p. 150. Further reference will appear in the text.

6 For discussions of Beckett's work in the media, see Esslin, Schneider's essay "On Directing *Film*," included with the typescript of *Film* (New York, 1969), pp. 63–94.

7 For instances when Beckett's works have been transferred from one genre to another, see Ruby Cohn, "Jumping Beckett's Genres," in *Just Play* (Princeton, N.J., 1980), pp. 207–229.

8 Letter from Samuel Beckett to his American publisher, 27 August 1957.

9 Samuel Beckett, *Dream of Fair to Middling Women*, unpublished novel, Reading University Library, Beckett Archive, MS 1227/7/16/9, p. 106. Further reference will appear in the text.

10 For a description of the contacts, see Esslin; Zilliacus, pp. 28–76; and Donald McWhinnie, "*All That Fall*," *Radio Times*, 11 January 1957, p. 4, and *The Art of Radio* (London, 1959).

11 Letter from Samuel Beckett to Nancy Cunard, 4 July 1956, rpt. in *No Symbols Where None Intended: A Catalogue of Books, Manuscripts, and Other Materials Relating to Samuel Beckett in the Collections of the Humanities Research Center* (Austin, Tex., 1984), p. 93.

12 As quoted in Esslin, 39.

13 Samuel Beckett, *The Unnamable*, in *Three Novels* (New York, 1955), p. 305. Further reference will appear in the text.

14 Samuel Beckett, *Fizzles* (New York, 1976), p. 37.

15 Samuel Beckett, *Waiting for Godot* (New York, 1954), p. 57.

16 Samuel Beckett, *All That Fall*, in *Collected Shorter Plays of Samuel Beckett* (London, 1984), p. 17.

17 Esslin (39) reports that the only change Beckett made in the original script was to alter the first line, which originally read: "All alone in that old crazy house."

18 Samuel Beckett, *Film* (New York, 1969), p. 11. Further reference will appear in the text.

19 As quoted in S.E. Gontarski, "*Film* and Formal Integrity," in *Samuel Beckett: Humanistic Perspectives*, eds. Morris Beja, S.E. Gontarski, and Pierre Astier (Columbus, O., 1983), p. 130.

20 As quoted in Gontarski, p. 135.

21 Samuel Beckett, *Ghost Trio*, in *Collected Shorter Plays of Samuel Beckett*, p. 248. Further reference will appear in the text.

22 In their *Ends and Odds*, Faber and Grove Press texts of *Ghost Trio* have different numbers of camera shots and wording.

23 Just as the rectangle is the central shape in *Ghost Trio*, the circle is the primary configuration in ... *but the clouds* ... and the square gives shape to *Quad I and II*.

Reading as Theatre: Understanding Defamiliarization in Beckett's Art

H. PORTER ABBOTT

> The only true voyage of discovery, the only really rejuvenating experience, would be not to visit strange lands but to possess other eyes, to see the universe through the eyes of another. (Proust[1])

To borrow an understatement from Charles R. Lyons, "the recited discourses in Beckett's late stage plays overpower the dramatised action." Expecting to see a play, we hear fragments of a story. The inversion of genre expectations is so insistent that part of the experience one undergoes is a genre question: Is this theatre or is it (again to use Lyons's words), "prose fiction enclosed in a theatrical conceit?"[2] One object of this essay is to make the case that this development in Beckett's work for the stage rests on the insight that reading itself is theatrical. But my principal object is to enlarge our understanding of what motivates Beckett's way of making strange – of which the reading/theatre fusion of the late plays is a highly characteristic example – and to suggest terms in which to frame that understanding. I shall focus on Beckett's play about reading, *Ohio Impromptu*.

I A Literary Convention Turns Inside Out

In the nineteenth-century novel, the use of an evening at the theatre as an occasion for mapping social relations received its richest development. From Balzac to Proust, novelists repeatedly bring us to a theatre and there direct our attention not so much to what is happening on stage as to what is happening in the audience. The device had great utility. As a visual representation of society, the theatre scene exceeded most novelistic venues (weddings, funerals, banquets, balls, salons, Sunday promenades) in its capacity to gather representative types into a single place, sufficiently compact to be commanded by the eye. In the theatre of the nineteenth-century audience, one could observe both the comparative elevation of these types and the chemistry of their interchange. In Balzac's *Père Goriot*, when Eugène de Rastignac escorts Mme de Beauséant to *Les Italiens*, the reader can join him in observing the sociology of love and money as the Count d'Ajuda Pinto momentarily abandons the box of the wealthy Rochefides for that of his old lover. At the same time, the reader can observe the obscure Rastignac insert himself into the devolving drama of a banker's wife and the Count de Marsay.

The device worked well in rendering a society for which identity was conceived in terms of visual spectacle – in theatrical terms of place, role, costume and convention – while its value was proportionally heightened when the nature and meaning of those terms were placed under excep-tional pressure, as they were throughout the nineteenth century. It was the fluidity and loopholes and general slippage of the social terms of place, role, and convention that gave the keenest fascination to what was going on in the theatre audience. For the readership, a great deal was at stake in this slippage. It is not surprising, then, that the finest and most elaborate example of this device – the twenty-five pages Proust devotes to an evening at the *Opéra* that opens the third volume of *A la recherche du temps perdu* – appeared in a work devoted to the waning years of the society that made it possible.

Proust's brilliant scene anticipates and counterbalances the chaotic postwar milieu that Marcel observes many years later in the Guermantes's drawing room during the closing pages of *A la recherche*. In his autobiogra-phy, Sartre drew on the same topological tradition to express his own understanding of the gulf between pre- and post-war social self-awareness when he juxtaposed two theatre audiences: that of nineteenth-century drama and that of twentieth-century cinema. Where the nineteenth-century bourgeois turned from the stage to see what he could take to be a coherent and reassuring image of society, the twentieth-century movie-goer awoke from the film to a world without form:

Where was I? In a school? In an official building? Not the slightest ornament: rows of flap-seats beneath which could be seen their springs, walls smeared with ochre, a floor strewn with cigarette stubs and gobs of spit. Confused murmurs filled the hall, language was reinvented, ...

The social hierarchy of the theatre had given my grandfather and late father, who were accustomed to second balconies, a taste for ceremonial. When many people are together, they must be separated by rites; otherwise, they slaughter each other. The movies proved the opposite. This mingled audience seemed united by a catastrophe rather than a festivity.[3]

Here Sartre anticipates the conclusion of Thomas Pynchon's *Gravity's Rainbow* where humanity is figured as an agglutinated mass of movie-goers, chanting in darkness with death only nanoseconds away. By stressing at the same time the magical power of film – "the delirium of a wall" (p. 77) – Sartre also anticipates Jean Baudrillard's theory of the postmodern condition, epitomized by the final depthlessness of Americans for whom nothing is real save what is rendered on a screen.[4]

Dougald McMillan and Martha Fehsenfeld have remarked how in *Eleuthéria*, the unpublished play Beckett wrote in 1947, the nineteenth-century bourgeois drawing-room with its cast of conventional characters was literally "'swept into the pit,'" clearing the stage for *Godot*.[5] Included in this general evacuation was a bored character named Spectator. In other words, it was a thorough house-cleaning which included in its understanding of theatre what we sometimes forget – the theatre audience. Swept into the pit is the complete theatrical situation which one finds so splendidly rendered in nineteenth-century fiction. Since *Eleuthéria*, the waning of audience form has become a common citation in Beckett, as, for example, when Vladimir identifies the audience as "the bog"[6] or when Clov peers at it through a telescope:

I see ... a multitude ... in transports ... of joy.
(*Pause.*)
That's what I call a magnifier.[7]

However, Beckett not only comments on the formal disintegration of the audience, he depends on it. In his work, the remnant of the old coherent audience is the canned applause of his 1982 play, *Catastrophe*. Exactly the same every night, it is displaced by the tentative, confused response of the real audience that follows its extinction. In 1952, before his theatre debut, Beckett told Roger Blin that the ideal audience for *En attendant Godot* would probably be an empty house.[8] There is more than hyperbole in this comment. Beckett's work requires emptiness in the theatre in the sense that it requires an openness to the unexpected. When the audience of the American première of *Godot* left the theatre in droves in Miami, they registered in their way the success of Alan Schneider's direction. The audience that week was a recrudescence of nineteenth-century socially structured self-awareness, and it was driven from the modern theatre.

Moving over to Beckett's prose fiction and searching it for some remnant of the device of the theatre audience, one finds only indeterminate observers – vague entities along the order of the "bog" in *Godot* – like the anonymous and inscrutable readers of Molloy's manuscript or those "above in the light" who are presumed to observe the creature of *How It Is.* "Remnants" is perhaps the wrong word for these entities because it suggests something vestigal, or accidentally left over, whereas their presence, however obscure, is so insistent that they have become a major formal element in Beckett's prose. At the same time, the pieces that Beckett has written for the stage since *Krapp's Last Tape* (1956) have, with very few exceptions, featured a listener or auditor: Krapp himself, Willie in *Happy Days*, the spotlight in *Play*, Joe in *Eh Joe*, Auditor in *Not I*, Listener in *That Time*, May in *Footfalls*, F in *Ghost Trio*, M in *... but the clouds...* , the Woman in *Rockaby*, the Dreamer in *Nacht und Träume*.[9]

The process begin in 1947 when Beckett swept the nineteenth-century theatre into the pit achieved one of its consummations in 1981 when Beckett seems to have gone on to displace not simply nineteenth-century theatre, but theatre itself, replacing it with the reading of a book. In the context of the novelistic topos we began with, *Ohio Impromptu* – a play that features a table, a hat, a book, a Reader and a Listener – provides the most interesting variation on Beckett's late plays of listening. Point for point, the situation in *Ohio Impromptu* is an absolute inversion of the nineteenth-century device of *theatrum theatri.* Where the latter was a presentation in prose narrative of the arena of staged performance, the former is a presentation on stage of the arena of prose narrative. I like to think that Beckett, with his fondness for antithesis, was aware of this inversion, but whether he was or not, I shall argue in what follows that this particular artistic move is not only powerfully expressive but throws into sharp relief two basic ways of understanding Beckett's strategies of defamiliarization.

II An Art of Radical Displacement

A fruitful place to start is with the immediate occasion that called the play forth – a conference of scholars in Columbus, Ohio.[10] It is hard not to entertain the idea that a dramatic piece consisting entirely of two ancient white-haired men, "*As alike in appearance as possible,*"[11] poring over a text, was intended to cast back an image, however refracted, of the audience for which it was composed – scholars whose professional life is spent poring over texts and reading them to each other. The suggestion is encouraged by the unusual topicality (for Beckett) of the piece's title, together with finer details that take on a resonance once this idea is entertained – details like Listener's requests to stop and go back over small critical points, and the precise textual reference to "page forty paragraph four" (p. 31).[12] In this perspective, the repeated phrase "the unspoken words" suggests the object of the entire interpretive enterprise: that is, those words which, when spoken, would release the meaning of the text. Conversely, were all the words spoken, interpretive scholars would be out of business. And this in turn may be the implied supplication of the play's concluding line (also repeated for emphasis): "Nothing is left to tell" (pp. 34–35).

Pierre Astier wrote that one of the departures of this impromptu from the impromptu tradition is that "Beckett does not seem to defend anything or attack anyone" in it.[13] But there is at the very least a suggestion of attack here, and it gives an acid touch to the final description of these sounders of textual depths: "Buried in who knows what profounds of mind" (p. 34). Beckett, after all, has had hard words for exegetes:

[W]hen it comes to journalists I feel the only line is to refuse to be involved in exegesis of any kind. And to insist on the extreme simplicity of dramatic situation and issue. If that's not enough for them, and it obviously isn't, it's plenty for us, and we have no elucidations to offer of mysteries that are all of their making. My work is a matter of fundamental sounds (no joke intended) made as fully as possible, and I accept responsibility for nothing else. If people want to have headaches among the overtones, let them. And provide their own aspirin. Hamm as stated, and Clov as stated, together as stated, nec tecum nec sine te, in such a place, and in such a world, that's all I can manage, more than I could.[14]

The person to whom these words were written was Alan Schneider, the same man who, 23 years later, directed the first performance of *Ohio Impromptu* at the conference in Columbus. After the performance, Schneider fielded questions from the audience and in his answers attended tenaciously to the play's empirical reality – to details of staging, costuming, props, and pacing – all the while astutely dodging invitations to engage in more transcendent modes of critique.

To read *Ohio Impromptu* strictly as a send-up of its scholarly audience is, of course, reductive. It depends on a willed underreading of the staged event, overlooking many of the play's elements to bring down pretty easy prey. The play, after all, was written by a scholar. According to professor Rudmose–Brown, his mentor at Trinity, Beckett was destined to be a "great professor."[15] The star pupil of his class in Romance Languages, Beckett had by the time he was 25 earned his Master of Arts, published a monograph on Marcel Proust, and actually begun a career as a Lecturer in French at Trinity. So if there is some faint shading of contempt for scholars in his offering to the Ohio conference, it is that finely honed contempt that only a fellow scholar can have. "I might have been a professor," says the narrator of *From an Abandoned Work.* "A very fair scholar I was too, no thought, but a great memory."[16]

I bring up these negative shadings, though, because they are not only undeniably present but play their role in inflecting (as they are inflected by) the work's other elements. It is essential that we see two dusty scholars poring over an ancient text – that we see their work as repetitive, ineffectual, laboriously academic – precisely because the story that they study is so emotionally strong. It is the old story of grief, of love lost, of the impossibility of reunion, told so compactly that it attains considerable density of feeling. What I am arguing here is that Beckett's capacity to bond incongruities of this sort is what provides the aesthetic charge of his work. The play, in other words, revives our common awareness of our condition by a process of making strange. This effect is well within the general conceptual framework of "defamiliarization."[17] But it is also a case of that extreme form of defamiliarization that I have called elsewhere "radical displacement."[18] One finds it frequently in Beckett and exceptionally so in this play. The argument that I have made regarding radical displacement is that this subset of defamiliarization turns on an incongruity managed in such a way that it is an apparent denial of the aesthetic object. By virtue of the resistance that that denial sets up in the audience, the full effect of the play, when it comes, comes with penetrating force.

As a threnody on the subject of love lost, *Ohio Impromptu* compares favorably (when performed well) with *Krapp's Last Tape* and the prose piece *Enough.* In all three, the furnishings or veneer of the work make it appear to be anything but a love story, yet, when the full impact of the work is felt, the resistance these furnishings provide can be seen in retrospect as an indispensable part of that effect. Thus, the vestige of slapstick in *Krapp* that Beckett has insisted on in all his tinkering with the play and that has proved such a challenge in a work of such lyrical depth at once frames and bonds with that depth. Similarly the extraterrestrial *bizarrerie* of *Enough* plays a vital part in our reacquaintance with the memory of love. And so, too, in *Ohio Impromptu,* as we watch, the power of the play enlarges with the growing likelihood that the dusty scholar is the passionate lover. Not just a dusty scholar, but a refracted caricature of scholars like those in the audience who read the same old stories of Beckett over and over again, looking and looking for what has not yet been seen. It is just here, in such unlikely breasts, that one finds such pain.

That said, though, it is important to stress that the material of resistance (all this equipage that suggests two scholars in a cell) is not simply instrumental in producing an effect "other" than this material – acting, in other words, primarily as a framing device. Rather, the final effect is synthesized, and in that sense inseparable from this material. We are not only reacquainted with an ancient emotion, but we see – through the agency of this material – how the emotion itself is strange. For this reason, I think, the irascibility and impatience that Alvin Epstein and Alan Mandell introduced into their versions of Reader, and that augmented the surface strangeness of the play, were quite appropriate.[19] They contributed shades of the boring, the aggravating, and the predictable to the play's complex structuring of grief – qualities that are commonly screened out in the representation of that emotion.

The extremity of Beckett's inversion of the novelistic *theatrum theatri* in this play deserves further comment. By extremity, I mean that Beckett did not simply replace the structured audience of theatre with the private reader of texts, but made that reader a kind of super-reader, that is, an interpretive scholar, one who reads over and over again, pausing over details, searching for "unspoken words." If, as I have argued, such negative academic connotations as repetition and nit-picking make an important contribution in both resisting the observer and contributing to the whole complex of feeling that the play constructs, the reader-scholar bears additional freight. Mockery is inextricably linked with sympathy for the scholarly attitude, sympathy that also comes from the inside. Beckett, like many of the great modernists, was a scholar who (despite his protestations of ignorance and bafflement) continued to wear his learning in almost everything he wrote. In his mature work, scholarship is important not for the erudite display it makes but as a signifier of the effort of scrutiny – the constant seeking of the truth in texts. Therefore, though it is essential that the mockery of scholarship be felt in this work, Linda Ben-Zvi has the emphasis right when she asserts that Beckett "is not parodying his critics, as other playwrights might have done; instead he is empathizing with them. Both he and they struggle toward clarity and sense."[20] The scholar, in short, is the epitome of the reader/listener – of that isolated, often rarefied and elite modernist audience whose artistic receptivity is at the opposite pole from that of the nineteenth-century bourgeois.

The difference was forecast early by Dostoevsky's Underground Man, a figure of comparable ambivalence, at once admirable and ridiculous, whose "disease of lucidity" confines him to the hermetic cell of his imaginings and sets him off against the "man of action" who accepts his role on the world stage and plays it with verve. The Underground Man suffers from terminal exegesis, the endless reading and rereading of his life story with no hope of crossing over into a reassuring world of fixed, unassailable meaning. The shadings of the scholar that characterize both figures in *Ohio Impromptu* situate them in this tradition while they reiterate a predominating Beckett figure: the one who knows he will never know yet never ceases to want to know. This obsessive reader (and writer) of texts appears to have transgressed the boundaries of what we commonly call Beckett's "prose fiction" and crowded his way out into what we commonly call Beckett's "theatre," to the point, in *Ohio Impromptu*, of taking over its entire theatrical space.

The theme of endlessly frustrated scrutiny, reiterated in this figure and in most other vestiges of scholarship that lace Beckett's work, is reiterated as well in the eyes that have proliferated in Beckett since Murphy trained his eyes from the vantage-point of a hair's breadth on the eyes of Mr. Endon.[21] There are the vulnerable, barely moving pale blue eyes of Ping ("eyes light blue almost white")[22]; the eyes of the searchers in *The Lost Ones* ("blue for preference as being the most perishable"); the "calm wastes" of the eyes of the last of the vanquished (also in *The Lost Ones*) in which the last of the searchers' eyes wander[23]; the black eye into which it seems there is a danger of disappearing without a trace like that of the woman in *All Strange Away* ("like say without hesitation hell gaping they part and the black eye appears")[24]; the pursuing camera eye of *Film*; the chrysolite eyes of his lover which Krapp sought to enter; the eyes that finally open for Croak in *Words and Music* and which, like those in *Krapp*, are linked to the womb. In these eyes and many more, Beckett elaborates the circle of identity that is played our between the poles of seeing and being seen.

I bring them up here because their reiteration also constitutes an endpoint that Beckett, with typical compaction, has achieved in distilling theatre from theatre. Just as eyes are the final reduction of the audience from its teeming nineteenth-century social complexity, so the short circuit of seeing and being seen are the final reduction of audience and performer which together make a theatre. At its most compact the drama played out is the drama of self-perception, in which these two necessary entities are wedged together in the tight little theatre of a single mind. This is how reading the story of oneself to oneself can be said to be the hard core of theatre. Beckett brings it to its greatest density when, in the last ten seconds of the play, after the sound of reading has ended, Reader and Listener "*raise their heads and look at each other. Unblinking. Expression-less*" (p. 35). In these closing seconds, theatre is stripped of expression and denied even the action of a blink. Yet if my reading of the larger progression in Beckett's work is correct, then what we have reached at the end of this play is a kind of still point at the core of theatre – a still point in which perception races in a circle.

These two perspectives on the "strangeness" of *Ohio Impromptu* serve the broader point of the first half of this essay: that Beckett defamiliarizes by a process of radical displacement, leading with an implicit denial of what becomes the burden of the piece. Moreover, this denial not only gives power to the final effect by its resistance to our understanding but bonds its resistance to the subject so that we see the strangeness in the familiar. By the repetitions and pedantry of scholarship we are reacquainted with grief; by the strict confinement to reading we are reacquainted with theatre. In both cases, the denial itself is a part of the return: we feel the pedantry of grief, the theatricality of reading.

III An Autographic Art

The terms of my discussion so far, and the view of Beckett they imply, accord well with the high modernist conception of the artist as aesthetic craftsman, gauging form to achieve effect, keeping himself well out of his art, save for the necessary appropriation of personal experience for aesthetic transmutation. This also jibes with much that we know about Beckett – his coming of age in the heyday of classical modernism, his early devotion to Joyce, his keen attention to formal considerations, his perfectionism, his impatience with personal inquiries. But Beckett was at least as complex as modernism, and in the rest of this essay on defamiliarization I want to cross over to the other side of the street to show how *Ohio Impromptu* is also a Proustian enterprise in self-writing.

The place to begin now is with what in current discourse might be called the play's autobiographical thematics – specifically with the fact that Reader is not reading just any story but what appears increasingly to be Listener's story or, more precisely still, the story of Reader's reading of Listener's story. The situation harmonizes closely with the words that conclude *Company* – a work composed at roughly the same time as *Ohio Impromptu* – and that seem in their turn to have the same reflexivity: "Till finally you hear how words are coming to an end. With every inane word a little nearer to the last. And how the fable too. The fable of one with you in the dark. The fable of one fabling of one with you in the dark."25

Compounding the effect of this thematic treatment of autobiography is the way *Ohio Impromptu* can be aligned with its author's situation – one who had produced "the same old study" over and over, to be read over and over, but now nearing the point when "Nothing is left to tell." It would have been difficult for Beckett not to have anticipated an awareness of this. Pierre Astier goes so far as to suggest that the hat on the table is all of Beckett's hats and the book all those books thought out under that hat: "All the texts filling the book would thus constitute a writer's lifework, a whole *oeuvre* representing in this case, I think, that of Beckett himself in the form of a make-believe compilation of all his writings so far." In buttressing this assertion with the point that *Ohio Impromptu* "encompasses intertextuality the whole range of [Beckett's] literary production," Astier repeats the observation that both Enoch Brater and John Pilling have made about *Company*.26

It is hard, in short, to be aware of these aspects of the work and to maintain an austere fidelity to the idea of authorial effacement. At the least, they raise the question of how the author of the larger text is implicated in that text. To answer this question, it is helpful to look at the highly personal false start Beckett made on *Ohio Impromptu*, which by good fortune (or design) was included on the back of one of the MS pages that he donated to the conference organizers and which they in turn published in the volume that came out of that conference. So immediate and personal are these few lines that they may conceivably have been the inspiration for the word "impromptu" that wound up in the title.

I am out on leave. Thrown out on leave.
Back to time, they said, for 24 hours.
Oh my God, I said, not that.
Slip [into] on this shroud, they said, lest you catch your death of cold again.
Certainly not, I said.
This cap, they said, for your [death's-head] skull.
Definitely not, I said.
The New World outlet, they said, in the State of Ohio. We cannot be more precise.
Pause.
Proceed straight to [Lima] the nearest campus, they said, and address them.
[Address] whom? I said.
The students, they said, and professors.
Oh my god, I said, not that.
Do not overstay your leave, they said, if yo do not wish it to be extended.

Pause.
What am I to say? I said.
Be yourself, they said, [you're ( )] stay yourself.
Myself? I said What are you insinuating?
[Yourself before, they said.]
Pause.
[And after.]
[*Pause.*]
[Not during? I said.] (pp. 191–192)

Given its title, one of the odd things about the final version of *Ohio Impromptu* is how deliberately programmed it seems. In the words of Linda Ben-Zvi, "there is nothing impromptu about the piece."[27] By contrast, in this false start Beckett appears to have picked up his pen to write with Stan Gontarski's request still ringing in his ears. The whole sequence of composition, then, from false start to finish, would appear to support Gontarski's argument in *The Intent of Undoing* that Beckett starts with personal material which he then proceeds to "undo" as he hammers out the finished art.[28] Perhaps, too, there is additional support for that argument in Beckett's delightful question: "Myself? ... What are you insinuating?" In other words, are you insinuating that I am ever myself in my public presentations? Do you presume to know me from my art?

But this question is not necessarily a rhetorical one. And even if it were, we would have no way, finally, of determining its implied answer, for it could just as easily be reformulated as "Am I ever *not* myself?" In fact, this accords with one of the ways to read *Not I* in which Mouth's futility of denial is understood to carry over reflexively to the author (of course it's her; of course it's Beckett). This interpretation also receives support from one conceivable reading of the "unreadable" question that concludes the false start in brackets (the false start of the false start):

[Yourself before, they said.]
Pause.
[And after.]
[*Pause.*]
[Not during? I said.]

Am I only myself offstage, not on? Or, Am I only the idea of myself gathered from the past or projected into the future, but not myself in the present?

Again, what makes this concluding question as delicate as the one that precedes it is that its implied suppositions seem equally indeterminate. It can be taken to imply that I am never myself, that I am always myself, that I am sometimes myself, that I am all of the above, or none. As I have argued elsewhere, the best reading of Beckett combines never and always.[29] In the rest of this essay, I want to show how the argument can be continued for *Ohio Impromptu*.

There is one point in the entire play when we hear a word that is not (presumably) written in the text that Reader reads. This is the word "Yes" and it comes in the following passage:

In this extremity his old terror of night laid hold on him again. After so long a lapse that as if never been. (*Pause. Looks closer.*) Yes, after so long a lapse that as if never been. Now with redoubled force ... (p. 31)

The word has become a crux of sorts, and most who write on the play have something to say about it.[30] But in the context of the evolution of this play from the immediate, spontaneous, highly personal sketch with which Beckett began to its opposite, the methodical, almost plodding, recitation of a written text which in turn is understood to be the nearly exact repetition of the same recitation as performed on many previous occasions – in such a context, this "Yes" is the last vestige of the impromptu. It is a faint trace of that susceptibility to free improvisation – the sudden appearance of the unanticipated – which one associates with the word Beckett chose to keep in the title.

This is especially important to bear in mind when one turns to the sentence that provokes Reader's "Yes": "After so long a lapse that as if never been." The impromptu quality of "Yes" reinforces the suggestion that, even after Reader's many readings, these written words have a capacity to startle, to cause scrutiny (*"Looks closer"*), to generate perhaps new thought. A further indication that this was on Beckett's mind originally is an additional "Hm" in the holograph MS after the second repetition of the curious sentence (p. 193).[31] The elimination of the "Hm" is in keeping with Beckett's austere subtlety, but the vestige of free play that remains tell us that reading – even the most ritualistic – is never merely repetition, that it can always spring surprises.

This emphasis gains plausibility (and importance) when one looks at the special peculiarity of the strange sentence in question. Not only does the sentence depart from all other sentences in the play, but the character of its perversity – especially the way it drops so many little assisting words:

"After so long a lapse [of time] that [it was] as if [it had] never been" – makes it quintessential late Beckett prose:

So true it is that when in the cylinder what little is possible is not so it is merely no longer so and in the least less the all of nothing if this notion is maintained. (1970)[32]

Sepulchral skull is this then its last state all set for always litter and dwarfs ruins and little body grey cloudless sky glutted dust verge upon verge hell air not a breath. (1974)[33]

Simply savour in advance with in mind the grisly cupboard its conceivable contents. (1981)[34]

First on back to unsay dim can go. (1983)[35]

In effect, the sentence is Beckett's signature. I like to picture Beckett signing it will a wry smile, knowing as always who is in the audience ("Scholars, take note. Who is it murders the language in this way?"). But this is serious fun and it echoes the fun Beckett had when he asked in the false start: "Myself? ... What are you insinuating?" What *can* be insinuated, when Reader hesitates over the words he reads, is what both is and is not, for want of a better term, Beckett's self. It is not Beckett's autobiographical self, which, as it is usually understood, is a retrospective self, packaged in a story, "Yourself before" rather than "During." But it *is* Beckett as he signs himself, his autobiographical self.

Moreover, there is action in this signature. Susan Brienza has argued quite rightly, in *Samuel Beckett's New Worlds*, that the dramatic action in Beckett's late work more than ever unfolds in the language.[36] The case I am making is that this is autographical action. It is, moreover, action that depends on us to happen, for it springs directly from our own collaborative engagement with Beckett's syntactic defamiliarization. It is, in short, Beckett "During," and by his sly wink in *Ohio Impromptu* he notifies us of his presence. If the reader "looks closely," he or she can see Beckett happening.

To show what I mean, let's look closely at a specimen of Beckett's late signature from *Stirrings Still*, one of the last things he wrote:

So on till stayed when to his ears from deep within oh how and here a word he could not catch it were to end where never till then. Rest then before again from not long to so long that perhaps never again and then again faint from deep within oh how and here that missing word again it were to end where never till then.[37]

How does one read prose as syntactically deranged as this? One process that would seem inevitable is some kind of unvoiced normalization working against the resistance of Beckett's omissions. Something which, voiced, might be transcribed as follows:

So on [he moved] till [he] stayed, when [there came] to his ears from deep within [the words,] "Oh how," and [then,] here [at this point, there came] a word he could not catch [which, if he could have caught it,] it were [would be/would mean] to end [there] where [he had] never [been] till then. [He would] rest then before [it came] again, [rest] from [a period anywhere from] not long to so long that [he thought] perhaps [he would] never [hear it] again, and then again [there came] faint from deep within [the words,] "Oh how," and [then] here [at this point there came] that missing word again [which, if he could only hear it,] it were [would be/would mean] to end [there] where [he had] never [been] till then.

This is not an attempt to render an adequate translation of the passage, but rather to indicate an operation that the English-speaking mind cannot avoid when it encounters such prose. In other words, we do not hear simply a variety of strangely pleasing sounds (which would have been easy enough for Beckett to construct) but we hear English as well. We hear it in the distance, beckoning, inviting us to make it predominate.

But if whatever "translation" we might come up with would not be an adequate rendering of the passage itself, then what is the status of the invitation to restore normal English? A partial answer is that it has the status of an instrument – something Beckett relies on to make verbal music. As such, English provides equipment we all share, a ground bass, against which Beckett can achieve new, aesthetically intriguing effects: "from not long to so long," "from deep within oh how," "it were to end where never till then." This jibes with the way Beckett's economies allow him to bring out rhythmic repetitions and rhyme: "when," "again." It also jibes with his frequently expressed sentiment that it is the shape, not the meaning, of a sentence that matters.[38]

If Beckett has pared language down to the point where it makes a strange music all his own, so recognizable that, in a play for scholars of his work, he can stop the "action" briefly to point to it – if this is the case, then the origins of this aesthetic may lie in Proust, an author Beckett read closely in his formative years. In a passage of *The Captive* in which Proust/Marcel argues for the inevitably autographical character of great art, he proposes an interesting embellishment on *symboliste* theory:

And, just as certain creatures are the last surviving testimony to a form of life which nature has discarded, I wondered whether music might not be the unique example of what might have been – if the invention of language, the formation of words, the analysis of ideas had not intervened – the communication between souls. It is like a possibility that has come to nothing; humanity has developed along other lines, those of spoken and written language. (p. 260)

Here Marcel is commenting on the individually specific "strange music" that great artists invariably pull out of themselves, a music which is no-where more indelibly their own than when they seek to go furthest afield.[39] One of the wonders of Beckett's career is just how far afield he succeeded in going. It is impossible to tell how much of the impetus (or reinforcement) for this came from Beckett's reading of Proust at the age of 23.[40] Still, this musical going afield fits snugly in the Proustian model. It also accords with the intuitive sense of many of Beckett's close readers – that in his very unexpectedness, the constancy of his self-overturning, lies his unmistakable persistence.

So it is not insignificant that, looking once more at the specimen signature from *Stirrings Still*, one finds again, as in *Ohio Impromptu* (as for that matter in so much that Beckett has written), a reflexive thematics of self-reading. In this passage with its missing words which we strain to comprehend, we read of the effort to comprehend language coming "faint from deep within," language that fixes its grip on the listener by its "missing word." If I am not mistaken, it is also at this point that the text reaches its greatest difficulty of access. Not only do we have the implied paradox of a word that is at once present and absent – "and here that missing word" – but we have to cope with Beckett's diabolic use of the subjunctive – "it were to end." In my version above, I rendered this as "[which, if he could only hear it,] it were [would be/would mean] to end." In other words, were he to hear that key word, an end would come. Even with this reading one must answer the question, An end to what? (the discourse? the movement? the search? the life?). But the same passage can be rendered with a different set of missing words: "[would that] it were to end." With this different normalization comes a different stress and an additional alternative for reading "it": Would that the discourse/move-ment/search/life were to end, or Would that the missing word were "to end." If the latter, the complete phrase coming "from deep within" would be, quite plausibly, "Oh how to end."

I have gone into these possibilities to show the kind of music – not only of sound but of meaning – that goes on in reading Beckett. But it depends on our own willingness to engage his syntactical defamiliarization. It is not an infinite play with signifiers but rather an energetic listening for possibilities as constrained by both context and the rules of language. At the same time, by working with Beckett's autographical cues and using this specimen signature from *Stirrings Still* as a gloss on *Ohio Impromptu*, I have sought to make the case that this special difficulty generates a continual reacquaintance with Beckett. As such, it is Beckett happening, Beckett "During," brought to being by the collaborative effort of our intelligence as it in turn is called into play by his exact notations.[41]

Briefly to sum up, when Beckett inverted the novelistic device of the theatre-evening, putting a Reader and a Listener on stage as sole *dramatis personae*, he not only staged the entire range of his audience (book readers, theatre listeners) but indicated where the action was. At the same time the inversion itself epitomized the artistic strategy of defamiliarization which Beckett inherited from modernist practice. Finally, it is possible to understand the resistance created by Beckett's defamiliarization in two different but parallel ways: as serving a reacquaintance with our shared condition and as serving Beckett's self-creation. The one accords well with the classical modernist model of an impersonal, distanced, craftsmanly art; the other accords well with Proustian late romanticism, until recently a muted, secondary strain in modernist commentary.[42] Beckett's susceptibility to both suggests the possibility of developing a more comprehensive model of modernist poetics.

NOTES

1   Marcel Proust, *The Captive*, trs. C.K. Scott Moncrieff and Terence Kilmartin (New York, 1981), p. 260. All further page references will be cited in the text.

2   Charles R. Lyons, "Beckett's Fundamental Theatre: the Plays from *Not I* to *What Where*," in *Beckett's Later Fiction and Drama: Texts for Company*, edd. James Acheson and Kateryna Arthur (London, 1987), pp. 83, 80.

3   Jean–Paul Sartre, *The Words*, tr. Bernard Frechtman (Greenwich, 1964), p. 76. All further page references will be cited in the text.

4   Jean Baudrillard, *Représentation et simulation* (Paris, 1981) and *Amérique* (Paris, 1986); portions of the first have been translated in *Simulations*, trs. Paul Foss, Paul Patton, and Philip Beitchman (New York, 1983); the latter has been translated as *America*, tr. Chris Turner (London and New York, 1988).

5   Dougald McMillan and Martha Fehsenfeld, *Beckett in the Theatre: The Author as practical Playwright and Director, Volume I: From* Waiting for Godot *to* Krapp's Last Tape (London and New York, 1988), p. 17.

6 Samuel Beckett, *Waiting for Godot* (New York, 1954), p. 10.

7 Samuel Beckett, *Endgame* (New York, 1958), p. 29.

8 Alec Reid, *All I Can Manage, More than I Could* (Dublin, 1968), p. 50.

9 See Bernard Beckerman, "Beckett and the Act of Listening" and Katherine Worth, "Beckett's Auditors: *Not I* to *Ohio Impromptu*," both in *Beckett at 80/ Beckett in Context*, ed. Enoch Brater (New York and Oxford, 1986), pp. 149–192.

10 *Ohio Impromptu* was written on request for the symposium "Samuel Beckett: Humanistic Perspectives" which took place on 7–9 May 1981 at the Ohio State University under the sponsorship of the College of Humanities. It was first performed on 9 May, directed by Alan Schneider with David Warrilow as Reader and Rand Mitchell as Listener.

11 Samuel Beckett, *Ohio Impromptu*, in *Rockaby and Other Short Pieces* (New York, 1981), p. 27. All further page references will be cited in the text.

12 In one of the holograph versions, there is an additional reference to an "appendix"; see *Samuel Beckett: Humanistic Perspectives*, edd. Morris Beja, S.E. Gontarski, and Pierre Astier (Columbus, 1983), p. 194. All further page references to these holograph versions will be cited in the text.

13 Pierre Astier, "Beckett's *Ohio Impromptu*: A View from the Isle of Swans," *Modern Drama*, 25 (1982), 332.

14 Samuel Beckett, *Disjecta: Miscellaneous Writings and a Dramatic Fragment*, ed. Ruby Cohn (London, 1983), p. 109.

15 Deirdre Bair, *Samuel Beckett: A Biography* (New York, 1978), p. 137.

16 Samuel Beckett, *Collected Shorter Prose: 1945–1980* (London, 1984), p. 131. The fuller quotation reads: "Fortunately my father died when I was a boy, otherwise I might have been a professor, he had his heart set on it. A very fair scholar I was too, no thought, but a great memory." In the actual chronology of events, Beckett quit his post at Trinity 15 December 1931, and his father died 26 June 1933.

17 For reading Beckett, the most useful and provocative description of defamiliarization is still that of Victor Shklovsky. Two of Shklovsky's important essays on defamiliarization (*ostranenie*) – "Art as Technique" and "Sterne's *Tristram Shandy*: Stylistic Commentary" – can be found in English in *Russian Formalist Criticism: Four Essays*, trs. Lee T. Lemon and Marion J. Reis (Lincoln, Neb., 1965), pp. 3–57. Shklovsky's fullest attempt to integrate the concept with his other ideas (*O teorii prozy*, 1925) has at last been made available in English as *Theory of Prose*, tr. Benjamin Sher (Elmwood Park, IL, 1990).

Helpful commentary on Shklovskian defamiliarization can be found in Lawrence Crawford, "Viktor Shklovskij: *Différance* in Defamiliarization," *Comparatie Literature*, 36 (Summer 1984), 209–219; Victor Ehrlich, *Russian Formalism: History, Doctrine* (The Hague, 1965), pp. 176–180; Daniel P. Gunn,

"Making Art Strange: A Commentary on Defamiliarization," *The Georgia Review,* 38 (Spring 1984), 25–33; Fredric Jameson, *The Prison-House of Language: A Critical Account of Structuralism and Russian Formalism* (Princeton, 1972), pp. 48–91; Leonard Orr, "Vraisemblance and Alienation Techniques: The Basis for Reflexivity in Fiction," *Journal of Narrative Technique,* 11 (Fall 1981), 199–215; and R.H. Stacy, *Defamiliarization in Language and Literature* (Syracuse, 1977).

   Related to Shklovsky's *ostranenie* is Brecht's *Verfremdung,* though I think the latter concept on the whole less useful in discussing Beckett whose focus, when compared with Brecht, seems determinedly metaphysical.

18 See H. Porter Abbott, "A Poetics of Radical Displacement: Samuel Beckett Coming up to Seventy," *Texas Studies in Literature and Language,* 17 (Spring 1975), 219–238.

19 For a different slant on Alvin Epstein's performance of Reader, see Jonathan Kalb's comparison of his and David Warrilow's versions of the role in *Beckett in performance* (Cambridge, 1989), pp. 48–62.

20 Linda Ben-Zvi, *Samuel Beckett* (Boston, 1986), p. 176.

21 Samuel Beckett, *Murphy* (New York, 1957), pp. 248–250.

22 *Collected Shorter Prose,* p. 149.

23 Ibid., pp. 170, 177.

24 Ibid., p. 124.

25 Samuel Beckett, *Company* (New York, 1980), pp. 62–63.

26 Astier, pp. 338, 339; Enoch Brater, "The *Company* Beckett Keeps: The Shape of Memory and One Fablist's Decay of Lying," in *Samuel Beckett: Humanistic Perspectives,* pp. 157–171; John Pilling, "*Company* by Samuel Beckett," *Journal of Beckett Studies,* 7 (Spring 1982), 127–131.

27 Ben-Zvi, p. 176.

28 S.E. Gontarski, *The Intent of Undoing in Samuel Beckett's Dramatic Texts* (Bloomington, 1985).

29 Abbott, "Narratricide: Samuel Beckett as Autographer," *Romance Studies,* II (Winter 1987), 35–46; "Tyranny and Theatricality: The Example of Samuel Beckett," *Theatre Journal,* 40 (March 1988), 77–87.

30 Kathleen O'Gorman writes that the word "Yes" indicates "a 'metanarrative' which to some extent calls into question the embedded narrative" ("The Speech Act in Beckett's *Ohio Impromptu,*" in '*Make Sense Who May': Essays on Samuel Beckett's Later Works,* Irish Literary Studies 30, edd. Robin J. Davis and Lance St. J. Butler [Gerrards Cross, 1988], p. 115); Kristin Morrison contrasts the repetition brought on by Reader's "Yes" with the six "significant" repetitions requested by Listener, making "Yes" primarily the verification of a "syntactically awkward" line (*Canters and Chronicles: The Use of Narrative in the*

Plays of Samuel Beckett and Harold Pinter [Chicago, 1983], pp. 121–122); Pierre Astier ventures that the "Yes" may simply have been occasioned by the "discovery in the text of such an unexpected and perfect alexandrine" (p. 334).

31 In his French version of the play, Beckett maintained the effect: "Si longtemps après que comme si jamais été. *(Un temps. Il regarde de plus près.)* Oui, si longtemps après que comme si jamais été." *Impromptu d'Ohio,* in *Catastrophe et autres dramaticules* (Paris, 1982), p. 63.

32 Samuel Beckett, *The Lost Ones,* in *Collected Shorter Prose,* p. 167.

33 Samuel Beckett, "Fizzle 8: For to End Yet Again," *Fizzles* (New York, 1976), p. 60.

34 Samuel Beckett, *Ill Seen Ill Said* (New York, 1981), p. 41.

35 Samuel Beckett, *Worstward Ho* (New York, 1983), p. 27.

36 Susan Brienza, *Samuel Beckett's New Worlds: Style in Metafiction* (Norman, OK, 1987).

37 Samuel Beckett, *Stirrings Still* (New York and London, 1988), p. 20.

38 Cited in Harold Hobson, "Samuel Beckett: Dramatist of the Year," *International Theatre Annual I* (1956), p. 153. For a useful compendium of Beckett's expression of similar or related sentiments see McMillan and Fehsenfeld, pp. 13–16.

39 "And it was precisely when he was striving with all his might to create something new that one recognized, beneath the apparent differences, the profound similarities and deliberate resemblances that existed in the body of a work" (*The Captive,* p. 257).

40 But see Nicholas Zurbrugg's extensive analysis of Beckett's rich misreading of Proust, *Beckett and Proust* (Gerrards Cross and Totowa, NJ, 1988).

41 Of the philosophical difficulties with defamiliarization in Shklovsky's treatment, the most frequently observed is the unresolved conflict between his use of defamiliarization as an effect of content – as in his famous argument that art "makes the stone stoney" with its implication that stoneyness is a quality somewhere in the world, approachable through art – and his use of it as a strictly formal event – as in his analysis of Sterne's reflexive "baring" of novelistic equipment in *Tristam Shandy.* The first favors a more or less stable ontology while the second would appear to abandon ontology for an exclusive epistemology. Renewal under the first is a continual return: under the second, a continual revolution.

In my own view, neither pole can be uncontaminated by the other, their differences boiling down perhaps to a slight adjustment in how we define defamiliarization: 1) the sensation of reacquaintance through the sensation of unfamiliarity, or 2) the sensation of reacquaintance as the sensation of unfamiliarity. The inability to make a clean break parallels the philosophical difficulty of making a clean break between memory and perception. In other words, without recognition there can be no unfamiliarity, and vice versa. The two main parts of my treatment of defamiliarization in Beckett fall roughly under the two slightly different definitions posed above. In my treatment of radical displacement, I definitely wish to stress a return. To do otherwise would be to suggest that grief, for example, has no reality outside of language. On the other hand, a constancy of unfamiliarity would appear to be the dominant aspect of Beckett's autographical action.

42 The major revaluation of modernism as an autographical art has emerged in feminist work on Woolf, Stein and H.D., but in the 1980s there have also been several efforts to extend the model to male modernist authors; see especially Steven Helmling, "Joyce: Autobiography, History, Narrative," *Kenyon Review*, 10 (Spring 1988), 91–109; Paul Jay, *Being in the Text* (Ithaca, 1984), pp. 115–160; Daniel R. Schwartz, "'I Was the World in Which I Walked': The Transformation of the British Novel," *University of Toronto Quarterly*, 51 (Spring 1982), 279–297.

Roundelay

SAMUEL BECKETT

on all that strand
at end of day
steps sole sound
long sole sound
until unbidden stay
then no sound
on all that strand
long no sound
until unbidden go
steps sole sound
long sole sound
on all that strand
at end of day

(1976)

Suggestions for Further Reading

Ibsen

Chamberlain, John S. *Ibsen: The Open Vision.* London, 1982.

Durbach, Errol. *'Ibsen the Romantic': Analogues of Paradise in the Later Plays.* Athens, Georgia, 1982.

Durbach, Errol, ed. *Ibsen and the Theatre.* London, 1980.

Haugen, Einar. *Ibsen's Drama: Author to Audience.* Minneapolis, 1979.

Holtan, Orley I. *Mythic Patterns in Ibsen's Last Plays.* Minneapolis, 1970.

Hornby, Richard. *Patterns in Ibsen's Middle Plays.* Lewisburg, Penn., 1981.

Johnston, Brian. *Text and Supertext in Ibsen's Drama.* University Park, Penn., 1989.

Lebowitz, Naomi. *Ibsen and the Great World.* Baton Rouge, 1990.

Marker, Frederick J., and Lise–Lone Marker. *Ibsen's Lively Art: A Performance Study of the Major Plays.* Cambridge and New York, 1989.

May, Keith M. *Ibsen and Shaw.* London, 1985.

McFarlane, James, ed. *The Cambridge Companion to Ibsen.* Cambridge and New York, 1994.

Meyer, Michael. *Henrik Ibsen.* 3 vols. London, 1967–71.

Northam, John. *Ibsen: A Critical Study.* Cambridge, 1973.

Thomas, David. *Henrik Ibsen.* London, 1983.

Valency, Maurice. *The Flower and the Castle.* New York, 1963.

Strindberg

Blackwell, M.J., ed. *Structures of Influence: A Comparative Approach to August Strindberg.* Chapel Hill, 1978.

Brandell, Gunnar. *Strindberg in Inferno,* trans. Barry Jacobs. Cambridge, Mass., 1974.

Carlson, Harry G. *Strindberg and the Poetry of Myth.* Berkeley, 1982.

Johnson, Walter. *August Strindberg.* Boston, 1976.

Lagercrantz, Olof. *August Strindberg.* New York, 1984.

Lamm, Martin. *August Strindberg,* trans. Harry G. Carlson. New York, 1971.

Meyer, Michael. *Strindberg: A Biography.* New York, 1985.

Morgan, Margery M. *August Strindberg.* London, 1985.

Robinson, Michael. *Strindberg and Autobiography: Writing and Reading a Life.* Norwich, 1986.

Sprinchorn, Evert. *Strindberg as Dramatist.* New Haven, 1982.

Steene, Birgitta. *The Greatest Fire: A Study of August Strindberg.* Carbondale, 1973.

Stockenström, Göran, ed. *Strindberg's Dramaturgy.* Minneapolis, 1988.

Törnqvist, Egil. *Strindbergian Drama: Themes and Structure.* Atlantic Highlands, N.J., 1982.

Törnqvist, Egil, and Barry Jacobs. *Strindberg's Miss Julie: A Play and Its Transpositions.* Norwich, 1988.

Pirandello

Bassanese, Fiora A. *Understanding Luigi Pirandello.* Columbia, 1997.

Bentley, Eric. *The Pirandello Commentaries.* Evanston, 1986.

Bloom, Harold, ed. *Luigi Pirandello.* New York and Philadelphia, 1989.

Cambon, Glauco, ed. *Pirandello: A Collection of Critical Essays.* Englewood Cliffs, 1967.

Caputi, Anthony. *Pirandello and the Crisis of Modern Consciousness.* Urbana and Chicago, 1988.

Di Gaetani, John Louis. *A Companion to Pirandello Studies.* New York, Westport, and London, 1991.

Firth, Felicity. *Pirandello in Performance.* Cambridge and Alexandria, 1990.

Guidice, Gaspare. *Luigi Pirandello.* Turin, 1963. Trans. as *Pirandello: A Biography* by Alistair Hamilton. London, New York, and Toronto, 1975.

Oliver, Roger W. *Dreams of Passion: The Theatre of Luigi Pirandello.* New York, 1979.

Paolucci, Anne. *Pirandello's Theatre: The Recovery of the Modern Stage for Dramatic Art.* Carbondale, 1974.

Ragusa, Olga. *Luigi Pirandello.* New York and London, 1968.

– *Pirandello: An Approach to His Theatre.* Edinburgh, 1980.

Sogliuzzo, A. Richard. *Luigi Pirandello Director: The Playwright in the Theatre.* Metuchen, N.J., 1982.

Starkie, Walter. *Luigi Pirandello.* London, 1926; 2d ed. London, 1937; rev. 3d ed. as *Luigi Pirandello, 1867–1936.* Berkeley, 1965.

Vittorini, Domenico. *The Drama of Luigi Pirandello.* Philadelphia, 1935; 2d ed. New York, 1957; rpt. New York, 1969.

Beckett

Ben-Zvi, Linda, ed. *Women in Beckett: Performance and Critical Perspectives.* Urbana and Chicago, 1990.

Brater, Enoch, ed. *Beckett at 80/Beckett in Context.* Oxford and New York, 1986.

Butler, Lance St. John, and Robin J. David, eds. *Rethinking Beckett: A Collection of Critical Essays.* London, 1990.

Cohn, Ruby. *Back to Beckett.* Princeton, 1973

– *Just Play Beckett's Theatre.* Princeton, 1980.

Federman, Raymond, and John Fletcher, eds. *Samuel Beckett and His Critics: An Essay in Bibliography.* Berkeley, London, and Los Angeles, 1970.

Fletcher, John. *Samuel Beckett's Art.* London, 1967.

Gontarski, S. E., ed. *The Beckett Studies Reader.* Gainesville, 1993.

Hesla, David H. *The Shape of Charos: An Interpretation of the Art of Samuel Beckett.* Minneapolis, 1971.

Kenner, Hugh. *A Reader's Guide to Samuel Beckett.* London, 1973.

– *Samuel Beckett: A Critical Study.* New York, 1961.

Knowlson, James. *Damned to Fame: The Life of Samuel Beckett.* New York, 1996.

– *Frescoes of the Skull: Later Prose and Drama of Samuel Beckett.* New York, 1980.

McMillan, Dougald, and Martha Fehsenfeld. *Beckett in the Theatre: The Author as Practical Playwright and Director. Volume 1: From "Waiting for Godot" to "Krapp's Last Tape."* London and New York, 1988.

Murphy, P.J., Werner Huber, Rolf Breuer, and Konrad Schoell, eds. *Critique of Beckett Criticism: A Guide to Research in English, French, and German.* Columbia, 1994.

Pilling, John, ed. *The Cambridge Companion to Beckett.* Cambridge and New York, 1994.

Contributors

H. Porter Abbott is Professor of English at the University of California, Santa Barbara. His publications include *The Fiction of Samuel Beckett: Form and Effect, Diary Fiction: Writing as Action,* and most recently *Beckett Writing Beckett: The Author in the Autograph.*

Milly S. Barranger, Alumni Distinguished Professor and Chair of the Department of Dramatic Art at University of North Carolina at Chapel Hill, has published articles on Southern women in American theatre, bio-bibliographies of Margaret Webster and Jessica Tandy, and books such as *Theatre: A Way of Seeing.* She is past president of the National Theatre Conference and the American Theatre Association.

Linda Ben-Zvi is Professor of English at Tel Aviv University. The author of numerous essays on American and European playwrights and a biography of Susan Glaspell, she is currently editing a complete edition of Glaspell's plays. Her books include *A Collection of Essays on Susan Glaspell; Vital Voices*, a collection of plays by American women playwrights; *Theatre in Israel*; and *Women in Beckett.*

Benjamin K. Bennett is Professor of German at University of Virginia. He is the author of *Modern Drama and German Classicism, Theater as Problem,* and book-length studies of Goethe and Hofmannsthal. His most recent book, on eighteenth-century German literature, is titled *Beyond Theory.* His forthcoming work includes a book to be called *All Theatre Is Revolutionary Theatre.*

Marvin Carlson, Professor of Theatre and Comparative Literature at the

Graduate School and University Center of CUNY, has published works on dramatic theory and nineteenth-century German and French theatre. His books include *Theories of the Theatre: A Historical and Critical Survey from the Greeks to the Present* and most recently *Performance: A Critical Introduction*.

Ruby Cohn, Professor Emeritus of Dramatic Art at the University of California, Davis, is a member of the editorial boards of *Modern Drama* and *Theatre Journal*. She has published extensively on twentieth-century drama and is the author of numerous texts on Beckett. Her recent books include *Anglo-American Interplay in Recent Drama* and *Retreats from Realism in Recent English Drama*.

James Fisher is Professor of Theatre at Wabash College, Indiana, and is the author of *The Theater of Yesterday and Tomorrow: Commedia dell'arte on the Modern Stage* and book-length studies of Al Jolson, Spencer Tracy, and Eddie Cantor. He is book review editor for *The Journal of Dramatic Theory* and editor of *The Puppetry Yearbook*.

John Fletcher is Professor of Modern Languages and European Studies at the University of East Anglia. He has published extensively on Samuel Beckett. In 1990 he was awarded the Scott Moncrieff Prize for translation from French. His recent critical writing includes work on Claude Simon, Alain Robbe-Gillet, and Iris Murdoch.

Elinor Fuchs teaches at Columbia University School and the Yale School of Drama. She is the author of *The Death of Character: Perspectives on Theater after Modernism*, winner of the George Jean Nathan Award in Dramatic Criticism (1996) and *Choice* Outstanding Book citation. Co-editor of the documentary play *Year One of the Empire* and editor of *Plays of the Holocaust: An International Anthology*, she has written articles that have appeared in numerous anthologies and journals as well as in *The Village Voice* and *The New York Times*.

Diane Filby Gillespie, Professor of English at Washington State University, Pullman, is the author of books and articles on twentieth-century dramatists and writers, especially Virginia Woolf. She has recently edited *Virginia Woolf's Roger Fry: A Biography* and co-edited *Virginia Woolf and the Arts: Selected Papers from the Sixth Annual Conference on Virginia Woolf*.

Brian Johnston is Professor of Drama at Carnegie Mellon University, Pittsburgh. He is the author of *The Ibsen Cycle, Text and Supertext in Ibsen's Drama*, and *To the Third Empire: Ibsen's Early Dramas*. His recent translations of Ibsen's entire Realist Twelve-Play Cycle, from *Pillars of Society* to *When We Dead Awaken*, are published by Smith and Krause (U.S.A.).

Andrew K. Kennedy is Professor of British Literature at University of Bergen, Norway. He is the author of *Dramatic Dialogue, Samuel Beckett*, and *Six Dramatists in Search of a Language*.

James R. Knowlson, Professor of French at the University of Reading and President of the Samuel Beckett Society, is the founder of and advisor to the Beckett International Foundation (formerly the Beckett Archive). His most recent work, *Damned to Fame: The Life of Samuel Beckett*, was awarded the George Freedley Memorial Award for the Outstanding Book on Theatre in 1996.

Anne Paolucci, Professor and Chair of English at St John's University, Jamaica, NY, has published widely on Pirandello and Albee. She is an award-winning playwright, poet, and short story writer and her editorial work includes *Justice Winsor: Native American Antiquities and Linguistics*.

R. Brian Parker is Professor Emeritus of English at Trinity College, University of Toronto and former Director of the Graduate Centre for the Study of Drama, University of Toronto. He is currently at work on a study of Tennessee Williams.

Marvin Rosenberg is Professor Emeritus of Dramatic Art, University of California, Berkeley. His major publications are *The Masks of Othello, The Masks of King Lear, The Masks of Macbeth, The Masks of Hamlet*, and this year, *The Adventures of a Shakespeare Scholar*.

Richard Schechner, Professor of Performance Studies at the Tisch School of the Arts, New York University, is editor of *TDR*, founding director of the Performance Group, and artistic director of East Coast Artists. He has written extensively on performance theory and avant-garde theatre. Among his books are *Environmental Theater, Between Theater and Anthropology*, and *The Future of Ritual: Writings of Culture and Performance*. His most recent award was a 1997 American Institute of Indian Studies Senior Research Fellowship.

Evert Sprinchorn, Professor Emeritus and former chairman of the Drama Department at Vassar College, Poughkeepsie, has written on Joyce, Shaw, and the Elizabethan stage. He is the author of *Strindberg as Dramatist* and has edited *Ibsen: Letters and Speeches* and *Wagner on Music and Drama.*

J.L. Styan is Snyder Professor Emeritus of English Literature and Professor Emeritus of Theatre at Northwestern University. In 1995 he received the Robert Lewis medal for Lifetime Achievement in Theatre Research, and his recent publications include *Restoration Comedy in Performance* and *The English Stage: A History of Drama and Performance.*

Hersh Zeifman, Associate Professor of English at York University, Toronto, is former co-editor of *Modern Drama* and former president of the Samuel Beckett Society. In addition to having written many articles on contemporary drama, he is editor of *David Hare: A Casebook* and co-editor of *Contemporary British Drama, 1970–1990.*

On the Editors

Christopher Innes is a Fellow of the Royal Society of Canada, a Fellow of the Royal Society of Arts (England), and Distinguished Research Professor at York University. The most recent of his various publications on modern theatre are *Modern British Drama: 1890–1990, Avant Garde Theatre: 1892–1992*, and *The Theatre of Gordon Craig.* He is the general editor for several series of monographs, including "Directors in Perspective," and was an editor of *Modern Drama* from 1987 to 1997.

Frederick J. Marker, Professor of English and Drama at the University of Toronto, has written extensively on many aspects of modern theatre and drama. His books include studies of Hans Christian Andersen, Kjeld Abell, Ingmar Bergman, Edward Gordon Craig, Henrik Ibsen, and others. His latest book, published in collaboration with Lise-Lone Marker, is *A History of Scandinavian Theatre.* He was the editor of *Modern Drama* from 1972 to 1976.

Karen Kitagawa, of York University, has prepared the contributors' notes and index for this volume.

Index